Praise for

DANGEROUS WEA.
DESPERATE STATES

Few problems raised by the new states of the former Soviet Union worry the outside world more than the seepage of nuclear and conventional arms and their ingredients into the wrong hands. Until now, however, we have not had an in-depth understanding of the policies and institutions governing the Russian, Ukrainian, Belarusian, and Kazakh control over critical exports. Written by an international group of highly expert authors, this is the first book to tackle the four key countries in great, yet accessible, detail. *Dangerous Weapons, Desperate States* is a crucial tool for addressing this crucial problem.

—Robert Legvold,
Professor of Political Science, Columbia University

Dangerous Weapons, Desperate States illuminates the economic roots of proliferation in the NIS and the domestic and international ineffectiveness that has failed to prevent its growth. The question remains whether the examples of export control failure and consequences of continued inaction outlined in this book will serve as a wake-up call for political leaders in the East and West.

—Kenneth N. Luongo,
Executive Director,
Russian American Nuclear Security Advisory Council

Dangerous Weapons, Desperate States is the most comprehensive review of export control developments in the former Soviet Union.

—Henry Sokolski,
Executive Director, Nonproliferation Education Policy Center

DANGEROUS WEAPONS, DESPERATE STATES

Russia, Belarus, Kazakstan, and Ukraine

GARY K. BERTSCH AND
WILLIAM C. POTTER, EDITORS

ROUTLEDGE

NEW YORK   LONDON

Published in 1999 by
Routledge
29 West 35th Street
New York, NY 10001

Published in Great Britain by
Routledge
11 New Fetter Lane
London EC4P 4EE

Library of Congress Cataloging-in-Publication Data

Dangerous weapons, desperate states: Russia, Belarus, Kazakstan, and Ukraine / edited by Gary K. Bertsch and William C. Potter.
        p.   cm.
    ISBN 0-415-92236-4.   ISBN 0-415-92237-2-p
    1. Disarmament.   2. Arms control—Former Soviet republics.   3. Weapons of mass destruction—Former Soviet republics.   4. Nuclear disarmament—Former Soviet republics.   I. Bertsch, Gary K.   II. Potter, William C.
JZ6009. F67D36   1999
327.1 ' 747 ' 0947—dc21   99-11361
                                                                                        CIP

CONTENTS

ACRONYMS

AG	Australia Group
BTWC	Biological and Toxin Weapons Convention
CFE	Conventional Forces in Europe Treaty
CIS	Commonwealth of Independent States
COCOM	Coordinating Committee for Multilateral Export Controls
CSCE	Conference on Security and Cooperation in Europe
CTR	Cooperative Threat Reduction (Nunn-Lugar) Program
CWC	Chemical Weapons Convention
DOE	U.S. Department of Energy
EU	European Union
FSB	Federal Security Service
FREEDOM	Freedom for Russia and the Emerging Eurasian Democracies and Open Markets
FSA	Freedom Support Act
FSU	Former Soviet Union
GDP	Gross Domestic Product
HEU	Highly Enriched Uranium
IAEA	International Atomic Energy Agency
ICBM	Inter-Continental Ballistic Missile
INF	Intermediate-Range Nuclear Forces
ITAR	International Traffic in Arms Regulations
MFA	Ministry of Foreign Affairs
MFER	Ministry of Foreign Economic Relations
MIC	Military Industrial Complex
MOD	Ministry of Defense
MOU	Memorandum of Understanding
MPC&A	Materials Protection, Control and Accounting
MTCR	Missile Technology Control Regime
NATO	North Atlantic Treaty Organization
NBC	Nuclear Biological Chemical
NGO	Non-Governmental Organization
NIS	New Independent States
NNWS	Non-Nuclear Weapons State
NPT	Nuclear Nonproliferation Treaty
NSG	Nuclear Suppliers Group
SEED	Support for East European Democracy
SNM	Special Nuclear Materials
UN	United Nations
USSR	Union of Soviet Socialist Republics
WA	Wassenaar Arrangement
WEU	West European Union
WMD	Weapons of Mass Destruction

PART I

EXPORT CONTROLS, TRADE, AND SECURITY

1

INTRODUCTION: THE CHALLENGE OF NIS EXPORT CONTROL DEVELOPMENT

Gary K. Bertsch
and William C. Potter

THE THREAT

Some may consider the title of this book—*Dangerous Weapons, Desperate States*—as hyperbole. It is not. The former Soviet Union developed a massive arsenal of lethal weapons—nuclear, chemical, biological, and conventional. During the Cold War, the USSR emerged as a military superpower. Along with the United States, it developed a vast array of weapons of mass destruction (WMD) whose use could put an end to all human life on the planet earth. The USSR also developed the capacity through intercontinental ballistic missiles (ICBMs) to deliver these weapons swiftly to all corners of the planet.

In the early 1990s the ideological, legal, and economic structure that supported Soviet military power quickly crumbled. The USSR collapsed and a struggling set of New Independent States (NIS) inherited this vast and dangerous arsenal. Russia alone inherited approximately 30,000 nuclear weapons, hundreds of tons of fissile material, 40,000 tons of chemical weapons, significant biological weapons capability, and the scientists and technological know-how to produce many additional weapons of mass destruction.

The transition to stable, productive economies in these NIS is proving to be incredibly difficult. Russia and other NIS are in desperate economic straits, as are the producers and custodians of WMD. National governments, individual ministries, and many defense firms and facilities are under enormous pressures to expand exports to generate revenues. Weapons and weapons-related materials and know-how are among the few commodities in the former Soviet Union for which there is an international demand backed by hard currency. In addition, in the chaotic new political and legal environment, corruption is rampant. New entrepreneurs are prepared to sell anything and everything to make a quick buck. Moreover, organized crime has expanded rapidly and often only a fine line separates state-sanctioned theft and exports and those of a nonstate variety. These criminal operations include the diversion, sale, and export of sensitive military hardware, technologies, and materials. Some of these transactions involve key components of weapons of mass destruction.

The institutions needed to control these threats in the early 1990s were either underdeveloped or nonexistent. With the exception of Russia, there was no governmental experience and little technical expertise in the NIS to control weapons proliferation. New states like Belarus, Kazakstan, and Ukraine had to create governments, institutions, laws, and regulations to control what threatened to become the largest weapons proliferation in human history. New officials had to be trained, export control systems created and put in place, and policies and procedures put into practice. This transformation required a change in attitudes and mind-sets, as well as regulations. Could this be done quickly enough to avoid what some considered to be the inevitable—the spread of the Soviet WMD arsenal to some of the world's most dangerous and irresponsible parties?

THE RESPONSE

During the peak of the Cold War, the United States and its allies pursued a policy of containment to prevent the spread of Soviet influence and military power. This task proved to be a costly but ultimately manageable one. Following the collapse of the Soviet Union in 1991, a U.S.-led coalition has promoted a new policy of "proliferation containment" globally and, in particular, vis-à-vis the NIS of the former Soviet Union. This policy seeks to curb the export, illicit or state-sanctioned, of a wide variety of military and dual-use items, including, but not limited to, nuclear material, technology, equipment, and services. The premise underlying the new approach to containment is that with the demise of the Soviet states, and in an environment of economic hardship, literally everything might be sold to anyone for the right price. Although some of the newly available export commodities, such as formerly classified KGB files, may constitute little threat to Western security interests, the dangers of "arms bazaars" in and weapons proliferation from the former Soviet Union are both real and serious.

Not surprisingly, the new policy of containment is viewed by many NIS officials with the same disdain as was the old policy by Soviet party apparatchiks. From the vantage point in Moscow, Minsk, and Kyiv, Washington tends not to practice what it preaches when it comes to export control policy, and is prone to confuse another country's economic needs and sound strategy for hard currency exports with a disregard for nonproliferation objectives. Indeed, policy-makers in the NIS are apt to remind their Western counterparts of their less than sterling record in the field of arms and nonproliferation exports (witness the U.S. leadership in global arms sales and U.S. government and/or corporation involvement in the nuclear weapons acquisition routes of India, Pakistan, and Iraq).

It may be impossible entirely to reconcile these competing perspectives, some of which derive from conflicting national interests and different evaluations of nonproliferation strategies and proliferation risks. Other differences, however, are probably a function of misconceptions and inadequate information. For example, despite the centrality of the issue of NIS export controls to the problem of proliferation threats from the former Soviet Union, little systematic research has been conducted on the topic. There is little knowledge of the actual (as opposed to formal) decision-making process in the nuclear and dual-use export sectors, or the relative importance attached to economic and nonproliferation objectives in export licensing decisions.

One of the difficulties in answering these and other weapons proliferation-related questions is that the export control process in the former Soviet Union today is in a tremendous state of flux. The general absence of comprehensive legislation governing the export of sensitive defense-related commodities, along with the revolutionary economic and political changes that have characterized many of the post-Soviet states, has contributed to a dynamic and confusing state of affairs.

This volume seeks to describe and analyze NIS weapons proliferation and export control developments. Drawing upon an international team of experts, the volume focuses on four of the key post-Soviet states—Belarus, Kazakstan, Russia, and Ukraine—and addresses a number of critical issues, including:

- What are the current export structures (that is, legal basis, institutional organization, licensing system, enforcement mechanism)?
- What are the major accomplishments and shortcomings?
- What are the domestic/bureaucratic politics of weapons trade and export controls and what is their impact on export behavior?
- What are the governments' attitudes toward international efforts (for example, the Nuclear Supplies Group, the Australia Group, the Missile Technology Control Regime, and the Wassenaar Arrangement)?

To the extent that NIS export behavior has been the subject of study in the past, the focus has generally been on transactions in the nuclear and conventional weapons sectors. A considerable literature, for example, has developed around the subject of illicit nuclear trade, although remarkably little systematic research has been conducted and reported.

This volume seeks to correct this imbalance by including the study of WMD, dual-use, and conventional arms promotion and control. Answers are sought for questions about the effect of economic pressures and defense conversion on arms export behavior, the factors responsible for the evolution of Russian and Ukrainian attitudes toward the Missile Technology Control Regime (MTCR), and the extent of convergence and divergence in U.S. and NIS perspectives on the desirability and means to control dual-use technologies in the post-Coordinating Committee for Multilateral Export Controls (COCOM) environment.

Norms and structure are important dimensions of the export control picture. Also significant, but frequently overlooked, are capabilities to implement policy once decisions are made. This study of NIS export control developments includes an assessment of the resources and political will available to the governments of the Soviet successor states, as well as the obstacles in the way of successful policy implementation. An effort also is made to discern the short- and longer-term implications of resource constraints in the export control sphere and whether or not Western assistance can or should be marshalled in this area.

NONPROLIFERATION STRATEGIES

Major strategies for controlling the spread of weapons and associated materials, equipment, and technologies from the NIS include (1) physical protection, (2) accounting and control, and (3) export controls. *Physical protection* involves securing the weaponry and/or associated items in order to avoid illicit movement or use by unauthorized persons. This approach is a natural and well-recognized response to help avoid weapons proliferation. *Accounting and control* involves keeping an inventory of all relevant weapons and associated items and assuring that they remain under authorized control. *Export controls* involve efforts to deny the illicit sale and to monitor and review the licensed sale of the controlled items noted above. As the chapters of this book note, export controls are becoming of increasing concern and importance.

The physical protection and accounting and control of weapons and associated items are important challenges requiring international attention. These two responses are particularly important in the context of the ongoing transition from a totalitarian Soviet state to more market-oriented and less centralized societies. Closed borders, control over the movement of people, and unrestricted policy surveillance made physical protection an easier task in the Soviet past.

Export controls, however, are a much larger and longer-term challenge requiring continuous attention and development to address the changing domestic and international environment. Thus far, this challenge is receiving far too little attention by both government officials and nongovernmental researchers.

THE BOOK

This book is a product of the efforts of the Center for International Trade and Security of the University of Georgia and the Center for Nonproliferation Studies of the Monterey Institute of International Studies to engage and encourage experts in the NIS to address the proliferation challenges in their part of the world. The University of Georgia and Monterey Institute programs are working with many young experts from these states, and some are contributors to this volume. In the following chapter of Part I, Vyachaslau Paznyak and Anatoli Rozanov of Belarus address the current security environment in the NIS and the prospects for nonproliferation export control development and cooperation. To begin Part II, Elina Kirichenko of Russia and William Potter examine the nuclear export control players and processes in Russia. Victor Zaborksy from Ukraine then takes a broader look at Ukrainian export control developments and challenges. Ural Latypov, Foreign Minister of Belarus, does the same for Belarus in the next chapter. Dastan Eleukenov of Kazakstan and Keith Wolfe address these issues regarding Kazakstan in the final chapter of Part II.

Part III of the book examines the problems and prospects surrounding the spread of weapons and efforts to control this proliferation from the NIS. Maria Katsva from Russia and Derek Averre of England begin with a chapter on the challenge of chemical and biological export control. Igor Khripunov from Russia examines the politics and economics of Russia's conventional arms export and control in the next chapter. Vladimir Orlov of Russia follows with a chapter on the problem of nuclear smuggling in Russia. Alexander Pikayev, also of Russia, addresses Russia's interests and efforts in controlling the spread of missiles and missile-related technology. Two Russians, Elina Kirichenko and Dmitriy Nikonov, conclude Part III with an assessment of Russia's role in the new and problematic regime for controlling conventional weapons and dual-use items, the Wassenaar Arrangement.

The editors would like to thank these contributors and the emerging community of nonproliferation specialists in the NIS for their efforts in helping promote research, study, and exchange on the issues addressed in this book. There is a critical need for more expertise and advanced research on these issues. We encourage these young experts to continue their important work. We also want to thank numerous foundations for their support of the programs making this book and the many related efforts possible. These include the Carnegie Corporation, the Compton Foundation, the Ford Foundation, the John P. and Catherine T. MacArthur Foundation, The John Merck Fund, The Ploughshares Fund, the Prospect Hill Foundation, the Rockefeller Financial Services, the Scherman Foundation, and the W. Alton Jones Foundation.

2

NIS SECURITY AND NONPROLIFERATION EXPORT CONTROLS

*Vyachaslau Paznyak
and Anatoli Rozanov*

The international security order has undergone tremendous change since the end of the Cold War. The world is faced today with an entirely new set of threats and opportunities. As a result, the need to readjust the proliferation control regimes and national export control arrangements has taken on a new sense of urgency.

This chapter will attempt to explain how the current international and domestic security environment in the New Independent States (NIS) of the former Soviet Union (FSU) affects the prospects for export control development and nonproliferation export controls. It will also examine how nonproliferation export controls can affect NIS security. Finally, it will consider the opportunities for NIS collaboration in nonproliferation export controls.

NIS AND SECURITY: IN SEARCH OF A STRATEGY

The disintegration of the Soviet Union and emergence of fifteen new states within its territory have produced uncertain and controversial results in terms of security. Surely, the collapse of communism, the start of a process of democratic transformation, and economic reform in most of the NIS were hopeful historical events. These shifts in their broad meaning have made it possible to seek world security on a more cooperative basis. At the same time, uncertainties and unpredictability associated with radical post-Soviet changes have considerably complicated the international security setting. The weakness of the new states and the rising economic, territorial, military, ethnic, and other problems in the NIS region created a potential source of instability.

Russia, Ukraine, Belarus, and their new neighbors face a challenge, as Robert Legvold put it, "greater than any confronted by any society in modern history."[1] The challenge is four-dimensional. These new states, first, are struggling to carry out a political revolution: to make over their authoritarian political systems as open, pluralistic democracies. Second, they all are trying to recast their basic economic orders, transforming planned and administered economies into free, market-driven ones. Third, they face a task of state-building. And, finally, many of the former Soviet republics need to turn diverse peoples occupying the area within their borders into cohesive nations.

The dissolution of the USSR signified a breakup of the entire Soviet defense and security system developed over decades. Rapid disorganization of the Soviet military power has led to a marked weakening of a sense of security on the part of Russia and some other NIS.

Basically, three main options were present for dealing with the problem of safeguarding security in the territory of the FSU: (1) to establish a collective security system embracing most of the NIS; (2) to rely mainly upon NIS national resources and mechanisms in search of security; and (3) to cooperate with and eventually to enter into existing Western security institutions that have proved their viability.

Since 1992, persistent efforts, initiated first of all by Russia, have been made in order to create a kind of security structure within the framework of the Commonwealth of Independent States (CIS). The principles of the CIS security system were laid down according to the Collective Security Treaty signed by the heads of six CIS states—Armenia, Kazakstan, Kyrgyzstan, Russia, Tajikistan, and Uzbekistan—at the meeting in Tashkent on May 15, 1992. Three CIS states—Azerbaijan, Georgia, and Belarus—acceded to the treaty in 1993. Ukraine, Moldova and Turkmenistan have decided not to join.

The Collective Security Treaty was not regarded as a very significant document by some experts. The problem with it (as with many other CIS documents) was that no adequate mechanism for its implementation was envisaged at the time of signing. Besides, not all member states were really interested in its implementation.

Russia has tried to activate the Collective Security Treaty and to develop on its basis a defense union within the CIS. On several occasions President Yeltsin has stressed that establishing the CIS security system was a priority task and has underscored Russia's special responsibility to the other CIS states.

On February 10, 1995, at the Almaty session of the CIS Council of Collective Security, the Concept of Collective Security was finally adopted.[2] According to the concept, the collective security of the participating states is to be based on the following principles:

- indivisibility of security, whereupon aggression against one participating state is to be viewed as aggression against all participating states;
- equal responsibility of participating states for maintaining security;
- observance of territorial integrity, respect of sovereignty, noninterference in internal affairs, and consideration of the interests of one another;
- collective defense on a regional basis;
- adoption of decisions on issues concerning collective security on the basis of consensus;
- correspondence of the composition and preparedness of forces and resources to the scale of the military threat.[3]

The participating states see a system of collective security as the aggregate of interstate and state bodies of administration and the forces and resources providing for defense of their interests, sovereignty, and territorial integrity on a common legal basis (with regard for national legislation).

The establishment of an effective collective security system may favorably affect the maintaining of stability in the CIS region. Such a system could provide conditions for tougher export control arrangements within the framework of the CIS. Enhanced regional cooperation might lead to developing a harmonized normative and legal basis for export controls, coordinating licensing procedures, and even establishing joint export control agencies. Closer political and military integration suggests a possibility of greater collaboration in "external" borders control and customs cooperation.

There has been a wide divergence of opinions in the West on the prospects of CIS military and political integration and its potential consequences. Most commentaries are rather negative with regard to a possible reintegration of the territory of the FSU and the defense union of the NIS. The arguments behind this stance are mainly that:

- reintegration will destroy the sovereignty of the states within the CIS;
- it will at the same time weaken democratic processes throughout the CIS;
- Russia, using its vast resources, which are incomparable to those of the other NIS, will start "flexing its muscles."[4]

Some Western observers (Zbigniew Brzezinski and others) claim that separate NIS with their own military structures are needed to balance the tendency for Moscow's position to gain strength. Within this attitude, advocating a long-term grand strategy of "consolidating geopolitical pluralism in the territory of the former Soviet Union,"[5] considerable emphasis is placed on supporting Ukraine's intention to be more independent from Moscow and to develop its own military force.

Ukraine's security strategy goes in line with what was mentioned above as the second option in safeguarding security of the NIS. Ukraine has refused to sign the CIS Collective Security Treaty and has instead opted in favor of a security policy that relies primarily upon national means and resources. Ukraine has indicated that it prefers to stay out of the process of the development of CIS structures, especially in the area of military security. A similar security policy is pursued by Moldova. Such an approach can eventually weaken export controls. Even if countries have strong national export control regimes, if they do not cooperate on this aspect of their security policy, controls are basically weakened.

The third option in developing security strategies of the NIS—to seek to join reliable and stable Western military-political institutions—cannot be regarded as realistic under present circumstances. Of course, the participation in the Euro-Atlantic Partnership Council and the Partnership for Peace initiated by NATO will bring the NIS closer to the Atlantic Alliance. But neither NATO nor the Western European Union (WEU) will be ready to spread the security umbrella over the NIS in the near future.

National security policies of the NIS, their priorities, and institutions are still in the process of formation. In practical terms, the concept of national security has already been worked out in some of the NIS. However, as a rule, this concept has not been properly put into shape through legislation.

In the opinion of a majority of NIS security experts who are dealing with the elaboration and formulation of the policies of the NIS in the area of national security, such policies should be based on the following general principles:

- national security cannot be ensured apart from the international security;
- national security is no longer confined to the military dimension, although it is an essential component; in the modern world, national security increasingly embraces political, economic, ecological, informational, and other factors that are tightly interrelated and that can, under certain conditions, constitute various threats.

Separate elements of the national security system have started functioning in the NIS. Coordinating bodies—Security Councils—have been established in many of the NIS. Some other institutions, forces, and structures are involved in the implementation of NIS security policies.

Many NIS have begun to cooperate with Western states on nonproliferation export controls. This cooperation may represent a form of integration and enhance international security.

DOMESTIC SECURITY TENSIONS

Export controls bring together a wide array of interests of individual entrepreneurs and businesses, economic and political lobbies, firms and industrial enterprises, various state agencies, and the state as a whole, as

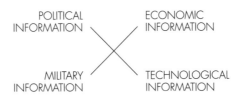

FIGURE 1 *Tensions among various aspects of national security involved in export control decision-making and policies*

well as the international community with its multiple alignments. This produces permanent tensions at various interest levels, the extent of which in turn depends on specific combinations of numerous factors. The most universal of these tensions for the NIS of the former Soviet Union seems to be the one between political-military and economic aspects of their security, on both the domestic and international levels. When reforming overmilitarized economies, NIS governments confront a dilemma: whether to join and fully cooperate with internationally recognized nonproliferation regimes, or to increase military and dual-use exports to survive.[6]

Besides, due to a concentration of export capabilities in the defense industries,[7] there is an interrelationship between the development of defense conversion strategies and export controls which makes the situation more complicated. The perceived need to provide for a rational reconciliation of national security interests with the economic interests of exporters in fact highlights decision-making problems and trade-offs between different aspects of national security: its political-military projections to the international environment while addressing domestic pressures. Unnecessary excessive restrictions of exports may backfire at the economic development of a country in question and affect its national security as a whole.[8] Most of these problems confront Western countries as well.[9]

Further, as there exists a measure of a bureaucratic conflict (see Figure 1) about the perceived national security interests among various governmental agencies, there is also a measure of compartmentalization of export control objectives pursued by different agencies, reflecting objectively existing problems and tensions and necessitating a compromising balance among them.[10]

INTERPLAY AMONG DOMESTIC AND INTERNATIONAL DIMENSIONS OF EXPORT CONTROLS: PROMOTING NIS SECURITY

The main objective[11] of export controls for the NIS in broad terms is perceived as the creation of favorable conditions for their integration in the international community,[12] facilitating foreign economic activities, safeguarding their economic interests, and consolidating national and international security by strengthening international nonproliferation regimes.[13] Creating export control systems in the NIS and making them consistent with international norms are preconditions for getting access to and cooperating in advanced technologies.[14]

Generally, nonproliferation export control efforts logically followed from the broader basic NIS nonproliferation policies with relation to their positions on the Nuclear Nonproliferation Treaty (NPT) and other international security arrangements. On the international side, this would both demonstrate the responsible approach of the NIS to international security concerns and their commitments and contribute to the consolidation of international nonproliferation regimes.[15]

Export controls have been promoted from exogenous international security issues to the status of security policy objectives, and in many instances have been "internalized" into NIS national security concepts. So, in a way, they have been developing together with the national security concepts and mechanisms of the NIS. Changes in NIS political systems and other domestic transformations have also, in some cases, brought export control issues to a higher profile.[16]

Along with the shaping of NIS security and their political and economic interests, a trend has been growing for them not to automatically copy export control systems of larger and more powerful states nor to uncritically follow every letter of international nonproliferation regimes. A solution to possible divergence of interests is seen in reciprocal consideration and accommodation of regime requirements and national interests.[17]

Figure 2 provides a generalized representation of a complex relationship between domestic security concerns and international nonproliferation export control arrangements. The perceived urgency and practical activities in the field, however, depend on several underlying factors:

- availability of sensitive materials or their deposits, technologies, equipment, stockpiles of armaments, and capacities for their production;[18]
- geographical position of the NIS and the corresponding possibility of using their territories for illicit trafficking,[19] as well as their proximity to the regions of proliferation concern;
- lack of domestic resources and the corresponding contribution of Western states in providing their expertise and material assistance to facilitate the creation of export control systems in the NIS;
- perceptions and prioritization of national interests and security threats by NIS governments.

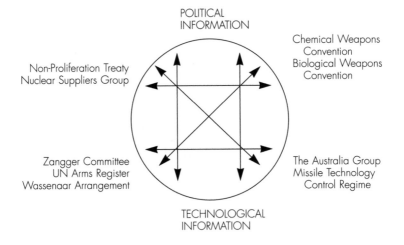

POLITICAL
INFORMATION

Chemical Weapons
Convention
Biological Weapons
Convention

Non-Proliferation Treaty
Nuclear Suppliers Group

Zangger Committee
UN Arms Register
Wassenaar Arrangement

The Australia Group
Missile Technology
Control Regime

TECHNOLOGICAL
INFORMATION

FIGURE 2   *Ramifications of national security interests with regard to the international nonproliferation export control arrangements*

Apparently, due to the interrelatedness of the domestic security dimension, development of national export controls also benefits other security areas. Thus, adoption of export control legislation and establishment of relevant mechanisms would serve to prevent and counter various criminal activities.

Conversely, close cooperation with Western counterparts on export controls facilitates communication of international experience to the developing security communities in the NIS, as well as the enhancement of their knowledge and perceptions of the present international security environment.

Yet another manifestation of a mutually complementing and reinforcing interaction of domestic and international export control aspects of security and other aspects can be seen in the fact that just as national export controls transcend the boundaries of any single country and bridge multilateral arrangements, along with preventing the spread of WMD they also promote cooperation and reinforce measures on such security issues as terrorism and contraband.

NONPROLIFERATION EXPORT CONTROLS IN THE NIS: PROBLEMS AND PROSPECTS

Discussion of the challenge of export controls in the NIS requires some preliminary clarifications. For practical purposes and policies it seems necessary to widen the scope of the notion rather than reduce it to the traditional sensitive area of issues relating to the weapons of mass destruction. The overall transitory situation in the economic systems of

CIS republics is one whereby underdeveloped legal, organizational, and technical means are complicated by confirmed and alleged cases of illegal economic activities, theft, smuggling, or transit via their territories of all kinds of goods and materials including radioactive ones; hence, the control over exports is of necessity indivisible from the control of imports. Further, it will overarch nuclear, chemical, biological, missile, and conventional dimensions.

Perceptions and practices of export controls are dependent not only on economic factors, but also on the type and formative stage of the particular political system of a state in discussion. As most NIS political systems evolved into presidential republics, key decisions on export controls as well as supervision over their implementation in many cases fell under the authority of presidential structures.

Security factors, while being an objective reality, translate into greater or smaller efforts being put into this business by the governing political elites, depending on their perceptions of linkages between both domestic and international security pressures and a correspondingly enhanced demand for developing export control mechanisms. A most vivid example of this is active efforts by Russia on export controls informed by the existing and potential domestic problems and regional as well as global implications of the proliferation of weapons of mass destruction and dual-use technologies.

External political factors are represented by the necessity of an adequate response to international challenges and requirements made in this field by the international community, as well as the need to comply with undertaken commitments. The role of a sound export control system will further grow in significance as economies of CIS republics become more open, on the one hand, and more integrated into the world economy, on the other.

After the collapse of the Soviet Union, Western nations experienced understandable premonitions about the spread of weapons of mass destruction outside the NIS—first of all fissile materials and corresponding technologies, and then the "brains" that had created them. Initial fears on this account have gradually subsided. Key republics such as Russia and Belarus from the very beginning had demonstrated responsible attitudes toward nonproliferation. Following a period of hesitation, Ukraine began to lean toward a similar approach. Kazakstan moved in the same direction.

Nevertheless, there can be no complete confidence that Russia and the other NIS will not present problems of proliferation in the future. One of the main reasons for this is the volatile economic situation that creates pressures to acquire foreign currency earnings, sometimes at any cost.

Another reason for proliferation that could potentially be very damaging is illegal acquisition of and trade in nuclear and other sensitive materials and technologies. Significant cases of alleged theft or diversions of highly enriched uranium (HEU) and plutonium are summarized by William C. Potter.[20]

Social tensions in Russia and other NIS, the proliferation of criminal organizations, and the corruption at all echelons of the bureaucratic elite "could lead to situations where well organized criminal groups and even individuals driven by greed could break the nonproliferation regime on their own, with the state being unable to stop them."[21]

In his statement before the Senate Select Committee on Intelligence on March 15, 1995, James F. Collins mentioned that "as we look to the future, we see the very real possibility that NIS organized crime could become involved in weapons-grade nuclear material smuggling."[22] So far, there is no convincing evidence that NIS organized crime has entered the field of such smuggling; the potential, however, is there. If not kept in check, the consequences will be disastrous.

Export controls are essential for a coherent and successful nonproliferation policy. Of course, export controls represent only one aspect of a comprehensive approach to nonproliferation. As Zachary S. Davis noted, "overemphasis on technology denial has many weaknesses, not the least of which is that export controls can never be completely 'leak proof.' Experience has shown that resourceful proliferators can find ways to circumvent export controls."[23] Yet export controls are a necessary and important means to counter proliferation. As a nonproliferation instrument, export controls, among other things, increase the probability that efforts to procure sensitive material will be uncovered and sinister intentions of would-be proliferators detected. While export controls are unlikely to stop a determined proliferant in the long run, they may buy important time in the shorter term—time that may be useful to bring other nonproliferation tools to bear.[24]

The effectiveness of global export controls will be greatly weakened unless Russia and the other former Soviet republics develop efficient export control systems and join and actively participate in the full set of multilateral nonproliferation control regimes.

Of all the NIS of the FSU, Russia has developed the most elaborate nonproliferation export control system. Nearly all the Soviet expertise, capability, databases, and other elements essential to export controls remain in Moscow. In Ukraine, Belarus, and Kazakhstan, as well as the other NIS, the state of export controls is considered to be more rudimentary than in Russia. Generally, in the words of Gary Bertsch, "the NIS lack nonproliferation cultures."[25]

The continuum of capabilities and interest in export controls in the NIS is broad indeed. They range from Belarus, which appears to be ready to create a Western-style system, through Russia, which has a functioning but not fully transparent or reliable system, to states such as Tajikistan, where formal export controls are in very early stages of development. Subsequent chapters of this book address these national developments more fully.[26]

CIS: REALITIES OF COLLABORATION IN NONPROLIFERATION EXPORT CONTROLS

At present CIS states have to tackle in their own ways several parallel interrelated tasks pertaining to export controls:

- creation of national systems of export controls;
- establishment and tuning up of bi- and multilateral legal and organizational mechanisms on the CIS level and ensuring their operation;
- specification of approaches to participating in the Wassenaar Arrangement.

The pace and character of progress in the above-indicated directions depend on the development of political and economic situation in CIS states, shaping of their national interests, and foreign political strategy. It goes without saying that, given the difference of interests and presence or absence of serious problems in relations with other CIS states, possibilities for solving those tasks may vary considerably.

Interdependence of CIS states in the sphere of export controls is determined by both centrifugal and integrationist trends in their political, security, and economic development. In distinction from the obvious economic interdependence of CIS states, in other areas it has been of a more relative character and will have a larger potential to grow along with the shaping of national systems of export controls and economic reintegration.

The priority of export control policies being nonproliferation of the weapons of mass destruction, the core element of interdependence of CIS states is their national and international security interests within the FSU and outside.

Interstate agreements reached on the CIS level are another element to be considered and are evidence of the realization of this interdependence.

The third element is the implementation of international commitments on export controls. On the one hand, commitments are supposed to be implemented. On the other, such implementation with regard to export controls is dependent upon compliance by counterparts.

The fourth, and still-developing, element of interdependence is sanctions against export control regime violators and the damage (political, economic, moral) that may follow for the violator party (a firm, an organization, and, eventually, the state).

Export control commitments of CIS member-states have been written down in numerous statutory and specialized agreements (see Appendix 1). The latter can be classified into several groups:

(*a*) general political and economic agreements;
(*b*) *specialized* agreements on:
- arms control and disarmament;
- cooperation in foreign economic activities;
- customs;

- protection of borders;
- security and military matters;
- military-technical issues;
- joint measures to combat crime;
- others, containing explicit and/or implicit export control clauses.

(*c*) agreements on export controls *per se* to date include only two:
  - Agreement "On Coordinating Activities on the Issues of Controlling the Exports of Raw Materials, Substances, Equipment, Technologies and Services, which May be Used for the Production of Weapons of Mass Destruction and Missile Means of their Delivery" of June 26, 1992, signed by Armenia, Belarus, Kazakstan, Kyrgyzstan, the Russian Federation, Tajikistan, and Ukraine, which binds the signatories to develop coordinated national export control systems based on control lists modeled after multilateral export control regimes;
  - the agreement among six CIS states (Armenia, Belarus, Kazakstan, Russia, Tajikistan, and Uzbekistan) on cooperation in the control of exports of material, equipment, technologies, and services related to the production of weapons of mass destruction signed on February 9, 1993.

Several meetings of the 1992 Agreement participants have taken place since then to foster a multilateral dialogue and establish interagency ties. From 1995 on, bilateral consultations on export controls intensified.

However, the continued crisis of the CIS brought about attempts to realize narrower but more concrete and practicable objectives. The Treaty on Deepening Integration in Economic and Humanitarian Fields, signed by Russia, Kazakstan, Belarus, and Kyrgyzstan on March 29, 1996, grew out of the 1995 initiative of the first three states on the establishment of the customs union. The Treaty of the Four set a still more ambitious goal of the creation of a "single economic space." To date efforts have been concentrated on the issues of payment, currency, and customs unions among member-states. Obviously, the development of the customs union is bound to lead to some forms of coordination on export controls.

The Russo-Belarusian Union, created on April 2, 1997, following the bilateral Treaty on the Formation of the Community of Belarus and Russia of April 2, 1996, marked a most advanced stage of integration compared to other CIS states. Special interstate structures have been formed to implement the Union Treaty. A program of coordinated activities in the field of foreign policy, a concept of joint defense policy, and some other joint documents adopted so far have initiated the process of unification of the two countries' legislative bases. Clearly, if Russo-Belarusian integration develops further, more identical security perceptions will have to be translated into identical security commitments, including equal participation in nonproliferation export control regimes. All the more so, Russia may be interested in bringing Belarusian standards to its own level. A special bilateral agreement on export controls is presently being developed by Belarus and Russia.

While the hitherto signed CIS export control arrangements have not been fully implemented, there are emerging problems pointing to the lack of concerted policies even within the newly established integration groupings. The customs union under the Treaty of the Four is suffering from poorly protected "outer borders." According to some estimates, the cost of reinforcing only the Belarusian border amounts to $47 million per year, while the customs committees of Russia and Belarus allocated in 1997 only $1 million.[27] The problem of controlling transfers of conventional weapons and dual-use items both within the CIS and on its borders has became more acute.[28]

Although these problems do not necessarily tell all about export control behavior of the NIS, they definitely indicate weaknesses in the practical implementation of national norms and international commitments.

Another area of inadequate cooperation and in fact of discord and often overt competition is the arms trade and attempts to sell dual-use technologies in international markets. This may be applied in some instances even to relations between Russia and Belarus. These developments confirm the limits and negative aspects of integration with respect to export controls as demonstrated by the EU, where differences of economic interests and lobbying of the weakened defense industries coupled with the abolition of national borders enhance the proliferation threat.[29]

Nonproliferation and export controls have become one of the central pillars in the entire post-Cold-War structure of international security. By strengthening and expanding domestic export control measures and harmonizing them with international norms and standards, NIS will contribute both to international security, which ever more rests on cooperative effort, and to their own security in the first place.

NOTES

1. Robert Legvold, "Western Europe and the Post-Soviet Challenge," in A. Clesse, R. Cooper, and Y. Sakamoto (eds.), *The International System After the Collapse of the East-West Order* (Dordrecht: Martinus Nijhoff, 1994).
2. "Declaration of Participating States of the Treaty on Collective Security," *Diplomaticheskiy Vestnic*, March 1995, no. 3, p. 33.
3. "Concept of Collective Security of Participating States of the Treaty on Collective Security," *Ibid.*, p. 35.
4. "Russia-CIS: Does the West's Position Need Modification?" Report of the Russian Federal Intelligence Service, *Rossiyskaya Gazeta*, September 22, 1994.
5. Zbigniew Brzezinski, "A Plan for Europe," *Foreign Affairs*, January/February 1995, p. 38.
6. Gary Bertsch and Igor Khripunov, "Nonproliferation Export Controls in the

Former Soviet Union: Assessment and Recommendations from a U.S. NGO," *The Monitor,* February 1995, p. 12.

7. See, for example, Yu. Simachev, "Export Controls in Russia," in *Export Controls in the New Independent States: Legislative and Administrative Challenges and Opportunities. Proceedings of the International Workshop, October 3–4, 1994. Minsk, Belarus* (Minsk: Eridan, 1995), pp. 24–25.

8. See U. Latypov, "Requirements to Legal Regulation of Export Control," in *Export Controls in the New Independent States,* pp. 95–96.

9. See Bertsch et al., *Controlling East-West Trade and Technology Transfer* (Duke, 1987).

10. See Yu. Simachev, "Export Controls in Russia," pp. 25–26.

11. For a discussion of a linkage between export control and security issues, see: Gary K. Bertsch, Richard T. Cupitt, and Steven Elliott-Gover (eds.), *International Cooperation on Nonproliferation Export Controls: Prospects for the 1990s and Beyond* (Ann Arbor: The University of Michigan Press, 1994); U.S. Congress, Office of Technology Assessment, *Proliferation and the Former Soviet Union,* OTA-ISS-605 (Washington, DC: U.S. Government Printing Office, September 1994); E. Kirichenko, "Export Controls in the System of National Security," in V. Paznyak (ed.), *European Integration and National Security of the NIS: Military-Political Aspects. Materials of an International Conference, June 10–12, 1993, Minsk* (Minsk: National Centre for Strategic Initiatives "East-West," 1993), pp. 64–65.

12. As an Estonian diplomat points out, the main impetus for the development of an export control system in Estonia "has been provided by the development of trade relations and the understanding of the fact that without rules Estonia cannot be part of the European game." See Indrek Tarand, "Estonia," in Harald Mueller (ed.), *Nuclear Export Controls in Europe* (Brussels: European Interuniversity Press, 1995), p. 270.

13. See Victor Pas'ko, "On the Development of Export Control System in the Republic of Belarus," in *Export Controls in the New Independent States,* p. 23.

14. See, for example, Evgenii Sharov, "Ukraine and the MTCR," *The Monitor,* vol. 1, no. 2 (Spring 1995), pp. 1; 21–22.

15. According to some Belarusian officials, creation of a reliable export control system will facilitate Belarus's early integration into both the systems of international security and economic cooperation. See Victor Pas'ko, "On the Development of Export Control System in the Republic of Belarus," p. 23.

16. After Belarus became a presidential republic in 1994, its Security Council became a collegiate body for nonproliferation and export control. It is responsible for considering issues of joining international nonproliferation agreements and authorization of major military and dual-use exports. See Ural Latypov, "The Shaping of Belarus' Export Control System," *The Monitor,* vol. 1, no. 2, 1995, p. 3.

17. See A. Baichorov, "Harmonization of NIS National Export Control Systems and International Nonproliferation Regimes," in *Export Controls in the New Independent States,* pp. 87–88.

18. For an inventory of nuclear materials, capabilities, and facilities in the FSU, see William C. Potter, *Nuclear Profiles of the Soviet Successor States,* Program for Nonproliferation Studies, Monterey Institute of International Studies, Monograph No. 1, May 1993; and *Nuclear Successor States of the Soviet Union,* Nuclear Weapon and Sensitive Export Status Report No. 2, December 1994, The Carnegie Endowment for International Peace, The Monterey Institute of International Studies.

19. According to a Latvian expert, for example, the main concern for all the Baltic republics is transit, but not exports or imports of strategic materials. See G. Kruminsh, "Legal and Practical Issues of the Realization of the Latvian National Export Control System," in *Export Controls in the New Independent States,* p. 63.

20. William C. Potter, "Before the Deluge? Assessing the Threat of Nuclear Leakage From the Post-Soviet States," *Arms Control Today,* vol. 25, no. 8, October 1995, pp. 9–16.

21. Andrei Shoumikhin, "View From Russia: The Weapons Stockpiles," *Comparative Strategy,* 1995, vol. 14, p. 214.

22. James F. Collins, "Crime in the New Independent States: The U.S. Response," Statement before the Senate Select Committee on Intelligence, Washington, DC, March 15, 1995, *Department of State Dispatch,* U.S. Department of State, April 3, 1995.

23. Zachary S. Davis, "Nuclear Proliferation and Nonproliferation Policy in the 1990s," in Michael T. Klare and Daniel C. Thomas (eds.), *World Security: Challenges for a New Century* (New York: St. Martin's Press, 1994), p. 124.

24. U.S. Congress, Office of Technology Assessment, *Export Controls and Nonproliferation Policy* (Washington, DC: U.S. Government Printing Office, May 1994), p. 11.

25. Gary Bertsch, "Introduction," *Restraining the Spread of the Soviet Arsenal: NIS Nonproliferation Export Controls, Status Report—1996* (Athens: The University of Georgia, 1997), p. 4.

26. A detailed analysis of national export control developments is also presented in Gary K. Bertsch and Suzette R. Grillot (eds.), *Arms on the Market: Reducing the Risk of Proliferation in the Former Soviet Union* (New York: Routledge, 1998).

27. *Belorusskaya Delovaya Gazeta,* April 17, 1997.

28. See Yevgeni Kulikov, "Russia's Cooperation on Export Controls with the Commonwealthof Independent States," *The Monitor: Nonproliferation, Demilitarization and Arms Control,* vol. 3, no. 2, Spring 1997, p. 27.

29. See Scott Jones, "An Enlarging Europe: Implications for EU Nonproliferation Export Controls," *The Monitor: Nonproliferation, Demilitarization and Arms Control.* vol. 3, no. 3, Summer 1997, pp. 15–17.

APPENDIX I

CHRONOLOGY OF RELEVANT AGREEMENTS WITHIN THE CIS TO EXPORT CONTROL

December 8, 1991	On the Creation of the CIS
December 21, 1991	Alma-Ata Declaration; On Joint Measures with Respect to Nuclear Weapons
December 30, 1991	On Joint Activities in the Exploration and Use of Space
February 14, 1992	On Regulating Trade and Economic Cooperation of CIS Member-States in 1992
March 13, 1992	On the Principles of Customs Policy; Regulations on the Customs Council
March 20, 1992	On the Principles of Providing Armed Forces of CIS Member-States with Armaments, Military Equipment and other Material Resources and on the Organization of R & D
May 15, 1992	Agreement between CIS Member-States with Respect to Chemical Weapons; On Cooperation in Foreign Economic Activities

June 26, 1992	On Coordinating Activities on the Issues of Controlling the Exports of Raw Materials, Substances, Equipment, Technologies and Services, which May be Used for the Production of Weapons of Mass Destruction and Missile Means of their Delivery; On the Main Principles of Cooperation in the Field of a Peaceful Use of Nuclear Energy; On the Exchange of Economic Information
July 6, 1992	Decision of CIS Member-States on their Accession to the Non-Proliferation Treaty
October 9, 1992	On the Principles of the Unification of the Economic Legislation of CIS Member-States
January 22, 1993	Statute Of the Commonwealth of Independent States
February 9, 1993	Agreement among Six CIS States on Cooperation in the Control of Exports of Materials, Equipment, Technologies, and Services Related to the Production of Weapons of Mass Destruction
April 28, 1993	Decision on the Council of the Heads of Foreign Economic Departments of CIS Member-States and Two Appendices Thereto
May 14, 1993	Regulation on the Coordinating and Consultative Committee of CIS Member-States and other Required Documents
September 24, 1993	Treaty on the Creation of the Economic Union; Regulation on the Council of Ministers for Foreign Affairs of CIS Member-States; Agreement on the Exchange of Information in the Field of Foreign Economic Activities; Rules for Identifying the Country of Origin of Commodities
December 23, 1993	Agreement on the General Conditions and Mechanism for the Support of Production Cooperation of Enterprises and Branches of Industry of CIS Member-States; Regulation on the Council of Heads of Customs Services of CIS Member-States
February 10, 1995	Decision of the Council of Collective Security on the Concept of Collective Security of the States-Parties to the Treaty on Collective Security; Decision of the Council of Collective Security on the Declaration of the States–Parties to the Treaty on Collective Security; Decision on the Basics of Customs Legislation of CIS Member-States
May 26, 1995	Agreement on Cooperation in the Sphere of the Protection of Borders of CIS Member-States with Non-Participating States

November 3, 1995	Decision on the Activities of Interstate and Intergovernmental Bodies of the CIS involved in the Coordination of Economic Issues;
	Agreement on the Unified List of Commodities for External Economic Activities of the CIS;
	Agreement on the Establishment of Common Scientific and Technological Space of CIS Member-States;
	Protocol Decision on the Organization of a Working Group for the Elaboration of the Draft Interstate Program of Joint Measures Aimed at Combating Organized Crime in the Territory of CIS Member-States
April 12, 1996	Agreement on Cooperation in Combating Crime in the Economic Sphere;
	Agreement on the Control over Transborder Transportation of Dangerous and Other Kinds of Wastes
May 17, 1996	Interstate Program on Joint Measures to Combat Organized Crime and Other Felonies in the Territory of CIS Member-States for the Period to 2000
March 27–28, 1997	Decision on the Establishment of the Council of the Heads of Security Agencies and Special Services of CIS Member-States
October 9, 1997	Concept of the Program of Military-Technical Cooperation of CIS Member-States;
	Statute of the Bureau for Combating Organized Crime and Other Felonies in the Territory of CIS Member-States

PART II

EXPORT CONTROL DEVELOPMENT IN THE NEW INDEPENDENT STATES

3

NUCLEAR EXPORT CONTROLS IN RUSSIA: THE PLAYERS AND THE PROCESS

Elina Kirichenko
and William C. Potter

Recent Russian nuclear export initiatives to Iran, China, and India have redirected Western attention from a narrow concentration on illicit nuclear trade involving the former Soviet Union to state-sanctioned commerce. This new focus, however, has not yet yielded much analysis of the Russian export control system.[1] Moreover, the small body of literature that does exist on the topic provides little insight on the process by which nuclear export decisions are made or information about the players involved. This chapter is an effort to remedy, at least in part, these deficiencies.

THE FORMAL STRUCTURE

As the inheritor of the well-developed Soviet export control structure, the Russian system from the outset possessed considerable technical know-how. Most of the changes that have been introduced since 1992, therefore, have involved efforts to reorganize the existing bureaucracy and to make the prior system more compatible with the rise of nongovernmental exporters and more market-based activities.

As might be expected under these circumstances of radical economic and political transformation, one finds a lack of congruence between formal export control responsibilities and the actual process by which decisions are made. This incongruence poses a major problem in analyzing the operation of the current export control system in Russia.

This difficulty of analysis is further complicated by the fact that the lack of congruence between formal and actual responsibility varies depending upon the export commodity in question. These caveats in mind, however, one can observe that nuclear export controls represent one of the principal components of Russia's broader export control system (other components deal with arms and missile exports, chemical and biological weapons-materials, and sensitive dual-use commodities, technology and materials). The foundation of the nuclear export control system consists of legal obligations, control lists, licensing procedures, and enforcement mechanisms.

Until Fall 1995, legal obligations referred principally to a body of Presidential Decrees *(ykazi)*, Presidential Directives *(rasporyazhenyi)*, and Governmental Regulations *(postanovleniya)*.[2] With several minor exceptions, the export control system lacked a foundation in national legislation.[3] This deficiency was remedied in part by the passage in 1995–1996 of three new laws. The first, "On State Regulation of Foreign Trade Activity" contains a short section (Article 16) on national export control policy. The second, "On the Use of Atomic Energy" has provisions relating to nuclear export controls.[4] In addition, a new Criminal Code was passed in April 1996 that contains a number of articles addressing export control violations and illegal handling of nuclear and radioactive materials.[5] A comprehensive draft law "On Export Controls" was circulated among relevant government ministries and agencies in 1997, and in summer 1998 it was finalized and submitted to the Duma.

Control lists specify those commodities, technologies, equipment, and material whose export requires licenses. These lists are prepared by experts of authorized state bodies, and are then approved by the Office of the Prime Minister and signed by the President. To date, five control lists have been adopted pertaining to: (1) dual-use nuclear-related material, equipment, and technology; (2) chemicals, equipment, and technologies that can be used for developing chemical weapons; (3) human, animal, and plant pathogens and equipment that can be used for developing biological weapons; (4) equipment, material, and technology that can be used for developing missiles and missile technology; and (5) selected types of materials, equipment, and technology used in the production of weapons and military hardware. In addition to these five control lists, there is a sixth list that covers nuclear materials, technologies, equipment, installations, and special non-nuclear materials (used for the production of nuclear materials), the export of which requires both licensing and special guarantees.

Licensing procedures specify the process of authorization of export of items covered by the control lists. The Ministry of Trade (the former Ministry of Foreign Economic Relations and Trade) has responsibility for issuing licenses, in consultation with other governmental bodies.

Export control enforcement encompasses activities such as border controls, customs inspection, and penalties for violations of export control regulations.

THE MAIN PLAYERS

The export control decision-making process in Russia has many tiers and involves numerous organizational actors including the president, parliament, the office of the prime minister, and a variety of executive state bodies. Their formal responsibilities are summarized below.

A. President

The president of the Russian Federation has broad constitutional powers to conduct foreign policy, including nonproliferation policy. Accordingly, his degree of commitment to nuclear nonproliferation greatly influences national export controls. Operationally, the president approves and signs export control lists and also issues decrees and directives.

B. Duma (Lower House of Parliament)

As noted previously, the legislative branch of government until recently has not played an active role in the formulation of national export control policy. It has, however, paid attention to some specific export issues, including the return of spent nuclear fuel, and Russia's participation in certain multilateral nonproliferation regimes such as the Missile Technology Control Regime (MTCR) and the Wassenaar Arrangement. The Duma also has affected export control developments by impeding the adoption of specific laws, as it did repeatedly with drafts of the Atomic Energy Act. As part of its efforts to extend its authority in different areas, however, the Duma increasingly has taken a more proactive stance on export control matters. This new posture was illustrated in hearings during 1994 and 1995 on the Law on State Regulation of Foreign Trade Activity.[6] A committee was established to try to reconcile the differences between the Duma and the President, and eventually a version that resembled the Ministry of Foreign Economic Relations proposal was accepted and signed by the President (October 13, 1995). Also indicative of the Duma's growing involvement in the formulation of national nonproliferation export control policy was its adoption on October 20, 1995, of Federal Law No. 170-FZ "On the Use of Atomic Energy."[7] The law contains several articles on the export and import of nuclear equipment, technology, material, and services.[8] A more comprehensive export control law was drafted by the Federal Service for Currency and Export Controls, and circulated to the relevant ministries and agencies for review in Fall 1997. However, initial reactions to the draft law were quite critical, and it was only submitted in a revised manner to the Duma for consideration and approval in 1998.

C. Office of the Prime Minister

The principal export control responsibilities of the Office of the Prime Minister of the Russian Federation are to approve bilateral agreements and contracts on cooperation with foreign countries in the nuclear and military-technology area, to issue export control regulations, and to approve control lists, which are then submitted to the president for signature. A division within the Department of Defense Industries in the Prime Minister's Office has responsibility for export control issues and maintains ties with other state bodies in this sphere.

D. Ministry of Atomic Energy (Minatom)

The most important executive body in the nuclear sector is Minatom, which derives its influence from formal regulations, the concentration of expertise within its ministry, and the personal connections of its senior leadership. Minatom's formal responsibilities in the export control sphere include the compilation of control lists for nuclear and dual use nuclear-related items, recommendations for the approval or denial of applications for export of all nuclear commodities and technologies, and the negotiations with foreign parties of nuclear contracts. The main bodies in Minatom with nuclear export control responsibilities are the Export Council (Exportnyi Sovet) and the Department for International Relations. The Export Council evaluates potential nuclear contracts; the Department reviews applications for nuclear export licenses. The decision of the Department is finalized by a Minatom deputy minister. The Department also is responsible for overseeing the implementation of international safeguards. Minatom has responsibility for approving the reexport or retransfer of critical nuclear items in agreement with Eksportkontrol. Another Minatom body, the Central Scientific Research Institute for Administration, Economics, and Information (Atominform), maintains a database on all nuclear exports and imports and conveys data on nuclear commerce to the IAEA. Minatom enterprises are required to apprise Atominform of their nuclear exports and imports.[9]

E. Governmental Export Control Commission

In order to coordinate state export control policy in pursuit of nonproliferation objectives, an intergovernmental Russian Federation Export Control Commission or Eksportkontrol was established by Presidential Decree No. 388 on April 11, 1992. Upon its creation, Eksportkontrol was given the task of drafting export control lists and, together with the Ministry of Foreign Affairs, conducting talks with representatives of the other CIS states for the purpose of coordinating export control activities. Eksportkontrol also was tasked to assist the Russian Federation Ministry of Justice in preparing proposals for the introduction of criminal and administrative penalties for the illegal export of items covered by the control lists. In addition, Eksportkontrol was charged with the responsibility for giving final approval for exports of specified material, equipment, technology, know-how, and services on the basis of the aforementioned five control lists. In May 1996 this responsibility was extended to cover sensitive nuclear items such as fissile material and enrichment and reprocessing technology. Under Government Regulation No. 574, the export license of such items can be issued only by the Ministry of Trade after approval of both Minatom and *Eksportkontrol*. Previously, only approval from Minatom was required.[10]

The interagency commission is chaired by the First Deputy Prime Minister and is comprised of the deputy chiefs of the following ministries and state bodies: Foreign Affairs, Defense, Atomic Energy (Minatom), Economics, Trade, State Committee on Nuclear and Radiation Safety (Gosatomnadzor), Science and Technology Policy, Academy of Sciences, Federal Security Service, Foreign Intelligence Service, and State Customs Committee. Staff support for *Eksportkontrol* is provided by the Department of Export Controls of the Federal Service of Currency and Export Control (FSCEC).[11]

F. Ministry of Trade

Next to Minatom, the most important player in the sphere of nuclear exports is the Ministry of Trade. It has formal responsibility for issuing licenses for the export of nuclear and dual-use nuclear-related commodities. In mid-1996, the Ministry also assumed the licensing responsibility of the Russian State Committee on Military-Technical Policy, which previously granted licenses for arms exports and import. Licensing authority for the export of nuclear commodities is concentrated in the Ministry's Department of Non-Tariff Regulation of Foreign Economic Activity, which maintains information on the applications of both nuclear and dual use items. The department has close ties with Minatom and sometimes serves as a bridge between that body and the working group of *Eksportkontrol*.

Licenses for the export of goods on five control lists are supposed to be provided only after approval is granted by the working group of the Russian Federation Export Control Commission. The Ministry of Trade also is charged with reviewing export control rules (in conjunction with the Export Control Commission), maintaining databases on export licenses and violations of national export regulations, issuing of import and end-user certificates, providing information on export control regulations, participating in negotiations and consultations on export controls with foreign governments, and applying administrative sanctions toward violations of export control regulations. The Ministry maintains offices in 62 regional divisions of the Russian Federation, but only issues licenses for items that have no proliferation significance. Critical nuclear and dual-use nuclear-related export licenses are issued by the Ministry of Trade's Department of Foreign Trade Regulation.

G. Federal Service of Currency and Export Controls

The Department of Export Controls of the Federal Service of Currency and Export Controls serves as the working group or secretariat for the Government Export Control Commission. Prior to its creation in August 1994, this department carried out a similar staff support function while lodged in the Ministry of Economics. The department was the principal party responsible for the development of the dual-use export control lists. It routinely prepares analyses and recommendations for the Export Control Commission, and prepares drafts of relevant decrees, regulations, and directives for the president and the government. Its representatives participate in negotiations and consultations on export control issues with foreign governments and in meetings of some multilateral export control regimes. Its special expertise continues to lie in the area of dual-use items, and its influence is greatest on licensing and reexport decisions in this realm.

The Federal Service, for most of its short existence, has been engaged in intense power struggles with other major export control organizational actors, and its influence on export policy has fluctuated considerably. In mid-1996, for example, it was in danger of dismantlement during the move to streamline the Russian executive branch. In late 1996 it also appeared that the export control function of the Federal Service would be transferred to the Ministry of Foreign Economic Relations. This move, however, ultimately was blocked, in part due to objections by some government officials that the transfer would have further aggravated the conflict of interest between the export promotion and export control missions of the Ministry of Foreign Economic Relations. It remains to be seen what impact if any the elevation of *Eksportkontrol* in 1997 to the status of a Governmental Commission and the assumption of the newly created position of Deputy Chairman of *Eksportkontrol* by the longtime head of the Federal Service's Department of Export Control will have on the latter body's influence.

H. Ministry of Foreign Affairs

Principal responsibility for overseeing the international aspects of export control policy resides formally in the Ministry of Foreign Affairs. The major organizational player on export control issues within the ministry is the Export Control Office under the Directorate for Security and Disarmament Issues. Also engaged in export control matters as a consequence of their responsibility for peaceful nuclear cooperation are the Division of Nuclear Nonproliferation and the International Atomic Energy Agency under the Department for International Science and Technology Cooperation. Representatives of the Ministry of Foreign Affairs participate in negotiations on international export control guidelines and regulations. They also participate in meetings of multilateral export control bodies and take part in bilateral negotiations and consultations on issues of import certificate procedures. Should the need arise, the ministry has the right to request on-site inspection abroad in order to determine the importer's compliance with the declared use of the item in question.

I. Federal Security Service (Federalnaya Sluzhba Besopastnosti, or FSB) and Foreign Intelligence Service (Sluzhba Vneshnei Razvedki, or SVR)

Both the FSB and SVR—successor organizations to the Soviet KGB—have special departments for nonproliferation and export control matters. These departments maintain close contact with Minatom and the Department of Export Control in the Federal Service for Currency and Export Control and provide these bodies with relevant intelligence information, especially as it pertains to illegal export of nuclear material by individuals and imports by prospective end users. These departments also interact with their counterparts internationally with the aim of curtailing illicit nuclear trade.

J. State Customs Committee

The State Customs Committee (GTK) has the task of monitoring the conformity of exports with licenses and customs declarations. It also is responsible for preparing and issuing delivery confirmation certificates and enforcing non-tariff regulations, including nonproliferation export controls.[12] A central office of the State Customs Committee in Moscow has responsibility for national GTK policy and participates in the interagency process in the development of federal export control regulations. There also are 18 regional administrative offices of the GTK, each of which has a division of non-tariff regulations with enforcement responsibility for nonproliferation export controls. The GTK also staffs 522 Customs checkpoints on the Russian border and at major points of entry and departure.[13]

K. State Committee on Nuclear and Radiation Safety (Gosatomnadzor)

Gosatomnadzor's responsibilities in the export control sphere relate primarily to the issuance of permits to enterprises for the production of nuclear or nuclear-related commodities. These permits are required before an export license can be granted by *Eksportkontrol.*[14] *Gosatomnadzor,* which was established by Presidential Decree in December 1991, also plays a significant indirect role in the regulation of nuclear exports due to its oversight responsibility in the sphere of physical protection, material control, and accountancy at civilian nuclear facilities in Russia.[15]

L. Russian Academy of Sciences

The Council on Export Controls of the Russian Academy of Sciences was established in June 1992 to provide expert scientific support for the administration of Russian export control policy. The Council's mandate was especially in the dual-use area, a topic that it also explored jointly with an export committee of the U.S. National Academy of Sciences.[16]

M. Center for Export Controls

The Center for Export Controls is a non-governmental entity established in 1994 at the initiative of a number of Russian governmental organizations including the Federal Service for Currency and Export Control, the Ministry of Foreign Affairs, and the Ministry of Foreign Economic Relations. The Center serves as a repository of information on Russian export control regulations and legislation. It also organizes nonproliferation export control workshops for Russian enterprises and offers consulting services in the export control realm. The Center maintains close ties with both U.S. and Russian governmental agencies with responsibilities for nuclear exports, as well as with non-governmental organizations and private businesses in the United States and Europe.

THE FORMAL PROCESS

The formal process by which export control decisions are made varies depending upon the item in question. The export licensing process for nuclear and "critical nuclear" products, as well as for nuclear-related dual-use material, equipment, and technology is described below.

A. Nuclear and Critical Nuclear Exports

The formal procedures for the export (and import) of nuclear and critical nuclear products are specified in Government Regulation No. 574 (May 8, 1996).[17] This document amends in a number of important respects Government Regulation No. 1005 (December 21, 1992), which previously had governed most nuclear exports. According to Government Regulation No. 574, critical nuclear products are defined as those nuclear materials, equipment, and related technology that are critical from the standpoint of the production of nuclear weapons. They include uranium enriched to more than 20 percent U-235, plutonium, equipment for uranium isotope separation, equipment for heavy water production, equipment for the conversion of enriched uranium and plutonium, and technologies associated with these critical nuclear products. The full list of nuclear material, equipment, special non-nuclear material, and related technology subject to export controls was approved by Presidential Decree No. 202 of February 14, 1996.[18]

Foreign trade in all such commodities is restricted to legal entities that have been approved by Gosatomnadzor to do business in the sphere of atomic energy. If a legal entity wishes to export a critical nuclear item, it must go through the four steps outlined below. If an entity wishes to export a non-critical nuclear item, steps number two and three may be bypassed.

1) Draft agreements concerning any nuclear transfers with foreign partners must be agreed upon *(soglasovani)* by all interested state agencies (including *Eksportkontrol,* Minatom, the Ministry of Trade, and the Ministry of Foreign Affairs).

2) If the item in question is a critical nuclear item, then a formal decision is required from the Office of Prime Minister in order to begin the official negotiation of a contract, agreement, or other arrangement.

3) Any export contract involving critical nuclear items must be evaluated by *Eksportkontrol.* At this stage, *Eksportkontrol* issues a conclusion confirming that the proposed contract is consistent with the domestic requirements and international obligations of the Russian Federation.

4) Once *Eksportkontrol* issues a positive conclusion regarding the realization of a contract, then any item delivered in the framework of that contract requires an export license. Export licenses are issued by the Ministry of Trade with the agreement of the Ministry of Atomic Energy.

Stated somewhat differently, critical nuclear exports are subject to multiple levels of control. The first level is the mandatory government decision permitting the negotiations. The second level involves the receipt by the exporter of a positive conclusion from *Eksportkontrol* regarding the export contract. The third level involves licensing on a case-by-case basis for the delivery of all nuclear items in the export contract. The addition of the second level of control, involving an assessment by *Eksportkontrol,* was introduced in May 1996 by Government Regulation No. 574 and represents a potentially significant dilution of Minatom's authority.

In order for *Eksportkontrol* to begin its evaluation of an export contract, an exporter must submit the following documents to the Federal Service on Currency and Export Control:[19]

a notarized copy of the certificate showing that the exporter is registered with the State;

a copy of the permit to handle nuclear materials issued to the exporter by Gosatomnadzor;

a copy of the agreement between the Russian manufacturer and the exporting organization, if the export of the critical nuclear item is performed through an intermediary;

documents containing a determination as to whether the nuclear export could convey information that is a state secret;

original documents from the government of the importing country that provide assurances that the imports: (1) will not be used for the manufacture of nuclear weapons or other nuclear explosives; (2) will be provided with physical protection at least equal to the standards recommended by the IAEA; and (3) will not be reexported without Russian approval.[20]

Once the Federal Service on Currency and Export Control has received the aforementioned documents, *Eksportkontrol* has 30 days to reach a conclusion regarding the proposed export. The Federal Service then forwards the determination to the exporter, Minatom, and the Ministry of Trade. If the exporter receives a positive decision from *Eksportkontrol*, it can initiate the application process with Minatom. In addition to the documents submitted to *Eksportkontrol*, the exporter also must provide Minatom with:

> an application for the issuance of a license;
> documents confirming the producer of the critical nuclear export and a permit for production issued to the manufacturer by Gosatomnadzor;
> documents confirming the absence of limitations on the part of the manufacturer for export of the nuclear objects abroad;
> a positive conclusion from *Eksportkontrol* regarding the possibility of implementing the proposed contract for the critical nuclear export.[21]

The Department of International Relations in Minatom reviews the documentation provided by the exporter. If the review is favorable and Minatom supports the license application, the recommendation is forwarded to the Ministry of Trade, which can grant the license if it concludes that the proposed export conforms to Russian economic policy. Critical nuclear products can only be exported under a one-time license, valid for a maximum of one year.

Minatom continues to be the major player in the decision-making process for licensing the export of non-critical nuclear products. An export license application for these items is sent to the Ministry of Trade's Department of Non-Tariff Regulation of Foreign Trade Activity only after Minatom has approved the application. This Department then sends its evaluation to the Ministry of Trade's central regional office, headquartered in Moscow, which is responsible for actually issuing the export license. Non-critical nuclear commodities can be exported under one-time and general licenses for up to one year. To date, only three general licenses are known to have been granted to the well-established exporter *Tekhsnabeksport*.

B. Dual-Use Nuclear Exports

The licensing process for dual-use nuclear exports resembles that for critical nuclear products. The principal difference is that the Ministry of

Trade can grant the license on the basis of a positive conclusion by *Eksportkontrol* and in the absence of Minatom approval.[22]

Procedures regulating dual-use nuclear exports are specified in Government Regulation No. 575 (May 8, 1996).[23] These procedures require that a prospective exporter submit the following documents to the Federal Service on Currency and Export Control in order for *Eksportkontrol* to reach a conclusion regarding the export license application:

> a letter that includes information identifying the owner of the dual-use nuclear item, and confirms that the export does not convey any information that is considered a state secret;
>
> a notarized copy of the certificate showing that the exporter is registered with the state;
>
> copies of the permits from Gosatomnadzor, issued to both the exporter and the owner of the dual-use nuclear item (if the exporter is not the owner) for the appropriate activity involving the dual-use commodity;
>
> an export license application, filled out in accordance with the requirements specified by the Russian Ministry of Trade;
>
> a copy of the contract for the proposed export of dual-use equipment, material or technology that specifies: (1) the purpose and place of application of the exported goods; (2) the end user of the exported goods; (3) a guarantee from the importer that neither the dual-use equipment, material, technology— nor reproductions of these items—will be used in the creation of nuclear explosive devices. If the export is to a non-nuclear-weapon state, the contract must include a guarantee from the importer that the dual-use equipment, material, or technology will not be used in any component of the nuclear fuel cycle, which has not been placed under IAEA safeguards. If the export is to a country that is not a member of the Nuclear Suppliers Group, the contract must include a guarantee from the importer that the dual-use equipment, material, or technology will not be re-exported without the written permission of Russia.
>
> an import certificate issued by the appropriate state agency of the country in which the end-use of the dual-use nuclear item will take place.

Once *Eksportkontrol* receives the aforementioned documentation, it has 30 days to issue a conclusion. In making that determination, *Eksportkontrol* is supposed to assess the proliferation implications of the commodity in question and the nonproliferation credentials of the recipient country.[24]

Once *Eksportkontrol* reaches a conclusion on the license application, the decision is forwarded by the Federal Service to both the exporter and the Ministry of Trade. In the case of a positive conclusion, the Ministry typically will issue a one-time license to the exporter.

THEORY VERSUS PRACTICE

Russia, by many standards, has developed an impressive export control system.[25] As described above, it has an especially well-developed set of institutions and formal procedures to govern the export of nuclear and nuclear-related commodities. Unlike the other post-Soviet states, it also benefited by the inheritance of most of the Soviet Union's expertise in the export control sector.

Notwithstanding these important assets and some indications of a growing maturity in the operation of Russia's export controls,[26] one also can point to serious problems in the implementation of Russian non-proliferation export controls. They pertain to the tension between non-proliferation and economic objectives, fractious bureaucratic politics, an underdeveloped legislative basis, inadequate enforcement measures, secrecy, and a stunted nonproliferation culture.

1. The Reverse Midas Touch

Russia today faces a dilemma common to other states with nuclear export capabilities and international nonproliferation obligations. What priority should it place on hard currency exports and proliferation restraint? The dilemma for Russia, however, is aggravated by the country's abundance of nuclear material, technology, equipment, and know-how and the dire economic situation of the government, including the nuclear sector. As such, there is a strong incentive to follow the reverse Midas touch—all that turns to gold we touch. Stated somewhat differently, it often has been difficult for the institutional advocates of nuclear export restraint to counter the proponents of more relaxed and opportunistic export policies.

One can observe instances of the subordination of nonproliferation to economic considerations in Russian nuclear trade initiatives toward Iran, China, and India. The latter case is particularly telling since it prompted Russia in 1996 to amend a domestic export control regulation that was at odds with the government's interpretation that the April 1992 Nuclear Suppliers Group guidelines were only applicable to contracts initiated after April 1992. The inconvenient regulation that might have legally precluded Russian nuclear exports to India was Government Regulation No. 1005 (December 21, 1992),[27] which specified that nuclear exports to non-nuclear weapon states could only be made if all of the recipient country's nuclear activity were under IAEA safeguards.[28] In contrast, Government Resolution No. 574 (May 8, 1996) conveniently amends Government Resolution No. 1005 and stipulates that so-called full-scope or comprehensive IAEA safeguards were only required under contracts concluded before April 4, 1992.[29] Under this grandfather clause, Russia has sought to argue that since an initial agreement to provide India with two VVER-1000 reactors was concluded in 1988, it was not subject to the 1992 full-scope safeguards requirement.[30]

2. Bureaucratic Politics

The lack of a strong legislative foundation for Russia's export control system contributes to constant and intense bureaucratic battles to alter by executive degree the nuclear export process and the relative authority of the different organizational actors. As the University of Georgia authors note, this bureaucratic infighting and continuous reshuffling have not been conducive to the orderly development and operation of the export control mechanism.[31]

The possibility for distortion or modification of the policy objectives intended by those who drafted export control decrees and regulations also is increased by the general lack of respect for law in Russia, the prevalence of corruption, and the relatively low standing of export controls in the hierarchy of national policy objectives of the Russian political leadership. The tendency for decisions in the Russian interagency process to be made on a case-by-case process within very broad guidelines also encourages export control decisions that are by way of exception (v poryadke isklyucheniya) and are based on political expediency rather than principle.[32]

This Russian approach, which often is characterized by permissive interpretations of legal restrictions under the rule that everything not expressly prohibited is permitted, also may involve extraordinary measures or extralegal initiatives that parallel the more formal, prescribed export control process. As described by Nikolai Sokov, a former Russian Foreign Ministry official, an enterprise that seeks to export a sensitive commodity, for example, might rely upon personal connections and try to raise the proposed deal with a member of the Export Control Commission, at the same time that it pursues the regular application process. Depending upon the source of the intervention, the Commission might be inclined to send a memorandum (zapiska) to other relevant agencies defending the export proposal on grounds of Russian national interests, the creation of jobs, etc. The memorandum also would likely assert that the initiative was consistent with Russia's international obligations and nonproliferation policy, or if it departed at all from these requirements, it did so only marginally. Therefore, the export should be approved. This special pleading could transform a routine review of the proposal according to established criteria into an interagency political negotiation, whose outcome depended more on the personal and organizational power of the players than on the established export control regulations. Although the lack of transparency in the Russian export control process makes it difficult to determine the applicability of Sokov's thesis to the nuclear export sphere, it would appear to be consistent with what we know about Russian nuclear trade initiatives to Iran and India. It also resembles the process by which decisions were taken regarding the sale of cryogenic engines to India.[33]

One recent legal development, which if actually applied, may counter in part the tendency for permissive interpretation of legal restrictions in the export sector, is the acceptance by the Russian government of the principle of so-called "catch all" requirements. This rule is designed to shift the burden of proof for exporting proliferation sensitive goods and technology to the exporter, even if the export in question may not be on a specific control list.[34]

3. Weak Enforcement

Perhaps the weakest link in the Russian export control system and the one that contributes most to the discrepancy between export control theory and practice is lax enforcement. Although the new Criminal Code (like its predecessor) contains provisions for the punishment of illegal exports of weapons of mass destruction and related material technology, equipment, and services, there appear to have been few prosecutions.[35] Given the seriousness of the offense, the prescribed punishment, even if implemented, would not likely serve as an effective deterrent. It ranges from a fine of $700 to $1,000, or the total salary of the convicted party for a seven- to twelve-month period, to between three to seven years of imprisonment.[36]

A number of factors account for the underdeveloped state of export control enforcement. They include: inadequate resources on the part of the State Customs Committee; that body's limited enforcement authority relative to its counterpart in the United States; the susceptibility of enforcement personnel to corruption due to low wages, delays in payment, and the prevalence of organized criminal activity; the porous, vast borders of Russia; and the low priority that the political leadership has placed on rectifying these difficulties.[37] Although the size of the State Customs Committee has grown substantially in recent years, there is little evidence that the increased number of customs officials has led to strengthened enforcement.

4. Nonproliferation Culture

One of the less tangible but most important elements of an effective nonproliferation export control system is a shared belief on the part of a broad spectrum of society in the danger of the spread of weapons of mass destruction and the need to control the export of sensitive material, equipment, technology, and services. These norms, unfortunately, are not yet deeply rooted in much of the Russian population that at best has only a faint understanding of the relevance of export controls to their daily life, in which they struggle to survive from one crisis to the next. In such a harsh environment that lacks a culture of nonproliferation, it is all the more important to foster the growth of a community of export control officials who give priority to nonproliferation considerations in their decision-making. Although some steps are being taken in this direction, such as the establishment of several new non-governmental organizations that focus on nonproliferation and export control issues, the challenge is enormous as is the cost of failure.

NOTES

This chapter was last revised and updated in November 1998.

1. The following is a partial list of English-language articles on Russian export controls. The most comprehensive study to date is the unpublished report by Emily Ewell and Holly Tomasik, *Nuclear Export Controls of the Russian Federation: A Status Report—December 1996*, prepared for the Office of Nonproliferation and Arms Control, U.S. Department of Energy, 1997; see also Y.V. Simachev and A.O. Kokorev, "Export Controls in Russia," a paper presented at the Workshop on Export Controls in the NIS: Legislative and Administrative Challenges and Opportunities, Minsk (October 3–4, 1994); Gary Bertsch and Igor Khripunov, "Nonproliferation Export Controls in the Former Soviet Union: Assessment and Recommendations from a U.S. NGO," *The Monitor: Nonproliferation, Remilitarization and Arms Control* (Summer 1997); Anna Otkina, "Comparative Legal Analysis of Russian Federation/United States System of Export Control and the Licensing Procedure for Dual-Use Technologies," an unpublished manuscript, Monterey, CA (May 1997); Gary Bertsch, ed., *Restraining the Spread of the Soviet Arsenal: NIS Nonproliferation Export Controls Status Report—1996* (University of Georgia Center for International Trade and Security, 1997); "Systems for Controlling Exports of Military Sensitive Items," in National Research Council, *Proliferation Concerns: Assessing U.S. Efforts to Help Contain Nuclear and Other Dangerous Materials and Technologies in the Former Soviet Union* (Washington, DC: National Academy Press, 1997), pp. 85–117; "Export Control in Russia," Yu. Drugor et al., *Reforms in Russia: Industrial Complex,* Part 1 (Moscow: Interdepartmental Analytical Center, 1995), pp. 56–72; Michael Newlin, "Export Controls and the CTR Program," in John M. Shields and William C. Potter, eds., *Dismantling the Cold War* (Cambridge, MA: The MIT Press, 1997), pp. 291–308; Elina Kirichenko, "The Evolution of Export Control Systems in the Soviet Union and Russia," in Gary Bertsch, Richard Cupitt, and Steven Elliot-Gower, eds., *International Cooperation on Nonproliferation Export Controls* (Ann Arbor: The University of Michigan Press, 1994), pp. 163–178; and Theodor Galdi, "Nonproliferation Export Controls in Eastern Europe and the Former Soviet Union," CRS Report for Congress, Congressional Research Service (October 25, 1994).

2. A complete list of these decrees, directives, and regulations is provided in Ewell and Tomasik, pp. 41–63. They also are accessible online in the NIS Nuclear Profiles Database, Center for Nonproliferation Studies, Monterey Institute of International Studies.

3 These exceptions were a 1992 customs law and Russian Federation Law No. 4902-1 (April 29, 1993) "On Amendments to the Criminal Procedures Code of the RFSFR." The latter law provided imprisonment and fines for violations of nonproliferation export control regulations.

4. The Atomic Energy Act initially was passed by the State Duma in July 1995, but was not signed by President Yeltsin. A very similar version subsequently was passed on October 20, 1995 and was signed by President Yeltsin on November

21, 1995. The text of the law appears in *Rossikaya Gazeta* (November 28, 1995).

5. Federal Law No. 63-FZ, "Criminal Code of the Russian Federation," was passed on June 13, 1996.

6. For the text of the law, see *Rossiyskaya Gazeta* (October 24, 1995), pp. 4–5.

7. The law was signed by President Yeltsin on November 21, 1995.

8. A more detailed discussion of this legislation is provided in Ewell and Tomasik, p. 42.

9. See Ewell and Tomasik, p. 9.

10. E. Kirichenko, "Russia's Export Control System: The Mechanism of Executive Branch Cooperation," *The Monitor*, vol. 1, no. 2, 1995, pp. 19–20. See also Ewell and Tomasik, pp. 59–60.

11. The Department of Export Controls moved to the FSCEC from the Ministry of Economics in August 1994 as a consequence of Governmental Regulation No. 1005 (August 30, 1994). See "On Matters of Organizing Export Controls in the Russian Federation." The precise composition of the commission has fluctuated as a result of the ongoing reorganization of the executive political structure.

12. Ewell and Tomasik, p. 12. See also Elena Budyaeva, "Customs Procedures in the Russian Federation for Dual-Use Goods, Services, Technologies, and Scientific-Technical Information," International Conference on Industry-Government Relations in Export Control, Moscow (December 18–19, 1996). Budyaeva heads the Department of Non-Tariff Regulation of the State Customs Committee.

13. Plotnikov, the GTK Representative, presentation at the seminar organized by the Moscow Center on Export Controls, September 1997.

14. "The Procedures for the Export and Import of Nuclear Materials, Equipment, Special Non-Nuclear Materials and Related Technologies," approved by Government Regulation No. 574 of May 8, 1996; and "On Endorsement of the Procedures of Issuing Temporary Permits by the State Committee for the Supervision of Nuclear and Radiation Safety *(Gosatomnadzor)* for Activities Related to the Export/Import of Nuclear Materials, Technology, Equipment, Assemblies, Specialized Non-Nuclear Materials, Radioactive Waste, and Spent Nuclear Materials," Gosatomnadzor Order *(Prikaz)* No. 128. [See Marina Belyaeva, "Russian Federation Control Over Export of Nuclear Materials," *The Russian Federation Nuclear Export Control System: Compendium* (Moscow, 1996), pp. 14–16 cited by Ewell and Tomasik, p. 15.]

15. For a detailed description of Gosatomnadzor's different responsibilities in the nuclear sector see Yuri Volodin, "Opisaniye i otsenka sistemy regulirovaniya i nadzor za uchetom, kontrolyem, i fizicheskoy zashchitoy yadernykh materialov v Gosatomnadzora Rossii" (trans: A Description and Evaluation of the System of Regulation and Oversight for Accounting, Control and Physical Protection of Nuclear Materials at Gosatomnadzor in Russia), unpublished paper written for the Center for Nonproliferation Studies, July 1997.

16. Ewell and Tomasik, pp. 15–16.

17. See Statute on the Procedures for Export and Import of Nuclear Materials, Equipment, Special Nonnuclear Materials, and Corresponding Technologies, in Ewell and Tomasik, pp. 135–143.

18. This decree superceded the previous nuclear export control list, first introduced in 1992.

19. These points are elaborated in Government Regulation No. 574, translated on pp. 136–139 in Ewell and Tomasik.

20. See Ewell and Tomasik, pp. 21–22, for an elaboration on these requirements.

21. The exporter need not submit to Minatom two documents that are required by *Eksportkontrol:* proof of registration with the State and proof that the export will not reveal State secrets. See Ewell and Tomasik, p. 22.

22. *Eksportkontrol* must approve the export license application. The views of Minatom can be solicited at the discretion of the Ministry of Trade and *Eksportkontrol.*

23. On Approval of the Statute Regulating Export from the Russian Federation of Dual-Use Equipment, Materials, and Related Technologies Applied for Nuclear Purposes. That document is reproduced in Ewell and Tomasik, pp. 147–157.

24. The precise criteria are found in Article 11 of the statute. See pp. 152–153 in Ewell and Tomasik.

25. A creative methodology for assessing national systems of export control, which is applied to the post-Soviet states, is provided by Cassady Craft and Suzette Grillot, Nonproliferation Tools and Methods for Evaluating National Systems of Export Control, in Bertsch, ed., *Restraining the Spread of the Soviet Arsenal*, pp. 80–91.

26. For a discussion of this trend see Michael Beck, Gary Bertsch, and Igor Khripunov, Russia, in Bertsch, ed., *Restraining the Spread of the Soviet Arsenal*, pp. 12–13. Among the signs identified by Beck et al. are a growing number of government edicts and ministerial institutions to enhance industry compliance with export control regulations. Also cited is the rapid expansion of the State Customs Committee.

27. The title of the regulation was On Approval of the Statute Regulating Exports and Imports of Nuclear Materials, Technology, Equipment, Installations, Special Non-nuclear Materials, Radioactive Sources of Ionizing Radiation and Isotopes.

28. Article Vb. of the regulation, "Procedures Regulating Exports and Imports of Nuclear Materials, Technology, Equipment, Installations, Special Non-Nuclear Materials, Radioactive Sources of Ionizing Radiation and Isotopes," approved by Government Resolution No. 1005 in 1992.

29. For the full text of this resolution see Ewell and Tomasik, pp. 133–143. The relevant language is on p. 136.

30. In January 1989, a tripartite agreement on safeguards was concluded with the participation of the IAEA with regards to the construction of a nuclear plant from the USSR in India (IAEA INFCIRC/360). The 1988 agreement initially was not implemented due to problems of financing, and then due to the disintegration of the USSR. See the Statement of the RF Ministry of Foreign Affairs of July 9, 1997, in *Yadernoye Rasprostraneniye*, July 1997; and also Marina Belyaeva, "O Nekotorykh Aktualnyk Problemakh Eksportnogo Kontrolya v Yadernoy Oblasti," *Yaderniy Kontrol*, October–November 1997, p. 43.

31. Beck et al., p. 13.

32. This Soviet/Russian bureaucratic tendency is developed by Nikolai Sokov, "The Export Control System in Russia: Why Does It Work the Way It Does?" unpublished manuscript, Center for Nonproliferation Studies, Monterey Institute of International Studies (December 1996), cited in Ewell and Tomasik, p. 36.

33. Alexander Pikayev, Leonard Spector, Elina Kirichenko, and Ryan Gibson, *Russia, the U.S. and the Missile Technology Control Regime*, Adelph: Paper 317 (London: International Institute for Strategic Studies, 1998) and Victor Mizin, "Russia's Missile Industry and U.S. Nonproliferation Options," *The Nonproliferation Review*, Spring–Summer 1998, pp. 36–47.

34. For a discussion of the "catch all" approach see Gary K. Bertsch, Richard T. Cupit, and Jakehiko Yamamoto, eds., *U.S. and Japanese Nonproliferation Export Controls: Theory, Description and Analysis* (New York: University Press of America), pp. 322–323.

35. On this point see Beck et al., p. 14. The relevant portions of the Criminal Code, adopted by the State Duma on May 24, 1996 are Articles 188 and 189. The new Criminal Code entered into force on January 1, 1997.

36. Ibid.

37. For an elaboration of some of these points see *Proliferation Concerns*, pp. 93–94.

4

EXPORT CONTROL
DEVELOPMENTS
IN UKRAINE

Victor Zaborksy

INTRODUCTION

Since its emergence as an independent state, Ukraine has been a problem country in the nonproliferation context. In the period 1992 to 1994, Ukraine was of great concern to the international community because of its ambiguous policy toward denuclearization and toward joining the Nuclear Non-Proliferation Treaty (NPT) as a nonnuclear-weapon state. These worries were alleviated after Ukraine's accession to the NPT on October 16, 1994, and its pledges to denuclearize. However, further proliferation threats have emerged, namely, that of nonproliferation export controls. Although the last of some 1,600 strategic warheads were removed to Russia on June 1, 1996, and the dismantlement of intercontinental strategic missiles (ICBMs) has begun, an industrial infrastructure producing nuclear, missile, and dual-use items, and the human expertise thereof, may contribute to the proliferation of weapons of mass destruction, thereby threatening global security. This chapter is intended to analyze Ukraine's export control goals, policies, mechanism, legal basis, and involvement in the international nonproliferation regimes.

Weapon-Related Commodities and Facilities in Ukraine

The high priority placed on developing an export control system commensurate with international standards in Ukraine would have hardly arisen had Ukraine not possessed the industrial facilities for producing components for weapons of mass destruction (WMD) on its territory. For this particular reason, Western governments have been concerned about Ukraine's slow movement toward developing an effective national export control system and are persuading the Ukrainian government in an effort to facilitate this process. The following is a brief overview of the commodities and facilities in Ukraine producing nuclear, missile, and dual-use items, as well as conventional weapons.[1]

NUCLEAR POWER PLANTS, RESEARCH REACTORS,
AND FUEL CYCLE FACILITIES

There are five nuclear power plants in Ukraine, located at Chernobyl, Khmelnitski, Rivne, Mykolaiv, and Zaporozhye, with 15 operational units. There are two research reactors in Ukraine at the Institute for Nuclear Research in Kyev and at High Marines School of the Ukrainian Ministry of Defense in Sevastopol. Also, Kharkiv Physical-Technical Institute possesses about 12 kilograms of uranium in bulk form enriched up to 90 percent. There are two principal uranium mining districts in Ukraine, located in the Kirovograd region and the Krivoy Rog region. All in all, there are about 60 facilities in Ukraine producing nuclear-related goods and technology.

MISSILE-RELATED FACILITIES

According to Valeriy Shmarov, the former Defense Minister of Ukraine, about 40 percent of the Soviet space complex's research and production capacity was located in Ukraine, and over 100 Ukrainian enterprises and research institutes had actively participated in the design and production of missiles and missile components.[2] The primary enterprises involved in Ukrainian missile industry are:

- Kharkiv Production Association Monolit, which had presumably been involved in a study to recode the guidance system of the strategic missiles in Ukraine. It also manufactures microminiature onboard computers and record-keepers for the *Mir* spacecraft;
- The Khartron Scientific and Production Association in Kharkiv, which in the past was involved in developing guidance systems for the Soviet ICBMs;
- The Yuzhmash Mechanical Plant in Dnepropetrovsk, the largest Soviet ICBM factory where Zenith and Cyclone rockets and the SS-18, SS-20, SS-23, and SS-24 missiles were built. Yuzhmash is also the world's largest facility of its kind;
- The Pavlograd Machine Building Plant, which had been producing solid-fuel rocket engines. Production of solid-fuel missiles at the plant stopped in 1991.

ENTERPRISES PRODUCING DUAL-USE ITEMS

The dual-use items being produced in Ukraine are of a concern in the context of missile and nuclear weapons proliferation.[3] Many of these items are on the "trigger lists" of the Missile Technology Control Regime

(MTCR) and the Nuclear Suppliers Group (NSG). The following enterprises, although mostly involved in the civilian sector, had been producing items that can be used in manufacturing missile weapons[4]:

- Kharkiv Production Association Kommunar had been producing missile and space guidance and control systems and relays for satellites;
- Novokramatorsk Machine Building Plant produces materials for the Buran-Energiya space complex and gravity bombs;
- Kyev Plant Arsenal had been producing elements of missile complexes, including precise measuring devices used to make monobloc lasers used in SS-18 ICBMs;
- Kyev Artem Production Association had been manufacturing air-to-air missiles and components for aircraft and missiles;
- Kyev Instrument Production Association had been producing instruments for space vehicles;
- Kyev Radio Plant had been producing control systems for missile complexes;
- Lvov Production Association Kinescope had been manufacturing aircraft flight control systems and missile complex control system elements;
- Pavlograd Chemical Plant Production Association had been producing missile fuel for the SS-24s and munitions.

Concerns over the nuclear-related dual-use products center primarily over Pridniprovsky Chemical Factory in Dneprodzerzhinsk, which produces heavy water and uranium oxide, as well as such dual-use items on the NSG list as zirconium, hafnium, and ion-exchange resin. Other facilities with unidentified locations produce such items from the NSG list as lasers, laser amplifiers, and oscillators; mass spectrometers and mass spectrometer ion sources; vacuum pumps; and neutron generator systems.[5]

FACILITIES PRODUCING CONVENTIONAL ARMS AND MUNITIONS

The facilities producing basic armaments and munitions in Ukraine are as follows:

- Chernigov Radio Instrument Plant Production Association produces combat aircraft control systems;
- Dnepropetrovsk Machine Building Plant produces systems for air defense and space communications;
- Feodosiya Research Institute of Aeroelastic Systems conducts research and development for military aircraft components and produces aeroelastic systems;
- Kharkiv Malyshev Plant produces armored vehicles;
- Kharkiv Tractor Plant produces armored vehicles and prime movers;
- Kharkiv Scientific Production Association Turboatom manufactures gas turbines for military jet aircraft and reduction gears for diesel engines used on military ships;

- Kyev Antonov Aviation Production Association produces military transport aircraft An-32 and An-124;
- Mykolaiv Black Sea Shipyard Production Association had been producing aircraft carriers.

EXPORT CONTROL LEGAL AND ADMINISTRATIVE INFRASTRUCTURE

Export Control Legal Basis

In 1991, the Ukrainian government started developing its export control system from scratch and thus far has not given priority to this issue in the context of its domestic political instability and severe economic crisis. However, the evolution of export control developments in Ukraine indicates that attention to export control issues is increasing, albeit rather slowly.

On April 16, 1991, the first Ukrainian Parliament adopted the Act on Foreign Economic Activity. Article 20 of the act specifies that the export and import of weapons, special components for their manufacture, explosive agents, nuclear material, technologies, equipment, installations, as well as other kinds of goods, technologies, and services that could be used for production of weapons require authorization by the Ukrainian state.[6] Adoption of this act took place at the time when the Soviet Union still formally existed. Although some provisions of the act touched upon export control issues, its main idea was to present Ukraine as a formally independent state and prevent uncontrolled withdrawals of commodities from Ukraine to Russia.

After the formal breakup of the Soviet Union in December 1991, the president and the Cabinet of Ministers of Ukraine picked up the initiative in developing Ukrainian export controls. Decree No. 153 of the Ukrainian Cabinet of Ministers of March 23, 1992, established the State Expert and Technical Commission. A principal task of the commission was to draft export control laws, but it was very slow in performing this duty and had done very little to that end. Presidential Decree No. 3 of January 3, 1993, superseded Decree No. 153 and established two new export control bodies: the Governmental Commission on Export Controls and the Expert and Technical Committee. In order to implement the Presidential Decree, the Cabinet of Ministers on March 4, 1993, issued Decree No. 6, On Establishing State Controls Over Exports/Imports of Arms, Military Material and Materials Needed for Their Production.

The major difference between the two Presidential Decrees of 1992 and 1993 is that according to the Decree No. 3 of 1993, the Governmental Commission on Export Control is the body representing 18 ministries and agencies on an equal basis, while the Expert and Technical Commission was clearly dominated by Ministry of Machine Building, Military-Industrial Complex and Conversion. This shift to collective decision-making on export control issues indicated the increased importance of export controls in the Ukrainian government's agenda, as well as meeting standards of international export control regimes. In the 1995 to 1997 period, the Cabinet of Ministers approved a number of decrees regulating exports of goods and technologies that may contribute to nuclear, chemical/biological, and missile proliferation as exports of dual-use goods and conventional arms. These decrees will be examined more closely in the respective sections of this chapter.

On December 28, 1996, President Kuchma issued Decree No. 1279/96, On Further Improvements in the State Export Controls, which transformed the Governmental Commission on Export Controls into the Governmental Commission on Export Control Policy; the Expert and Technical Committee was renamed the State Service on Export Control (SSEC), which is granted a ministerial status and is directly subordinated to the Cabinet of Ministers of Ukraine. The ultimate stage in terms of the legal basis would be the Law on Export Control, a comprehensive long-term concept to be passed by the Parliament of Ukraine. However, understanding that passing such a law will be a time-consuming process, President Kuchma on February 13, 1998, issued Decree No. 117/98, On Procedures for Export Control in Ukraine. The draft of the decree was originally developed in mid-1996, and it took the government almost two years to settle all the disputes and disagreements around it. This decree can be considered a step forward in terms of increasing effectiveness of the export control system in the country for a number of reasons. First, this is a long-awaited comprehensive single document stating the government's goals, objectives, and procedures of export controls. Second, for early-warning purposes, the export control authorities are to be notified about plans to negotiate contracts with foreign partners. Paragraph 18 of the decree states: "To begin negotiations regarding the signing of foreign economic agreements (contracts) on the export of controlled goods, as well as other goods subject to limited transfers to certain foreign countries, an exporter is first to seek permission from the State Service on Export Control to conduct such negotiations." Third, so-called "catchall" provisions have been introduced. Paragraph 14 of the decree reads: "An exporter must consult the State Service on Export Control if the exporter knows or comes to learn of the possibility that the goods intended for export will be used to develop weapons of mass destruction, their delivery means, or conventional arms, despite the fact that said goods are not included in the control lists." The decree is more likely to serve as a temporary document regulating export controls in Ukraine until Parliament passes the Law on Export Control. The time framework for adopting the Law on Export Control by Parliament is unclear. Meanwhile, the export control system in Ukraine is legally based on the decrees of the Executive Branch, and the State Service on Export Control and the Governmental Commission on Export Control Policy are the major players in this system.

State Service on Export Control (SSEC)

The State Service on Export Control is the main executive organ on export controls in Ukraine. According to the December 28, 1996, Presidential Decree, "The chairman of the State Service on Export Control of Ukraine is to be made equal in rank, payment, material and domestic support, and medical and transport services to the position of minister, the deputy chairmen to deputy ministers, and the heads of structural subdivisions of the Service to the corresponding categories of ministry employees." SSEC has the following responsibilities:

- organization and implementation of state control to ensure the national security of Ukraine, its compliance with international agreements on nonproliferation of WMD and their delivery means, as well as limitations in conventional arms transfers;
- development and implementation of measures to ensure protection of national interests in export controls;
- addressing the issue of feasibility of international transfers of controlled items;
- maintaining control over the use of controlled items in declared purposes;
- registration of legal entities and individuals whose activities are related to exports, imports, and transit of controlled items;
- drafting legislative and normative acts related to regulating export control activities;
- development and maintenance of a functioning automated state export control system;
- implementation of cooperation with relevant agencies of foreign countries and international export control regimes;
- preparation of materials for consideration by the Governmental Commission on Export Control Policy related to the area of its expertise.

Governmental Commission on Export Control Policy (GCECP)

This commission is made up of representatives from the following ministries and agencies at the level of heads or deputy heads: Foreign Affairs; Foreign Economic Relations and Trade; Defense; Economy; Machine Building, Military-Industrial Complex and Conversion;[7] Internal Affairs; Security Service; the Center for Strategic Planning and Analysis under the National Council on Security and Defense; SSEC; State Customs Service; and the State Committee on Border Protection. The commission is responsible for:

- facilitating interagency coordination in the area of export control;

- consideration of issues of imposing limitations or restrictions of exports, imports, or transit of controlled goods in accordance with Ukraine's international obligations and national security interests;
- addressing case-specific issues of international transfers of controlled items;
- consideration of materials needed by the President or the Cabinet of Ministers of Ukraine for decision-making within their area of competence.

The commission meets at least once a month. The commission's decisions on issues not covered by legislation are considered legally binding for all ministries, agencies, industry, and organizations.[8]

Licensing

Eventually, licensing is supposed to become a responsibility solely of the SSEC.[9] However, as of April 1998, SSEC has shared the task of issuing licenses with GCECP, due to the absence of a clear-cut division of powers between the two bodies on a working level. Currently, export of nuclear goods and technologies and conventional arms is licensed by GCECP, whereas imports and transits of all goods and exports of dual-use items are licensed by SSEC. A license is required for exports; imports; reexport; transit turnover; export of scientific and engineering product related to commodities subject to export control; related agency operations on exports/imports; creation of joint ventures for design, development, and production of commodities that can be used for developing arms and military equipment; export and import by passengers; and export and import as contributions to the growth of trade and industry enterprises in cases of international cooperation.

As of January 1998, the right to export goods subject to export control was given to *Ukrspetsexport*—the only arms trading company in Ukraine—and eight individual enterprises. In 1997, 46 individual enterprises applied for permission to be independent exporters, but according to the SSEC officials, only 2 percent of them qualified for independent trade.[10]

Under bilateral agreements inherited from the former Soviet military-industrial complex, Ukraine transfers some items to Russia without licenses. Appropriate Ukrainian ministries prepare lists of items that are to be approved but not licensed. Copies of the approved lists are forwarded to customs points, which check shipments across Ukrainian borders. However, most transactions between the two counties involving items subject to export control require licenses.

Enterprises apply for license directly to the SSEC, which, while reviewing the application, may confer with appropriate ministries. When submitting a license application for export, import, and transit of indigenous commodities and technologies controlled by international regimes, the applicant must attach to it the following documents: international import certificate; end-user certificate; copy of the contract; and specifications, if required. When an enterprise applies for a license for the first time, it also must submit to the SSEC for official registration a copy of its statute and a list of goods it produces. Both ministries and the SSEC weigh the technical, political, economic, and military factors in making the license decision. According to the Ukrainian Cabinet of Ministers' decrees regulating export, import, and transit of commodities that can be used to develop nuclear, chemical/biological, and missile weapons, the following factors are taken into account in making the license decision: nonproliferation standards; capabilities and objectives of the nuclear, chemical/biological, and missile/space programs in the recipient states; criticality of the goods to be exported in terms of ability to develop weapons of mass destruction and their delivery means; assessment of the end use of transferred goods; and applicability of relevant multilateral arrangements.[11] These decrees provide that the licensing decision is to be made within 30 days after the submission of a complete application. However, due to submission of incomplete applications and long bureaucratic procedures, the average period for reviewing the license application is two to three months, and sometimes up to one year. To provide initial screenings and to facilitate the license application reviewing, nine regional SSEC offices are due to be established. The final decisions on issuing licenses, however, are to be made by the main SSEC office in Kyev.[12]

The issue of the license can be refused or revoked if: (1) licensing violates or jeopardizes the international commitments of Ukraine; (2) the Ukrainian or the foreign importer/exporter violates international regulations; (3) the sales of goods and technologies jeopardize economic interests or national security of Ukraine; (4) the applicant presented false information in the submitted application and/or additionally requested documents.

Enforcement

Formally, the government has a broad scope of powers (inspection of documents, shipments, accounts, seizure of goods, physical inspection of cargoes at border points, and so on), but in practice the execution of these powers is far from perfect. Sometimes the SSEC is incapable of verifying submitted documents due to a limited number of qualified officers. Also, if at the prelicense check stage the SSEC discovers purposely misleading information submitted by the Ukrainian exporter or importer, there is no law to prosecute the violator. In undertaking prelicense checks, the SSEC requests the Foreign Ministry to check end use and end-user certificates of foreign companies. However, the limited number of Ukrainian embassies abroad (about 60), inadequate financing, and lack of trained personnel decrease the quality of such checks. Overall, Ukraine has been limited by its lack of information and has had to rely on outside sources. Interpol, for example, has apparently helped Ukrainian authorities check licenses for goods destined for Yugoslavia, and the U.S. Defense Department has been asked to provide information on suspect countries and importers.[13] The potential for official corruption at different agencies involved in export controls is high, especially for low-paid customs officers. Poor equipment at border points contributes to the potential for smuggling.

In compliance with Section 228.6 of the Penal Code of Ukraine, the violation of established procedures for export of commodities, raw materials, equipment, and technologies that can be used for creation of missile, nuclear, chemical, and other types of armament, special military equipment, or services related to creation of arms, military, and special equipment, and illegal export of the above-mentioned items and related spare parts and ammunition is punishable by imprisonment of up to eight years and confiscation of property. This amendment to the Penal Code was made in 1993, and since that time there has been no precedent of prosecuting violators of export control procedures. Such a precedent is unlikely to occur until the Law on Export Control is adopted. However, there have been cases where customs officials uncovered smuggling, and the smugglers were subsequently prosecuted. Also, the Ukrainian Security Services has uncovered cases of spying and attempts by foreign nationals illegally to obtain sensitive technology. In late January 1996, three Chinese nationals were caught in Dnepropetrovsk as they obtained a series of papers on the design of engines for intercontinental ballistic missiles with the intention of smuggling them to China. The Chinese were expelled from Ukraine on the basis of Article 32 of the Law on the Legal Status of Foreigners for "actions contrary to the interest of national security" of Ukraine.[14]

EXPORT CONTROL AS A CHALLENGE TO THE UKRAINIAN GOVERNMENT

Export Control as a Political Challenge

The major political challenge is that people with very little experience in state-building and state-governing have faced such a sophisticated and complex problem as developing an effective export control system. One should not consider the development of the export control system in Ukraine apart from the general political, economic, and legal environments of the country, which are currently all rather unfavorable for a number of reasons.

Ukraine is rather slow in developing its national export control system in part because it has never had a community of nonproliferation experts among government, research institutions, and lawyers; and, consequently, now lacks skilled professionals in the export control area. Some officials dealing with export control questions are bureaucrats of the old *nomenklatura,* and they lack an understanding of the goals and objectives of the contemporary nonproliferation regimes and national export control systems. Ukrainian leaders have made numerous declarations of their commitment to nonproliferation; however, moving from general and vague political commitments to nonproliferation to their practical implementation through developing a national export control system has turned out to be a difficult task. Many government, and especially industrial, officials are very hard to convince that the proliferation of weapons of mass destruction will threaten Ukraine's national security. What they sense is that Ukraine is being pressured to restrict its export in order to protect Western, particularly U.S., security and trade interests. However, these sentiments have slowly begun to change over the last couple of years, and in the Presidential Decree of December 28, 1996, it is stated, for the first time, that strict export control is needed "to maintain Ukraine's national security."

Domestic political instability also hinders the development of the export control system in Ukraine. Rivalry between President Leonid Kuchma and Rada, the Ukrainian Parliament, over the legislation of separation of powers in 1995 and 1996 made Rada deputies very skeptical of all the moves initiated by the president and the government. The president has frequently criticized lawmakers for dragging their feet on establishing a legislative base for economic reform and crime-fighting, which are of vital importance for establishing effective national exports in Ukraine. The new post-Soviet Constitution, adopted in June 1996, provided a general separation of powers between the executive and legislative branches and was expected to stop the rivalry between the two branches. However, in August 1997, Parliament drafted three bills (which eventually did not pass) on amendments to the Constitution, which would curtail the president's powers and considerably extend Parliament's rights.[15] The Parliament elected on March 29, 1998, with much stronger Communist and left-wing representation, is likely to be even more reluctant to make any significant progress in the area of export control. Given this, the tension between Parliament and the president is likely to continue, which will consequently affect the passing of legislation on export controls.

From a proliferation standpoint, a serious concern arises from the presence of corruption coupled with organized crime. President Kuchma has admitted that "corruption has infected a significant part of the state apparatus."[16] As a response, the National Bureau of Investigation was created in July 1997, but combating this challenge has been of limited effect thus far. Many high-ranking officials are taking advantage of the absence of comprehensive export control legislation. The presumption that "everything is legal unless prohibited by law" makes them reluctant to make changes in the Ukrainian civil and criminal codes regarding export controls.

Weapons-related smuggling is a relatively new field for the Ukrainian mafia. However, the evolving business culture in Ukraine suggests that much weapons and weapons-related trade may bypass the export control licensing process. Exporters may prefer not to go through authorized export channels and apply for a license, but rather simply smuggle the goods through the porous borders of the former Soviet Union. When they do request a license, they may resort to bribery, mispresentation of the facts, or mislabeling.[17]

Export Control as an Economic Challenge to Ukraine

Developing an export control regime while in the process of decentralizing and expanding the trade based on a market model is another challenge to the Ukrainian government. The severe economic crisis in Ukraine has threatened the political survival of the president, the government, and Parliament, and it is very hard to make a decision to restrict exports, since exports create jobs and are expected to improve the Ukrainian economy. "Today we possess enormous scientific, technical and staff potential and are able to produce competitive products for both domestic and foreign customers. And the armaments market has always existed and will exist for many more years, and it would be unwise not to take advantage of this fact," said Victor Petrov, former Minister of The Ministry Machine Building, the Military-Industrial Complex and Defense Conversion.[18]

Ukraine inherited the second-largest portion of the former Soviet defense industry. Military production in the Ukrainian Soviet Socialist Republic (SSR) constituted an estimated one third of the total Soviet military production and 38 percent of Ukraine's total industrial production. Government sources suggest that 1,840 research centers and enterprises and 2.7 million people—5 percent of Ukraine's total population—are engaged in military production, with 700 of these enterprises, employing 1.3 million people, producing exclusively for the military.[19]

The conversion of the Ukrainian heavily militarized economy has been very slow and painful. Government financing of the military-industrial complex stopped suddenly, and the factories were not ready for it and are currently struggling to survive. The unsuccessful experience of conversion of the military-industrial complex has forced industry directors to seek new military-related contracts. The Yuzhmash plant in Dnepropetrovsk had started, unsuccessfully, producing street cars and trolleybuses and is lobbying the Ukrainian government in order to preserve its missile production capabilities and to expand space activities. The Kharkiv-based Malyshev Machine-Building Plant (KMBP), formerly the largest tank factory in Ukraine, had tried, also unsuccessfully, to produce and trade motorcycles and trailers in 1992 and 1993. It was fortunate to sign a contract with Pakistan in 1996 for the export of 320 T-80UD tanks worth $600 million, which has been keeping the enterprise afloat. The Khartron factory seems to be more successful in locating new contracts, since it has been engaged in the design and production of automatic control systems for Ukrainian nuclear power plants. However, Khartron directors have been seeking new contracts within the framework of the Ukrainian National Space Program.[20] Participation in the space launch program and Defense Ministry procurements have also been attractive to the Mykolaiv Shipbuilding Plant, which has been studying the feasibility of converting an aircraft carrier into a carrier-rocket marine launching pad for the Defense Ministry.[21]

The unsuccessful experience of conversion of the military-industrial complex has forced industry directors to seek new contracts, even if they pose a proliferation threat. Both government and industry managers have been tempted by quick profits resulting from the export of military-related products. Few in the defense industry and industries producing dual-use products respect the notion of export controls and, therefore, might increase the sale of internationally controlled goods and technologies in order to survive.

The most recent case of Ukraine's intention to export turbines for a nuclear power plant in Iran supports the point. In April 1997, President Kuchma promised the United States and Israel that Ukraine would not supply a $50-million-worth turbine for the Büshehr nuclear power plant in Iran and pledged never to do anything that would help Iran, Iraq, or Libya develop weapons of mass destruction. However, opposition to this decision from the plants involved in the Iranian deal was so strong that Kuchma recanted and stated in November 1997 that Ukraine's participation in the Büshehr project "is not in the nuclear cycle but in electricity. Ukraine's position is clear—we are looking for jobs for Ukrainian factories." Kuchma asked the United States to drop its opposition to Ukrainian participation in the project.[22]

There is little transparency between the government and industry, and industry remains uninformed and confused. There are a number of examples: the Azot Chemical Plant in Dneprodzerzhinsk applied for license to set up a joint venture with a Panamanian company to produce and export heavy water;[23] the arms manufacturing company Montazhelectro, on its own initiative, offered to construct missile launchers for Libya.[24] These examples demonstrate that industry managers have little knowledge about international nonproliferation export control regimes and that industry internal compliance mechanisms, if they exist at all, are at the early stages of development.

One analyst suggests that since "it is a conflict of interest for the government to own the firms whose exports are being regulated . . . the defense enterprises must be privatized."[25] This suggestion can hardly be put into practice in the foreseeable future. In June 1997, the Ukrainian Parliament approved a plan to privatize 4,222 large and medium-sized enterprises, discarding, first of all, enterprises that are considered a burden to the economy. Facilities related to nuclear energy and missile and conventional arms production are very unlikely to be privatized in the near future. Enterprises of the military-industrial complex are considered potentially profitable, and the government will hardly give them up.[26] However, even if these enterprises are privatized, they could still present a proliferation threat because the "anything goes" mentality may encourage managers to seek hard currency by exporting internationally restricted products rather than shifting production to civilian ventures or complying with export restrictions.

PARTICIPATION IN THE MULTILATERAL NONPROLIFERATION REGIMES

Ukraine, the Nuclear Non-Proliferation Treaty, and the Nuclear Suppliers Group

On November 16, 1994, the Ukrainian Parliament approved Ukraine's accession to the Non-Proliferation Treaty (NPT), contingent only upon receiving security guarantees from the nuclear nations. Guarantees from the United States, Russia, and the United Kingdom were provided in a memorandum at the Conference on Security and Cooperation in Europe on December 5, 1994, in Budapest. France and China provided security guarantees to Ukraine in separate documents. Thus Ukraine formally became a nonnuclear-weapon state, party to the NPT, on December 5, 1994.

In September 1994, Ukraine signed agreement on full-scope safeguards with the IAEA. This agreement came into force on January 13, 1995. The agreement provides IAEA inspection of all Ukrainian peaceful nuclear activities. The first *ad hoc* inspections began in February 1995, and since then inspections have taken place every two months. The Ministry of Environmental Protection and Nuclear Safety is formally responsible for inventory and control of nuclear materials in Ukraine. In late September 1995, the Ukrainian government set up a body within the Ministry of Environmental Protection and Nuclear Safety to monitor safety precautions at nuclear power plants, nuclear waste storage sites, and nuclear fuel production facilities. The new body is called the Main State Directorate for Control Over Nuclear Safety.[27] Also, the United States has established a $22.5-million project to assist Ukraine in establishing a national fissile material protection, control, and accountability system (MPC&A). MPC&A improvements have been taking place at the Kharkiv Physical-Technical Institute, the South Ukraine Nuclear Power Plant in Mykolaiv, the Sevastopol High Marines School Research Reactors, and the Kyev Institute for Nuclear Research.[28]

When Ukraine ratified the NPT and signed the agreement on full-scope safeguards with the IAEA, it hoped to open the door to NSG membership. However, the absence of a legal basis controlling the export of nuclear materials and technologies and of a list of controlled items were factors preventing Ukraine's admission to the NSG. The initial draft of the list was prepared in the spring of 1993 by the former Ukrainian State Committee on Nuclear and Radiation Safety, but it took the Ukrainian government about three years to review and implement it.[29]

Finally, on March 12, 1996, Ukraine's Cabinet of Ministers issued Decree No. 302, which approved "Regulations on the Procedure for Controls on the Export, Import and Transit of Commodities Which May Relate to Nuclear Activities and May be Used to Develop Nuclear Weapons." The decree also provided a list of items subject to export/import/transit controls and licensing that is an inherent part of the regulations. With that decree issued, all legal obstacles to Ukraine's joining the NSG were removed, and at the May 1996 NSG meeting in Buenos Aires, Argentina, Ukraine joined the NSG as a full-fledged member.

One of the consequences of Ukraine's membership was that the NSG established a group of experts on export control at the Kyev-based Institute for Nuclear Research, which is considered by the SSEC as its resource for technical expertise and assistance related to nuclear and dual-use technologies and materials. Two U.S. nuclear facilities— Argonne National Laboratory and Los Alamos National Laboratory— have been assisting this group in terms of expertise and financial support. Argonne has allocated $40,000 to train nuclear export control experts, and Los Alamos has allocated $65,000 to create a database on Ukrainian nuclear enterprises for the SSEC. Both projects are operated through the U.S. Department of Energy.[30]

It was presumed that Nuclear Suppliers Group (NSG) membership would allow Ukraine to access markets for peaceful nuclear material use, legally export items on the NSG "trigger list," and create an image of Ukraine as a devoted supporter of nuclear nonproliferation. However, developments over the sales of Ukrainian turbines to Iran, mentioned earlier, have demonstrated how easily commercial interests may come to conflict with nonproliferation goals. In respect of the turbines deal, Ukraine turned out to be "caught in the middle of a U.S.-Russian tug of war," as Yuri Scherbak, Ukrainian Ambassador in Washington, put it,[31] where both the United States and Russia were applying "sticks" and "carrots." In exchange for dropping the Iranian deal, the Clinton administration offered the Ukrainian government a package of small business loans, Export-Import Bank credits, joint ventures, and space cooperation. The United States also offered to sign an accord with Ukraine on peaceful nuclear cooperation which would provide U.S. technology and fuel to Ukraine. At the same time, the U.S. officials warned that if Ukraine goes forward with the deal, Ukraine would not get the loans and credits, the U.S. administration would not sign an agreement on nuclear cooperation with Ukraine, and the U.S.-Ukrainian economic and political partnership would be reduced to a minimum level. In its turn, the Russian government warned Ukraine that if it backs out of the deal, Russia would not order components for its nuclear power reactors from Ukraine in the future. As a "carrot," Russia offered its own credits and technology to Ukraine to complete the construction of two reactors at Rivne and Khmelnitski and to supply the fuel to operate them.[32]

The Ukrainian government's decision on the Iranian deal was not an easy one. Ukraine's 15 nuclear reactors annually require fuel rods worth $320 million. Ukraine does not have uranium reprocessing facilities and has to buy nuclear fuel from abroad. Nuclear power plants in Ukraine provide about 50 percent of the country's electricity, and the option of creating a nuclear fuel cycle is being discussed. However, according to one Ukrainian official, the program to mine and process uranium would cost Ukraine $682 million, and is now considered economically unviable.

In 1997, Russia sent $167-million-worth of nuclear fuel to Ukraine, which was the last portion of the "warheads for free fuel" deal under the Trilateral Statement of 1994.[33] Beginning in early 1998, Ukraine has been looking for external suppliers. Russia and the United States are the first candidates. Both Russia and the United States are interested in playing a major role in the lucrative modernization of the Ukrainian nuclear energy sector and fuel supplies, but the whole set of complex political, economic, and security issues accompanying the Iranian deal had complicated the relationship among the three countries. Eventually the U.S. stick-and-carrot policy won out, and on March 6, 1998, during U.S. Secretary of State Madeleine Albright's visit to Kyev, President Kuchma announced that Ukraine would abandon plans to supply turbines for the completion of the Iranian nuclear plant. Resulting from Ukraine's dropping the Iranian deal, an agreement on cooperation in the peaceful use of nuclear energy was signed in May 1998 by Ukrainian Foreign Minister Boris Tarasyuk and the U.S. Ambassador to Ukraine, Stephen Pifer.

Ukraine and the Missile Technology Control Regime

Historically, most of the civilian sector of the Soviet space program was in Russia, while in Ukraine, a major part of the scientific and industrial space complex was involved in developing and producing the missiles which formed the backbone of the strategic forces of the former Soviet Union. Yuzhmash and its affiliated Yuzhnoye Design Bureau had been the principal Ukrainian facilities involved in the design and production of the ICBMs, as well as *Zenith* and *Cyclone* launch vehicles, electronic intelligence satellites, and ballistic missile early-warning satellites and radars. All in all, over 100 Ukrainian enterprises and research centers had been actively participating in the design and manufacture of space machinery since the beginning of the Soviet space program.[34]

Since the collapse of the Soviet Union in 1991, Ukraine's space industry has been under severe financial strain because of reduced orders and loss of steady revenue. Yuzhmash has suffered the most losses. According to its Designer General, Yuri Alexeev, the facility's combined workforce has declined from 52,000 in 1991 to 34,000 in early 1996.[35] Participation in Western commercial ventures has helped to keep the enterprise afloat, as has its newly acquired role as the destruction facility for SS-19 ICBMs, made possible by the U.S. Cooperative Threat Reduction (CTR) Program.

Nevertheless, current levels of production and financial support are far below past levels, eliciting fears that Ukraine's edge of technology and know-how may be lost. The National Space Agency of Ukraine was established in 1992, and since 1993 the National Space Program (NSP) has been included in the country's budget. The NSP received a favorable jolt in 1994, when Leonid Kuchma, who was Yuzhmash Director General for about a decade, was elected president of Ukraine. The presidential team is composed of people from the Dnepropetrovsk region devoted to the promotion of the space/missile sector in Ukraine.

Ukraine's approach to the MTCR has been in line with its general policy of preserving its missile and space industries. Ukraine inherited a large arsenal of missiles, including 46 10-warhead SS-24 ICBMs and 130 six-warhead SS-19 ICBMs, both with a range of 10,000 km; AS-15 air-launched cruise missiles; SS-21 short-range missiles (with a range of 120 km); and some 130 SS-1 Scud-B missiles (with a 300-km range). Dealing with their missile legacy, the Ukrainian negotiators have chosen the strategy: "Everything which is not prohibited by arms control and reduction treaties is allowed." According to this strategy, under the Intermediate-range Nuclear Forces (INF) Treaty, Ukraine, as one of the Soviet successor states, is obligated not to produce, test, or deploy short-range (500 to 1000 km) and intermediate-range (1000 to 5500 km) missiles. The Lisbon Protocol of May 23, 1992, made Ukraine a party to the START-1 treaty, which provides that 36 percent of launchers of the former Soviet Union be eliminated, and bans some other types of missiles. Parliament's resolution of November 18, 1993, stated that only 36 percent of launchers on the territory of Ukraine should be eliminated, and the rest could be used for launching civilian payloads into space.

Based on these interpretations of the treaties, the Ukrainian government had been insisting on its legal right to keep the Scud-B missiles now deployed and to develop and deploy nonnuclear varieties of the following missile systems:

- ground-launched ballistic and cruise missiles with ranges up to 500 km (310 miles);
- air-launched cruise missiles with ranges up to 600 km (372 miles);
- sea-launched cruise or ballistic missiles with no range limitations.

The Ukrainian government, under the START-1 treaty, acquiesced to the destruction of all its missile silos, and decided to destroy its SS-19 missiles and transfer to Russia its SS-24 missiles. The most disputable issue left was the fate of medium-range Scud and Scud-type missiles with a range of 300 to 500 km. Since late 1994, immediately after Ukraine joined the NPT as a nonnuclear-weapon state, political and military circles in Ukraine have been discussing the possibility of producing and deploying short- and medium-range missiles, considering these systems to be legitimate means of deterrence in light of the country's nonnuclear status. The Ukrainian military continues to discuss this option, arguing that such missiles, carrying high-accuracy, conventionally armed warheads, would provide a more effective and less costly deterrent than a defensive posture that relies on tanks and aircraft, an argument that is highly appealing to the cash-poor Ukrainian Defense Ministry. So far, the idea of developing and deploying missiles is being debated only in general terms, and no numbers and types of missiles have been publicly mentioned.

In the U.S.-Ukrainian Memorandum of Understanding (MOU) signed in Washington, DC, on May 13, 1994, Ukraine agreed to conduct its missile-related exports according to the criteria and standards of the MTCR. Under the terms of the memorandum, Ukraine was to develop a missile-related export control list in compliance with MTCR requirements. On July 27, 1995, Ukraine's Cabinet of Ministers approved the Regulations Guiding the Control over Export, Import and Transit of Missile Technology Items, as Well as of Equipment, Materials and Technology Used in the Manufacture of Missile Weapons. The regulations specify that the export, import, and transit of the following items are to be controlled: completed missile systems; unmanned air vehicles capable of carrying payloads of at least 300 km; and equipment, materials, and technologies that can be used to manufacture these vehicles. This decree also approved the list of controlled missile-related goods and technologies. It consists of two parts: Category I, which includes missiles capable of carrying payloads of at least 500 kg a distance of at least 300 km as well as equipment and technologies most significant for manufacturing missile weapons, and Category II, which includes missiles capable of carrying payloads for at least 300 km and not included in Category I, as well as respective equipment and technologies. Export of items referred to in Category I are to be under strict restriction, while restrictions on export of items of Category II are less severe.

However, the prospects of Ukraine's full membership in the regime were unclear due to U.S. membership criteria. On September 27, 1993, President Clinton issued a new policy regarding U.S. efforts to prevent the proliferation of weapons of mass destruction and their delivery systems. The new policy called for strong support for the MTCR, noting that the United States "will support prudent expansion of the MTCR membership to include additional countries that subscribe to international nonproliferation standards, enforce effective export controls and abandon offensive ballistic missile programs."[36] All future MTCR members, in order for membership to be agreed by the United States, will have to observe these constraints.

That meant that Ukraine, in order to become an MTCR member,

should have renounced its right to produce tactical missiles of a range of 300 to 500 km and air- and sea-based cruise missiles and removed Scud missiles still on its territory. The Ukrainian government was strongly opposed to this request, arguing that: (1) the MTCR is essentially an export control regime and not a disarmament agreement; (2) Ukraine may potentially need these missiles (except for ICBMs) for strengthening its defense capability; (3) such a request is of a discriminatory nature, since it is not applied to all MTCR members; (4) this U.S. request was not supported by other MTCR members; and (5) Ukraine had been producing Category 1 missiles since early 1960s, and the Yuzhmash Plant and Yuzhnoye Design Bureau in Dnepropetrovsk have outstanding technological potential and human expertise in this area. Discontinuing production of Category I missiles may cause mass unemployment in the region and consequently lead to social challenges.[37]

Production of missiles at Yuzhmash has reportedly been suspended. However, psychologically, it was difficult to make a decision to give up this production once and forever. Such a decision was especially difficult to make for President Leonid Kuchma, with his Yuzhmash background. For Kuchma, that could have meant clashes with the "Dnepropetrovsk lobby," with the military, and with Parliament. (Parliament ratified START-1 and NPT on the condition that the president would not give up the nation's missile capability.) Many in Ukraine felt a kind of psychological trauma because of having been forced by the West to denuclearize, and strongly opposed making another concession by giving up a part of the nation's missile potential. As one Ukrainian diplomat put it, "The Americans have denuclearized Ukraine; now they want us to give up our missile program. What will they demand next—to give up machine guns?"[38] Supporting these sentiments, President Kuchma kept stating that "despite U.S. objections, Ukraine will continue the development and production of medium-range missiles capable of destroying targets at a distance of 300 to 500 km."[39]

Ukraine's perception of the missile proliferation threat differs from that of the United States. Ukraine does not have security interests in different parts of the world, nor has it military allies and respected obligations. Acquisition of longer-range missiles by Iran, Iraq, North Korea, Syria, or Libya would not directly affect the military security interests of Ukraine. As Alexander Negoda, Director General of the National Space Agency of Ukraine put it, "For other countries, transfer of their missile technologies means transfer of secrets and a threat to their national security interests. For Ukraine, there is no direct threat to its national security from the sales of its missiles and related technologies. That makes Ukraine a unique country. In fact, having taken obligations on missile nonproliferation, Ukraine contributes to the security of other countries more than it does for its own security."[40] Although supporting the international missile nonproliferation efforts in general terms, the Ukrainian government does not have strong national security incentives to be ultimately devoted to the MTCR objectives.

Some press reports have suggested that Ukraine's nonproliferation credentials may merit closer examination. In mid-1996, the U.S. government expressed concerns that Ukraine was selling SS-18 missile technology to China by calling it civilian space cooperation. In response, President Kuchma argued that Ukraine viewed China as its most valuable partner in the area of space cooperation. At the same time he stated that Ukraine had rebuffed Chinese efforts to purchase Ukrainian SLV technology, but he offered to sell rocket hardware to Beijing.[41] In late 1996, reports on Ukraine's missile sales to Libya contributed further to doubts as to Ukraine's export control credentials. It was reported that Ukraine agreed to sell SS-21 or Scud-B missiles to Libya for $510 million.[42] Export of Scud-Bs would violate Ukraine's pledges to the MTCR, since the range of these missiles is greater than 300 km. Export of SS-21s with the range of 120 km would also be illegal under the new 1993 MTCR guidelines, which provide for a strong presumption of denial of transfers of any missiles, if there are strong reasons to believe that they would be used for the delivery of weapons of mass destruction. Libya is believed to have the capability to produce chemical warheads. Ukrainian officials ruled out the possibility of selling these missiles to Libya. In early 1996, the Russian press suggested that Ukraine offered SS-21 missiles to Pakistan and unspecified missiles to India, which also would be inadmissible under the MTCR, given the nuclear programs in these countries.[43] All these alleged Ukrainian deals lead one to believe that Kyev's intention to profit from exports of its surplus missiles and missile technological and industrial potential is real.

As a result of these dynamics, Ukraine was facing a serious dilemma: comply with the U.S. conditions for full membership in the MTCR—with the resultant prospect for increased space cooperation with other regime members, thereby improving the position of one of the country's most important industries—or continue to be an MTCR "adherent," preserving the right to develop a limited range of military missiles, but thereby restricting cooperative endeavors that could be crucial to the survival of the country's space industry. Kyev officials had been demonstrating that in the "launchers or missiles" dilemma, priority had been given to space cooperation, since it is believed that Ukraine's space industry can improve the very difficult economic situation the country now faces, as well as promote other related sectors of the economy and contribute to Ukraine's international standing.

The stalemate over Kyev's full membership in the regime, which continued from 1994, was finally resolved in March 1998, when Secretary of State Madeleine Albright brought to Ukraine a package of "carrots" to talk Kyev out of the turbine deal with Iran. The Joint U.S.-Ukrainian

Statement, signed in Kyev on March 6, 1998, by Madeleine Albright and the Ukrainian Foreign Minister Hennadiy Udovenko, reads that the parties agreed "that the cause of missile nonproliferation would be best served by Ukraine's membership in the Missile Technology Control Regime (MTCR). To that end, the United States indicated that it has no reservations regarding Ukrainian membership in the MTCR, and that the United States supported immediate Ukrainian membership in the MTCR." Both sides have agreed that Ukraine, while being a full-fledged member of the regime, will keep its Scud missiles through the end of their service lives, and should not forswear future production of short-range missiles should it find it necessary.[44]

According to the Joint Statement, Ukraine's membership in the MTCR will result in "an expansion of mutually beneficial space cooperation, performed in a manner consistent with the countries' arms control and nonproliferation commitment and the prospects that launches of U.S. commercial satellites on Ukrainian rockets would not be constrained by quotas." In the follow-up to Secretary Albright's visit to Kyev, Ukraine and the United States will be discussing the strengthening of export controls, including the adoption of "catchall" controls, which means denying the export of any item—even items not on a control list—if it is destined for a WMD or missile program. Because space cooperation often involves sensitive technologies, the United States and Ukraine agreed on two new understandings on technology security that will facilitate future cooperation. First, Albright and Udovenko signed a Technology Safeguard Agreement (TSA), which lays out procedures that will ensure that the sensitive technologies incorporated in U.S.-made satellites will be protected when those satellites are launched on Ukrainian rockets. Second, the U.S. and Ukraine agreed on procedures to protect Ukrainian MTCR-controlled technology transferred to the United States for the Sea Launch project.

Ukraine and Chemical Weapons

Soviet officials listed no chemical weapons storage facilities outside of what is now Russian territory in the data they exchanged under the 1989 Memorandum of Understanding between the United States and the Soviet Union. A February 1993 House Armed Services Report on the chemical weapons threat cited several experts who did not list former Soviet republics other than Russia as possessing chemical weapons.[45] According to Ukrainian Greenpeace officials, in the former Soviet Union chemical weapons had been tested on Ukrainian territory near Odessa and Sevastopol. Also, there was a factory in Zaporozhye producing poisonous substances. Those substances had been stored in Zolotonosha, Cherkassy, Krivoy Rog, Ochakov, Fastov, and Kremenchug.[46]

According to General Victor Lytvak, head of the Ukrainian Defense Ministry's department for radiation, chemical, and biological protection, Ukraine does not presently have any chemical or biological weapons on its territory, although it has an insignificant amount of relevant substances for laboratory research.[47] Ukraine has not joined the May 15, 1992, CIS Chemical Weapons Agreement. The nine state parties to the agreement agreed that "CIS member states will pursue coordinated policy on control over the export of dual-use chemicals which are produced for peaceful purposes but can be used for production of chemical weapons and technologies for their production" (Article 5). Ukraine had no objections against this particular provision; however, it disagreed with the provision that under this agreement Russia assumes obligations for destroying chemical weapons and other CIS countries are to participate in funding such destruction. The cost-sharing of the destruction of Russian chemical weapons was supposed to be regulated by a separate agreement which, however, has never been signed.[48]

Ukraine signed the Chemical Weapons Convention (CWC) on January 13, 1993, the very first day the convention was open for signature, but has not ratified it as of yet. Ukrainian Foreign Ministry officials have stated that the reason for the delay of the ratification of the CWC is the uncertainty over the Soviet chemical weapons buried in the Black Sea after World War II. If they turn out to be buried in the sea bed that is formally part of Ukrainian territory, Ukraine would be responsible for the destruction of these weapons and respective costs. In order to avoid this, the Ukrainian government is negotiating with Russia on a number of political, military, legal, and environmental issues.

Developing national Ukrainian legislation on exports of chemical goods and technologies took more than two years, mostly because of insufficient cooperation between the government and industry and because it was not a priority issue in the government's agenda. By the Decree No. 384 of April 22, 1997, the Cabinet of Ministers of Ukraine approved the Regulations on Controls Over Export, Import, and Transit of Goods, Which May Be Used For Production of Chemical, Bacteriological (Biological), and Toxin Weapons. The regulations also include a list of controlled goods and technologies that consists of three parts and is identical to the "trigger list" of the Australia Group.

Sensitive chemicals can be produced at chemical plants in Odessa, Severodonetsk, Dneprodzerzhinsk, and Shostka. However, according to Ukrainian government officials, there have been no applications to export chemicals which can be used in weapons manufacturing for at least the last four years.[49] In March 1997, Hong Kong and Taiwanese newspapers accused Ukraine of selling 500 tons of sarin nerve gas to China. Ukrainian officials called the reports "groundless conjectures," and Western experts also regarded the charges with skepticism.[50]

Ukraine's Conventional Arms Exports

"We signed contracts almost every two to three days last year," said Mr.

Andrei Kukin, Director General of Ukrspetsexport, Ukraine's main arms-trading company, stating that 170 arms contracts, worth more than $1 billion, were signed in 1997, thereby making Ukraine the world's twentieth largest arms exporter.[51] The 1997 deals can be viewed as a real success, given the $600 million arms export revenue in 1996 and less than $100 million in 1995.[52] These figures are difficult to verify or compare with figures from Russian and U.S. experts mainly because countries use different variables to calculate the total amount. Nevertheless, what is more important is the undeniable fact that for the last two years Ukraine has been successfully breaking into the world's arms market.

Experts argue that Ukrainian arms export potential in early 1992 was $8 to 10 billion annually, which, if used to full capacity, could eventually provide a significant contribution to economic development in Ukraine. However, decreasing domestic military procurement, undefined national priorities, lack of a clear strategy of marketing arms, a small number of analysts in this area, as well as interagency disputes over the sharing of arms export revenues, have prevented this optimistic prospect from full realization over the first years of Ukraine's independence. The three original arms exporting firms—Progress, directed by the Security Service and the Ministry of Interior; Ukrinmash, subordinate to the Ministry of Machine Building, Military-Industrial Complex and Conversion and selling reserves of the Defense Ministry; and Ukroboronservice, directed by the Ministry of Foreign Economic Relations—had their own objectives, policies, and strategies, and some of their officials had been charged with corruption and misuse of revenue.

In the first years of independence, export controls as a long-term policy goal practically did not exist. In the early 1990s, there was a number of press reports alleging that Ukrainian firms had been selling arms to belligerent countries, sometimes violating international embargoes on arms sales. Allegedly, Ukrainian entities were exporting tanks and combat aircraft to Azerbaijan, MiG-29 fighters to South Africa, and unspecified weapons to Angola and South Yemen. The most scandalous was the charge of exporting weapons to Croats and Muslim forces in Bosnia.[53] Reportedly, "gray market" dealers, but not the Ukrainian government, were responsible for most of those sales. According to Ukrainian police and security service officials, the three arms exporting firms and respective ministries served as a legitimate "roof" for arms dealers and were in charge of no more than 20 percent of arms exports from Ukraine. The remaining 80 percent of sales went through arms dealers who used their connections in the president's team, ministries, and Parliament.[54]

To combat the chaos in the area of arms exports and rechannel the revenue from individuals' accounts to the state budget, on June 5, 1996, the Council on National Security and Defense under the president made a decision to create a single arms-trading company responsible directly to the government. The arms firms' managing ministries were reportedly against the change, as all decision-making and profits were to be remanded to the government and not to the individual agencies. Despite the opposition, the government proceeded, and in November 1996 the three firms merged into one new company, Ukrspetsexport, managed by the Prime Minister's Office. According to the Ukrspetsexport officials, a centralized trading authority is necessary to prevent the illegal export of all types of weapons and sensitive technologies from Ukraine and to ensure compliance with the obligations under the Wassenaar Arrangement. Another driving force for that decision was the necessity to concentrate all conventional arms exports into one organization in order to increase arms sales significantly in the world market.

There are three major means of expanding conventional arms and arms-related exports. The first is to manufacture brand-new weapons and equipment specifically for export. The $650 million contract signed in August 1996 to supply Pakistan with 320 T-80UD tanks within four years is a real breakthrough for Ukraine. Islamabad's first major purchase of land weapons from a former Soviet republic is Kyev's biggest arms sale to date. The first 15 tanks were delivered from stock, followed by new tanks produced on the revived production line at the Malyshev Plant in Kharkiv. Export procurements are the most desirable option for the Ukrainian government and arms-producing enterprises, because besides revenue, they provide jobs to those unpaid workers still formally on the payroll and bring back to work those who had to quit. The Pakistan deal literally brought the Malyshev Plant back to life. The plant had produced 800 tanks in 1991, only 43 in 1992, and none in 1993 and 1994. In 1995, it managed to produce only three tanks for the IDEX-95 exhibition, the world's largest arms fair.[55] After signing the deal with Pakistan, newspapers in Kharkiv have been overflowing with adverts for jobs at the plant with salaries three times the country's $90-per-month average. Inspired by the contract with Islamabad, Ukraine has offered its new T-84 tank at a tender to Turkey, which plans to buy 1,000 tanks as part of its military modernization efforts. According to Andriy Kukin, former director of Ukrspetsexport, Ukraine has good chances to win the tender, since its T-84 costs $2 to 2.5 million, which is about half the price of the U.S., German, French, and Italian equivalents.[56] In the years to come, stresses Mr. Alexander Kovalenko, Ukrspetsexport Deputy Director, tanks will remain Kyev's main military export. At the same time, Ukraine is trying, with some success, to enter the aircraft market. It is pushing the production of the An-32 transport aircraft, An-71 early-warning aircraft, and An-70, a military version of the passenger jetliner, designed jointly by the Kyev-based Antonov Production Association and the Russian firm Aviakor.

The second source of arms for sale is excess weapons. At the time of the collapse of the Soviet Union, there were 37 divisions armed with

9,293 tanks, 11,346 armored personnel vehicles, 18,240 artillery systems, and 22 Tu-95 H Bear and 20 Tu-160 Blackjack strategic bombers on Ukranian territory, not to mention military equipment and supplies enough to equip five fronts for offensive combat. The total cash value of all inherited military assets was an estimated $89 billion.[57] Ukraine's international disarmament obligations and diminished domestic needs have made much of these arsenals excessive. Under the 1991 Conventional Forces in Europe (CFE) Treaty, Ukraine is obligated to destroy 1,972 tanks, 1,577 armored personnel vehicles, 1,562 artillery systems, and 560 combat aircraft. The cash equivalent thereof is $7 to 11 billion.[58] Under the CFE Treaty provisions, some of these weapons can be cascaded to other European countries whose quota allows additional supplies of arms. Moreover, the Ukrainian armed forces are being gradually downsized from 750,000 in 1991 to 250,000 by the year 2000, which will release arms and equipment ready for dumping on the arms market. All in all, according to Volodymyr Mukhin, head of Ukraine's Parliamentary Committee on Defense and Security, Ukraine possesses enough surplus weapons "to feed the country for the next 10 to 20 years." No matter how realistic this statement is, the fact is that Ukraine, having been on the front line against NATO during the Cold War, has inherited an enormous arsenal of weapons and is ready to sell much of it. Having started with exports of bombs, grenades, torpedoes, and cartridges, Ukraine eventually began to sell small quantities of heavier weapons such as main battle tanks, transport aircraft, air-to-air missiles, and helicopters. The Stockholm International Peace Research Institute (SIPRI) 1997 Conventional Weapon Database listed 16 countries that have bought weapons and equipment from Ukraine since 1991.[59] To that list should be added the most recent contract with Syria, which purchased 200 Soviet-made T-55 tanks,[60] and $24-million-worth of exports of 600 military trucks to India.[61]

The third source of revenue is servicing, repairing, and upgrading weapons for foreign customers. According to some estimates, the former Soviet Union had exported arms and military equipment, the cash value of which is an estimated $200 billion, to more than 70 countries.[62] Much of it requires upgrade and repair, and Ukraine has inherited a large net of arms service and repair facilities. About 15,000 Soviet-made tanks had been sold to dozens of countries and can be upgraded with Ukrainian 1,200 hp engines and other features. Ukrainian facilities can service, repair, and upgrade aircraft and helicopters exported by the Soviet Union to more than 40 countries (excluding the NIS).[63]

Besides the natural commercial competition in the arms market, Ukraine, in searching for new contracts, has been experiencing pressure from Russia. Russian government and industry officials, viewing Ukraine as an arms sales competitor, have been threatening not to cooperate with Ukraine in the production of weapons Ukraine is willing to export.

Angered over the Ukrainian tank deal with Pakistan, Russia threatened in early 1997 to cut supplies of tank cannons and optical and navigation equipment for the T-80UD, which at that time was 30 percent Russian-made.[64] The official reason for Russian displeasure was that Russia is actively pursuing arms sales to India, Pakistan's major rival; consequently, supplying weapons parts destined for Pakistan would put Russia in an "ambiguous position."[65] Ukraine, in its turn, reminded Russia that it produces and supplies engines for the Russian top-of-the-line KA-50 Black Shark helicopters and electronic equipment for C-300 air defense systems, aggressively advertised at arms fairs.[66] Having understood that the dependence is mutual, and that Ukraine can find another supplier or start indigenous production of parts, in June 1997 Russia dropped its opposition to the tank deal. Having learned the lessons of the first Russian-Ukrainian "arms trade war," both sides will likely refrain from overt blackmail, although they will view each other as a competitor rather than as a partner in joint arms production and exports and will therefore try to reduce dependence on each other.

Although the goal of the Ukrainian government is to expand its arms exports from a quarter of its total exports to a third,[67] it feels obligated to be in compliance with exports' antipode—export controls. Significant progress in this area has been made over the last couple of years. The major step regarding controls on exports of conventional arms was joining the Wassenaar Arrangement. At the early stages of negotiating a post-COCOM regime, Ukrainian officials had stated that Ukraine would like to become an original member of a new export control arrangement. However, originally Ukraine did not want to yield to the U.S. request to accept an obligation not to export armaments and dual-use items to Iran, Iraq, Libya, and North Korea. Disputes mostly centered around exports to Iran. Nevertheless, eventually U.S.-Ukrainian negotiations on this issue resulted in a compromise, the terms of which both countries agreed not to make public.[68] The Wassenaar Arrangement on Export Controls for Conventional Arms and Dual-Use Goods and Technologies was formally set up at the July 11 to 12, 1996, plenary session in Vienna, Austria. Thirty-three nations, Ukraine included, became the original members of the new regime.[69]

At the domestic level, arms exports are regulated by the 1996 Decree of the Cabinet of Ministers of Ukraine, the Regulations On the Procedure for Controlling Exports, Import and Transit of Certain Types of Goods, Hardware, Materials, Software, and Technologies which Can Be Used in Manufacturing of Weapons, Military or Special Equipment. The regulations specify that the grounds for denying a license to export arms are, among others, "jeopardizing the interests of Ukraine in terms of defense, economy, international affairs, state security, as well as Ukraine's obligations under international agreements." The February

1998 Decree, signed by President Leonid Kuchma, has made export controls even more restrictive. It specifies that not only arms transfers, but also starting negotiations with a foreign customer, require special permission from authorized government agencies. According to Ukrainian Foreign Ministry officials, Ukraine observes embargoes on arms sales to Angola, Afghanistan, Iraq, Liberia, Libya, Somalia, and Sierra Leone. Also, as an OSCE member, Ukraine refrains from arms transfers that would lessen the security of other members or prolong military conflicts.[70] The State Service on Export Control (SSEC) is the body in charge of licensing conventional arms exports. To facilitate the license reviewing process, SSEC is planning to open four regional offices, including one at the Malyshev plant.

Out of the whole complex of exports of weapon-related goods and technologies, exports of conventional arms, munitions, and equipment are viewed by the Ukrainian government as most lucrative in terms of revenue and least risky in terms of nonproliferation criticism. Nonproliferation restrictions regarding conventional arms exports are much less severe than those related to nuclear, missile, and chemical/biological weapons. Trying to reach $10 billion annually in arms exports by the year 2000, a goal reportedly set up by President Leonid Kuchma, no matter how realistic it seems, Ukrainian arms exporters are seeking new markets in the Arabian peninsula, Southeast Asia, Africa, and Latin America, offering everything sellable, from heavy battle tanks to light handguns.[71] By the end of 1998, all Ukrainian police forces were to be equipped with a new Fort-12 9-mm pistol being manufactured at the Vinnytsa-based Fort weapon factory. The new pistol will accept a Parabellum 9-mm round, an international standard ammunition, which will make it suitable for export. "That is the main reason we are planning to develop a Parabellum pistol," says Volodymyr Mikhailov, a Fort official. "That way the weapon becomes marketable outside the country. And export is the only real source of income right now."[72]

CONCLUSION

Formally, the present export control system in Ukraine has a legal basis, a licensing body, and an enforcement mechanism. However, all these elements are far from being effective since they are poorly organized, manned, equipped, and financed. The immaturity of the Ukrainian government in the area of state-building and the political instability and economic crisis in the country are serious challenges to creating an effective export control system. The absence of immediate military threats to Ukrainian security, caused by the proliferation of weapons of mass destruction, also decreases the awareness by political leadership in Ukraine of the importance of export controls. The Ukrainian government is still shaping its national security interests, evaluating its military and civilian heritage left after the collapse of the Soviet Union, and figuring out how to use this heritage as a bargaining chip in negotiations with the West. Kyev is reluctant to take any obligations that would cut down its industrial, technological, and export potential, preclude some options in military developments, and limit its room for maneuver in the future. Debates over Ukraine's joining the NPT, the Wassenaar Arrangement, and the MTCR are cases in point.

At the same time, the desire to be recognized as a civilized, democratic state and to create a favorable trade and investment climate, combined with Western assistance, encouragement, and pressure, creates the positive forces promoting the development of nonproliferation export controls in Ukraine. Along with efforts on a governmental level, a community of nongovernmental export control experts is also emerging. In March 1997, the Ukrainian Scientific and Technical Center on the Export and Import of Special Technologies, Hardware, and Materials was created. The center serves as a gathering point for export control policy, technical, and scientific experts. The evolution of export control developments in Ukraine indicates that attention to these issues is increasing. In general, this evolution could be considered "normal" for a state with an overmilitarized but generally poor economy, slow bureaucratic decision-making, corruption, and political instability.

NOTES

1. Much of the information on nuclear and missile-related facilities is taken from William Potter, *Nuclear Profiles of the Soviet Successor States*, Monograph No. 1, Monterey Institute of International Studies (May 1993), pp. 83–90.
2. *The Nonproliferation Review* (Fall 1994), p. 200.
3. For more information on Ukraine's dual-use and conventional arms production, see "Investment Opportunities in Ukrainian Defense Conversion," prepared by U.S. Department of Commerce. Bureau of Export Administration, July 20, 1994, pp. 7–71.
4. The description of production of these enterprises is referred to the past, since in most cases it is hard to estimate their current involvement in the Ukrainian missile industry.
5. Most of the information on nuclear-related dual-use items was obtained during an interview with a Institute for Nuclear Research official in Kyev in September 1996.
6. Theodore Galdi and Brian Stanton, *Nonproliferation Export Controls in Eastern Europe and the Former Soviet Union*, CRS Report for Congress (October 25, 1994), p. 12.
7. By President Kuchma's decree of July 25, 1997, the Ministry of Machine Building, Military-Industrial Complex and Conversion and the Ministry of Industry were liquidated and recreated into one ministry—the Ministry of Industrial Policy.
8. Information on SSEC and GCECP is drawn from Victor Vaschilin, "State Export Control in Ukraine," *The Monitor: Nonproliferation, Demilitarization and Arms Control*, vol. 3, no. 3, p. 13.

9. This subsection is based on the following sources: "Managing Export Control in Latvia and Ukraine," *A Trip Report of the LAWS/WCNP NIS Export Control Project* (August 8–12, 1994), pp. 7–10; Sergei Svistil, "Ukraine," in *Worldwide Guide to Export Controls*, 1994/1995 Edition; Sergei Svistil, "Developing Export Control System in Ukraine," *The Monitor: Nonproliferation, Disarmament and Arms Control*, Fall 1995, pp. 74–83; and the author's interviews with Ukrainian government officials.

10. "Ukraine's Export Control System and Its Legal Basis," presentation by Mr. Victor Vaschilin, Chair, State Service on Export Control, at the conference "Interaction Between Industries and Export Control Agencies in Ukraine," Kyev, November 18, 1997.

11. For details, see the following Decrees of the Cabinet of Ministers of Ukraine: Regulations on the Procedure for Controls on the Export, Import, and Transit of Commodities Which May Relate to Nuclear Activities and May Be Used to Develop Nuclear Weapons, Decree No. 302 of March 12, 1996, Article 15; Regulations on the Procedure for Controls on the Export, Import, and Transit of Missile Items, As Well as of Equipment, Materials and Technologies Which May Be Used to Develop Missile Weapons, Decree No. 563 of July 27, 1995, Article 14; Regulations on the Procedure for Controls on the Export, Import, and Transit of Commodities Which May Be Used to Develop Chemical, Bacteriological (Biological) and Toxin Weapons, Decree No. 384 of April 22, 1997, Article 16.

12. Victor Vaschilin, presentation.

13. "Managing Export Controls in Latvia and Ukraine," *A Trip Report of the LAWS/WCNP NIS Export Control Project* (August 8–12, 1994), p. 8.

14. For details see FBIS-SOV-96-021, January 31, 1996, p. 54; *OMRI Daily Digest*, no. 22, part 2 (January 31, 1996); *OMRI Daily Digest*, no. 32, part 2 (February 14, 1996).

15. For details, see Viktor Demidenko, "Ukrainian MPs Out to Limit Presidential Powers," *RIA-Novosti Hotline* (August 28, 1997), issue 39.

16. "Kuchma ousts officials in corruption cleanup," *KievPost* (February 20–26, 1997), p. 1.

17. See: Gary Bertsch and Igor Khripunov, *Restraining the Spread of the Soviet Arsenal*, A Status Report (Center for International Trade and Security, University of Georgia, October 1995), p. 5.

18. FBIS-SOV-95-050, March 15, 1995, p. 57.

19. Christopher Hummel, "Ukrainian Arms Makers Are Left on Their Own," *Radio Free Europe/Radio Liberty Research Report*, vol. 1. no. 32 (August 14, 1992), p. 33.

20. *Holos Ukrayiny* (January 27, 1995), p. 3.

21. *FBIS-SOV-94-215*, November 5, 1994, p. 30.

22. "World Leaders Raise Funds for Chernobyl Safety," *Kyiv Post* (November 21, 1997) p. 3.

23. Sergei Svistil, "Developing Export Control System in Ukraine," *Proceedings of the International Workshop Export Controls in the New Independent States: Legislative and Administrative Challenges and Opportunities, October 3–4, 1994, Minsk* (Minsk, Eridan, 1995), p. 82.

24. For more information, see Bill Gertz, "Kiev Imperils U.S. Aid with Libya Arms Deal," *Washington Times* (December 9, 1996), pp. A1, A12; *OMRI Daily Digest*, no. 239, part II (December 12, 1996) *Deutsche Presse-Agentur* (February 1, 1997).

25. Sarah Jacobson, "A Comparison of Russia and Ukranian Export Control Regimes," *Nonproliferation Analysis*, vol. I, issue 1, Summer 1995. p. 18.

26. On November 22, 1996, the Ukrainian Parliament voted to suspend the privatization of 208 state-owned enterprises deemed "strategically important" until laws governing investments in such businesses are adopted. The parliament also decided to increase the number of state-owned enterprises barred from privatization from 1,475 to 7,111. See *OMRI Daily Digest*, no. 228, part 2 (November 25, 1996).

27. *OMRI Daily Digest*, no. 191, part 2 (October 2, 1995).

28. *The Nuclear Roundtable*. Background Documents. "The Cooperative Threat

Reduction Assistance to Ukraine." Cooperative Threat Reduction Program, Department of Defense. January 16, 1997. Online.

29. See "Nuclear Security in Kazakhstan and Ukraine: An Interview with Vladimir Shkolnik and Nicolai Steiberg," *The Nonproliferation Review*, vol. 2, no. 1 (Fall 1994), p. 46.

30. Interview with Dr. Sergei Yatskevitch, the U.S. Department of Energy liaison and lead analyst at the Institute for Nuclear Research, conducted in November 1997 in Kiev.

31. David Ottaway and Dan Morgan, "U.S., Ukraine at Odds Over the Nuclear Technology Transfer," *Washington Post* (February 8, 1998), p. A25.

32. Ottaway and Morgan, "U.S., Ukraine," p. A25.

33. "Free Nuclear Fuel Supplies Stop Next Year," *Kiev Post* (March 6–12, 1997), p. 23.

34. William C. Potter, "Interview with Vladymir Shkolnik and N. Steinberg: Nuclear Security in Kazakstan and Ukraine." *The Nonproliferation Review* (Fall 1994), p. 200.

35. Yuri Alexeev's presentation at the workshop Non-Proliferation Strategies for Ukraine's Aerospace Industries, Dnepropetrovsk, May 24, 1996.

36. Cited in Deborah A. Ozga, "A Chronology of the Missile Technology Control Regime," *The Nonproliferation Review* (Winter 1994), p. 89.

37. Ukrainian government and industry officials expressed these arguments at an international workshop Non-Proliferation Strategies for Ukraine's Aerospace Industries, which took place in Kyev on May 23, 1996, and in which the author participated.

38. Interview with Ukrainian Foreign Ministry officials conducted in April 1995.

39. FBIS-SOV-97-137, May 17, 1997.

40. Alexander Negoda, presentation at the international workshop Non-Proliferation Strategies for Ukraine's Aerospace Industries, Kyev, May 23, 1996.

41. Peter de Selding, "Ukraine Proposes Collaboration with WEU," *Space News* (June 10–16), 1996, p. 3.

42. Bill Gertz, "Kiev Imperils U.S. Aid with Libya Arms Deal," *Washington Times* (December 9, 1996), pp. A1, A12.

43. See Aleksandr Sychev, *Izvestiya* (April 16, 1996), cited in "Ballistic, Cruise Missiles, and Missile Defense Systems: Trade and Significant Developments" (February–June, 1996). *The Nonproliferation Review* (Fall 1996), p. 169.

44. For more details, see Howard Diamond, "U.S., Ukraine Sign Nuclear Accord, Agree on MTCR Accession," *Arms Control Today* (March 1998). Online.

45. Amy Smithson, *The Chemical Weapons Convention Handbook*, no. 2 (September 1993), p. 44.

46. *Kievskie Vedomosti* (April 6, 1995), p. 7, "Officials disclose CW cashe" (no author).

47. FBIS-SOV-95-225, November 22, 1995, p. 51.

48. See Igor Khripunov, "Russia's Chemical Weapons Demilitarization: Post-Soviet Prospects and Challenges," presentation at the Fourth Annual International Conference on Controlling Arms. Philadelphia, Pennsylvania, June 19–22, 1995.

49. Interview with an SSEC official in June 1997.

50. *OMRI Daily Digest* no. 44, part II (March 4, 1997).

51. Pyotr Yudin, "Ukraine Takes Aim at Russia In Arms Exports," *Defense News* (February 16–22, 1998), p. 30.

52. *Ibid.*

53. Gennadiy Klyuchikov, "Shadow Arms Trade Is Flourishing in Ukraine," *Nezavisimoye Voennoe Obozrenie* (Independent Military Review) (February 1–7, 1997), p. 6.

54. *Ibid.*, p. 6.

55. Vladimir Chumak, "Ukraine and Conventional Arms Exports," *Export of Conventional Arms*, PIR Center, Moscow, No. 1–2 (January–February 1997), p. 13.

56. Rostislav Khotin, "Feature Ukraine Tank Maker Tests Diplomacy As Output Rises," *Reuters* (December 1, 1997), Online.

57. Gennadiy Klyuchikov, *op. cit.*, p. 6.
58. Vladimir Chumak, "Ukraine and Conventional Arms Exports," p. 14.
59. *SIPRI Conventional Weapon Database* (1997). Special thanks to Ian Anthony (SIPRI) for making this data available.
60. "Syria, in Arms Build-up, Buys 200 Advanced Tanks from Ukraine," Agence France-Presse (December 17, 1997). Online.
61. "Ukraine to Sell Military Trucks to India," *Radio Free Europe/Radio Liberty Newsline*, vol. 1, no. 141, part II (October 17, 1997).
62. Vladimir Chumak, "Ukraine and Conventional Arms Export," p. 14.
63. *Ibid.*, p. 14; Rostislav Khotin, *op. cit.*
64. Since late 1997, all the components for the UD-80 tank have been produced at Ukrainian enterprises.
65. Mary Mycio, "Kyiv Defensive over Tank Deal," *Kyiv Post* (May 1, 1997). Online.
66. Sergei Zgurets, "Armor Is Strong and Tanks Are Fast!", *Delovaya Nedelya* (Business Week), Kyev (June 23–30, 1997), p. 13.
67. Taras Kuzio, "Ukraine's Arms Sales Continue to Expand," *Jane's Intelligence Review* (March 1997), p. 108.
68. Interviews with Ukrainian government officials conducted in September 1996 in Kyev.
69. Wassenaar's original members include the following countries: Argentina, Australia, Austria, Belgium, Bulgaria, Canada, the Czech Republic, Denmark, Finland, France, Germany, Greece, Hungary, Ireland, Italy, Japan, Luxembourg, the Netherlands, New Zealand, Norway, Poland, Portugal, the Republic of Korea, Romania, the Russian Federation, the Slovak Republic, Spain, Sweden, Switzerland, Turkey, Ukraine, the United Kingdom, and the United States.
70. Michail Osnach, "International Obligations of Ukraine in the Area of International Transfers of Arms and Dual-Use Goods," presentation at the conference Interaction Between Enterprises and Governmental Organs of Export Control, Kyev (November 18, 1997).
71. Taras Kuzio, *op. cit.*, p. 110.
72. Stefan Korshak, "Ukraine: Locally Produced Pistols Boost Trade," *Radio Free Europe/Radio Liberty* (January 22, 1998). Online.

5

THE BELARUSIAN EXPORT
CONTROL SYSTEM

Ural Latypov

FACTORS AFFECTING THE DEVELOPMENT OF THE
BELARUSIAN EXPORT CONTROL SYSTEM

After gaining independence in 1991, the Republic of Belarus began creating, basically from scratch, its own export control system and the legal foundation for it. Previously, when the Belorussian Soviet Socialist Republic was a part of the Soviet Union, the republic did not have its own legislation regulating issues of foreign trade and export control. This sphere was totally controlled by Moscow, the Soviet Union government, and central ministries and departments.

The remains of the old Soviet Union system in this sphere of activity, inherited by the republic, have by now lost their significance, since they were designed to operate under a socialist, administratively regulated economy. Despite the newness and complexity of the problem and an insufficient number of qualified specialists, a relatively reliable export control system was created and began operating in the republic in 1992 to 1993.

In order to understand correctly the current status and prospects of the Belarusian export control system, it is important to consider the fact that it was created and is now developing under considerable influence of the Russian Federation and the United States. And each of these countries do it in their own way.

Russian approaches to export regulation affect the Belarusian export control system because of the close economic connection between the countries. New, important steps have been taken since 1995 for further development of Belarusian-Russian relationships, which, without doubt, will touch upon the issues of export control. The discussion is now about further development of the customs union and the unity of regulating the common customs territory.

Despite the fact that both Belarus and Russia still maintain their own export control systems, some amendments will be needed in the next several years toward their unification. Presently the four parties to the customs union—Russia, Belarus, Kazakstan and Kyrghyzstan—are working on an agreed approach to this issue.

As a result of the colossal economic dependence of Belarus on Russia, the former has been virtually mimicking Russian steps on the formation of the export control system, while adapting them to its own requirements. The principle similarity of the two systems of government administration and remaining personal contacts among experts have allowed and still allow Belarus to acquire Russian experience easily and without much alteration.

It would not be a mistake to argue that due to growing economic integration and several other factors, it is impossible for Belarus to have an export control system that would differ significantly from the Russian one. Moreover, if the tendency for integration continues, the Belarusian and the Russian systems will become more interlinked. Organizationally, this may manifest itself in the creation of joint data banks or in other forms. At the same time, due to Belarusian leadership's adherence to independence, the official unification of the two systems (at least in the near future) is not expected.

While the influence of Russia on development of the Belarusian export control system occurs almost spontaneously, without direct efforts on the part of Russia, the case with the United States is completely different.

Two points should be mentioned here. First, Belarus cannot without serious adaptation acquire the American export control experience due to fundamental differences in economies, state structure, and legal systems. Secondly, economic relations between Belarus and the United States are still so weak that there can be no automatic influence of the American export control system on the Belarusian one. Nevertheless, the American influence is quite comparable to the Russian one on the level of direct effect on the Belarusian export control system.

Unlike the Russian one, the American influence results mainly from direct efforts on the part of the government and nongovernmental institutions of the United States. There are two components in this influence: intellectual and financial.

The current understanding by the Belarusian state officials of the necessity, goals, and functioning of export control systems was achieved primarily through conferences, seminars, and other types of education provided by the Americans. We can note a great usefulness of informational materials and training booklets sent from the United States. Beside the efforts of the American government, Belarus strongly perceives the influence of the American academic and research organizations such as the University of Georgia and the Monterey Institute of International Studies. Material assistance, rendered in the framework of the Nunn-Lugar Program, still plays an important role in the growing effectiveness of the Belarusian export control system, although the nature and span of the program turned out slightly different from what had been expected.

It should be noted that the American and Russian efforts on the development of the Belarusian export control system complement rather than contradict each other. No matter how strong the influence from abroad, the nature and peculiarity of the Belarusian export control system is primarily determined by internal factors.

The Belarusian economy combines the state, still regulated, and private components. Although the state still owns the principal industrial enterprises, the share of the private sector is growing slowly but steadily. This tendency, in turn, requires modifications of the export control system, which more and more has to orient itself to the conditions of private business.

Of great importance is the change in the form of government in the country: under the new Constitution, Belarus became a presidential republic.[1] Consequently, a transformation occurred in the system of government administration, including the system of export control.

LEGAL REGULATION OF THE BELARUSIAN EXPORT CONTROL SYSTEM

The entire Belarusian legal system was inherited from the Soviet Union, and the legal foundation of the export control system is no exception. But the Soviet legislature was developed basically to meet the needs of the administrative economy and the state monopoly on foreign trade; therefore it could not be effectively used to regulate exports in the conditions of emerging market structures and to give the right to export to enterprises with various forms of ownership. Under these circumstances, the government of Belarus was compelled to choose to regulate exports by means of administrative acts—the decisions of the government.

The Belarusian government has taken a number of decisive measures to enforce a legal basis of export controls to act in accordance with multilateral regimes' guidelines. In November 1997, the House of Representatives and, in December 1997, The Council of the Republic of Belarus adopted the Export Controls Law. The law was signed by the president on January 6, 1998. It was published in *The National Economic Weekly* No. 4. The law incorporates the experiences of Russia, Poland, Germany, and the United States, as well as the recommendations of foreign and domestic nongovernmental institutions. The Center for International Trade and Security, Georgia University, the Lawyers Alliance for World Security, Washington D.C., and the Monterey Institute of International Studies have made substantial contributions to the development of this law. The Export Controls Law is a kind of framework law that stipulates general rules and regulations and forms the state basis of an export control system governed by the principles of legality and transparency. According to the law, the term "export control" covers establishment and implementation of the permission order of import into the customs territory of the Republic of Belarus and the use, transit, and export of the export control objects outside its bounds.

It is indicated that export control in our country is exercised with the purposes of providing national security and protecting economic interests, fulfilling obligations under international treaties, and supporting international efforts for nonproliferation of mass destruction weapons and conventional arms.

The export control system in the Republic of Belarus is based on the following principles: implementation of the state control over transfer through the customs border of export control objects liable to international and national control; publicity and accessibility of information on order, rules, tasks, and principles of the export control system and measures of liability for violations in this field of export control; and harmonization of procedures and rules of export control with international norms and practice.

The Export Control Act applies to the relations in which state bodies, legal entities, natural persons, and officials are involved in the process of foreign economic activity. It also applies to cases where actions or agreements made or signed by Belarusian state bodies or legal entities and natural persons outside the country contribute to the proliferation of mass destruction weapons and conventional arms or inflict damage to our national security or political and economic interests.

The law gives authority to impose criminal and/or civil penalties for violations in this field. But it also protects the rights of exporters or any entity or natural person involved. One of the most important principles of international experience in export control—control over the end use of exported and imported items—is stated by the act. According to the law, the Ministry of Foreign Economic Relations, together with interested agencies, is authorized to conduct prelicense and postshipment end-use checks. The law determines the lists of export control objects, and these newly adopted lists are fully harmonized with those of multilateral regimes of nonproliferation. The interagency coordinator and authority responsible for issuing licenses is the Ministry of Foreign Economic Relations, which consults the interested ministries and agencies so that political sensitivity and proliferation concerns are duly considered before a decision is made. In any event a validated license is required for export of all controlled items. The adopted law gives an opportunity to ensure the coordination of exporters' interests with the requirements of regional and international security and will promote our republic's active participation in world trade.

PRINCIPAL STATE BODIES THAT PARTICIPATE IN REGULATING AND CONTROLLING EXPORTS

The export control and regulation system in Belarus has much in common with comparable systems of other nations (Canada, the United States, and others). At the same time, there are significant differences that need to be known and considered. It should be emphasized here that not all such differences should be treated as imperfections. The most important evaluator of the system should be its effectiveness in maintaining export limitations in the difficult political and socioeconomic situation that the republic finds itself in today.

The originality of the Belarusian export control system is caused primarily by the following factors:

- ownership of the overwhelming part of the national economy by the government; hence most of the exporters are government enterprises;
- a specific structure of government administration and the division of functions among state bodies in Belarus, inherited from the former Soviet Union;
- incomplete formation of the government administration structure as a whole and of the export control system in particular.

The state export control and regulation system includes the following components. The Security Council is a collective body that deals with all principal issues of nonproliferation export controls. It is by statute a consulting body, but due to the membership—it is headed by the president and includes the prime minister, foreign and defense ministers, and several other key figures—all its decisions are implemented. The Security Council considers such issues as joining the international nonproliferation agreements and the feasibility of single large exports of weapons and dual-use goods. The decisions of the Security Council are legally implemented through presidential decrees; thus the Belarusian state export control system now has two new important components: the president and his Security Council.

The State Committee on Economy and Planning (*Goseconomplan*) is an organ of interdepartmental regulation that has no analogs in the West. It continues to play an important role in governing the Belarusian economy, most of it, as mentioned earlier, belonging to the state. In the area of export control, *Goseconomplan* does the following:

- considers and adopts quotas on the export of Belarusian-made goods. The quotas established by *Goseconomplan* are mandatory for all governmental and nongovernmental structures that deal with exports;
- makes amendments during the year to the quotas and lists of quoted goods on its own accord or by suggestion from interested ministries and departments;

- participates in the development of the lists of goods that are subject to export limitations;
- participates in decision-making on licensing exports of specific goods.

The Ministry of Foreign Economic Relations (MFER) was created in March of 1994 as a replacement to the State Committee on Foreign Economic Relations (SCEFR) (in 1998, MFER was merged with the Ministry of Foreign Affairs and the Ministry for the Affairs of the Commonwealth of Independent States). The functions of MFER in direct regulation and control of exports are as follows:

- export licensing. MFER has an exclusive right to issue licenses for goods that are subject to limitation.
- determining the proper procedure of licensing, the list of documents required for obtaining the license;
- creation and maintenance of the republic's database for all licenses ever issued, regardless of their origin, and their implementation.

Along with direct export administration, MFER also has a decisive role in policy-making in this sphere and the creation of legal foundations for export control. These functions of MFER can be grouped into the following categories:

- working out suggestions for the Council of Ministers and the Supreme Soviet on improving the export control and administration;
- making official proposals (together with the Foreign Ministry) on participation in international nonproliferation regimes;
- developing (together with the Ministry of Justice and other departments) draft government decisions and legislature on all issues of export control and administration.

In comparing the roles of the Ministry of Foreign Economic Relations of the Republic of Belarus and the U.S. Department of Commerce (DOC), one cannot overlook the existing differences. Compared to the DOC, MFER has much less authority. While the DOC's Export Control Bureau has a structure that allows it (together with other departments) to influence the entire export cycle, from prelicense inspection to confirmation of the end reception of the product, and identify violations of export limitations, the MFER Division on Nontariff Regulations has insufficient manpower, authority, and funds for such an undertaking. Under these circumstances, it is conceivable that the process of formation of MFER structures should incorporate (within the limits of the Belarusian system of government administration) the experience of the DOC's Export Control Bureau. At the same time, it can be observed that MFER cannot be fully granted the authority that the Export Control bureau has, particularly in the area of implementation. As is widely known, the Division for Enforcement of Export Limitations employs special agents who have the right to conduct undercover operations, carry out arrests, and implement other investigative actions. Granting such privileges to one of MFER's divisions is unlikely, at least in the observable future, due to the existing distribution of functions among the state bodies in the country. Information-gathering using undercover sources has been a prerogative of only a few departments of the government. Despite expansion of their number by including the Tax Police, the Law on Law Enforcing and Investigative Activities gives such a right to only a limited number of organs (the Committee for State Security, the Internal Ministry, and so on) Due to that fact, the question of strengthening the measures of export limitation will most likely be resolved through attracting the departments that already have such prerogatives, rather than granting these prerogatives to MFER.

The Ministry of Foreign Affairs (MFA) functions in export control and administration as follows:

- generating and introducing to the government and Parliament proposals on foreign policy priorities, including issues of exports and their control;
- generating proposals and implementation of practical measures for Belarus's joining the international treaties and nonproliferation regimes, and working out the drafts of such international documents;
- generating proposals and participating in decision-making on limiting exports to certain countries and on participation in embargoes imposed by the U.N. in relation to certain states;
- participating in decision-making on principal export deals.

General issues of export control are supervised by the MFA's International Security Division.

Unlike the U.S. State Department, Belarusian MFA is not authorized to issue export licenses. The degree of MFA's influence on export control is significantly connected with the fact that the Belarusian diplomatic service is still in its early stage of development. Belarus has embassies and consulates in only a few countries, and their staff is limited by low funds, allocated to the diplomatic corps. Due to that fact, Belarusian diplomatic and consular representatives have limited abilities to gather information on end users of exported goods and other relevant information.

The role of the Ministry of Defense (MD) in Belarusian export controls is determined mainly by the process of reform that the armed forces are now undergoing, and the conversion of the military industry. Having inherited over 200,000 personnel and substantial weapons reserves from the former Soviet Union, Belarus must now decrease both the number of troops (to 100,000 as of 1995) and weapons. This fact creates the possibility (when no international agreement is violated) of sales of excess weapons and military hardware on the world market. The functions of the MD in the area of export controls are the following:

- participating in working out the control lists of goods subject to limitations;
- issuing licenses for the development, production, and sales of munitions, military hardware, and other specific goods;
- participating in decision-making on issuing licenses for export of weapons' munitions, military equipment, hardware and their parts, and other specific goods.

The presence of a license, issued in accordance with the Decision of the Council of Ministers from December 16, 1991, No. 386, Procedures for Issuing Special Permits (Licenses) to the Subjects of Economic Activity for Some Types of Activities according to the Decision of the Council of Ministers of the Republic of Belarus from September 22, 1992, No. 573, is a mandatory condition for obtaining the export license.

The State Customs Committee (SCC), created after Belarus gained independence, now oversees the customs checkpoints. Participation of the SCC in export controls is as follows:

- discovery and arrest of smuggling operations, including smuggling of specific goods;
- conduct of preliminary investigation of smuggling, with further transfer of the resulting materials to the state security organs; it should be noted here that, unlike the U.S. Customs, the Belarusian SCC does not have the authority to gather information during the investigative and preliminary inquiry stages.

The Border Guards (BG) of the Republic of Belarus are engaged in controlling the movements of individuals across 69 checkpoints and guarding the national boundaries. According to the Law on Law Enforcing and Investigative Activities, BG divisions have the authority to gather information, using all their operational capabilities, about all planned and actual acts of border violation, a fact that expands substantially the ability of this service to prevent any unauthorized transfer of specific goods across the border. According to the present legislation, the BG has the following functions:

- discovery and arrest of illegal export of specific goods across the national border;
- conduct of preliminary investigation of border violations, including those connected with the illegal export of specific goods, with further transfer of the found information to the state security organs for further investigation. The importance of the BG in providing real implementation of export control has increased with the growing crime rates in the CIS countries. In many cases the perpetrators are trying to ship the cargo across the border without proper licensing and without going through customs checkpoints. Such types of felonies can be stopped almost exclusively by BG.

The State Security Committee (SSC) has functions comparable to those of the American intelligence service and the FBI. As far as the export controls are concerned, its functions are as follows:

- providing the nation's leadership with all available information necessary for the development and conduct of export control and administration;
- participating in drafting the normative acts that regulate export control, including the lists of controlled goods and countries of destination;
- participating in decision-making regarding the principal export transactions of specific goods (coordination);
- counteracting the activities of foreign secret services aimed at illegal export of controlled goods (services);
- detecting and conducting preliminary investigation of smuggling operations including those involving export controlled goods, with further transfer of these matters into the court.

The Law on the State Security Committee of the Republic of Belarus passed the first reading in the Supreme Soviet in 1993 and was adopted with amendments in 1994. This department remains one of the most effective instruments capable of detecting and pressing criminal charges against individuals who violate export control regulations.

PROCEDURES AND PROVISIONS FOR LICENSING EXPORT OF SPECIFIC GOODS AND SERVICES

Licensing as a way to regulate exports first began being used in Belarus in 1991 and was carried out initially in accordance with the legislature and normative acts of the former Soviet Union. Presently, the licensing is regulated by the normative acts of the Belarusian government, as discussed above.

According to these acts, issuing licenses for export of specific goods is a prerogative of the Ministry of Foreign Economic Relations (previously the State Committee on External Economic Relations). During 1992 to 1993, the State Committee issued a number of licenses for export of weapons, military hardware, equipment, and their parts. According to the present legislature, more than 47 companies in Belarus have the right to export goods that are subject to export controls and have licenses for these exports from the Defense Ministry. Generally, these are enterprises, associations, and corporations that produce or repair weapons and military hardware. The presence of a license from the Belarusian Ministry of Defense is a prerequisite for obtaining a license for export of weapons and military hardware.

The export of weapons, military hardware, and their parts into areas of military conflicts and unstable political situations, as well as reexport and the use of weapons beyond the territory of the importing country, are prohibited without a special permit from the government of the Republic of Belarus. The export of narcotics, hallucinogens, and toxins, which are listed in List I of the U.N. Convention on Hallucinogens, is also prohibited.

A positive decision on issuing a license for export of weapons, military hardware, means of delivery of WMD, materials, and special parts used in the development of WMD is made by the MFER only after coordinating discussions with the Ministry of Defense, State Industrial Committee, Foreign Ministry, State Security Committee, Academy of Science, and *Goseconomplan*. The presence of an import certificate of the end user is a requirement for issuing a license.

Import and export of industrial property (inventions, industrial samples, working models) and scientific and technical achievements that have no legal protection, including those on magnetic and other carriers, can be carried out only with the agreement of the State Patent Service of the Republic of Belarus, a subdivision of the government.

In order to obtain a license, a declarant provides the following:

- an application addressed to the head of the organization issuing the license;
- a contract (agreement);
- an international import certificate.

If necessary, MFER may require additional documents. An international import certificate is issued by an authorized agency of the end-user country (MFER in the Republic of Belarus), and should contain the following guarantees:

- that the imported goods and their replicas will not be reexported without written consent of the exporter;
- the assurance of the importer country that these goods and their replicas will not be used for the development of WMD;
- the assurance of the importer country not to use the goods in any activity related to the nuclear fuel cycle that is not guaranteed by the IAEA.

In the event that the exports are current technologies, goods, and services containing information on discoveries, inventions, and results of research, and also in the event that the exported goods cannot be positively identified as a dual-use commodities, MFER sends inquiries to suitable organizations in order to obtain their expert conclusions on the matter.

An incorrectly filed application, failure to provide the necessary guarantees on the part of the importer, providing limited or insufficient information on the purchase, unsupported price reduction, or other amendments in the contracts that may damage the interests of the Republic of Belarus may be a basis for rejecting the application.

The presence of information from the state investigative bodies that the importer has violated international nonproliferation agreements on prohibition of a particular weapon of mass destruction and the means of its delivery, or of proven facts that the importer has smuggled, purchased, and used such commodities illegally for the purposes of developing WMD may also constitute the grounds for rejection. A rejection should be well supported, and a written notification should be sent to the declarant. Both exporters and importers begin all customs procedures only after obtaining the license.

The adoption of the seven control lists already presented to the government may become an important step in increasing the effectiveness of the republic's export control. These lists are as follows:

- List I, Nuclear weapons, materials, and equipment related to nuclear activities and the related dual-use technologies;
- List II, Chemical weapons and equipment for their production;
- List III, Bacteriological (biological) weapons and equipment for their production;
- List IV, Means of delivery of nuclear, chemical, and bacteriological weapons;
- List V, Conventional weapons;
- List VI, Certain raw materials, materials and equipment, inventions, technologies, know-how, and results of research and design used in the development of weapons and military hardware;
- List VII, Dual-use commodities.

Considering the above measures of export control it should be noted that export administration should at the same time facilitate the right of the individuals to participate in international trade. Implementation of this right depends substantially on swift and fair consideration of license applications, and is also a circumstance that affects greatly the formation of the market economy in Belarus. From this point of view, it might be a good idea to create a computer network for handling export license applications and relevant information, which would, just as does its prototype, in the American government, provide full information on every application at every stage of its consideration; also needed is a computer network to track export license applications. Direct assistance on the part of the United States in the creation of such computer systems would in the long run facilitate the right of individuals to participate in free export trade and the establishment of a market economy in the republic.

LEGAL FOUNDATION OF RESPONSIBILITY FOR EXPORT CONTROL VIOLATIONS IN THE REPUBLIC OF BELARUS

Establishing and enforcing responsibility for export control violations is the condition *sine qua non* of any effective export control system. While considering this issue, it should be noted that the Belarusian legislature continues to preserve the characteristics of the FSU legal system, which was oriented to the needs of the command economy. Because of that, and also due to historical traditions, the legal system of Belarus differs significantly from those of the Western nations. Presently, virtually all branches of the legal system are undergoing a process of reformation, but it is far from complete.

Responsibility for Criminal Prosecution
of Export Control Violations

The existing Criminal Code of Belarus[2] does not directly provide for the responsibility for export control violations, which is not surprising, considering the fact that the Belarusian Criminal Code was adopted in 1961. The code is constantly being amended, but none of the amendments directly relates to the issues of export control. A draft new code passed the first reading in the Supreme Soviet in 1993,[3] was amended in 1994, and is much more adapted to the requirements of a market economy. Nevertheless, this draft does not provide for responsibility for criminal prosecution of export control violations. According to the members of the working group that drafted the code, there are several reasons for that. The first, and, perhaps the most important, is that export control is not yet viewed as worthy of criminal prosecution if violated. The second reason is the absence of a law on export control and administration the violation of which could invoke criminal prosecution.

Due to these, and also a number of other less significant reasons, the draft Criminal Code does not provide sufficient legal foundation for prosecuting individuals who conduct illegal export of nuclear and other hazardous materials. It should be noted first of all that the draft has significantly amended the article on smuggling (Article 185):

> Smuggling, that is transfer across the customs border of the Republic of Belarus of narcotics, poisonous, toxic, virulent, hallucinogenic, radioactive and explosive substances, weapons and munitions, special materials and equipment of military designation, unbeknownst by the customs, or concealed from such, and also the transfer of items and valuables are forbidden or limited for transfer across the border of the Republic of Belarus in large quantities.

Inclusion of a special list of materials into the article gives this law a direction that can be actively used against smuggling of particularly hazardous materials that are also subject of such limitations under international nonproliferation regimes. Along with that, the following articles of the draft can be used for criminal prosecution of individuals who violate export controls: Violation of Regulations on the Oversight of Nuclear Materials (Art. 269), Violation of Regulations in the Oversight of Biological and Toxic Agents (Art. 277), Violation of Regulations on the Oversight of Virulent and Toxic Substances (Art. 279), Violation of Regulations on the Oversight of Hazardous Chemical Substances (Art. 280), and so on. All these articles also provide for the responsibility of monitoring the illegal trafficking of radioactive materials, biological and toxic agents, and other mentioned hazardous substances.

At the same time, it is obvious that the above norms cannot compensate for the absence in the new draft of an article that directly establishes responsibility for export control violations. It would be expedient therefore to include an article on the illegal export of commodities, scientific and technical information, and services used for the development of weapons, military hardware, and weapons of mass destruction into Chapter XX of the new Criminal Code. This article could contain the following two parts:

- export of raw materials, materials, equipment, technologies, scientific and technical information, and services that can be used for the development of weapons and military hardware and are subject to export limitation;
- export of raw materials, materials, equipment, technologies, scientific and technical information, and services that can be used for the development of nuclear, chemical, and biological weapons, or missile means of their delivery by missiles, and are subject to export limitations.

Emphasis on these two sections of the article is imperative in order to differentiate the responsibility for export control violators of WMD and missile technology and make the punishment for such violations more severe.

It is clear, at the same time, that the establishment of appropriate levels of criminal responsibility for export control violations depends on the adoption of the Law on Export Control and Administration and the adoption of the lists of controlled commodities. The notion of "illegal export" that appears in the present draft article is too general. Moreover, all export regulations provisions in Belarus do belong to the category not of laws but of administrative acts—decisions of the government. With the adoption of the Law on Export Control and Administration, it would be possible to establish responsibility for its violations. And it could be expedient to establish responsibility not only for the illegal export of controlled commodities, but also for premeditated actions of the exporter that had a knowledge of the end user of the exported goods and services being a controlled country, and for concealment by the exporter while obtaining the license of the knowledge that the exported commodities are used in the controlled countries for military or other purposes listed in the Law on Export Control and Administration.

Introduction of such articles may have a deterrent effect on potential violators, as well as a preventive function. Even more significant is the fact that the introduction of such articles would mean more possibilities for the law enforcement organizations to conduct investigative activities in this area. Until the Criminal Code provides for such criminal activities, the law enforcement organizations are not responsible for their interruption. The inclusion of such norms into the Criminal Code will facilitate the detection and prevention of the most serious export control violations.

Administrative Responsibility for Export Control Violations

Administrative responsibility in Belarus is regulated by the Code of the Republic of Belarus on Administrative Offense. Chapter 14A of this Code, Administrative Offenses on the Due Customs Regulation Procedures (administrative customs offenses), contains 14 articles that establish various degrees of responsibility for violations in transporting commodities across the border.[4] Adopted on February 3, 1993, the Customs Code of the Republic of Belarus provides due procedure for such violations.[5]

The Administrative Code does not contain provisions for direct responsibility for export control violations. In order to fill the gap, the government of Belarus has adopted its Decision No. 733 of October 26, 1993, which establishes responsibility for violating the due procedure for quoting and licensing of exports and imports of goods and services. This normative act establishes fines for export of goods and services that require a special license, without obtaining such, and for providing knowingly misleading information when applying for a license or making amendments to the license after obtaining it without the knowledge of the issuing organ.

Beside the above-mentioned, Decision No. 733 provides fines for five other violations of the licensing procedure. The same decision provides that the fines are gathered by special representatives of the Department of Economic Control attached to the government of Belarus. The grounds for fining could be the results of the department's inspections and information received from other organizations.

NOTES

1. Constitution of the Republic of Belarus, Minsk, 1994.
2. The Criminal Code of the Republic of Belarus, Minsk, 1984.
3. The Criminal Code of the Republic of Belarus (draft), Minsk, 1993.
4. The Code of the Republic of Belarus on Administrative Offense, Minsk, 1993.
5. The Customs Code of the Republic of Belarus, Minsk, 1993.

6

EXPORT CONTROLS IN THE REPUBLIC OF KAZAKSTAN

Dastan Eleukenov
and Keith D. Wolfe

INTRODUCTION

Kazakstan strongly supports strengthening nonproliferation measures worldwide, especially nuclear nonproliferation. This problem is especially close to Kazakstan, which in the past has adopted cardinal decisions in the field of nuclear policy. Kazakstan was the first country in the world to shut down an active nuclear test site and in addition was the first state to ratify START-1. Kazakstan welcomes the interests of the international community in working together with the former Soviet countries of Belarus, Kazakstan, and Ukraine, all of which have fulfilled their commitment to withdraw all nuclear warheads from their territory. This is really a historical step toward a sincere and large reduction of the nuclear threat and the creation of a unified security space in the former Soviet region.

In Almaty in early December 1997, the deputy foreign ministers of Central Asian states hosted a meeting under the rubric of the Conference on Interaction and Confidence Building Measures in Asia (CICA) process. Representatives from almost 20 Asian states adopted the Final Communiqué produced at this session. In particular, they agreed to discuss a diverse set of issues in detail such as disarmament, nonproliferation of WMD, arms control, security and confidence-building measures (CBMs), and peaceful and equitable settlement of disputes. Given the size and diversity of the Asian continent, the importance of such efforts cannot be overestimated.

Mindful of its obligations under the Non-Proliferation Treaty (NPT), Kazakstan has expressed its intention to work closely with other states to urge universal adherence to the NPT and to realize fully the goals and provisions stated in the preamble and throughout all provisions of the treaty. Kazakstan also wholly supports the objectives of the IAEA and the strengthening of IAEA safeguards. It recognizes the importance of maintaining effective nuclear material physical protection, control, and accounting in accordance with international standards. Toward this goal, Kazakstan receives assistance from numerous countries throughout Europe, North America, and Asia, such as Japan.

In possessing large stocks of uranium that today comprise approximately 25 percent of the world's authentically ascertained supply, Kazakstan provided 31 percent of all uranium used in the former Soviet Union. Kazakstan produced 85 percent of the fuel used in Soviet nuclear power plants. In addition, Kazakstan inherited a significant potential for producing beryllium, tantalum, and other sensitive metals, including rare and rare earth metals. In essence, the production of uranium and the manufacture of fuel pellets and rare metals have defined the contents of nuclear export for Kazakstan. Since independence was solidified in 1992, Kazakstan has independently exported both nuclear and dual-use products.

Because Kazakstan has taken to exporting sensitive items and technologies independently, implementing export controls is regarded as one of the most important directions of state policy to secure the nonproliferation of weapons of mass destruction. Kazakstan has accomplished a great deal in this effort in a relatively short period of time.

December 1993 was truly the takeoff point for establishing an export control system in Kazakstan. Parliament ratified the NPT on December 14, 1993, while U.S. Vice President Albert Gore was visiting Kazakstan. Gore's visit concluded with a package of Kazakstani-American agreements that were signed on December 13, 1993. The package included an agreement between the Ministry of Defense of Kazakstan and the U.S. Department of Defense, providing Kazakstan with assistance toward upgrading its national export control system to prevent the proliferation of weapons of mass destruction, including the technologies and know-how related to these weapons.

These two almost-simultaneous events of joining the NPT and signing the agreements with the U.S. greatly stimulated the creation of an export control system in Kazakstan. All export control developments that have taken place in Kazakstan subsequently bear the fingerprints of these two critical events coinciding with Gore's high-level visit to Almaty.

EXPORT CONTROL DEVELOPMENTS IN KAZAKSTAN

Analytically, the process of creating an export control system in Kazakstan has come through three fairly distinct stages:

1. December 1991 to December 1993;
2. December 1993 to May 1996;
3. May 1996 to the present day.

This chronology reflects the basic events in the history of Kazakstani export control, including gaining independence, joining the NPT, beginning to cooperate on export control with other countries, and the passage and implementation of an export control law by the Kazakstani Parliament. However, the described chronology is schematic. The point is that the creation of an export control system in Kazakstan involved different efforts simultaneously.

During the first stage, efforts were undertaken to control exports in two senses. The first was to develop the framework of a general state system. Secondly, a framework for the creation of a system to control nuclear sensitive materials was established, which is of vital importance for any state such as Kazakstan that possesses nuclear-related technologies.

It would not be accurate to say that during this first stage of development from independence to the joining of the NPT, there was no control over the export of nuclear materials or other dual-use goods in the country. For example, as early as December 1991 (in fact, immediately after gaining independence), the Cabinet of Ministers of the Republic of Kazakstan adopted Decree No. 804, On the Licensing Procedures for Shipping Goods from the Republic of Kazakstan.

Since that time, a number of governmental decrees have been made to regulate exports, including the so-called "goods of state importance." The term "goods of state importance" covered nuclear materials, dual-use goods, armaments, and military hardware (the term may be viewed as an equivalent for the term "special goods" used in Belarus and Ukraine). During this period, the term "goods of strategic importance" was also used in Kazakstan, but the meaning had nothing to do with the goods commonly subject to nonproliferation export controls. Currently, neither of these terms is used in Kazakstan.

To get a better picture of export controls in Kazakstan during its first two stages of development, we will present a list of decrees and legal acts passed by the government to regulate exports from the country. These decrees were the legal basis for export control up until the passage of an export control law in June 1996:

1. No. 804, dated December 27, 1991;
2. No. 118, dated February 16, 1993;
3. No. 43, dated April 26, 1994;
4. No. 66, dated January 19, 1995;
5. No. 1002, dated July 20, 1995;
6. No. 298, dated March 12, 1996.

The list does not contain decrees that made only minor changes in the corresponding decrees of the government. It is obvious that the legal basis of export controls in Kazakstan has changed frequently. The causes of this phenomenon (which is common for many countries) are numerous. For example, two introductions of new decrees in 1995 were connected to the creation of the Customs Union between Belarus, Kazakstan, and Russia (Kyrgyzstan subsequently joined as a member). Also, working toward the goal of creating a market economy in Kazakstan, a planned liberalization of external economic activity was pursued. However, the mechanism of control over the export of dual-use goods, armaments, and military hardware has remained largely intact. The following is a description of the export procedures in the Republic of Kazakstan as they came into being, which provides guidance for our understanding of the current system.

It is noteworthy that at first the governmental decrees were symmetrical with regard to export and import. This was apparently because the commercial approach dominated over the political one in controlling exports and imports and was dictated by the need to protect the internal market.

Until March 1995, there was no interagency bureau overseeing export controls in Kazakstan. However, we can state firmly that the Ministry of Industry and Trade (MIT), currently called the Ministry of Energy, Industry, and Trade, was the main agency charged with export controls in Kazakstan, though not the only agency responsible for issuing export licenses. It has also continually controlled, directly or indirectly, the export of armaments and military hardware, except for a short period in 1995 when a special agency called the Committee on Defense Industry was created, charged to oversee the military-industrial complex, and subsequently incorporated into the MIT.

According to the Decree of the President No. 1311, dated July 30, 1993, the export and reexport of goods of state importance could be undertaken only by state external trading companies (SETC) established under the MIT. In all, 11 SETCs were established by the fall of 1994. Under the MIT at the end of 1993, SETC *Ulan* was established, which had exclusive rights to export and import armaments and military hardware. Then in 1994, another SETC, *Kazakstan Sauda*, was granted the right to trade used military hardware. Since that time, the sphere has been changed organizationally.

In the realm of nuclear export, the national joint stock firm, KATEP (subsequently reformed into *KazAtomProm*), responsible for the nuclear industry, played the major role. The company was not among the SETCs and, therefore, could not export goods of state importance because some of the KATEP shares were privately owned. KATEP carried out its operations in the nuclear market through SETC *Ulan*. As Kazakstan was building its independence, the government apparently preferred to export and import goods of state importance exclusively through state-owned enterprises. Before the export control system was designed, this policy was justified. It is important to note that with the establishment of the Kazakstan Atomic Energy Agency (KAEA) in 1992, nuclear export in Kazakstan now takes place only if cleared by the agency. In addition, from the very beginning the activities of the KAEA were very close to the existing standards of ensuring a commitment to nuclear nonproliferation, including through the use of control of sensitive exports.

Despite its central role, the MIT could not coordinate its activities with the Ministry of Foreign Affairs and other agencies. For example, the MIT lacked information for differentiating between export destination countries. The necessity of establishing a special agency to coordinate export control in Kazakstan was gradually becoming apparent. As a result, the government adopted Decree No. 338, On Measures of Further Developing the Export Control System in the Republic of Kazakstan, dated March 24, 1995, which created the State Export Control Commission of the Republic of Kazakstan. The preamble states that the decree was made "in order to protect the strategic interests of the Republic of Kazakstan, fulfill its international obligations, and further develop and perfect the export control system."

Among the major tasks of the State Export Control Commission of the Republic of Kazakstan are: (1) coordinating the state's export control activities; (2) creating and maintaining the legal and normative basis for export controls in Kazakstan; (3) developing and adopting the organizational and methodological materials pertaining to export control with which all residents and nonresidents in the Republic of Kazakstan must comply; (4) coordinating decision-making on the issuing, suspending, or revoking of export licenses by ministries and agencies; (5) reviewing the results of work by executive bodies of the State Export Control Commission; and (6) making decisions on controversial questions.

According to this decree, the corresponding departments of the Ministry of Energy, Industry, and Trade, the Committee on Defense Industry, the Atomic Energy Agency, the Ministry of Defense, the Ministry of Science, and the Ministry of Ecology and Biological Resources, are the executive bodies of the State Export Control Commission of the Republic of Kazakstan with respect to related lists of goods, activities, and services. They were ordered to work out the necessary control lists.

An important feature of the above decree is that the Ministry of Foreign Affairs had to play a modest yet complex and important role in the system of state export controls. It was entrusted to work out a list of the states on which export restrictions were placed for particular goods, activities, and services. Also, the Ministry of Foreign Affairs was expected to participate in delivering information about potential foreign importers to the commission.

Generally speaking, although not all of the principles of the decree were implemented before the law on export controls was discussed in the Parliament, the adoption of Decree No. 338 may be regarded as a timely demonstration by the government of its serious plans to create an effective export control system in Kazakstan. It showed the commitment the central government had to creating a well-run and complimentary system of export control, including all relevant state agencies and ministries. In practice, however, the commission could be deemed a failure. Leading up to the passage of the state's export control law, the commission only very rarely met, and currently, while on paper still existent, in reality, the commission has died a quiet and unnoticed death. Of course, from a technical point of view, it is not entirely necessary to have such a commission. Nevertheless, a resurrection of this concept could be useful, and in the near future it may become an effective tool for improving the interagency coordination of export control policy.

EXISTING EXPORT CONTROL PROCEDURES IN THE REPUBLIC OF KAZAKSTAN

The legislative core of export controls in Kazakstan is the Law on Export Control of Arms, Military Equipment, and Dual-Purpose Products, signed into law on June 18, 1996. In fact Kazakstan was the first country in the former Soviet Union to pass comprehensive legislation on nonproliferation export controls. As its preamble states, this law establishes the principles and procedures of export control over arms and military equipment, raw materials, intermediate goods, equipment, technology, scientific and technological information, and services linked with their production and use in the interests both of international security and the national security of the Republic of Kazakstan, as well as a strengthening of the procedures of the nonproliferation of weapons of mass destruction.

This legislation grants the necessary powers to the government regulatory institutions responsible for export control over the export (or reexport) of arms and military equipment, dual-use products including nuclear materials, as well as transit cargoes of a similar nature. It establishes regulations for obtaining the required information from producers, exporters, and commercial middlemen, including information about the end use and end users of products subject to export control. This legislation also gives state regulatory institutions that are authorized to conduct export control operations the power to investigate, license, and reject applications for the export of above-mentioned products.

The law broadly defines the items subject to export control, including weapons and military technology, nuclear and dual-use nuclear materials, chemical and biological agents that could be used in the creation of chemical or biological weapons, missile technologies, military scientific and technical information, as well as any other products determined by the Government of Kazakstan. The control lists for the country were created in Decree No. 298, discussed further below. The law specifically states that nuclear exports must be placed under IAEA safeguards and addresses issues of reexport and transit.

It is necessary to mention that during the drafting of the law,

Kazakstan used the experience of American experts as called for under the agreement between the Kazakstani and U.S. defense ministries that provided U.S. assistance for the creation of an export control system designed to prevent the proliferation of weapons of mass destruction from Kazakstan. In addition, Kazakstan's export control law served as a model for a very similar law used in Tajikistan for export control.

The law serves as the solid basis for developing a series of regulations in the field of export controls. However, at least two major changes of the structure of the Kazakstani government have taken place since the law entered into force. Therefore, some delay occurred in developing a new regulatory basis to fully implement the law. Meanwhile, a number of governmental regulations remain effective. At present, the most important are the following ones.

1. Decree of the Government of the Republic of Kazakstan No. 298, dated March 12, 1996, provided for a single procedure for the export and import of goods, activities, and services mandatory for all businesses in the Republic of Kazakstan, regardless of the form of ownership. The law on export control continued these same practices and, even through governmental changes and ministerial reorganization, the same basic procedures remain today.

The Procedures for Issuance of Licenses for the Export and Import of Goods, Activities, and Services in the Republic of Kazakstan were approved by this decree. The decree is effective only in connection with goods specified in the control lists attached to the decree. Any other goods not on the control lists are sold and purchased without licenses. The only agency currently having the right to issue licenses is the Ministry of Energy, Industry, and Trade (MEIT, renamed from the old Ministry of Industry and Trade but carrying out the same basic functions of the old MIT) and its bureaus in the regions.

2. Government Resolution No. 183 On the Export and Import of Nuclear Materials. Technologies, Equipment, Facilities, Special Non-Nuclear Materials; Dual-Use Equipment, Materials, and Technologies; Radioactive Materials; and Isotope Products, issued on March 9, 1993. This resolution sets forth the requirements for nuclear exports and outlines the responsibilities of the Kazakstan Atomic Energy Agency in the sphere of nuclear export control. Although this resolution was enacted before Kazakstan officially acceded to the NPT, Article IV specifically requires that nuclear exports be carried out in accordance with the provisions of the NPT. Lists of controlled nuclear and dual-use nuclear materials, which are consistent with Nuclear Supplier's Group lists, are set forth in Appendices 1 and 2.

3. *Government Resolution No. 1037* On the Licensing of the Export and Import of Goods (Works, Services) in the Republic of Kazakstan, issued

on June 30, 1997. This resolution is the seventh and final in a series of resolutions, each superseding the next, outlining the licensing procedures for exporting controlled goods in Kazakstan. The resolution explains the export licensing procedures, as well as including control lists for all goods requiring either special permission from the government and/or an export license before they can be exported. The list of goods requiring special permission from the government includes military equipment and technologies, nuclear materials and technologies, radioactive materials, and radioactive waste. The list of goods requiring an export license includes all materials and dual-use materials that could be used in the production of a weapon of mass destruction. License and application forms are provided as well. The same basic procedures are as outlined above in Decree No. 298.

References to export control also are found in the Law on Use of Atomic Energy (effective since April 1997). This law codified the legal basis and regulatory principles regarding the use of atomic energy in Kazakstan. Section 4 specifically addresses export and import questions in two articles. Article 19 states that export and import of goods and services in the sphere of use of atomic energy are controlled by relevant state organs in accordance with the national legislation and international obligations of the Republic of Kazakstan. Article 20 states that the procedures for exporting and importing nuclear materials, technologies, equipment and facilities, special nonnuclear materials, sources of ionizing radiation, radioactive materials, and radioactive waste are set forth in the legislation of the Republic of Kazakstan.

Export Control Authority

Fortunately, drafters of the Kazakstan export control law foresaw the possible restructuring of the government and the necessary changes to the system that would be required as a result. The law gives the government a necessary degree of flexibility. As mentioned above, according to existing practice, the recently created MEIT is the key body in terms of licensing exports. Currently, there are discussions taking place within MEIT to create a special Export Control Service in the Ministry.

A decision on the issuance or denial of a license is made by MEIT and, if necessary, is cleared by the related ministries and agencies, no later than 10 days after an application was registered. A denial should be justified and returned to an applicant in written form. Authorized state executive agencies may suspend or revoke previously issued licenses if businesses do not comply with export and import regulations. Licenses are issued for a period of up to a year. Two copies of all licenses are issued, and they have several levels of counterfeit protection. The first copy is handed to an exporter to present to a customs office, and the second copy goes directly to MEIT. Standard practice is that a license issued for one exporter cannot be transferred to another one. Customs then uses the license issued by MEIT as the basis for the processing and export of a licensed good from the territory of the country.

In the issuance of a license, the Ministry of Science and the State Technical Committee of the Republic of Kazakstan for Protection of Information play vital roles. These bodies are important actors in the license review process, and if they decide to not approve a license, then the Cabinet of Ministers will not issue the license. It is noteworthy that the Atomic Energy Agency and the National Aerospace Agency are parts of the Ministry of Science, and thus play a day-to-day role in license review of nuclear-sensitive and missile-related exports.

Explosives, detonators, and small arms are exported only if cleared by the Ministry of Internal Affairs. Normative and technical documentation for military commodities can be exported only if cleared by the Ministry of Defense Committee on Defense Industry and the State Technical Commission on Protection of Information. The export of rare earth metals, as well as their raw materials, alloys, and combinations, are possible only if cleared by the Ministry of Science.

According to the established practice, the Customs Committee, together with corresponding law enforcement agencies, prevents, through a comprehensive inspection of vehicles, goods without necessary documents from being shipped from the territory of Kazakstan.

As a rule, the above-mentioned decrees of the government of the Republic of Kazakstan do not distinguish between the CIS countries, the Baltic States, or the countries of the "far abroad." However, there are other governmental decrees and interstate agreements that distinguish trade relations with the countries of the "near abroad" from those with the countries of the "far abroad." It is necessary to mention the Customs Union between Belarus, Kazakstan, Russia, and Kyrgyzstan here. It should be stressed that, on the whole, Kazakstani trade relations with the "near abroad" are strictly economic relationships and have nothing to do with export control policy in the generally accepted meaning of the term.

As far as the export of armaments and military hardware is concerned, it is implemented by the Republican State Enterprise (RSE) *Kazvoentekhimpeks* created by the Committee on Defense Industry within the Ministry of Defense of the Republic of Kazakstan. Among its tasks are: (1) purchasing and selling of armaments and munitions, military hardware and technology, spare parts and equipment; (2) organizing, collecting, and selling of aerospace solid waste, as well as ferrous and nonferrous metal scrap, and metal scrap of military origin; and (3) conducting export/import operations with military commodities. RSE *Kazvoentekhimpeks* is granted the right to conduct export/import operations with the above-mentioned commodities.

Ensuring missiles and missile technology export controls is somewhat different. As is known, the Baikonour space center, the only true missile-related facility within Kazakstan, is leased out to Russia, and bilateral treaties and agreements regulate its activities. However, these circumstances do not preclude Kazakstan from participating in the MTCR in the future.

In addition to the above, the new Agency of Strategic Planning and Reforms, which incorporated a considerable part of the former Ministry of Economy, will evidently play an increasing role in export control policy as well. It is responsible for reviewing licenses based on the likely economic impact a given export is likely to have on the country in the future. As economic considerations continue to take more prominent positions within the government, the agency's role is likely to increase in importance.

Enforcement and Penalties

On January 1, 1998, a new Criminal Code of the Republic of Kazakstan entered into force. It provides punishment for violations of the export control law. According to the Criminal Code, production, proliferation, and use of weapons of mass destruction qualify as a crime against peace and security of mankind (Articles 158 and 159). The illegal export of technologies, scientific and technical information and services used for creation of WMD, and arms is penalized severely, including confiscation of goods, imposition of fines, and possible subjection to criminal liability (Article 243). Other items relevant to export control include violations of customs legislation and thefts, taken into account by Articles 250 and 255. Finally, violations of export control legislation could be connected with Articles 247 to 249 and 209, which cover violations of the rules of management of radioactive materials, economic smuggling, and so on.

MEMBERSHIP IN NONPROLIFERATION CONTROL REGIMES

Kazakstan is a nonnuclear-weapon state party to the NPT, and, accordingly, all exports of nuclear goods and technologies are placed under IAEA safeguards in the country of destination. Kazakstan signed a safeguards agreement with the IAEA on July 26, 1994, and the agreement entered into force in August 11, 1995.

Kazakstan is, however, not yet a member of the Nuclear Suppliers Group (NSG), but its export control lists of nuclear materials, equipment, and technology are based on the NSG lists. Kazakstan has expressed an interest in joining the NSG and continues to work toward this goal. Kazakstan is not a member of the MTCR or an adherent to its standards. At the same time, given the considerable space exploration technologies on its territory, the possibility of Kazakstan membership in the MTCR should be a question for the future.

Kazakstan is a party to the Agreement on the Basic Principles of Cooperation in the Field of Peaceful Use of Nuclear Energy (Minsk

Accord) of June 26, 1992, between CIS member states. In addition, on February 9, 1993, Kazakstan reached an agreement with five other CIS states to cooperate in controlling exports relevant to manufacturing weapons of mass destruction. Kazakstan signed the Chemical Weapons Convention (CWC), but has yet to ratify the convention, and joining the Biological Weapons Convention (BWC) is currently under consideration. The financial requirements of participation in both conventions appear to be a difficult point because of the current economic situation in Kazakstan.

INTO THE FUTURE

As one can see from the delineation above, Kazakstan has come a long way in the development of its export control system. This is because it has been a priority within the government. This will continue into the future so that Kazakstan can move toward an even more complete export control system. For this to come about, there are several areas where the export control system will need to move ahead.

One of the more important hurdles in front of the export control authorities in Kazakstan is the lack of implementation of regulations directing the export control structure. While Kazakstan is ahead in that it is the first CIS state to pass an export control law and have it signed by its president, legal authorities are still lacking in the state. With sets of implementing regulations, which are currently being developed in a multiagency effort, the export control structure in Kazakstan will become much more complete.

Another direction from which Kazakstan can gain much is in taking an even more active role within the international nonproliferation regime community than the high level of interaction it currently has. Kazakstan believes strongly in playing an international role in its nonproliferation efforts. While it is too early to say that Kazakstan is close to achieving membership in some of the above-mentioned regimes, it is also important to point out that this is an integral part of the state's future plans, showing once again the government's commitment to nonproliferation and export control.

Another very important aspect in the ongoing development of export controls in Kazakstan is also well on its way toward becoming a reality. It has been recognized for some time that a more modern means of communications between both licensing organizations as well as between licensers and enforcement bodies was needed in Kazakstan. As a result of successful cooperation between the United States and Kazakstan governments, an automated export control system is currently under development and should be running by the fall of 1998 (moving of the capital of Kazakstan to Astana added some additional time to the realization of the system). This will provide for a significant improvement in the lines of communication, but further computerization will be needed to bring the export control system up to desired standards. An example comes in the fact that the system will not sufficiently be in coordination with customs authorities at the borders. Another example is that Kazakstan has only now begun compiling databases on recipients of Kazakstani products and technologies, as well as on other pertinent matters. The creation of databases on items such as exports, imports, suppliers, and recipients will go a long ways toward making the licensing process faster and more thorough.

With its export control law and with a government dedicated to building upon and improving the export control system in Kazakstan, we should see only more improvement in this area in the years to come. Even with the standard problems facing any export control system in a state such as this, including a lack of sufficient staff, a lack of as much training as would be ideal for both licensers and enforcement personnel, and a lack of necessary funding to carry out all relevant tasks to the export control processes, Kazakstan is moving ahead toward building one of the premier export control systems in the region. This can be explained by the direct and serious efforts of the presiding government to implement policies that protect against the proliferation of weapons of mass destruction, of which export control plays an important part.

PART III

PROBLEMS
AND PROSPECTS OF
EXPORT CONTROL
AND CURBING
THE SPREAD OF WEAPONS

7

CHEMICAL AND BIOLOGICAL WEAPONS EXPORT CONTROLS

Maria Katsva and
Derek Averre

INTRODUCTION

The attack by the Aum Shinrikyo cult on the Tokyo metro using a chemical nerve agent awakened international attention to the potential of chemical and biological weapons (CBW)[1] in terrorist and other offensive actions by small groups involved in limited-conflict situations. The threat posed by CBW in regional armed conflicts has been widely recognized since the use of chemical weapons by Iraq in the war with Iran in the 1980s, and the dangers of proliferation have been accentuated by the discovery of the extent of the Iraqi CBW program in the last few years.

The task of combating proliferation has been given added urgency by the new international security situation in the post-Cold-War period. In particular, the disintegration of the Soviet Union—the world's main producer of CBW—and the ensuing political and economic instability in the Newly Independent States (NIS) highlighted the need for a comprehensive response to possible proliferation from the region, including the establishment of an export control system. The issue is complicated by continuing uncertainty, not only about the dual-use nature of many of the materials and technologies included in export control schedules, but also about the chemical and biological (CB) capabilities of the NIS, the extent to which the Soviet Union's offensive military programs have been dismantled or converted, and the difficulties of monitoring production and verifying compliance with national controls in these countries.

The term "proliferation" is used to describe many facets of the problem of the spread of armaments, and especially weapons of mass destruction (WMD): "vertical" proliferation within a possessor state, including possible qualitative developments in CB agents and means of delivery;[2] the leakage of materials from production or research facilities for illegal transfer to groups wishing to use them for military purposes; the creation by terrorist or other antisocial groups of offensive means; the transfer of know-how via brain drain or through personal (or indeed electronic) contact between scientists; or the illicit export from one country to another of dual-use materials or technologies by evading export controls. This chapter restricts itself necessarily to the last of these, although the problem is placed in wider context.

As one leading authority on CBW has pointed out, as far as this class of weapon is concerned the term "proliferator" has even been employed to describe countries that are a long way from possessing CBW but have the intention to acquire them. He goes on to argue that:

> although capacity for waging [chemical and biological warfare] is spreading to more and more countries, and although a part of the spread is indeed due to the conscious desire of renegade states such as Iraq actually to wield CBW weapons, the greater part is simply an unfortunate side-effect of a process that is otherwise beneficial and anyway impossible to stop: the diffusion of competence in applied chemistry and biology from the rich to the poor parts of the world. The concern about CBW proliferation lies, basically, in the fact that the diffusion is taking place within what seems to be an environment of diminishing restraint on the use of chemical weapons.

He suggests a working definition to identify the problem as a whole: "a loosening of inhibitions against using CBW weapons within an environment of easier access to them."[3]

We provide a brief overview of CB export controls in the Soviet period and go on to describe policy and legislation in this sphere in the NIS since 1991 and the history of their involvement in the major international nonproliferation initiatives—the Chemical Weapons Convention, the Biological and Toxin Weapons Convention, and the Australia Group. The status of the chemical and biotechnology industries in the NIS is described and an analysis made of production and research and development (R&D) capabilities relevant to proliferation concerns. This analysis provides the background to the task—always difficult in view of differing opinions on how easy it is to manufacture CBW on the basis of civilian industry[4]—of assessing the current and potential effectiveness of CB export controls in the NIS. Finally this matter is discussed in relation to broader issues of security and foreign trade policy in the NIS and to the collective disarmament and nonproliferation initiatives of the 1990s.

SOVIET CB EXPORT CONTROLS

Indications of rising concern about CW proliferation on the part of the Soviet authorities came in the mid-1980s. In January 1986, the USSR

Council of Ministers approved a statute on the export of dual-use chemicals that emphasized "due regard for the Soviet Union's obligations under the 1925 Geneva Protocol" and made mandatory the receipt from the importing country of guarantees that the chemicals would not be directly or indirectly used to manufacture CW and would be reexported only with the written consent of the relevant Soviet foreign trade organization. Draft contracts with foreign partners as regards these guarantees were to be agreed with the Soviet Ministry of Foreign Affairs. Any violation of these terms was to lead to the cessation of shipments to the offending country until the foreign trade organization and the Ministry of Foreign Affairs investigated the breach. A single list of dual-use chemicals was annexed to the statute.[5]

This statute was superseded in 1989 by one that was aimed at bringing the Soviet Union more in line with systems existing in other leading industrialized countries. This new statute contained two lists of dual-use chemicals; exports of items on the first list were to be carried out by the Foreign Trade Organization *Soyuzkhimeksport*, with draft contracts having been agreed by the Ministries of Foreign Economic Relations and Foreign Affairs after ensuring end-use safeguards, while items on the second list could be exported by various types of organizations on licenses issued by the Ministry of Chemical and Petrochemical Industry. The other main amendment to the 1986 statute was the prohibition of exports to countries violating the ban on the use of CW laid out in the 1925 Geneva Convention. A third list covering 12 dual-use production technologies subject to licensing by the State Committee for Science and Technology and exported through *Soyuzkhimeksport* was established under a separate act.[6]

The publication of these acts accompanied diplomatic initiatives that addressed the issue of CW proliferation and use. On March 3 to 6, 1986, U.S.-Soviet bilateral talks took place on chemical export controls. Progress was understandably slow, but two years later a joint communique from the Gorbachev-Reagan Moscow summit stressed the need for concrete solutions to the problem of ensuring effective verification of a CW convention, and called on all nations with a dual-use chemicals capability to institute stringent export controls to inhibit the proliferation of CW. There was also an attempt by the Soviet Union to secure an agreement among Comecon states to exercise controls over exports of technologies to countries interested in developing a CW capability.[7] These events, together with the Gorbachev administration's openness (albeit limited) about the Soviet CW effort,[8] represented important progress in terms of arms control and a substantial change in Soviet attitudes toward CW.[9]

Existing export control regimes were restructured during 1991 to embrace items in all areas of proliferation concern, and a new coordinating body, the USSR Commission for State Export Controls—a forerunner of the Russian Federation Export Control Commission—was established to develop an export control policy for national security and foreign policy purposes. The Office of Export Controls, set up in the early 1980s within the USSR State Planning Commission *Gosplan*,[10] continued its executive functions and reviewed export control schedules of nuclear, missile, chemical, and biological items specifically for nonproliferation purposes. In addition to the three lists covering chemical G&T (goods and technology), a schedule covering biological organisms was introduced that included a number of basic categories of viruses, bacteria, plant and animal pathogens, and so on.[11]

An authoritative source argues that, despite the establishment of this embryonic or prototype nonproliferation export control system, "there was no explicit rationale for Soviet export controls"[12]—the issue was not discussed by the Supreme Soviet at all, and there was only limited input from foreign policy and trade specialists—and the agencies involved were not concerned with creating an effective enforcement mechanism. In the Soviet system, the relevant government agencies had the power to approve or prevent any trade activity and worked largely according to administrative nontransparent criteria that furthered their own departmental interests. The efficiency of the system was poor, particularly during *perestroika*, when firms were eager to export their technologies.

With the end of the Cold War and the evolution of a new international security situation that brought with it very different problems, the Soviet authorities began to consider the proliferation issue and national export control policy in greater depth and to cooperate with multilateral organizations, including the Australia Group. The radical political and economic changes following the events of August 1991 and the subsequent breakup of the Soviet system hastened the introduction of a much more comprehensive nonproliferation effort.

CB EXPORT CONTROL POLICY AND LEGISLATION IN THE NIS

The thrust of the systems of export controls being developed in Russia and certain other NIS differs from that of the Soviet Union. With the collapse of the Soviet system, these countries were faced for the first time in the modern era with important choices in economic and security policy; one of these was striking an appropriate and delicate balance between the liberalization of foreign trade as part of a free-market economy and the introduction of comprehensive and effective export controls to prevent the proliferation of sensitive G&T.

The Russian Federation (RF), which inherited by far the greatest part of the USSR's chemical and biotechnology industry, took upon itself Soviet commitments and obligations in the sphere of disarmament and moved quickly to create an export control framework for CB G&T. The establishment in April 1992 of the RF Export Control Commission, that was charged with coordinating export control policy and drafting lists of controlled items, was followed by a decree in July of that year promulgating an interim schedule of materials, equipment, technologies, and scientific information used in weapons manufacture that were subject to licensing and establishing the licensing procedures involved.[13] This schedule included one specific pharmaceutical item and production technology for certain biological toxins and chemical neurotoxins. More comprehensive registers of dual-use CB G&T requiring similar controls and subject to the same licensing procedures were subsequently issued that, together with the introduction of more definite controls on nuclear and missile items, brought Russia broadly in line with international practice on exports of G&T usable in weapons of mass destruction.

The first Russian dual-use chemicals list appeared in September 1992.[14] This was superseded by a more detailed list compiled in accordance with Australia Group recommendations in December 1994; Section 1 covers chemicals, Section 2 covers equipment, and Section 3 covers related production technologies.[15] The directives that established these lists were accompanied by resolutions of the Cabinet of Ministers that approved the licensing procedures for exports of dual-use chemical G&T.[16] An initial list of bacteriological and toxin materials was issued in November 1992;[17] this was also superseded by one that follows the recommendations of the Australia Group.[18] Controls on the export of missile technology that could be used to deliver WMD warheads—a vital element in nonproliferation measures due to technological advances in recent years—have also been instituted.[19]

Other NIS have also made progress in developing export control systems and establishing schedules. Among the seven control lists presented to the Belarusian government for approval are two dealing specifically with CW and BW and equipment for their production, and one dealing with means of delivery of nuclear, chemical, and biological weapons.[20] The Ukrainian government, which did not in fact sign the May 1992 CIS Chemical Weapons Agreement requiring the signatories to coordinate policy on monitoring dual-use chemical export controls due to a dispute with Russia over funding the CW destruction program, has introduced a decree to control exports of CB and toxin weapons which includes appended lists of controlled items.[21] In 1995 the foundations for controls over CB G&T were laid by the Kazak government, whose permission is required for all exports of weapons-related items. Included on the schedules of licensed items are "materials, equipment and technologies that are intended for peaceful purposes but can be used for the development of missile, nuclear, chemical or other weapons of mass destruction"; any decision on licensing these items by the Kazak Ministry of Economy and Trade is to be coordinated with the state Committee for the Defense Industry and the State Technical Commission on Information Protection.[22]

The Russian export control system is backed up by legal penalties for violating regulations. The RF Criminal Code, which was adopted by the State Duma on May 24, 1996, and entered into force on January 1, 1997, punishes the contraband transfer of CBW and CB items subject to export control through the RF state borders by imprisonment for between three and 12 years, depending on circumstances, with possible forfeiture of the violator's property (Article 188). The illegal export of controlled technologies, scientific and technical information, and services in the CBW sphere is also punishable by imprisonment (from three to seven years) or hefty fines (Article 189).[23] The legal penalties for violations in the other NIS are less well established. In Ukraine the Penal Code was amended in 1993 to provide for the prosecution, with imprisonment for up to eight years, of those violating export controls of G&T usable in nuclear, missile, and CB armaments, but there are unlikely to be any prosecutions until the law on export controls is adopted.[24] The draft Criminal Code of Belarus includes in the definition of smuggling the transfer abroad of poisonous and toxic substances as well as "special materials and equipment of military designation," but legal amendments specifying criminal prosecution for the illegal export of export-controlled G&T have apparently not yet been completed.[25] Proposals for amendments to the Criminal Code of Kazakstan to introduce criminal penalties for export control violations had not been endorsed by the government as of early 1997.[26]

THE NIS AND MULTILATERAL CB
EXPORT CONTROL ARRANGEMENTS

The relative importance of export controls in nonproliferation regimes is disputed, but the technical and procedural provisions contained in the 1993 Chemical Weapons Convention (CWC)—the first multilateral treaty affecting a large civilian industrial sector, the 1972 Biological and Toxin Weapons Convention (BTWC), and the multilateral suppliers agreement commonly known as the Australia Group (AG) have been crucial to the development of CB nonproliferation in the NIS.

A number of articles in the CWC, which was opened for signature on January 13, 1993,[27] and entered into force on April 29, 1997, following the sixty-fifth ratification on October 31, 1996, focus on export controls and restrictions on transfers of chemicals. Article 1 binds states parties never to "transfer, directly or indirectly, chemical weapons to anyone" or "to assist, encourage or induce, in any way, anyone to engage in any activity prohibited to a State Party under this Convention," and goes on to define CW, toxic chemicals, and precursors in Article II. The transfer of dual-use chemicals is controlled and monitored but not prohibited by the CWC; however, Article XI obliges parties to make their national chemicals trade regulations "consistent with the object and purpose" of the CWC. An annex contains three lists of chemicals that are to be under control or restriction. Schedule 1 incorporates high-risk chemicals that have little or no application in nonweapons use and are actual warfare agents or immediate nerve agent precursors; these must in no circumstances be transferred to any nonparty to the CWC, and stringent controls are placed on transfers to states parties.

Chemicals in Schedule 2 pose a significant risk and are key precursors in CW production or toxic chemicals that can be used to produce warfare agents. They can be transferred to nonparty states up to three years after the CWC enters into force, provided end-use and non-reexport guarantees are given, and thereafter only to states parties. Initial and annual declarations must be made providing aggregate national data on Schedule 2 chemicals produced, processed, consumed, imported, and exported, and for each facility producing them in quantities above the declaration threshold.

Schedule 3 items are dual-use chemicals that are often produced in large commercial quantities for peaceful purposes and can be transferred to nonparties providing end-use and non-reexport guarantees are provided; there are similar requirements on declarations as for Schedule 2 chemicals, but the declaration thresholds are much higher.[28] Also, other plants producing more than 30 tons of organic chemicals containing phosphorus, sulphur, or fluorine (PSF) and those making more than 200 tons of non-PSF organic chemicals have to be declared.

The BTWC, ratified in 1975 by the USSR, similarly bans the development, production, stockpiling, and transfer of BW agents, but is widely perceived to be vitiated by the impossibility of outlawing research for defensive or peaceful purposes and the lack of a monitoring and verification regime (such as that envisaged by the CWC) to ensure compliance. Furthermore, recent developments in biotechnology and genetic engineering have led to a spread of capabilities—a great deal of relevant information is published in the open literature—and the dual-use nature of much of the technology involved means that materials potentially used in BW have widespread legitimate application that could benefit developing countries and, it is argued by some, should not be denied them. There is a considerable problem in ensuring detection of the small quantities of biological and toxin agents which suffice to present a weapons threat and in monitoring new agents. BW proliferation has nevertheless been slowed by the application of specific supply-side export controls applied through national regulations and by the coordinated efforts of members of the AG.[29]

The AG, an informal organization that does not impose transfer restrictions on its members but relies on voluntary implementation of national export controls, has provided an important forum for coordination and information exchange and for harmonizing national control lists. Over the years since its inception in 1985, it has developed guideline lists of key pre-cursors and a "warning list" of chemicals used in CW manufacture which has contributed to restricting their transfer to potential proliferators. Opinion on the efficacy of the AG varies; as an informal arrangement, it lacks sanctions against states (including its members) that ignore its provi-sions. Industrially developed nations have regarded it as an interim mea-sure pending the establishment of a verifiable CW convention, and spe-cialists have concluded that a determined country could fairly easily cir-cumvent its provisions and acquire the chemicals and technology to pro-duce some CW indigenously.[30] However, it is generally agreed that it has raised awareness about CW proliferation, and its supporters argue that it has retarded CW development and may in some cases have forced coun-tries to reconsider their CW programs.

Its experience was also useful in the establishment of the CWC; in fact the AG may well survive until the CWC is perceived to be operating satis-factorily and the BTWC is developed into a stronger verifiable regime, which may be several years in the future. The current precursor list con-tains 54 specific chemicals, and registers of dual-use equipment and tech-nology that AG members are expected to control have been added. Since 1990 the AG has also addressed biological agents, technology, and equip-ment and has developed three lists covering human, plant, and animal pathogens and a list of dual-use biotechnology equipment.[31]

Soviet interest at the turn of the decade in cooperating with the AG was an important stimulus to the development of national export con-trol policy and procedures and of lists of CB G&T. The USSR participat-ed in its seminars (the first in December 1990) organized to encourage central and east European states to prepare or improve their export con-trol legislation, and since 1991 Russia has had regular working contacts with the group. The Yeltsin administration, motivated both by support for AG nonproliferation aims and by chemicals trade interests, has demonstrated its adherence to AG principles by bringing the RF's export control lists in line with the AG's. However, Russia is not yet a for-mal member of the AG. There are still concerns among its members about inadequate controls over exports of precursors, and doubts remain about Russia's commitment to join the group, due in part to the lack of interagency consensus on the issue of controls.

Russia finally ratified the CWC in October 1997 despite concerns, par-ticularly among certain groups in the State Duma and Federation Council, over its requirements regarding the timetable for destruction of her 40,000 tons of CW stockpiles and the costs involved. It was realized that nonratification would have had implications for Russia's contribu-tion to the chemical disarmament process in general. Although Russia's national export controls would still place a legal requirement not to transfer dual-use chemicals illegally, the monitoring and on-site verifica-tion of chemicals production necessary to ensure the accuracy of data reported by manufacturers in compliance with the CWC would not be possible, and the suspicion would remain that production of certain chemicals could be diverted to CW manufacture. From the commercial point of view, not being party to the CWC would have left Russia liable to restrictions on trade with member states in chemicals on the CWC lists and chemical technology.[32] Russian policy advisers also warned of the loss of political influence in the international arena that would result from nonratification.[33]

There is some concern in the Russian chemical industry over the reporting of information on chemical production under the provisions in the CWC. Some industry representatives see this as the disclosure of sensitive commercial data to a body whose responsibilities are uncertain; they were attempting to block ratification pending improvements in protecting such information.[34]

THE CHEMICAL AND BIOTECHNOLOGY INDUSTRIES IN THE NIS

Recognizing the extent of the proliferation potential in terms of industrial capacity for scheduled CB materials and the technological level of the relevant industries is important in assessing the likely scale of monitoring and verification efforts and understanding the problems involved. Despite these countries' relative weakness in certain spheres, the size and complexity of the chemical and biotechnology industries in the NIS are considerable. Then chairman of the RF Committee for Chemical and Biological Weapons Convention Problems, Pavel Syutkin, has stated that compiling a database of chemicals for the purposes of the CWC will be an onerous task; this is made harder by the fact that most of the Russian enterprises producing precursors and dual-use chemicals are now independent joint stock companies making their own production and investment policies, and by the fact that there have been gaps and inaccuracies in statistical reporting since the disintegration of the Soviet system. While there is still a large measure of state control over enterprises in most of the other NIS, ownership of industry there may also pass into independent private hands.

The Chemical Industry

Syutkin has provided a general estimate of the number of Russian facilities of interest to the CWC. Facilities that formerly produced CWC Schedule 1 chemicals—in other words, chemical warfare agents or key final-stage precursors—can be numbered in single figures and those capable of producing Schedule 2 and 3 chemicals in dozens, while there are "hundreds" of enterprises manufacturing organic chemicals, including PSF compounds.[35] A closer look is needed at this statement.

A recent account has identified seven facilities, out of "about 20 CWPF [production facilities] and filling plants" declared by the

Russians, which were engaged in post-World-War-II manufacture of actual CW: the Kaprolaktam, Orgsteklo, and Korund production associations in Dzerzhinsk, the State Scientific-Research Institute for Organic Chemistry and Technology (*GosNIIOKhT*) in Moscow, its branch at Volsk-17, and the Khimprom production associations in Volgograd (formerly the S.M.Kirov plant) and Novocheboksarsk.[36] Of these, the first three produced "old" CW; Kaprolaktam manufactured iprite (mustard gas) and lewisite; Orgsteklo produced hydrocyanic acid; and Korund produced hydrocyanic acid and (at least during the war years) phosgene.[37] Manufacture of these chemicals was apparently discontinued some time ago;[38] according to chemical industry directories, they have in recent years been engaged in the large-scale manufacture of industrial chemicals. Korund is of interest to CWC and AG lists since it has the capacity to manufacture potassium cyanide, sodium cyanide, and thionyl chloride, as well as sulphur and phosphorus-containing compounds. In the Orgsteklo production profile are small volumes of organic fluorine compounds and cyanide-based intermediates. Kaprolaktam produces basic industrial chemicals such as caprolactam, acetylene, chlor- and dichlorethane, trichlorethylene, ethylene glycol, epichlorhydrin, monochloramine, and isopropyl alcohol.

The Volgograd and Novocheboksarsk Khimprom enterprises, two of the largest concerns in Russia, are of major interest to CWC since they used to manufacture organophosphorus nerve agents and still produce important dual-use chemicals and large quantities of organic compounds. The Volgograd facility started up industrial manufacture of sarin in 1959 and of soman in 1967.[39] According to official sources, manufacture was discontinued some time before 1987 (although Vil Mirzayanov, the man who "blew the whistle" on the Soviet binary CW program, has claimed that Soman was produced after 1987[40]), and recent accounts indicate that the CW plant has been dismantled.[41] The Volgograd Khimprom company manufactures phosphorus oxychloride, phosphorus trichloride, dimethyl phosphite, and sulphur chloride, as well as a range of organic phosphorus- (until recently including insecticides) and fluorine-containing compounds, and may have the capability to produce other CWC/AG listed chemicals. Khimprom Novocheboksarsk, located in the Chuvash republic, produced Soviet V-gas until 1987; according to the former head of the Committee for CBW Convention Problems, it is the only former CW facility to have been preserved.[42] The company manufactures phosphorus oxychloride, phosphorus trichloride, and dimethyl phosphite as well as phosphorus-based compounds (including insecticides), sulphonyl urea herbicides, chlorine-caustic products, dyestuffs and their intermediates, veterinary compounds, and other intermediate chemicals.

GosNIIOKhT was the Soviet Union's primary CW R&D institution[43] and had a small pilot plant for the production of prototype CW. It had three branches: the branch at Volsk-17, otherwise known as Shikhany-1 (close to the Shikhany-2, or Volsk-18, CW testing range) and since 1992 called the State Institute for Technology of Organic Synthesis (*GITOS*), and two more at Novocheboksarsk and Volgograd. These four sites apparently carried out virtually all applied CW research and development, including on the alleged binary CW program, before industrial or pilot production took place at Novocheboksarsk, Volgograd, and (presumably for smaller runs) Volsk-17.[44] *GosNIIOKhT* has reportedly fallen victim to the drop in defense allocations since 1992; its personnel has been reduced and some of its facilities vacated and, according to its director, research has been wholly reoriented to chemical defense and the development of nonmilitary pharmaceutical and other compounds. In addition *GosNIIOKhT* was designated by the Russian government as the head institute in cooperation with U.S. agencies and contractors under the chemical demilitarization assistance program. The Moscow branch is involved in work in phosphorus and fluorine chemistry.[45]

There is some difficulty in providing an accurate assessment of Russian manufacture of CWC Schedule 2 and 3 and AG list chemicals due to the lack of reliable data and the fact that in the post-Soviet-reform period some plants are being forced to reprofile production to eliminate loss-making capacity. From an examination of available chemical industry databases and directories it is possible to identify around 20 industrial facilities, including the plants mentioned above, which are producing or have until recently produced the compounds in question on a commercial scale; up to 18 substances can be positively identified. However, it is possible that there are other companies manufacturing such compounds and that other listed chemicals that do not appear in the open commercial literature can be produced. It is also the case that the number of plants producing PSF compounds and discrete organic chemicals in Russia is well over 100, if not the hundreds mentioned by Syutkin; large-scale production or capacity exists for phosphatic mineral fertilizers, chlorofluorocarbons, plant protection agents, pharmaceutical chemicals, and a range of other organic industrial chemicals.[46]

In spite of the relative weakness, compared with leading Western countries, of Soviet chemical engineering, there is some expertise in this sphere. Precise data are lacking, but a number of facilities manufacturing sensitive chemicals have quite sophisticated equipment, some of it produced indigenously. There were specific institutes designing equipment for the Soviet CW program, one of which—*Giprosintez* in Volgograd—is currently bidding to design CW destruction equipment.

A recent U.S. Department of Defense report states that Ukraine, Kazakstan, and Belarus have no known CBW programs and no intention of establishing them. There are, however, a number of facilities in these and other NIS of proliferation concern. A number of NIS plants outside of Russia can be positively identified as manufacturers of CWC/AG listed compounds, and several of these states, particularly Ukraine, Kazakstan, Belarus, and Uzbekistan, have substantial industrial production of organic chemicals spread among dozens of facilities. One such facility, the Khimprom enterprise in Pavlodar, Kazakstan, which has capacity for phosphorus compounds (including phosphorus trichloride) as well as manufacturing organic synthesis products, was reportedly planned as the site of a CW facility toward the end of the Soviet period.[47]

The Biotechnology Industry

A series of disclosures in 1992, starting with the admission by Yeltsin on January 29, that there had been "a lag in implementing" the BTWC,[48] revealed that the Soviet Union had created a large-scale offensive BW program ("at least an order of magnitude larger than those of the USA and the UK"[49]) on the basis of an extensive indigenous microbiology industry—indeed, part of the program was carried out in ostensibly civilian facilities—and emphasized the difficulties faced by the international community in reliably tracking developments for military purposes in this branch of science.

The RF Ministry of Defense inherited a network of military microbiological facilities that could be divided into two branches: a larger one subordinate to the Main Directorate for Radiation, Chemical and Biological Defense, and a second one administered by the Main Military-Medical Directorate. The main organization under the former directorate is the Scientific-Research Institute of Microbiology in Kirov, which appears from the scientific literature to concentrate on vaccines against plague and which manages at least two other military microbiological facilities (as well as, in former times, a proving ground and field testing laboratories). One of these is the Center for Military-Technical Problems of Anti-Bacteriological Defense in Ekaterinburg, formerly Sverdlovsk, which in the 1960s produced pathogenic agents suitable for use as BW and now appears to be occupied with biological defense research and with monitoring worldwide proliferation of BW. This was the source of the notorious anthrax outbreak of 1979 which led to the curtailment of certain of its activities.

The second facility is the Center of Virology in Sergiev Posad, formerly Zagorsk, also a former center for R&D into pathogenic agents and now engaged in developing prophylaxis and treatment methods for dangerous diseases as well as in biological protection and decontamination. This center was also responsible for field testing laboratories in Aralsk, Kazakstan, and on Vozrozhdenye Island in the Aral Sea. Today only one BW-related facility is known to be subordinate to the Main Military-Medical Directorate; the Scientific-Research Institute of Military Medicine in St. Petersburg, now one of the leading centers for defense against nuclear and CBW, engaged in testing vaccines and developing mass immunization and prophylactic methods and means of detecting pathogenic agents.

Running alongside the BW program at the above-mentioned facilities was the organization *Biopreparat*, which was created in 1973 and became important in financing and managing Soviet BW R&D. Now a Russian joint stock company, it has emerged as the country's leading biotechnology organization, with around 50 research and production facilities, which controls what is reputed to be the world's second largest antibiotics industry and manufactures a range of biopharmaceuticals and veterinary products.[50] Several centers within the *Biopreparat* organization were involved in biological warfare: the State Scientific Center of Applied Microbiology in Obolensk (work included vaccines against highly pathogenic viruses including recombinant preparations against plague and anthrax and molecular preparations against anthrax and legionnaire's disease); the Institute of Immunological Design in Lyubuchany, Moscow district (involved in the full cycle of basic and applied R&D, fermentation, and production, and whose work included detection of and developing vaccine against tularaemia); the Scientific-Research Institute of Molecular Biology in Koltsovo, which incorporated the State Scientific Center of Virology and Biotechnology *Vektor* (vaccines against highly pathogenic viruses including Marburg, Ebola, Lassa, Crimean-Congo hemorrhagic fever, Eastern equine encephalitis, and others); and the Institute of High Purity Preparations in St. Petersburg. Some sources have pointed out the difficulty of being certain about the number of facilities involved in BW, various estimates of which put the number at between nine and 20 (including those mentioned above).[51]

Starting with the April 1992 decree "On Ensuring the Implementation of International Pledges in the Sphere of Biological Weapons," the Yeltsin administration has taken a number of measures that purport to eliminate offensive microbiological R&D in Russia, including opening up facilities to inspection, introducing administrative changes to make *Biopreparat* more accountable to civilian bodies, and converting facilities to peaceful programs to boost the country's performance in pharmaceuticals and biotechnology.[52] To contribute to confidence-building, Russia, the U.S., and the U.K. in September 1992 agreed upon a set of measures to address concerns about Russia's compliance with the BWTC, including reciprocal inspection visits to BW facilities.[53]

Welcome though these developments are as far as demilitarizing the BW effort is concerned, the size of the biotechnology industry built up over the years (and Soviet BW facilities apparently played an important part in developing parts of the civilian microbiological sector) means that there will be continuing concern over the potential for proliferation. There is a large number of facilities that might need to be monitored for illicit activities under a verifiable BWTC. One source refers to "a national committee and a national program for biotechnology [which] encompassed 150 institutes in the former Soviet Union";[54] however, an expert analyst has put the figure considerably higher, estimating the number of small production facilities with a fermenter at several hundred in Russia alone, and has stated that a lot of dual-use equipment used in the former Soviet biotechnology industry was produced indigenously.[55] It is worth noting that inspection visits to Russian facilities under the above-mentioned agreement with the U.S. and U.K. have failed to remove all concerns about an offensive BW program in Russia. The NIS's capabilities in biotechnology are not limited to Russia. One defense analyst reports the BW status of Belarus, Kazakstan, and Ukraine as (respectively) "capable," "unlikely possessor," and "capable(?)/unlikely possessor."[56] In the case of Kazakstan, however, U.S. intelligence has also speculated about the possible military nature of work carried out at a facility in Stepnogorsk. In any case there is also a substantial biotechnology industry in the NIS outside of Russia, with perhaps 150 facilities in Ukraine, several dozen in Belarus and Kazakstan, and some centers in all of the other states.[57]

ASSESSMENT OF THE EFFECTIVENESS OF CB EXPORT CONTROLS IN THE NIS

The establishment of export control systems in the NIS in a period of rapid and in many respects fundamental political and economic change, and at a time of accelerating technological development that profoundly affects the extensive chemical and biotechnology industries described above, is understandably not without its problems. The financial and administrative burden at the government level of providing trained and competent personnel, infrastructure, and equipment to monitor compliance with CB nonproliferation measures will be difficult enough for the NIS at the current time. Informing and educating inexperienced and possibly recalcitrant manufacturers who are faced with a slump in domestic demand and are hard pressed to maximize profits, with the aim of encouraging industry to assume some of the responsibility for the transfer of sensitive items, will be an added drain on resources. It will also be difficult to overcome residual reluctance in the defense establishment to be transparent about weapons-related work. The dilemmas that the political and industrial-technical elite in these countries may face between control over and transfer of dual-use G&T may well be more difficult to solve than in the West. Assessments about the potential for proliferation are made even more problematic by the difficulty in separating fact from speculation and disinformation for propaganda and other purposes, particularly in countries such as the NIS with a tradition of secrecy in defense matters, where information was (and sometimes still is) tightly controlled by interest groups.

Initial progress has been made on securing the cooperation of the chemical industry in Russia. The current head of the Committee for CBW Convention Problems has referred to a seminar set up by his organization to explain the CWC to industrialists and scientists in the chemical sector as well as local authorities, although much work remains to be done on a system of reporting and data collection.[58] The Center on Export Controls, an independent nongovernmental organization (NGO) based in Moscow which has links with overseas NGOs working on export control issues, has hitherto been involved mainly with nuclear proliferation and has only recently initiated work in the CB sphere.[59] There remains a danger that the latter may be overshadowed by the former. Progress has been made in Belarus, which ratified the CWC in July 1996; a regional seminar on national implementation was held in Minsk in 1995.[60] There is not much evidence of extensive programs to involve industry in the other NIS, although Russia and Uzbekistan have attended an Asian regional seminar on national implementation of the CWC that addressed matters of industrial verification and chemical industry outreach.[61]

One case highlights the concerns widely felt about the possibility of NIS export controls being breached. The former chairman of the Committee for CBW Convention Problems and a leading figure in the Soviet CW program,[62] Anatolii Kuntsevich, was accused of illegally exporting around 800 kilograms of a CW precursor to Syria in November 1993. The case is murky for a number of reasons,[63] particularly because of the possibility of political provocation—the affair was made public by the Federal Security Service (FSB) prior to the December 1995 elections, when Kuntsevich was standing as a Zhirinovsky Liberal-Democratic candidate to the State Duma.[64] Vil Mirzayanov has reported information received from a former colleague at *GosNIIOKhT* that Kuntsevich was in charge of an agreement signed with the Syrian Center of Ecological Protection in October 1992 under which Russia has shipped to Syria "laboratory cabinets, vacuum pumps, and other laboratory equipment, all of which could be used for purposes other than environmental work," and thereby "may have facilitated the establishment of a conduit for the transfer of chemical weapons related knowledge and/or materials."[65] It is no surprise, in view of the above, that Syria was recently accused by Israel of creating nerve agents with the help of Russian scientists. Libya and Iraq have also been identified as possible recipients for chemical materials and know-how,[66] while speculation has been forthcoming about Russian assistance to Iranian BW programs.[67]

While the Kuntsevich affair makes the concern widely expressed by Western security agencies and proliferation analysts understandable, uncertainty as to the real facts of the case (and indeed of the others referred to above) illustrates the difficulty in making a reliable assessment of the dangers of proliferation through breaches of export controls by NIS suppliers. Any such assessment would have to focus on the complex motivations of potential recipients and the levels of competence in CB technology they have already attained, something beyond the scope of this chapter. This is, of course, a universal problem, as the well-documented cases of German exports of dual-use chemical technology and other incidents demonstrate; export controls will never be foolproof, and any breaches hitherto by companies in Russia and the NIS may not be any worse than such cases. This prompts us to focus on the main problems specific to the NIS that may make proliferation more of a threat.

A major problem yet to be faced may be the inadequacy of judicial procedures in the NIS. Export controls have to be enforced by national authorities, with the ultimate sanction being legal penalties imposed by the courts. One source describes how the application of certain controls by the German authorities over the export of chemical equipment in 1984 "were found wanting in the courts"; when a German company was denied a license to export what was put forward as a pesticide facility to Iraq the company took the case to court and won.[68] There were a number of other cases where sanctions were imposed on businessmen, of course. Nevertheless it does not take a great deal of imagination to envisage a situation where an underresourced and overstretched national authority in an NIS is faced with bearing the costs of an action by an aggressive and wealthy private commercial concern, skeptical about the value of trade controls and prepared to take a risk in order not to lose out on business, in a courtroom where judicial expertise in complex matters of commercial law is limited. How many such cases might have to be fought is a question that cannot be answered with any certainty.

Ensuring the effective working of underresourced, understaffed, and inadequately trained customs services in the NIS is likely to be a continuing problem.[69] In the immediate post-Soviet period, Russia acted to forestall the illicit export of controlled G&T through other NIS with weaker controls by drafting its regime so that exports to the latter follow the same procedures and require the same guarantees as for any other export destination—in other words, to make export controls begin at the RF borders.[70] Since then, negotiations have been held with the customs services of certain other NIS with the aim of unifying customs policy and practice. Customs cooperation doubtless represents a saving in terms of finance and resourcing; however, establishing a coordinated policy on key requirements—common lists of items, common criteria for the issue of licenses, coordinating and strengthening licensing and enforcement procedures—is proving difficult. Russian officials have emphasized that regular consultations on export controls are being held "to create conditions under which international obligations of our countries in the framework of a unified economic space would be guaranteed,"[71] but the history of the CIS, with its poor record on implementing agreements, leaves room for doubt over the success of the initiative.[72]

There is a particular problem in customs controls over exports of chemical agents, which are widely regarded as more difficult to detect than nuclear materials. Occasional random inspections are obviously not an adequate response to the possibility of smuggling export-controlled chemicals, and it requires time and expensive equipment to make a complete evaluation of chemical substances concealed in sealed containers—and indeed of the quantities declared on the license application—to avoid cheating. Indeed, it may be unrealistic to expect that every outbound shipment of chemicals from the NIS can be inspected; one account describes how, in the 1980s, U.S. customs relied mainly on intelligence, undercover operations, and public awareness programs to combat chemicals proliferation, and stopped a shipment only when there were doubts over the end user or destination or obvious irregularities in documentation.[73] Nevertheless the U.S. experience emphasizes both the need for adequate training and resourcing of NIS customs officials and that effective border control is only one link in a chain comprising strict licensing and enforcement procedures, intelligence-gathering, and industry outreach.

U.S. assistance via the Nunn-Lugar Cooperative Threat Reduction (CTR) program for export controls in the NIS has been extremely important; one source has argued that the "immediate impact of reduction or elimination of CTR assistance would be to dramatically increase the danger that nuclear and other weapons materials, technologies and expertise would be diverted to the global arms market."[74] CTR assistance has been provided not only for export controls development, of course, and herein lies part of the problem: export controls are competing for resources with other proliferation concerns, for example, the need for physical protection of CW stockpiles and improvements in the system of accountability.[75] A senior State Customs Committee official lamented the fact that no extra state funding was provided in 1996 for nuclear G&T controls while assistance under the CTR program had dried up.[76]

Resources have also been directed at averting a "brain drain" of scientists who worked on former Soviet WMD programs. While there have been no irrefutable cases of CBW scientists being involved in the offensive programs of proliferant states, the danger is considered to exist.[77] Estimates of the number of scientists actively engaged in CBW work in the former Soviet Union have varied considerably. A director of the International Science and Technology Center (ISTC) in Moscow declared that there are 60,000 scientists of proliferation concern in the NIS, including 10,000 from CBW programs.[78] This figure is presumably extrapolated from the numbers of staff employed on research at known CBW institutes (and perhaps in fundamental chemistry linked with physiologically active agents), and as such is a reasonable estimate. Such estimates may be misleading in assessing the extent of the threat and must be treated with caution, however; according to one scientist from *GosNIIOKhT*, the strict secrecy that operated in the Soviet defense complex meant that specialists concentrated on their own narrow sphere of work and were often unaware of what their colleagues were doing.[79] While it is true that only a few of the right specialists could represent a proliferation danger, it may be that few individuals have the breadth and depth of experience to pose a credible proliferation threat in terms of building a complete CBW program. Commentators warning of mass recruitments of CBW specialists also often ignore the complex motivations, linked with concerns about national security and scientific prestige, behind scientists' contributions to the Soviet WMD effort; it may well be that, despite current difficulties, the lack of such motivations would prompt most scientists to refuse to work on offensive programs for foreign regimes.

The creation of the ISTCs in Moscow and Ukraine, designed to provide weapons specialists with opportunities to engage in nonmilitary projects and thereby reduce the incentive to sell their expertise elsewhere, has been the main specific initiative by the West to reduce this threat. While welcome, the activity of the ISTC has hitherto been much more oriented toward scientists in the nuclear and missile than the CB sphere,[80] and there is some doubt about whether its programs are achieving the desired aim. Nevertheless the potential for the ISTC to promote collaboration with biotechnology institutes in the NIS and to "help promote indigenous expertise in export control by facilitating the development of export control centers at the industrial level" has been identified.[81]

A Russian intelligence report has argued that supporting peaceful research does not remove the threat of a brain drain and has advocated administrative and legislative measures on a multilateral basis, including a ban on emigration by those directly involved in developing such weapons, as well as widespread use of intelligence methods to monitor potential emigration.[82] Links with foreign intelligence services to monitor proliferation matters have reportedly been established. Regarding legislation on the transfer of know-how, an RF presidential decree signed in November 1995 has stipulated a list of information regarded as a state secret and subject to the Law on State Secrets, including information about the development of dual-use technologies and "about the use for military purposes of dual-use agents and technologies."[83]

Perhaps the most difficult issue in the proliferation debate is that of striking a balance between control over the export of G&T and managing a responsible transfer policy that satisfies the commercial and technological needs of both suppliers and recipients. As a leading authority has argued, the main pathway of proliferation is the purchase on the open market, ostensibly for peaceful purposes, of know-how, plant, and precursor chemicals; in a highly competitive world market, any vacuum in supply due to some countries adhering to export controls will be filled by others who recognize no such restraints.[84] The internationalization of controls through the CWC addresses this problem, and export controls can help to make trade more transparent, but because of the nature of dual-use CB G&T, they cannot provide a perfect solution to proliferation problems, and various demand-side restraints must be considered. The rapid development of dual-use biotechnologies in particular makes it important to find ways to minimize the dangers of proliferation and alleviate security concerns about offensive BW use while narrowing the scope of export controls and legitimizing transfers for peaceful purposes under conditions of transparency.[85]

This chapter has made clear the formal commitment of Russia and some of the other NIS to nonproliferation export controls. However, a tension still exists between their adherence to regimes and the urgent need to exploit their scientific and industrial capabilities on global markets. The tension is made greater by the fact that some of the NIS's traditional markets are in countries that give cause for greatest proliferation concern; industrial lobbies force the governments of the NIS to take a different view of the status of these countries, as the recent controversies over Russia's nuclear cooperation with Iran and support for lifting trade sanctions against Iraq demonstrate. There is no cast-iron Western consensus on trading with such as Iran and Iraq, of course, and Russia is not alone in pursuing her national interests. These interests can be both economic and political; exports of G&T and technological cooperation can be important in expanding influence with a country or countries of a region. Again, a good example is Russia's military-technical cooperation with India, which has refused to accede to nonproliferation regimes because of perceived discrimination by Western industrialized nations against countries in the South. Future NIS trade policy on dual-use G&T trade will thus depend on a number of variables: the extent to which they can gain access to mainstream trade between the major trading nations, pressure from domestic industrial lobbies (including the defense industry), and the pursuit of security through cooperation with certain countries of strategic importance.

There is evidence to support the claim that Russia is more inclined toward influencing supposedly "unstable" countries through diplomatic activity and economic and technical incentives, including developing cooperation in dual-use technologies for peaceful purposes and contributing to an improved climate for nonproliferation in the countries in question. A problem arises from the fact that this approach conflicts with the view expounded by some in the West, both at government and policy advisory level. One standard work on nonproliferation export controls, while stating that "a comprehensive approach has to encompass a host of instruments, including diplomacy, arms control, political confidence-building, export restrictions and sanctions, economic and military aid incentives," and military power projection and defensive measures, argues that "certain of these autocratic regimes—Iraq, Libya, Iran, and North Korea—should be singularized, their activities should be publicized globally, and all forms of trade with them should be discouraged. . . . [T]hey are pariah states, terrorizing their neighbours and their own citizens, and should be treated accordingly."[86]

The implications of all this may well be felt in trade in CB G&T. As developments in these technologies grow apace and markets for peaceful applications expand in some of the less-developed countries, NIS with limited domestic markets will be impelled to maximize their potential through exports. Rather than a threat, however, this may—if the issues involved are openly debated in international fora—in fact be an opportunity, bringing the dilemma of trade and technology control into sharper focus.

Although assessing the prospect of "vertical" proliferation in the NIS is beyond the remit of this chapter, the issue has wider implications for the spread of CBW capabilities across NIS borders. Some facilities in Russia, inevitably in view of their past activities and the general technological level of the chemical industry, match the picture of those which could be converted to CW production in terms of equipment and auxiliary technology available and access to raw materials and key starting chemicals, and could be difficult to detect because of their location in a multipurpose chemical complex.[87] The potential for proliferation stemming from the extensive NIS biotechnology effort has already been outlined. In a situation where the role of CBW in national security is not as clear-cut in the minds of defense planners and nationalist or conservative political groups as it is in those of diplomats negotiating arms control agreements, and where the tradition of secrecy in the defense establishment has been compounded by a breakdown in political control over it, concern still exists about the possibility of a resumption of clandestine programs that could result in the creation of channels for the transfer of CBW abroad. Environmentalists and other nongovernmental groups critical of state policy were in the Soviet Union and often still are regarded as "enemies" or "rebels" by the authorities.[88] The transparency and accountability of government agencies involved in chemical disarmament and chemical defense are important to the success of nonproliferation; whether the degree of maturity of NIS political systems can guarantee these commodities remains to be seen.

CONCLUSIONS

Two aspects of the CB proliferation threat from the NIS can be considered in making a concluding assessment. The first is technological. The intrinsic dual-use nature and widespread availability of many key CB materials and technologies, coupled with a strong climate of opinion in favor of making them accessible to countries wishing to use them for commercial purposes, are general problems faced by developed industrialized nations. The problems are considerable in Russia and some other NIS because of the extent of their weapons-related chemical and biotechnological capabilities. The governments of these countries are evidently aware of the danger of CB proliferation and, although these spheres have not received as much attention as nuclear and missile technology, measures have been introduced to conform to international practice on CB export controls. There is a need to continue to provide assistance to the NIS and enlist their cooperation in international efforts to keep pace with technological developments in the CB sphere with a view to furthering nonproliferation.

The second aspect centers on the political, economic, and security issues peculiar to the NIS that intrude into nonproliferation policy. At the national level, there is some doubt whether their governments are capable of giving due attention to nonproliferation efforts, given the financial and administrative pressures they are experiencing and the lack of cohesion and consensus between agencies among which the tasks of constructing a comprehensive export control system are shared. At industry level, the urgent need of market-orientated companies to realize their potential in terms of sales of G&T abroad may, particularly if sanctions are perceived to be avoidable and government does not provide a strong lead, prompt them to ignore legal guidelines and act on the principle of "no questions asked" when trading in sensitive items.

The current official position on nonproliferation makes it unlikely that there will in the foreseeable future be any large-scale transfer of CB agents or technologies for obvious offensive purposes from the NIS. Nor, in the opinion of the present writers, can we expect a mass exodus of CBW specialists eager to put their expertise at the service of any regime prepared to pay for it. Much more likely are cases similar to the Kuntsevich affair described above: the transfer of chemicals apparently destined for use in pharmaceuticals, insecticides, plasticizers (as Kuntsevich in fact claimed), or other compounds, or of equipment ostensibly for the manufacture of these compounds or for purposes such as the treatment of environmentally harmful agents. The scope for sensitive trade in microbiological agents and technology may be even greater. The danger of such transfers being facilitated by uncoordinated government activity, weak judicial enforcement of export control legislation, and nontransparent trading practices does exist in the NIS. Much work remains to be done to reduce this danger.

NOTES

The authors would like to acknowledge the helpful comments made on a draft of this chapter by Dr. Igor Khripunov, Associate Director of the Center for International Trade and Security, University of Georgia.

1. CBW is used in this chapter to refer broadly to both the finished article and, in terms of export controls, to materials and technologies used in their manufacture.
2. E.M. Spiers, *Chemical and Biological Weapons, A Study of Proliferation* (New York: Macmillan, 1994), p. 1.
3. J. Perry Robinson, "Chemical and Biological Weapons Proliferation and Control," in *Proliferation and Export Controls: An Analysis of Sensitive Technologies and Countries of Concern* (Deltac/Saferworld, 1995), pp. 32–33.
4. For a discussion of this, see Perry Robinson, *op. cit.*, and Spiers, *op. cit.*, pp. 27–29.
5. *International Affairs (Moscow)* (April 1986), pp. 151–152.

6. *Vneshnyaya torgovlya*, 11 (1989), pp. 50–51.

7. The "Leipzig Group" formed under this initiative first met in June 1987 and had made some progress on introducing formal controls over dual-use chemicals and technologies in the Warsaw Pact states (except Romania) by 1989 before it expired with the political changes in central and eastern Europe. See S.N. Kisselev, "The Former USSR and Nonproliferation of Chemical Weapons," in H.G. Brauch, H.J. van der Graaf, J. Grin, and W.A. Smit (eds.), *Controlling the Development and Spread of Military Technology*, (VU University Press, 1992), p. 217; B. Morel, "How Effective is the Australia Group?" in K. Bailey, R. Rudney (eds.), *Proliferation and Export Controls* (University Press of America, 1993), p. 58.

8. This included hosting an international delegation at the Shikhany testing site in April 1987 to inspect facilities and munitions, and the April 1989 bilateral U.S.-Soviet Wyoming, "Memorandum of Understanding Regarding a Bilateral Verification Experiment and Data Exchange Related to Prohibition of Chemical Weapons," which provided for an exchange of data on CW types and quantities, method of storage, location of storage and production facilities, and the opportunity for both sides to visit the other's storage and production sites. See J. Krause, C.K. Mallory, *Chemical Weapons in Soviet Military Doctrine* (Westview Press, 1992), pp. 153–154.

9. See *ibid.*, chapter 7.

10. E. Kirichenko, *Soviet Export Control Policies* (mimeo draft paper, 1992), p. 4.

11. *Ibid.*, pp. 8–10. This source notes that the Council of Ministers confirmed only the nuclear and chemical lists.

12. *Ibid.*, p. 11.

13. *Commersant* (September 29, 1992), pp. 25–27. It is perhaps worth noting that the Export Control Commission, composed of the deputy heads of the leading government agencies dealing with trade, industry, security, defense, and intelligence, did not formally incorporate representatives of state bodies dealing with the chemical and biotechnology industries.

14 Presidential Directive No. 508-rp of September 16, 1992, On the Introduction of Control over the Export from the Russian Federation of Chemical Substances and Technologies which Have Peaceful Purposes but Can Be Used in Developing Chemical Weapons; see *Rossiiskaya gazeta* (September 30, 1992) pp. 3–4. Like the 1989 Soviet statute, this act disallowed exports to countries violating the Geneva Convention ban on CW use.

15. Presidential Directive No. 621-rp of December 7, 1994; see *Ekonomika i zhizn'*, 52 (1994), pp. 5–6, 1 (1995), p. 10 and 2 (1995) p. 11.

16. Resolutions No. 734 of September 18, 1992, and No. 50 of January 16, 1995.

17. This similarly ruled out exports of biological materials to countries violating the Geneva Convention or the 1972 Bacteriological and Toxin Weapons Convention; Directive No. 711-rp of November 17, 1992; see *Rossiiskie vesti* (December 5, 1992) p. 3.

18. Directive No. 298-rp of June 14, 1994; see L. Lyashenko, "We Are Carrying on an Open Dialogue," *Rossiiskaya gazeta* (June 24, 1994) p. 4. Licensing procedures were confirmed by Cabinet of Ministers Resolution No. 892 of November 20, 1992, superseded by No. 1098 of September 26, 1994. For a translation of documents defining procedures for the export of G&T used in CB and toxin weapons, see *The Monitor* (Centre for International Trade and Security at the University of Georgia), 1, 3 (Summer 1995), pp. 26–27, 28–29.

19. An original list consistent with the Missile Technology Control Regime (MTCR) was published in 1993, followed by an expanded list incorporating amendments to the MTCR technical appendix and confirmed by Directive No. 193-rp of April 25, 1995 (see *Rossiiskaya gazeta* [May 4, 1995], p. 10). The expanded list was published in *Ekonomika i zhizn'* (1995) 26, p. 29; 28, pp. 28–29; 30, pp. 28–29; 32, pp. 28–29; 34, p. 28; and 36, p. 29.

20. U. Latypov, "The Belarusian Export Control System," *The Monitor*, 2, 1–2 (Winter-Spring 1996), pp. 13–17. For more on export controls in Belarus, see A. Makavchik, "Belarus' Export Control Developments and Participation in Multilateral Nonproliferation Regimes," *The Monitor*, 3/4, 4/1 (Fall 1997/Winter 1998), pp. 35–37. The Belarusian "Export Control Act and Regulations on Import/Export and Transfer of Scheduled Chemicals" are slated to begin operating in early 1998 (p. 36).

21. Decree of Cabinet of Ministers of Ukraine No. 384, April 22, 1997; see *The Monitor*, 3/4, 4/1 (Fall 1997/Winter 1998), pp. 46–51. For a description of the Ukrainian export control system in general, see V. Vaschilin, "State Export Controls in Ukraine," *The Monitor*, 3, 3 (Summer 1997), pp. 12–14. One source reports that there were no applications for Ukrainian export licenses for dual-use chemicals in the 1992 to 1995 period; V.L. Zaborsky, *Ukraine's Emerging Export Control System: Challenges and Prospects* (Athens: Center for International Trade and Security, University of Georgia, January 1996), pp. 41. The nine states parties to the CIS CW agreement agreed that "member states will pursue coordinated policy on control over the export of dual-use chemicals which are produced for peaceful purposes but can be used for production of chemical weapons and technologies for their production" (Article 5). There appears to have been little further activity within CIS structures since 1992.

22. M. Ustyugov, "Problems of Developing an Export Control System in Kazakhstan," *The Monitor*, 2, 1–2 (Winter-Spring 1996), pp. 8–10. This list came under Kazak Cabinet of Ministers Decision No. 1896 of December 30, 1995, which formed an amendment to No. 1002 of July 20, 1995. A Law on the Export Control of Arms, Military Hardware and Dual-Use Products was introduced on June 18, 1996. A Georgian export control law is expected to come into force in spring 1998; see D. Bakradze and M. Kudava, "Export Control System in the Republic of Georgia," *The Monitor*, 3/4, 4/1 (Fall 1997/Winter 1998), pp. 37–39. Among the remaining NIS, progress on introducing CB export controls has been limited. See chapters by L. Anderson and C.B. Craft in G. Bertsch (ed.), *Restraining the Spread of the Soviet Arsenal: NIS Nonproliferation Export Controls, Status Report* (Athens: CITS, University of Georgia, 1997).

23. *The Monitor*, 2, 4 (Fall 1996), pp. 33–34.

24. Zaborsky, *op. cit.*, pp. 14–15.

25. Latypov, *op. cit.*, pp. 16–17; Makavchik, *op. cit.*, p. 36. The penalty envisaged is up to 10 years imprisonment and fines up to 50 times the monthly wage.

26. Ustyugov, *op. cit.*, p. 10.

27. Fourteen NIS had signed the CWC by the end of 1993, the exception being Uzbekistan, which finally signed it in November 1995. As of December 3, 1997, instruments of ratification had been deposited by Turkmenistan, Tajikistan, Armenia, Georgia, Moldova, Belarus, Latvia, Uzbekistan, and Russia; *The CBW Conventions Bulletin*, 38 (December 1997), p. 15.

28. For details see *SIPRI Yearbook 1995: Armaments, Disarmament and International Security*, pp. 609–611. Schedule 1 chemicals must be destroyed except for a total of one tonne for research purposes to be stored at one declared facility which is subject to systematic inspection. Schedule 2 reporting thresholds are 100 kg for toxic chemicals and one ton for precursors. Facilities producing 30 tons of Schedule 3 chemicals must be declared and those producing 200 tons are subject to random inspection.

29. *Ibid.*, pp. 613–614. For a discussion of the issues involved in controlling BW proliferation, see E. Geissler and J.P. Woodall (eds.), *Control of Dual-Threat Agents: The Vaccines for Peace Programme* (SIPRI CBW Studies Report No. 15) (OUP, 1994) (especially ch. 3). For an account of recent developments on introducing a verification protocol to the BTWC, see T. Toth, "A Window of Opportunity for the

BWC Ad Hoc Group," *The CBW Conventions Bulletin,* 37 (September 1997), pp. 1–5; "Strengthening the Biological and Toxin Weapons Convention," *The CBW Conventions Bulletin,* 38 (December 1997), pp. 16–21.

30. Spiers, *op. cit.,* p. 63; J.P. Perry Robinson, "The Australia Group: A Description and Assessment" in Brauch *et al., op. cit.,* pp. 168–169.

31. *SIPRI Yearbook 1995,* pp. 608–609, 614–615. See pp. 611–612 for a discussion on the evolution of the AG with respect to the CWC. The current AG schedules are (i) the Export Control List for Chemical Weapons Precursors (extended from 50 to 54 chemicals in June 1992); (ii) Control List of Dual-Use Chemical Manufacturing Facilities and Equipment and Related Technology (revised June 1993); (iii) List of Biological Agents for Export Control (revised list agreed in June 1993); (iv) List of Animal Pathogens for Export Control (December 1992); (v) List of Dual-Use Biological Equipment for Export Control (June 1993); (iv) List of Plant Pathogens for Export Control (June 1993); Perry Robinson, *Proliferation and Export Controls* . . . , p. 43. For a full description of items in the CB lists as of June 1994, see *Chemical and Biological Weapons Reader* (U.S. Arms Control and Disarmament Agency, June 1994), pp. 61–76.

32. This is a common concern. The president of the U.S. Chemical Manufacturers Association has estimated that around $600 million per annum of U.S. exports would be affected by a CWC trade ban; F.L. Webber, "The U.S. Chemical Industry Stake in the Chemical Weapons Convention," *Chemical Weapons Convention Bulletin,* 34 (December 1996), pp. 1–2. The NIS's exports of downstream industrial chemicals are lower than those of the U.S. and other major chemicals traders, but recent sources indicate that Russian losses under a CWC trade ban could be $100 million per annum or more, which represents a substantial part of exports of organic chemicals. Imports of chemical intermediates and sophisticated chemical technology important to Russian industry would also be threatened; see S. Kortunov, "Russia Should Be a Fully Fledged Member of the OPCW," *Khimicheskoe oruzhie i problemy ego unichtozheniya,* 4 (Summer/Fall 1997), p. 4; A. Kalyadin, "Russian Policy Dilemmas in the Sphere of Chemical Disarmament," *ibid.,* p. 13.

33. Kortunov, *op. cit.,* pp. 4, 6. A May 1996 report by the RF Foreign Intelligence Service warned of the problems that chemical arms control would face in the event of nonratification by Russia and the U.S., including possible retardation of the development of the BTWC; *Khimicheskoe oruzhie i problemy ego unichtozheniya,* 2 (Fall 1996), p. 9.

34. Interview by author with a representative of the RF State Committee for the Chemical and Petrochemical Industry, August 1996 (the committee has since been incorporated into the RF Ministry of Industry).

35. *Khimicheskoe oruzhie i problemy ego unichtozheniya,* 2 (Fall 1996), p. 1. It is worth noting that prior to the breakup of the USSR these facilities were not subordinated to the core defense complex ministries but to the Ministry of the Chemical Industry, although the latter was engaged in important military-related work and its forerunners sprang from the Military-Chemical Trust, which initially oversaw the industrial manufacture of Soviet CW. See L. Fedorov, *Chemical Weapons in Russia: History, Ecology, Policy,* mimeo draft, Russian Center for Ecological Policy (Moscow, 1994), pp. 8–9.

36. J. Tucker, "Former Soviet Chemical Weapons Plants," *The Nonproliferation Review,* 4, 1 (Fall 1996), pp. 79–80. These production associations (the standard Soviet term for industrial enterprises) are now joint stock companies.

37. Fedorov, *op. cit.,* p. 23.

38. Tucker, *op. cit.,* p. 80, V. Berezko, "Destroying Chemical Weapons Is No Cheaper than Producing Them," *Krasnaya zvezda* (August 3, 1995), p. 2. In this interview a

senior official stated that "the chemical plant in Dzerzhinsk . . . has been producing peaceful products for a long time now," but did not specify which facility.

39. Fedorov, *op. cit.*, p. 22. He notes that experimental production of V-gas was also established there in the 1940s and 1950s.

40. *BBC Summary of World Broadcasts*, part 1, "Former USSR" (November 4, 1992), p. C1/1 (hereafter *SWB*).

41. See A. Kuntsevich, "Ratifying the Convention without International Support Is Impossible, I Propose Declaring a Moratorium," *Khimicheskoe oruzhie i problemy ego unichtozheniya*, 2 (Fall 1996), p. 19. Kuntsevich mentioned that the Volgograd CW plant had already been dismantled and civilian production set up on the site. However, an agreement has only recently been reached formally to convert the CW plant into a joint U.S.-Russian civilian production facility; see *Chemical Weapons Convention Bulletin*, 34 (December 1996), pp. 15–16, 20. Russia has consistently voiced its concern about the cost of destroying former CW facilities and has campaigned for their conversion; see *SIPRI Yearbook 1996*, p. 679, and Tucker, *op. cit.*

42. Kuntsevich, *op. cit.* An agreement signed by the RF Prime Minister Chernomyrdin and the prime minister of the Chuvash republic reportedly includes provision for "the destruction or conversion to civilian uses of facilities for the production of chemical weapons at Khimprom joint stock company"; *Chemical Weapons Convention Bulletin*, 33 (September 1996), p. 18 (TASS report).

43. *GosNIIOKhT* (also referred to as *GSNIIOKhT* or *GRNIIOKhT*) was mentioned in the most comprehensive early survey of Soviet chemical and biological warfare facilities under the name "Scientific-Research Institute No. 42," which prepared prototype experimental batches of toxic agents and filled munitions; W. Hirsch, *Soviet BW and CW Preparations and Capabilities*, mimeo (Washington D.C., Training & Intelligence Division, U.S. Army Chemical Corps, 1951), p. 120. The institute produced the first experimental batch of mustard gas in 1924, and was also known for a time as GSNII-403; Fedorov, *op. cit.*, pp. 10, 74.

44 Amy E. Smithson, V. Mirzayanov, R. Lajoie, and M. Krepon, *Chemical Weapons Disarmament in Russia: Problems and Prospects*, Henry L. Stimson Report No. 17 (October 1995), pp. 22–28. Fedorov (*op. cit.*, p. 14) mentions that the Novocheboksarsk branch was closed in the mid-1980s.

45. M. Rebrov, "Who Is Polluting with Chemicals?" *Krasnaya zvezda* (June 16, 1993), p. 2. According to a recent report, *GITOS* is faring even worse than *GosNIIOKhT*, mainly since it has not been earmarked for work on CW stockpiles destruction; see *Ogonek*, 3 (January 1998), pp. 27–29.

46. The products identified are hydrogen fluoride, sodium fluoride, sodium bifluoride, potassium fluoride, potassium bifluoride, ammonium bifluoride, dimethyl phosphite, phosphorus oxychloride, phosphorus trichloride, phosphorus pentasulphide, chloropicrin, triethanolamine, dimethylethanolamine, dimethylamine, potassium cyanide, sodium cyanide, thionyl chloride, and sodium sulphide. In addition, phosgene can be produced in Uzbekistan and perhaps also in Russia, and the technology to produce the Schedule 2 substance PFIB exists in Russia. A Russian source has in fact claimed that there are over 30 Russian enterprises capable of manufacturing Schedule 3 chemicals and over 400 making "concrete (*sic*) organic chemicals and chemicals containing fluorine, sulphur and phosphorus"; Kalyadin, *op. cit.*, p. 14.

47. L. Fedorov, "After the Picnic," *Segodnya* (July 5, 1994), p. 10.

48. M. Leitenberg, "The Conversion of Biological Warfare Research and Development Facilities to Peaceful Uses," in Geissler, Woodall, *Control of Dual-Threat Agents*, p. 77. Leitenberg also mentions (p. 79) the revelation that the military had developed "aeriel bombs and rocket warheads" capable of carrying certain BW.

49. *Ibid.*, p. 81.
50. This information is taken from a close study of conversion in the Russian micro-biological sector; A. Rimmington, "From Military to Industrial Complex? The Conversion of Biological Weapons' Facilities in the Russian Federation," *Contemporary Security Policy*, 17, 1 (April 1996), pp. 83–87. The same issue (pp. 1–79) also contains an article by M. Leitenberg, "Biological Weapons and Arms Control," with sections on the USSR's and Russia's involvement in BW programs and an analysis of BW proliferation.
51. Leitenberg, *op. cit.*, pp. 80–81, 89–102. See also Rimmington, *op. cit.*, p. 108, for a brief history of the first three of these key BW facilities subordinate to *Biopreparat*.
52. Rimmington, *op. cit.*, pp. 88–89.
53. *SIPRI Yearbook 1996*, p. 691.
54. Leitenberg, *op. cit.*, p. 99.
55. Interview with Dr. A. Rimmington, Birmingham University, December 19, 1996. Dr. Rimmington mentioned that his book *Ex-USSR Biotechnology Industry* 1st edition (revised) (Technology Detail, August 1993), in which over 200 facilities and institutes are listed for Russia and around 50 for Ukraine, probably includes only around a half of the biotechnology facilities in the NIS.
56. Geissler, in *Control of Dual-Threat Agents* p. 16, based on J. Reed, *Defense Exports: Current Concerns*, A Jane's Special Brief (Jane's Consultancy Services, April 1993).
57. Interview with Dr. Rimmington; see also Rimmington, *Ex-USSR Biotechnology Industry*.
58. *Khimicheskoe oruzhie i problemy ego unichtozheniya*, 2 (Fall 1996), p. 1; *Yadernyi kontrol*, 13 (January 1996), p. 6.
59. Conversation with the director, Mr. A. Bulochnikov, April 6, 1998.
60. *SIPRI Yearbook 1996*, p. 681.
61. *Chemical Weapons Convention Bulletin*, 34 (December 1996), p. 32.
62. Kuntsevich rose to become deputy head of the chemical troops under Gorbachev; A. Dolgikh, "Chemical Weapons: Is It Easy to Eliminate Them?" *Krasnaya zvezda* (October 22, 1993), p. 2.
63. See L. Berres and A. Koretskii, "Mikhail Barsukov Has Poisoned a Chemist's Life," *Kommersant—Daily* (October 24, 1995), p. 14. This source claims that the export of another 5 tons of a dual-use compound was stopped by the counterintelligence agencies early in 1994; it also speculates that the timing of the revelation—before a Yeltsin-Clinton meeting—was to demonstrate to the U.S. what can happen when the chemical defense establishment is deprived of funding, and that Kuntsevich will never be convicted because he knows too much about Russia's CW past. In fact all charges against him were formally withdrawn in October 1996.
64. L. Berres, "Disgraced Academician Seeks Meeting with Head of FSB," *Kommersant—Daily* (November 11, 1995), p. 20. This source states that, according to the FSB, the substance in question was phosphorus trichloride; Mirzayanov mentioned in testimony to the U.S. Senate that the substance shipped was methylphosphonyl dichloride; *Chemical Weapons Convention Bulletin*, 30 (December 1995), p. 25. It is worth noting that the security services have been accused of staging provocations in a number of cases, including the contraband export of nuclear materials.
65. Smithson et al., *op. cit.*, p. 32.
66. *Jamestown Foundation Monitor*, 2, 217 (November 19, 1996).
67. *Sunday Times* (August 27, 1995) (quoted in *Chemical Weapons Convention Bulletin*, 30 [December 1995], p. 17).
68. Spiers, *op. cit.*, p. 54.
69. The RF State Customs Committee includes two departments dealing with CB issues: the Export Control Department and a department dealing with special equipment.

70. Government Resolution No. 854 of November 6, 1992, "On the Licensing of Export and Imports of Goods, Works and Services on the Territory of the Russian Federation," included (in Appendix 5) "materials, equipment and technologies which have a peaceful application but which can be used in the creation of missile, nuclear, chemical and other types of weapons of mass destruction" and referred specifically to the CIS, Azerbaijan, Georgia (both of which later joined the CIS), Latvia, Lithuania, and Estonia as countries for which a license is needed to export goods; *Rossiiskaya gazeta* (November 24, 1992), pp. 4–5. A subsequent decree concerning the supply of armaments, military technology, and items for military and dual-use applications in line with U.N. Security Council decisions also effectively treated the CIS members as foreign countries; *Rossiiskaya gazeta* (February 25, 1993), p. 6.

71. Ye. Kulikov, "Russia's Cooperation on Export Controls with the Commonwealth of Independent States," *The Monitor*, 3, 2 (Spring 1997), p. 26.

72. These problems are discussed further in I. Khripunov, "Industry-Government Relations in Russia's Export Control," *The Monitor*, 3, 1 (Winter 1997), p. 28; I. Khripunov and S. Pushkarev, "Disintegration and Integration: Implications for Export Controls," *Restraining the Spread of the Soviet Arsenal*, pp. 74–79.

73. Spiers, *op. cit.*, pp. 56–57.

74. J.M. Shields, "Conference Findings on the Nunn-Lugar Cooperative Threat Reduction Program: Donor and Recipient Country Perspectives," *The Nonproliferation Review* (Fall 1995), p. 72.

75. A.E. Smithson, "Improving the Security of Russia's Chemical Weapons Stockpile," in Smithson et al., *op. cit.*, pp. 5–20. Vil Mirzayanov has described the inadequate protection of storage facilities and poor accountability that also exist at *GosNIIOKhT* (interview with author September 12, 1996).

76. *The Monitor*, 2, 4 (Fall 1996), p. 24.

77. According to Russian sources, research groups active in the former Soviet BW program have been invited by "certain countries" or "foreign representatives of Third-World countries"; S.V. Netesov, "The Scientific and Production Association Vector: The Current Situation," in Geissler, Woodall, *Control of Dual-Threat Agents*, pp. 137–138; *SWB* (April 29, 1992), p. C2/5 (report from *Izvestiya*).

78. *Chemical Weapons Convention Bulletin* (June 1996), p. 32.

79. See D.L. Averre, "The Mirzayanov Affair: Russia's Military-Chemical Complex," *European Security*, 4, 2 (Summer 1995), p. 280. It is interesting that, while Vil Mirzayanov has stated that 200 people are familiar with the production technologies of binary chemical warfare agents in Russia, one of his former colleagues estimated that "no more than 20 people" at the institute knew of the testing of the new binary agents developed in the 1980s, from which one may infer that no more than this number know enough to constitute an immediate proliferation threat; see O. Vishnyakov, "I made the binary bomb," *Novoe vremya*, 50 (1992), p. 47.

80. As of March 1996 the Moscow ISTC had funded 236 projects involving over 12,000 scientists in five NIS, 63 percent of which were from the nuclear sector, 16 percent from the missile complex, 3 percent from CW, and 4 percent from BW research; less than 10 percent of funds supported CBW scientists. The report from which these data are taken found that "the level of ISTC activity with biological and chemical warfare institutes is not proportional to the threat," and recommends placing more emphasis on CBW institutes in ISTC activities; *An Assessment of the International Science and Technology Center*, National Research Council (National Academy Press, Washington D.C., 1996), pp. 7, 17, 23. In discussing the Ukrainian Center, the report also states that "although there is no evidence now of biological or chemical warfare activities in Ukraine, there are a number of chemical and biological scientists who have the potential to con-

tribute to such activities in facilities where such research could be carried out" (p. 24). In the ISTC 1997 Annual Report (sourced on the Internet), of the 496 projects approved, total allocations $155.1 million, 68 were in chemistry and biotechnology with allocations of $16.0 million, or 10.3 percent of the total; however, closer investigation reveals that not all the CB projects involve institutions potentially related to CBW work.

81. *An Assessment*, pp. 21–22.

82. *A New Challenge after the "Cold War": The Spread of Mass Destruction Weapons*, JPRS Report: Proliferation Issues (FBIS draft translation), 1993, pp. 12–13. In fact administrative measures limiting freedom of movement and contact with the West have been introduced at some nuclear facilities; A. L'vov, "Nuclear Special Forces," *Rossiiskaya gazeta* (April 22, 1995), p. 4. A comprehensive legal basis for such measures appears not to have been created, however, nor is there any indication that this has been extended to include CBW scientists. The emphasis in this Russian report on the importance of intelligence in general in countering proliferation is echoed by a recent report by the U.S. Department of Defense; see *Proliferation: Threat and Response* (Office of the Secretary of Defense, April 1996) p. 55.

83. *Rossiiskaya gazeta* (December 27, 1995), p. 5 (section 20). For the Law on State Secrets (up to date, with amendments) see *Zakon* (*Izvestiya* publication), 2 (February 1998), pp. 9–20.

84. Perry Robinson, *Proliferation and Export Controls*, p. 40–41.

85. See Geissler, Woodall, *Control of Dual-Threat Agents,* for the debate surrounding the "Vaccines for Peace" Program, a proposal to establish an international program for the development and use of vaccines against dual-threat agents, which in the view of its authors provides for greater transparency about biological research—thereby strengthening international norms against biological warfare—and contributes to improving global health care by reducing the biotechnology gap between North and South. Another authoritative source provides a timely reminder that "[export controls] are not trade restrictions, but trade enablers. The trade that results is not controlled in a traditional sense, but licensed. The export control system is most accurately described as a system that licenses and renders transparent trade in dual-use materials. . . . [T]he proper focus of debate is not whether such controls should exist but how they can be applied fairly and efficiently, what modes of coordination among exporters are legitimate and necessary, and how potential consensus can be achieved. . . . concerning the proper balance between the obligation not to assist others to make forbidden weapons and the obligation to promote international cooperation in militarily sensitive materials and technologies for peaceful purposes"; B. Roberts, "Rethinking Chemical and Biological Export Controls," *The Monitor*, 3, 1 (Winter 1997), p. 11.

86. Bailey, Rudney, *op. cit.*, p. xviii.

87. See R. Trapp, *Verification under the Chemical Weapons Convention: On-Site Inspection in Chemical Industry Facilities* (SIPRI CBW Studies Report No. 14) (OUP 1993), pp. 54–56, 83–86.

88. The former term has been used by the chairperson of the Duma Committee for Ecology to characterize perceived defense establishment attitudes toward her colleagues' activities; the latter term was, interestingly, used by the former head of the Radiation, Chemical and Biological Defense Troops to describe critics of the Defense Ministry's plans for chemical disarmament. See *Khimicheskoe oruzhie i problemy ego unichtozheniya*, 2 (Fall 1996), p. 13; *Yadernyi kontrol*, 13 (January 1996), pp. 3–4.

8

THE POLITICS AND ECONOMICS OF RUSSIA'S CONVENTIONAL ARMS TRANSFERS

Igor Khripunov

This chapter examines Russia's basic motivation in exporting conventional arms and reviews the evolving legal basis and decision-making mechanism as a tool intended to control this process of transfers consistent with national interests and international obligations. In order to prognosticate Russia's responses to possible arms control initiatives, it is important to provide insight into the inner workings of the mechanism that focuses on key government departments and agencies as well as lobbying groups and other actors that tend to promote their own interpretation of national interests. This is particularly relevant for Russia, whose economic situation is still bleak and interagency coordination inherently weak.

This chapter has four sections. The first covers the transition from Soviet ideologically based weapon exports to the current nonideologically motivated approach. The second reviews the status of the defense industry as the driving force behind the export. The third section describes the three currently practiced types of Russian arms transfers, or, in other words, the main features and goals of military-technical cooperation with other countries. The fourth section explores continuous experimentation with different models of arms transfer controls, with a special emphasis on the model that began to emerge in July to August 1997.

One definitional issue requires clarification. Since the terms "weapon exports" and "weapon transfers," as traditionally applied to the former Soviet Union, would be rather misleading in a post-Cold-War framework, they must be understood in a new, wider, international context. They are often used in this chapter interchangeably with another term, "military-technical cooperation." Though the latter was coined long ago mostly for political convenience, it remains widely used in government documents, media reports, and academic papers, and can well capture the new Russian reality of arms transfers. It more accurately reflects Russia's status as weapon manufacturer and exporter in transition toward increasing involvement in internationalization and globalization of its defense production. Hence, military-technical cooperation is generally defined here as a combination of weapon sales, servicing, licensed production, technology transfers, and, of particular importance in this chapter, codevelopment, coproduction, and joint marketing schemes. For example, Russia can now independently manufacture only one fifth of its standard assortment of weapon systems without relying on major inputs from most other New Independent States (NIS), whose defense industries constituted in the past one single Soviet military-industrial complex.

TRANSITION TO THE NONDEOLOGICAL WEAPON TRANSFERS

During the Cold War period, export of conventional weapons served the important objective of acquiring and maintaining ideological and political spheres of influence. The United States and the USSR routinely provided ideologically motivated security assistance, supplying their client states with heavily subsidized—and in many cases free—weapons, military hardware, services, and training. At that time, the Soviet government treated any information related to weapon transfers as highly classified. Recent publications indicate that those transfers were of little commercial value and were used as an ideological/political tool. According to an official Russian source, in 1990 the USSR exported over $16-billion-worth of weapons, out of which cash receipts totalled only $900 million.[1]

With the end of the Cold War and collapse of Communism, the basic motivations behind conventional weapons transfers underwent dramatic changes. The ideological motivation behind Soviet weapon exports withered away. With still largely undefined national security and foreign policy interests, Russia was seeking a new rationale for continued weapons transfers. Then came the rude awakening and realization that the United States had been aggressively becoming the primary weapons supplier, accounting for almost half of global arms exports. Also gone was the naïve suggestion expressed earlier by Foreign Minister Andrei Kozyrev that the U.S. government should cooperate with Russia and assist it in finding new weapons markets in order to shift the Russian focus from problem countries to more stable and reliable countries. This shift effectively helped the Yeltsin government put an end to the internal debate regarding the relationship between arms export and its morality. There emerged a growing consensus that successful efforts to increase the share of Russian weapons sold in world markets would not only ensure the survival of the problem-prone military-industrial complex, but also facilitate the revival of the entire national economy.

It can be argued that in the subsequent period most Russian decision-makers started to view military-technical cooperation as a major component of overall military cooperation with other countries, an important part of its national defense policy, and a useful foreign policy tool. To some extent, weapon sales, in addition to nuclear power and space cooperation, are needed to help ensure Russia's position as a great power. The main problem was and is how to use this tool efficiently yet safely in pursuance of Russia's national interests while the country is living through a turbulent time of transition and nation-building.

Commercialization, or what some Russian observers have termed "mercantilization," of arms transfers had quite a fertile soil as a new philosophy of conducting weapons business. It is significant that in February 1994, in the first ever State of the Union address before both chambers of the Federal Assembly, President Yeltsin conditioned Russia's commitment to the control of international weapons transfers by referring to a loose notion of "observance of the Russian commercial interests in this area."[2] He returned to this subject in his 1994 address to the U.N. General Assembly, proposing to launch a multilateral discussion of the issues regarding the regulation of the international weapons and military hardware markets. Since then, he has shown little interest in discussing this subject again.

However, a radical shift from ideological considerations as the basis for weapons transfers to the cash-on-delivery approach has brought about, in combination with other negative factors, a disastrous effect on the actual volume of sales. According to the London-based International Institute for Strategic Studies (IISS), Russia's share in global trade dropped to 7.5 percent in 1992 ($2.6 billion). For comparison, in 1988 the USSR exported $27.4-billion-worth of weapons, which was equal to 35.6 percent of the world market. The latest estimate of Russia's performance for 1996 is 8.6 percent of global arms trade, or $3.4 billion, meaning that Russia was trailing the United States (42.6 percent), the United Kingdom (22.1 percent), and France (14.1 percent).[3] Russian statistical sources are classified, with government officials often quoting Stockholm International Peace Research Institute (SIPRI) data. However, the SIPRI methodology was designed as a trend-measuring device, permitting the measurement of changes in the total flow of major weapons and their geographical pattern rather than reflecting a commercial value of transfers. In Russia's case, the SIPRI approach conveniently enabled officials to quote annual figures well above the actual cost and revenues. For example, SIPRI's estimate for Russia's aggregate export was $2.9 billion in 1992 and $4.5 billion in 1996.

Under pressure from nongovernmental experts and the media, the Russian government had to revise the publicly announced figures and present them in a more realistic way. In April 1998, Yevgenii Ananyev, at that time General Director of the Rosvooruzhenie arms trading company, reluctantly admitted that of the officially provided figure of $3.5 billion for 1996, Russia's actual revenues were slightly more than $2 billion, with the rest accounting for barter trade and debt payments. His estimate of actual revenues for 1997 was at the same level. However, there are signs that the veil of secrecy in this area will not only persist but also extend further. A Presidential Decree issued in January 1998 identifying what should constitute a state secret referred to information regarding military-technical cooperation with other countries as falling under this category. It is hardly surprising that several weeks later, at a press conference, Yakov Urinson, at that time Vice Premier and Minister of Economics in charge of military-technical cooperation, flatly refused to discuss current statistical data for weapons trade. In his words, "everything connected with the export of armaments, the more so connected with the portfolio of orders, is confidential information and should not be widely discussed in the press."[4]

DEFENSE INDUSTRY AND ARMS EXPORT

The Soviet military industrial complex was developed to support global expansion and promote the political and military interests of the USSR in its confrontation with the economically more powerful and advanced West. The disintegration of the Soviet Union brought about a severe systemic crisis in the Soviet defense industry. Russia inherited about 70 percent of the Soviet military-industrial complex. As such, Russia had little difficulty in persuading most of its former collaborators and subcontractors in former Soviet republics, who without continued cooperation faced the bleak prospect of major restructuring and retooling, to resume defense cooperation.

Regardless of their geographic location, defense design and production facilities were originally established to service the national security requirements of one single Soviet state. For example, the Kazakstan component of the former Soviet military-industrial complex traditionally specialized in supplying and servicing the Soviet Navy. Although independent Kazakstan has been trying to establish its own navy in the Caspian Sea, its needs would be too limited to keep its national defense industry solvent. According to data provided by Russia's defense experts, air defense S-300 PM systems were coproduced by 103 plants in Russia, Armenia, Belarus, and Ukraine. Production of T-72 tanks and MIG-29 fighter aircraft involved 700 and 568 plants, respectively, in several republics. Nuclear-powered strategic submarines were jointly manufactured by 2,000 plants, out of which 1,300 are now located in Russia, over 550 in Ukraine, 83 in Belarus, five in Kazakstan, four in Armenia, three in Moldova, and two in Kyrgyzstan.[5]

The Soviet military-industrial complex was the most powerful lobbying group with easy access to the top party leaders. After the end of the Cold War, the complex lost most of its leverage. As Russian politics evolved, the most powerful lobby became occupied by the oil and gas complex, largely because this industry accounted for over three fourths of Russia's annual budget revenue.[6] Secondly came powerful financial groups that would not mind serving weapons export deals but were undoubtedly developing a much wider agenda. That the relative position of the defense industry further weakened is evidenced by the way that the government agency charged with it has been reformed. This agency originally existed as a state committee for defense industries, which in May 1996 was upgraded to a full ministry, only to be abolished and integrated into the Ministry of Economics one year later. Each transition brought about periods of instability, personnel changes, and conflicting administrative reforms.

Russia's military output dropped by over 80 percent by the late 1990s as compared with 1991, and over two million employees had to leave the military-industrial complex. Its facilities currently operate at 10 to 15 percent of their capacity, and almost half of the equipment is rated as obsolete. Pay in the military-industrial complex is 40 percent lower than that of Russian industry as a whole.[7] According to Deputy Minister of Economics Vladimir Salov, in 1997 Russia's output of arms and military equipment plummeted by 31 percent over the previous year. The defense sector recorded an across-the-board fall in production of 16 percent. Salov said that orders that had not been paid for were increasing and debts to defense suppliers had tripled in the two years since January 1996 to about $3 billion.[8]

In the absence of any consistent policy to restructure Russia's defense industry and long-term funding for defense conversion, its managers had no other alternative but to rely even more heavily on the export of weapons and military hardware. As of 1997 to 1998, export revenues accounted for 62 percent of all the funding channeled into the Russian defense industry. In other words, the defense industry was becoming more focused on export options rather than the declining domestic demand. In an unusually frank interview, Academician Evgenii Fedosov, Director of the Research Institute of Aviation Systems, complained that the Defense Ministry should back off from its "overzealous" role in determining what can and cannot be transferred to foreign clients because "*de facto* the Defense Ministry is no longer a major buyer. Its procurement share ranges from 10 to 20 percent, while India and China account for up to 80 percent."[9]

The Russian government has a clear stake in stimulating defense exports for one more reason: it constitutes one half of all products manufactured by Russia's otherwise uncompetitive machine-building industry and sold in world markets. The share of machines and equipment in Russia's exports further dropped to 7.6 percent in 1997.[10] Foreign contracts for Russian-manufactured defense products were expected to provide employment to about 1.4 million workers in the defense industry until 2000. In 1996 alone, Rosvooruzhenie, which until August 1997 was Russia's only arms trading intermediary, generated about 70 percent of all contracts awarded to Russian weapons manufacturers. On the other hand, there were indications that the overall military-technical policy for the defense industry has been shaped not by designated federal bodies, but rather by the evolving demand of world markets often in conflict with Russia's national security interests.[11]

That there exists a rapidly growing gap between the recently approved Program for the Development of Weapons and Military Hardware until 2005 and the actual procurement orders was explicitly admitted by First Deputy Defense Minister Nikolai Mikhailov. Nevertheless, in the absence of adequate funding he had no better advice to defense industry managers than to urge them even more vigorously to "promote weapon exports in order to keep afloat until the system of procurement orders could be revived" (in his estimation, in 2001 at the earliest). In the meantime, export of weapons and military hardware with a view to generating "extra budgetary money for restructuring the armed forces and their technical modernization" was recognized by him as one of several priorities for 1998.[12]

Russia's interests in weapons sales and resultant vulnerabilities are not unique compared to those of other major weapon producers, but they remain alarming because of Russia's still overmilitarized economy, economic stagnation, and dramatically decreased GNP. Russia is striving to climb to the top of the list of largest weapons exporters, even though it is not in the top 15 to 20 industrial nations in terms of GNP or general economic performance.

THREE TYPES OF RUSSIAN MILITARY-TECHNICAL COOPERATION WITH FOREIGN COUNTRIES

After the demise of the Warsaw Pact and disintegration of the Soviet Union, Russia has developed three distinct types of military-technical cooperation with other countries.

Military-Technical Cooperation with CIS Countries

This type of cooperation is focused on reintegrating the defense industries of the former Soviet republics that are Commonwealth of Independent States (CIS) members. Russia's military doctrine of November 1993 put special emphasis on this dimension of military-technical cooperation by saying that "Russia prioritizes the importance of restoring and expanding on a mutually beneficial basis the cooperative efforts of the production facilities which are part of the defense industrial potential and related sci-entific-research institutions of the CIS countries."[13] CIS military-technical cooperation is hardly a revenue-making activity for Russia, but it is safe to assume that, in the view of Russian strategists, this cooperation should ide-ally serve important security purposes in addition to keeping the Russian defense industry afloat and relatively competitive.

Far from being a full-fledged alliance, Russian-CIS military-technical cooperation is carried out under a formal multilateral agreement (the 1992 Mutual Security Treaty) and involves weapons transfers and com-mercial sales, joint operation of military facilities and infrastructure, leas-ing of bases, training, and continued codevelopment and coproduction. Among several other decision-making bodies in the framework of the CIS Headquarters for Coordinating Military Cooperation set up under the Mutual Security Treaty is a committee for military-technical cooperation tasked with developing relevant programs and practical arrangements. This committee has drafted a concept of military-technical cooperation that was approved by the Council of the Heads of the CIS governments. At its April 1998 session, the committee, which usually convened every three months, adopted a long-term plan for military-technical coopera-tion until 2001, covering, among other things, the operation and expan-sion of the radar surveillance and identification system. The ten partici-pating countries (Azerbaijan, Armenia, Belarus, Georgia, Kazakstan, Kyrgyzstan, Russia, Tajikistan, Uzbekistan, and Ukraine) also agreed to upgrade the status of the committee by placing it under the auspices of the Council of CIS Defense Ministers. The armament chief of Russia's armed forces was expected to become its new chairman.[14]

There is at least one major pitfall in the way Russia visualizes the evo-lution of this type of military-technical cooperation in line with its national interests. With the establishment of sovereign states replacing the Soviet Union, they have naturally developed their own arms export-ing agencies and national policies in this field that often place them at odds with Russia. The bulk of their sales come from the stockpiles that originally belonged to the Soviet armed forces, though in some cases national manufacturers opted for independent development and pro-duction rather than cooperative efforts with Russian counterparts.

As most former Soviet republics deplete their previous stockpiles of weapons, the main issue is whether their national defense industries will stay competitive. A leader in this regard is Ukraine, which has been aggressively diversifying its weapon trade. According to Ukraine's official sources, its export revenues in 1997 were over $600 million. It is selling weapons and military hardware to over 50 countries.[15] In 1996, Ukraine signed a contract with Pakistan involving a sale of 320 Ukraine-manufac-tured T-80UD tanks for a total of about $650 million. The 1997 *SIPRI Yearbook* rated Ukraine as the world's tenth largest exporter (following

Belarus in ninth place). According to the U.S. Congressional Research Service, Ukraine ranked sixth in arms sales agreements with developing nations in 1996, with a total of $800 million in contracts.[16] The latest data from the U.S. Arms Control and Disarmament Agency released in September 1997 placed Ukraine as the world's thirteenth largest arms exporter in 1995, with $160 million in sales, though Ukraine itself cited $74 million in 1995 sales. These discrepancies apparently resulted from massive unaccounted transfers. A commission of the Supreme Rada (Ukraine's Parliament) concluded in 1998, after a yearlong investigation, that during the period from 1992 to 1996, weapons and military hardware were sold or disposed of without adequate controls and accounting procedures, in violation of the existing regulations and at a profit for some individuals.[17] It does not mean, however, that Russia and Ukraine do not share common interests in promoting their joint products for export. Their bilateral project of the AN-70 military transport aircraft was submitted, for example, to a group of seven Western European countries developing the Future Large Aircraft (FLA) program. Russia and Ukraine proposed to integrate their already available technologies in this international program, which was originally expected to cost about $22 billion, with a per-plane price tag of about $75 million.

Belarus's standing seems less promising. It has been selling mostly previously stockpiled Soviet weapons, and its recent success may be short-lived. It is dependent on the Russian defense industry more than Ukraine is, and its major niche would be in developing more intense military-technical cooperation, taking advantage, in particular, of the Russian-Belarusian Union and increasingly acting as a go-between when Russia may prefer not to be directly and publicly associated with some particular sales. Kazakstan's defense industry is in an even more stagnant state. Kazakstan's 1997 arms sales, including locally produced torpedoes, mines, and firearms, are estimated at $17 million. Its Defense Minister indicated in April 1998 that his country "was planning to earn tens of million of dollars by selling outdated weapons and ammunition it had inherited from the former Soviet Union to Third World countries."[18] At the same time, the government shows little interest in the revival of the defense industry and is promoting further privatization of its 43 defense plants, urging foreign investors to participate.

Military-Technical Cooperation with Third-World Countries

The second type of military-technical cooperation involves weapons export, licensed production, services, and training for old and new recipients mostly in Asia, the Middle East, and South America. This type of cooperation is undoubtedly very important to Russia as a revenue source. However, it is unlikely to alleviate the across-the-board deplorable state of Russia's defense industry. According to Russian government sources, there are only a few cash-generating export producers—18 enterprises account for 80 percent of total exports.[19] On top of that, the Duma Defense Committee found out in 1998 that export revenues were not shared with manufacturers as specified by relevant arrangements, and in some cases were misappropriated. For example, as of early 1998, some manufacturers had not yet received what was due to them for 1996. The committee drafted a resolution that recommended holding random audits of how export revenues were handled, including their transfer to actual producers.[20] Those few exporters who successfully sell their products could not only stay afloat, but also implement a more long-term strategy. The Sukhoi Design Bureau's budget is largely dependent on its export performance—70 percent comes from export revenues while only 30 percent comes from state procurement orders (for each aircraft sold, it receives 5 percent of its selling price). In 1997 all salaries to its personnel were paid from the export revenues. As a result, the Sukhoi Bureau has developed a potential to export at least twice as much as it is currently exporting. Shukhoi has been offering for export over eight modifications of the SU-27.[21]

Among major items sold or promoted worldwide are T-72 and T-80 main battle tanks, armored vehicles, Kilo-class diesel-powered submarines, SU-27 and MiG-29 aircraft and their modifications, Mil and Kamov helicopter gunships, S-300V and S-300 PMU air defense systems, shoulder-fired *Igla* (Needle) portable air defense weapons, and many others. Out of 58 recipient countries of Russian-manufactured weapons and military hardware, China and India account for almost three fourths of Russia's exports and enjoy the status of "strategic partners." Both countries have agreements on military-technical cooperation with Russia (in October 1997 it was decided to extend the agreement with India until 2010) and have been acquiring on a massive scale, fighter aircraft, Kilo-class diesel submarines, and advanced air defense systems, to mention just a few. In 1997, there were signs that the commodity structure of Russia's defense exports to these two countries was undergoing changes. The share of air force weapons and military hardware began to shrink, while at the same time, exports for the navy were growing. It is believed that the share of naval weaponry in Russian exports has reached 15 percent. There was also an increase in the export of air defense systems.

China and India provide a good example of how wide-ranging and extensive Russia's military-technical cooperation approach can be regarding some Third-World countries. In addition to Chinese and Indian armed forces being dependent on Russian supplies and technologies, Russia, as the primary supplier, and these two recipients are teaming up in mutually beneficial codevelopment and coproduction projects. For example, India is planning to modernize jointly with Russia the existing SU-30 MK as a SU-30 MKI, which will have a new generation of India-designated onboard avionics and other support systems currently unavailable for Russia, due to economic and financial hardships in its defense industry. Russia has concluded agreements on military and technical cooperation with several other Third-World countries whose scope is, however, smaller and the implementation of which is almost exclusively cash-oriented.

An important feature of Russia's weapons trade in this category is its emphasis on exporting the most sophisticated and state-of-the-art systems. In an article dated late 1996, Aleksandr Kotelkin, former General Director of Rosvooruzhenie, wrote of this practice approvingly:

> If previously the Soviet Union did not deliver, as a rule, the newest models of arms to other countries, today Russia sells modern, high-tech models. Also, these deliveries are occurring simultaneously with the introduction of these weapons systems in Russia's armed forces. This is an important difference between Russia's export policy and U.S. policy. The United States often sells other than the best weapons systems abroad, and most often sells either used arms or arms which have been in the arsenal for many years.[22]

In the continued environment of financial austerity, the Mil Helicopter Manufacturing Company, a leading producer of a wide range of military and civilian helicopters, was desperately promoting sales of its two newest models, Mi-28 and Mi-28N. According to its officials, the company has to sell its best products to foreign customers even before the Russian armed forces have a chance to operate them. The Ministry of Defense could afford to procure a total of three Mi-28s and eight Ka-50s (Black Shark).[23] There are numerous other examples where superior weapon systems were exported or authorized for export before they were inducted in Russia's armed forces.

In the Russian decision-making process these were and still are hard choices, often giving rise to interdepartmental bickering. An official formerly employed by the dissolved Ministry of Defense Industries who also served in high-level Soviet and Russian defense industry and arms trading bodies, identified the Ministry of Defense, General Staff, and Foreign Intelligence Service as interagency players opposed more often than others on national security grounds to export deals involving transfer of advanced weapon systems. Most other ministries and agencies with responsibilities for dealing with the defense industry usually prevail in authorizing such transfers.[24]

That the interagency process involves tough bargaining among the agencies is also evidenced by some recent publications and statements. One is an article by Lieutenant General Nikolai Zlenko, Deputy Head of the Defense Ministry's Department for International Military Cooperation, published in the May-June 1998 issue of *The Military Parade*.[25] He laments that during the period of transition to a market economy, the number of state institutions "capable of defending the state's interest in a disinterested and efficient way is decreasing." While the "nonmilitary" agencies are understandably mostly profit-oriented, the Ministry of Defense, according to Zlenko, is less interested in profit. The most important task for the Ministry is to prevent the use of Russian-made arms against Russia or its allies in possible armed conflict, which may disrupt the balance of forces in a given region and damage Russia's national security interests. Zlenko proudly indicates that as a result "only 50–60 percent of armaments proposed for export are allowed to be sold." The interagency work regarding weapon transfers is highly classified, and this claim cannot be independently verified. However, his concluding remarks, that "a mechanism for determining requirements for weapons proposed to export" is yet to be set up, provide evidence that the relevant decision-making process is still poorly organized.

The Ministry of Defense, as the designated agency responsible for preventing possible damage to national security as a result of export operations, faces a serious dilemma. By authorizing the export of sophisticated weapons that could be hypothetically turned against Russia, the ministry tends to chose the lesser evil. Despite opening up a channel for the spread of dangerous weapons and technologies, this option keeps afloat the manufacturers that use the revenues, in the absence of adequate funding from the state budget, to modernize and produce weapons intended for induction in Russia's armed forces. Otherwise, by severely restricting such exports on national security grounds, the Ministry of Defense would undercut the defense industrial base and leave the armed forces with only a fraction of modern weapons so needed for their ongoing restructuring.

A 1995 deal making available to China a complete production facility for the SU-27 aircraft gives a good example of such controversial issues. Under this license, China begins manufacturing SU-27 jet fighters in 1999. Some Russian aviation industry analysts have characterized this license agreement as "an act of outrageous stupidity."[26] However, the deal provided at about 150 design bureaus and defense plants work that is much needed in the absence of domestic procurement.

The conflict between Russia's immediate economic needs and its long-term interests has not gone unnoticed. Aleksandr Konovalov, head of the Moscow-based Center for Military Policy, characterized the China deal as one case where Russia's actions were perhaps "too pragmatic," placing "present economic interests over national security."[27] But critics like Konovalov are in the minority. An engineer from the Komsomolsk-on-Amur Aircraft Manufacturing Company (KnAAPO), which was contracted to put together this production facility to be transferred to China, was rather ambiguous in a personal interview about his own attitude, especially as a resident of Russia's Far East, where his company was located. He reluctantly admitted that transferring state-of-the-art weaponry to the Chinese across the border can potentially pose a threat, and he had serious doubts about the way the deal was structured. However, his line of reasoning was that Moscow-based government officials who allegedly approved the deal must have carefully evaluated all possible contingencies, and he now cares most about getting paid regularly to feed his family.[28] Others argue that exports actually improve Russia's security. Pavel Felgengauer, a leading Moscow-based security analyst, believes that the weapons trade with China, Iran, and India will help Russia stabilize the situation in Central Asia and thus secure on a long-term basis Russia's vulnerable southern borders.[29]

As Russian-Chinese strategic partnership expands, there are grounds to expect other tr`nsfers. It was reported on December 1998 that the Chinese government approached Russia with a cost-sharing offer to jointly complete the design and start production of what is known as Russia's fifth generation fighter MFI (multifunctional fighter) project 1.42. Its prototype was yet to be flight tested but Russian aviation sources claimed that this new fighter would be comparable, if not superior, to the U.S. F-22.

Military-Technical Cooperation with Industrialized Countries

The rationale behind Russia's growing interest in this type of military-technical cooperation with other countries is a new product of the post-Cold-War period. It would be naive to expect that Russia can easily succeed in selling complete weapon systems to industrialized countries, though there are some success stories. However, engaging Western governments and companies in joint projects or technology exchanges has other, important, long-term benefits. Such cooperation might eventually generate R&D-related savings, facilitate marketing prospects, and pave the way for some other dual-use or civilian projects to follow suit. To some extent, engaging Western governments in joint programs was Russia's response to the globalization trends in defense production worldwide and reflects its willingness to acquire, before it is too late, a niche in the evolving international division of labor.[30]

The rationale behind Russia's growing interest in this type of military-technical cooperation is not only export-motivated. It is common knowledge that each subsequent weapon system would cost from two to three times more than its predecessor. Being only at the initial stage of restructuring and modernizing its armed forces, Russia is hardly in a position to rearm on its own, given its ongoing financial and economic crisis. Moreover, there is hardly any justification for Russia in this post-Cold-War world to remain self-sufficient, as was the case with the Soviet Union, in manufacturing the entire range of weapons and military hardware. Gennadii Gornostayev, researcher from a think tank operated by the Ministry of Economics, wrote that, whether Russia wanted it or not, it would have to abandon any hope that it could continue independently developing and producing new generations of weapons and military hardware, as the Soviet Union did, and limit its relationship with other countries to their sales only. According to Gornostayev, "Russia's potential to provide new generations of weapons to its armed forces will be determined, to a great extent, by the scale of its external military-economic relations," thus extending well beyond the national borders Russia's domestic military-economic programs.[31]

The landscape of Russia's military-technical cooperation with industrial countries is highly diverse in terms of intensity, political priority, and usefulness. Heralded as a success story is the implementation of the Russian-French agreement on military-technical cooperation signed in February 1994. Both sides refer to the MiG-AT fighter trainer as the best example of such cooperation. The MiG-AT was developed jointly with the French companies Snecma Turbomeca and Sextant Avionique and manufactured in Russia. However, the marketing efforts are yet to yield substantive results.

Altogether, there are about twenty specific projects in the framework of Russian-French cooperation. One of them involved the upgrading of the Soviet-manufactured *Grad* (Hail) multiple rocket launch systems. As a result, a new solid rocket fuel was introduced which made it possible to extend the range from 14 miles to 24 miles and increase the accuracy.[32] Another one was presented at the Eurosatory-98. The French company Cilas and a Russian Tula-based design bureau improved the performance of the Soviet-developed laser-guided artillery system Krasnopol. The companies involved in this project claimed that the new upgraded Krasnopol-M was far superior to its U.S. counterpart, Copperhead.[33] There is an ongoing codevelopment project with the participation of Russia's Granat design bureau focused on laser technologies with military applications. It was reported that France had purchased from Russia a prototype of the battlefield laser.[34]

Similar but in some cases lower-profile agreements on military-technical cooperation have been facilitating Russia's relationship in this field with Germany, Italy, Britain, and several other industrialized countries. The starting point for Russian-German cooperation was technical assistance in serving MiG-29 aircraft left over after the demise of the German Democratic Republic. However, Russia's hopes that Germany might consider the purchase of additional MiGs were dashed for economic and political considerations after its government decided to procure Eurofighters instead. Then came the idea of pooling efforts with Germany's Daimler-Benz Aerospace (DASA) for marketing the new upgraded MiG-29 SMT. Rosvooruzhenie was a major funding source to produce the MiG-29 SMT modification as a multifunctional combat aircraft (air defense, attack, reconnaissance, and airborne command post). Its motivation and rationale for funding was that the MiG-29 SMT could become an excellent product for export. It is also planned to introduce the MiG-29 SMT into Russia's Air Force as a by-product of this project. In late May 1998 the MiG-29 SMT was displayed at the ILA-98 aerospace show in Berlin. According to presidential aide Evgenii Shaposhnikov, the German partners approached other European states that still operate MiG-29s with an upgrading offer to be carried out by joint Russian-German company MAPS (MiG Aircraft Production Support).[35]

The German government became the main driving force (alongside France) behind the idea of integrating Russia and Ukraine into the multilateral Future Large Aircraft (FLA) project by contributing to it the AN-70 military transport aircraft design and technologies. After a May 13, 1998, decision by other FLA partners to exclude the Antonov consortium from the FLA, Chancellor Helmut Kohl halted funding for the German FLA contractor to continue participation in the aircraft design phase until this company completed a new study of a potential alternative approach involving the AN-70.[36]

An agreement on military-technical cooperation with Italy was signed in November 1996. It served as a framework for Italy's limited participation in the development of the YAK-130 trainer. Otherwise, the ongoing high-level exchanges show few signs of vigorous activity in the field of military-technical cooperation between these two countries. In November 1997, Russia and Britain set up a joint commission for their defense ministries, under whose auspices both sides agreed to develop and implement projects on military-technical cooperation.

Russia's military-technical cooperation with Israel is more visible but has serious limitations. Both countries have been successfully selling the idea of high-quality and inexpensive Russian-manufactured platforms bolstered by advanced Israeli technologies. All joint projects are export-oriented to third countries. The most recent example is a contract between Russia's Rosvooruzhenie and Israel's Aircraft Industries Ltd. (IAI), under which the Il-76 cargo plane is converted into an early-warning airborne platform for the Chinese Air Force. However, Russian-Israeli military-technical cooperation is politically vulnerable. Under existing bilateral arrangements, Israel has to clear with the United States any significant transfer of advanced technologies, and domestically the government is under pressure to stay away from military-technical cooperation with Russia until there is convincing evidence that it is not involved in leaking missile technologies to Iran.

The U.S. approach was a two-stage plan starting with an umbrella agreement for cooperating in dual-use technologies. Under this scheme, only after the dual-use technologies agreement was signed would a second agreement on military-technical cooperation be negotiated. According to a U.S. Department of Defense (DOD) official interviewed in June and December 1997 who was involved over the previous two years in these bilateral contacts, the U.S. experience in negotiating with the Russian side was "rather frustrating." There was a recurrent pattern of Russians first agreeing upon a draft and then avoiding its signing at a later stage. For example, in May 1997 when the Russian Defense Minister visited Washington, D.C., the U.S. negotiators expected to finalize the draft and sign it. The Russian delegation, however, backed off. In hope of expediting a solution, the U.S. administration succeeded in placing this item on the agenda of the Gore-Chernomyrdin Commission. Russian officials explained such delays to their U.S. counterparts by the fact that, in the absence of an appropriate legal basis protecting intellectual property and copyrights, any Russian-U.S. agreement was unlikely to work. In the view of the interviewee, other pitfalls in the way of successful negotiations were the continued restructuring of the Ministry of Defense, leading to the reappointment of several successive negotiators who were new to the process, and the lingering Cold War mentality among the mid-level Russian military, which made the general atmosphere less conducive to mutual trust.[37]

In addition to bilateral channels, Russia has repeatedly attempted to promote this type of military-technical cooperation in a multilateral context. Speaking before the Western European Union (WEU) Parliamentary Assembly in Paris on December 1, 1994, then Foreign Minister Andrey Kozyrev proposed a broad program of such cooperation that included, among other things, direct contacts between Russia's Rosvooruzhenie and relevant WEU bodies. The concept of Russia's special status with NATO, continuously advocated by the Russian leadership prior to 1997 as a major precondition for fully implementing the Partnership for Peace program, presupposed wider military-technical cooperation. In the highly emotional negotiating process in 1996 to 1997 to develop the text of what is now known as the Founding Act on Mutual Relations, Cooperation and Security between NATO and Russia, Foreign Minister Yevgenii Primakov reportedly raised specific arms trade issues as one of the conditions for Russia to accept the document. Apparently, this clause, which was designed to open up NATO markets to Russian-manufactured weapons, was rejected by NATO negotiators.

However, the Founding Act, signed on May 17, 1997, contained several other provisions that were inserted mostly on Russia's insistence and could easily be interpreted as laying the groundwork for military-technical cooperation in the NATO framework. Section III of the act (Areas for Consultation and Cooperation) incorporated such provisions as "pursuing possible armaments-related cooperation through association of Russia with NATO's Conference of National Armaments Directors"; "developing mutually agreed cooperative projects in defense-related economic, environmental and scientific fields"; "possible cooperation in Theatre Missile Defense"; and so on. Initially, the way NATO was moving ahead in implementing the provisions on military-technical cooperation was in conflict with Russia's interpretation of these provisions. The reports coming out of the NATO-Russia Permanent Joint Council (PJC), established under the Founding Act, have indicated that, as of early 1998, the two sides were widely apart in pursuing their goals. However, subsequent developments indicated that the two sides were making some progress in finding a compromise—at least, a Russian representative has reportedly started to attend meetings of National Armaments Directors. However, it would not be realistic to expect a major breakthrough both bilaterally and multilaterally. A major obstacle barring such industrial cooperation is, in the view of Heinrich Vogel, Director of the Federal Institute for Russian, East European and International Studies in Germany, Russia's failure to understand the critical importance of managing the interplay between research and development, industrial performance, and marketing. "The gap in integrating these skills has not closed," wrote Vogel in *Defense News*.[38]

However, an even more important political reason for slow progress is lack of mutual trust among participants. As long as mutual suspicions and recriminations persist, military-technical cooperation will be hostage to them. On the other hand, it would be an illusion to expect that military-technical cooperation can become by itself a source of confidence-building and thereby independently shape the political agenda. Pending an improvement in the strategic, political, and economic environment, military-technical cooperation between Russia and the West is likely to remain limited.

LEGAL BASIS AND DECISION-MAKING

After becoming an independent state, Russia declared itself the continuation state rather than a successor state, meaning that its commitment to assume all major obligations of the Soviet Union included, above all, its nuclear power status and Security Council seat in the U.N. It also accepted those few international obligations that existed at that time in the area of conventional weapon transfers, including the sanctions imposed by the U.N. Security Council and its relevant P-5 arrangements. Subsequently, in December 1995, Russia became a founding member of the Wassenaar Arrangement on Export Controls for Conventional Arms and Dual-Use Goods and Technologies.[39]

On the policy side, five major objectives of Russia's military-technical cooperation with foreign countries were outlined in the November 1993 Military Doctrine. They were: (1) strengthen Russia's military-political positions in different regions of the world; (2) raise hard currency for the state needs, defense conversion projects, defense production, destruction and disposal of weapons, and restructuring of the defense industries; (3) maintain at the required level Russia's export potential as regards conventional weapons and military hardware; (4) develop a scientific and experimental basis for the defense industries, and their scientific research and design institutions and organizations; and (5) provide social support for the personnel of industrial plants, institutions, and organizations that develop and produce weapons, military and special hardware, and other items.[40] The above Russian list was strikingly similar to the U.S. five objectives of weapons transfers included in the White House Guidelines for Conventional Arms Transfers Policy dated February 17, 1995.[41]

In reality, it would not be an exaggeration to say that profit-making was and remains the dominate motive of any Russian policy action. Interagency coordination seemed to be lacking in the context of the Cypress deal. While Russian diplomats were discussing at the United Nations possible commitments not to introduce new weapon systems in Cypress, Rosvooruzhenie struck a deal to deliver to the island $400-million-worth of state-of-the-art S-300 air defense units. There was little coordination even inside the arms trading community. While it was understood that the Cypress deal would seriously complicate Russia's relations with Turkey, time and money were nevertheless spent by other hopeful Russian weapon manufacturers who submitted their proposals to the Turkish government in response to its requests for bids concerning, in particular, battle tanks and helicopters. By the same token, the perseverance of some Russian exporters to sell weapons to Syria was in conflict with their colleagues' stake in nurturing mutually beneficial military-technical cooperation with Israel. Supplying weapons to both sides at war or similar adverserial situations often requires farsightedness, meticulous advanced planning, and diplomatic skills.

As to the implementation side, throughout Russia's short post-Soviet history, its legal basis and the mechanisms intended to ensure state control in the area of weapon exports were continuously revamped under the impact of economic imperatives or as a result of intervention by strong personalities, pressure groups, and, to some extent, ulterior motives of some major actors involved.

Liberal Multiactor Model

Immediately after the August 1991 coup that paved the way for the disintegration of the Soviet Union, the old institutions were unable effectively to control transfers of weapons and enforce relevant laws and regulations. The first two years (1992 to 1993) were characterized by arrangements to restructure the previous trading patterns in an attempt to find the right balance between centralized control and market freedoms for manufacturers. The Ministry of Foreign Economic Relations was tasked with issuing export licenses. There was an increasing number of entities possessing the right to sell defense-related items and services, including Oboronexport, Spetsvneshtekhnika, Voentekh, and others. Russian regions (there are altogether 89 administrative units) largely dependent on weapons production were trying to get special privileges allowing them to conduct weapon sales on their own and retain the bulk of revenues as a way of relieving their economic pressures and promoting defense conversion. For example, by a Presidential Decree in March

1992, the Udmurt Republic was empowered at one point to export military items, and experimented for a while, but without much success.

As a result, the first stage in the evolution of Russia's weapons transfer system might bear the name of "liberal multiactor model." This model's lack of organization and specific guidelines created significant problems for Russian arms exporters. On the one hand, competing in the same product, producers brought down the price; on the other, the confused and disoriented buyers did not know whom to turn to for a specific item. There appeared numerous organizational difficulties in servicing weapons and military contracts: while previously the entire process was coordinated and supervised by one or two state agencies, in 1992 and 1993 several were involved.[42] Though the May 1992 Presidential Decree, On Russia's Military-Technical Cooperation, established an interagency commission as part of the overall objective of maintaining tight state control, these efforts failed in the conditions that prevailed in Russia at that period of time.

Indeed, lack of accounting and inadequate enforcement gave rise to widespread corruption and even pilferage. According to a State Duma source, in 1992 alone, over 1,000 railway cars, each loaded with 20 tons of artillery shells, "disappeared without trace" in the North Caucasus military district.[43] Consider Voentekh, a state company that was registered in October 1992 with the full support of the Ministry of Defense. Its purpose was to sell used military hardware, with profits going to meet some of the social needs of servicemen. But from the beginning, Voentekh also traded in the latest military technologies. In 1992, Voentekh was involved in the sale of the latest Russian-manufactured T-80 tanks and the Tunguska air defense system, even though the export of these weapons was prohibited by law. Armed with a counterfeit license, in 1993 Voentekh tried but failed to sell the former Yugoslavia 2,000 assault rifles and a million rounds of ammunition. The following year, in violation of both Russian and Sri Lankan law, the company transferred (via Ukraine) armored vehicles and small arms to a buyer in Sri Lanka. There are indications that the weapons fell into the hands of the separatist Tamil Tigers, further destablizing the Sri Lankan situation.[44] It is not surprising that during this period official revenues from weapons sales were visibly declining.

Centralized Uniactor Model

Against this bleak background, there was clearly a need for streamlining the weapons export mechanism. The initial move, which can be called "centralized uniactor model," came with the establishment in November 1993 of Rosvooruzhenie as a specialized company for exports and imports of armaments. Though several exporting companies retained some of their rights, Rosvooruzhenie dominated the scene. This model was largely masterminded and meticulously developed by Aleksandr Korzhakov, head of the Presidential Security Service. He promoted his former employee Aleksandr Kotelkin to become the Director General of Rosvooruzhenie, replacing in this position Victor Samoylov, formerly a military advisor to the Vice Premier Vladimir Shumeiko. In June 1994, President Yeltsin appointed Boris Kuzyk, another Korzhakov protegee, as a presidential aide on military-technical cooperation who was supposed to manage the entire system from above, on behalf of the president, albeit president's security chief Korzhakov. The building of this centralized model was completed in December 1994 with the establishment of a State Committee for Military-Technical Policy as a ministry-level structure directly subordinated not to the prime minister, but to the president. At the same time, the work of the committee was to be supervised by Oleg Soskovets, First Vice Premier, who was a long-standing and trusted friend of Aleksandr Korzhakov.

Under Yeltsin's Decree No. 2251, dated December 30, 1994, this committee's unprecedentedly wide scope of reference included not only the development and carrying out of state policy in the area of military-technical cooperation with other countries, but also coordination of weapon programs, conversion of the production facilities of the military-industrial complex, and disposition of weapons and military hardware. By the same Decree No. 2251, the Interagency Commission on Military-Technical Cooperation was disbanded as a freestanding agency, and its functions were transferred to the Coordinating Interagency Council for Military-Technical Policy to be set up under the auspices of the new committee and to be chaired by Oleg Soskovets. That the driving force behind the restructuring was Aleksandr Korzhakov and his men was evidenced by a provision of the decree (altered in a subsequent revision) specifically authorizing the assignment to the committee of staff members from his Presidential Security Service. Most of the new players from top to bottom, including Sergei Svechnikov who was appointed Committee Chairman, had a common background of military intelligence or security service. As this model was finalized, it had three distinct decision-making levels: the president, the government, and a group of designated agencies and organizations with the Committee for Military-Technical Policy playing the leading role. Yeltsin's Decree No. 1008 on military-technical cooperation, dated October 5, 1995, served as the legal basis of this centralized model.

There was a consensus among most Russian observers that this new "centralized uniactor model" demonstrated some real advantages as compared to its predecessor, with much more diffused powers and internal competition. Despite a continued shrinkage of the global market, Russia succeeded in expanding its relative share. A government insider and professor of Russia's Academy of Military Sciences, Aleksandr Rybas, approvingly referred to the "exceptionally rational structure and effective operation" of this model.[45] In the view of one of Russia's nongovernmental experts, Konstantin Makienko, an implicit linkage between the military-technical cooperation and presidential security structures undoubtedly had a positive effect on Russia's stronger position on the world arms market. The Security Service, one of the few effective government structures at that time, managed to curtail the level of criminal presence in arms trade, increased discipline, and suppressed imminent institutional and personal competition. This centralization of military-technical cooperation became, perhaps, one of the factors deterring the declining levels of arms exports and facilitating their subsequent growth.[46]

This model, however, had one inherent deficiency that was about to undermine it from within. The idea of achieving an absolute monopoly position was in conflict with the general trends of economic demonopolization and free marketing advocated by liberal-minded government leaders. Regional leaders and enterprise directors continued to lobby in favor of gaining extensive rights in the area of military-technical cooperation. As a result, despite the opposition from the arms trading elite, eight military-industrial plants were granted, during that short period of time, the right to independent marketing and sales of their products in the world markets. Then in June 1996, after Yeltsin fired Korzhakov and Soskovets as a result of which Anatolii Chubais's competing liberal-minded team came to power, the "centralized uniactor model" showed signs of strain. The dismantlement of the model started later with the abolishing of the Committee for Military-Technical Policy. The committee's functions were transferred to the Ministry of Foreign Economic Relations.

However, this did not mean an immediate demise of the whole model because, among other things, two key personalities—Kuzyk and Kotelkin—retained for the time being their positions (the former was relieved from the presidential staff in February 1998 "for redundancy," while the latter lost his directorship at Rosvooruzhenie in August 1997, was transferred to the Ministry of Foreign Economic Relations and fired in January 1998 because of "downsizing of the personnel"). One of the reasons for this delay was that they developed good working relations with Aleksandr Lebed, who agreed in the summer of 1996 not to run against Yeltsin in the second round of the presidential elections, largely in exchange for a powerful position of Security Council Secretary in Yeltsin's administration. One of his many ambitions in this new job was either to include Russia's military-technical cooperation in the Council's scope of reference or to play a vital role in its conceptualization and implementation. Also, Yeltsin's prolonged illness and surgery in late 1996 and early 1997 prevented the opponents of Korzhakov's model from delivering a quick, deadly blow.

Centralized Multiactor Model

In the meantime, Yeltsin's new entourage was preparing the groundwork for a new model and new rules of the game. An increasingly important role in controlling several major components of this system was subsequently played by a relative newcomer, Yakov Urinson, who in his capacity of First Vice Premier and Minister of Economics supervised the Ministry of Foreign Economic Relations, which had earlier absorbed the Committee for Military-Technical Policy but did not completely inherit its original and far-ranging functions. In March 1997, the Ministry of Defense Industries was abolished and transferred to Urinson's Ministry of Economics, making whatever residual leverage the defense industry had retained even weaker.

A puzzle that has not been completely solved is why the model that enabled Russia to increase its weapons sales from $1.7 billion in 1994 to over $3 billion in 1996, with the share of hard currency revenues reaching the $2-billion level, was targeted for dismantlement and the people responsible for its success literally dumped. The longest holdover, Boris Kuzyk, consistently attempted until his last day in office to present the dismantlement of the previous model as a preplanned and carefully coordinated process involving him and like-minded people. In one of his last interviews in the capacity of a presidential aide in December 1997, Kuzyk claimed that despite its drastic restructuring, Russia's military-technical cooperation was a smoothly evolving process started in 1993 and, contrary to the obvious, the president's decisions "have not fundamentally changed" anything.[47] The editorial board of the monthly that published the interview openly questioned Kuzyk's business-as-usual interpretation of the ongoing changes. Its own version was that the reform of the system of military-technical cooperation came "as a result of serious banking intrigues." According to this scenario, former employees of the MAPO-bank took advantage of their well-established contacts in the presidential administration in order to "kick out the key personalities" in the arms trade with whom the competing UNEXIM bank was associated, thus creating for the MAPO-bank a new niche in this lucrative business.[48]

Numerous theories emerged in response to these developments providing a testimony of how unpredictable Russian politics may be and how hard it is sometimes to rationalize its basic motivation. For example, Ruslan Pukhov, Director of the Center for Analysis of Strategies and Technologies, did not believe that there was a long-term strategy of military-technical cooperation in Russia. He discounted the likelihood of the Kremlin leadership following a well-coordinated and comprehensive decision-making process. Pukhov believed that major structural and personnel decisions were made "on the Byzantine principle of proximity to the President." Whoever has a chance to bring across to him an attractively packaged idea may carry the day. This situation often led to unpredictable, if not dangerous, zigzagging in policy and its implementation.[49] There was also a corruption theory presented by the government sponsored daily *Rossiiskaya Gazeta.* Its staff correspondent Viktor Klenov alleged that Kuzyk and Kotelkin were involved in a number of shady deals including the use of a small private bank through which they laundered considerable sums of money. Also, a private shipping company, Kargotrans, was established with Kotelkin's personal involvement. The company received lucrative contracts from Rosvooruzhenie to transport military cargoes outside Russia at rates much higher than those prevailing in the market. Payments to the company were transferred through an intricate network of offshore banks, making it difficult to trace them. There is no information whether these allegations were formally confirmed and legal proceedings were instituted against some leaders of the arms export elite.[50] Conspiracy theory was further advanced by the pro-Communist forces, which had great respect for Kotelkin's well-publicized attempts to upstage the United States as arms exporters. Their leftist newspaper, *Zavtra,* attributed his removal to the pressure put on the Russian leadership by the United States showing increasing concern about Russia's successes in weapons markets.[51]

Among other speculations, perhaps the most plausible was that Rosvooruzhenie became the dominating arms trading agency with its own agenda, reluctantly letting manufacturers act independently. At the same time, drawing on its extensive cash flows and taking advantage of the virtually bankrupt status of the Defense Ministry, Rosvooruzhenie developed ways to impose its vision and priorities on national R&D and weapons production. There was a growing gap between the Rosvooruzhenie policy and the perception of Russia's national security interests by other interagency players.[52]

The approval in June 1997 by the Federal Assembly of the federal law On Military-Technical Cooperation with Foreign Countries, which was vetoed by President Yeltsin a month later, accelerated the advent of the next stage in the evolution of Russia's policy in this area. The controversy over this law dated from early 1995, when the Duma Defense Committee developed its draft. Concurrently, a competing draft text was formulated by the presidential staff and submitted to the Duma in November 1995 after the Duma's own version passed the first reading. However, the Duma Council decided to treat the government draft as an amendment to its own draft and instructed the Defense Committee to focus on preparing the text for the second reading. After its approval by both chambers, the presidential administration insisted on Yeltsin exercising his veto power because, in its view, the legislature pulled the blanket too much to itself, acquiring, as a result, "excessive and unconstitutional powers in the area of military-technical cooperation."[53] In his letter to the leadership of the

Federal Assembly dated July 22, 1997, President Yeltsin explained the rationale behind his veto. The letter contained a long list of what was qualified as discrepancies and conflicts within the existing legal basis in terms of substance and procedure. Yeltsin objected, among other things, to a provision of the law that "restricted the powers of the President in making decisions on the export to individual countries of military products not included in the list of military products allowed to be exported." Instead, as the Federal Assembly insisted, such exports would be regulated by federal laws only, "which does not correspond to the current practice of exporting military products and to the principle of the separation of powers."[54]

On September 5, 1997, the Duma tried but failed to overcome Yeltsin's veto. The law was finally adopted in the summer of 1998. However, the prolonged absence of a dedicated federal law that would regulate this sensitive area was a clear indication that, in addition to the interagency wranglings and personality clashes, there was another dimension of the problem—lack of common understanding and cooperation between the legislature, on one hand, and the presidential administration and executive branch, on the other.

After President Yeltsin exercised his veto power on July 22, 1997, there was clearly a need for his own initiative to fill in the legal vacuum and lay down a framework for a new model. Despite the growing importance of legislatively approved laws, Presidential Decrees in Russia have acquired increased significance under the 1993 Constitution. Pending the adoption of federal laws, quite a time-consuming process in any democracy, Presidential Decrees in Russia are intended to serve as an important source of law. Article 11 stipulates that the Russian President occupies a special and separate position from the other branches of government: "State power in the Russian Federation shall be exercised by the Russian Federation President, the Federal Assembly, the Russian Federation government and Russian Federation courts." The Constitution assigns to the president the fundamentally important task not only of coordinating the functions of state bodies, but also of ensuring that the functions performed by the legislative, executive, and judicial branches confirm to legal requirements. Article 115 of the Constitution assigns Presidential Decrees, which may be of "normative" nature, a status comparable to federal laws. Article 80 lists the issues on which the president may exercise his prerogative, but the wording is so general that it is open to wide interpretation and, consequently, controversy.

The way the new arrangements were conceptualized and shaped throughout 1997 and 1998 gives grounds to categorize them as falling into the "centralized multiactor model." The transition to this model started with Presidential Decree No. 792 of July 28, 1997, On Some Measures for Improving the Management of Military-Technical

Cooperation, which shifted the control of Russia's military-technical cooperation in general and coordination of Rosvooruzhenie activity in particular from the president to the prime minister.[55]

This decree was followed in August 1997 by a package of others. Decree No. 907, dated August 20, 1997, On Measures for Strengthening the State Control of Foreign Trade Activity in the Area of Military-Technical Cooperation, served as an umbrella document. It changed the status of Rosvooruzhenie into "a federal state unitary enterprise." In addition to Rosvooruzhenie, two more intermediaries were authorized to operate: Promexport, which changed its status to a federal state military enterprise like Rosvooruzhenie, and Rossiiskie Tekhnologii (this entity was yet to be set up). New revised statutes of Rosvooruzhenie and Promexport were approved by Government Resolution No. 1658, dated December 31, 1997.[56] It took longer—until February 1998—for Rossiiskie Tekhnologii (Russian Technologies) to emerge. The August 1997 package of Presidential Decrees, in particular, Decrees No. 908, 909, and 910, gave some rough idea about possible division of labor among the three: Rosvooruzhenie would specialize in major export deals involving new weapon systems; Promexport would focus on surplus weapons and spare parts; Rossiiskie Tekhnologii would be involved in protecting Russia's copyrights, technology transfers, and R&D-related contracts. In reality, as their statutes were finalized, the borderlines between these intermediaries became blurred. The decrees failed to provide clearly defined areas for them to operate, which should be a prerequisite to avoid duplication and competition. In a fight for survival, each of the three would seem anxious to grasp any contract even if it did not fit into its originally defined scope of reference. A good case in point is the May 12, 1998 press conference by Yurii Khozyainov, First Deputy Director of Rosvooruzhenie. Among future priorities he listed at the press conference was the conclusion of smaller and medium-sized contracts; more involvement in supplying spare parts and components for the weapon systems already transferred; and export promotion of "intellectual products,"—R&D and military technologies that were yet to be industrially introduced.[57]

Under the same umbrella Decree No. 907, the Ministry of Defense not only retained its function of training foreign military personnel and technicians but also was granted the right to sell surplus weapons ("those released from the armed forces as a result of the reforms").[58] As of mid-1998, Russia's Air Force alone was planning to sell about 600 surplus aircraft (MiG-27, MiG-23, SU-22, L-39, and others) as well as older S-200 and S-125 air defense systems. They were offered worldwide at unprecedentedly low prices.[59] India has already demonstrated an interest in acquiring used air defense systems for training purposes. The umbrella Decree No. 907 also replaced the existing interagency mechanism with a coordinating interagency council for military-technical cooperation. An important innovation introduced by the decree was the establishment of supervising councils whose mandate would be to control the activity of the three unitary enterprises. The government also acquired a final say in the selection of financial institutions to be contracted for servicing the deals concluded by these enterprises.

Decree No. 907 had three attachments: (a) Provision for Controlling Russia's Trade in Military Products; (b) Procedure for Granting to Russia's Organizations the Right to Trade with Other Countries in Military Products; and (c) Statute of the Coordinating Interagency Council for Military-Technical Cooperation.[60]

The Provision requested the Coordinating Council to develop by January 1998 two lists (No. 1 and No. 2). List No. 1 would cover all military products permitted for export to foreign buyers, specifying which of these items can be licensed for production outside Russia. It would also define the scope of military R&D allowed to be carried out on a contractual basis for foreign customers. List No. 2 would incorporate the countries to which the items in List No. 1 are permitted to be transfered. However, some countries in List No. 2 may not be eligible to import the entire range of List No. 1 items.

Similar lists existed during the Soviet period. They were revised and updated on an annual basis, but nevertheless each major new contract required approval by the General Secretary of the Communist Party. However, with the updated lists available to key decision-makers, such approvals were a mere formality in most cases. The 1992 Presidential Decree on military-technical cooperation provided for the same procedure of maintaining lists but, as reported in the Russian media, the last time the lists were updated was 1993. As a result, each new contract was to be approved on its merits by the president, which greatly enhanced the role of its staff responsible for submitting relevant documentation.[61] The January 1998 deadline set by the Presidential Decree for drafting and finalizing the lists had not been met. At a June 1998 conference on arms export held in Moscow and attended by representatives of over 200 defense plants, participants urged the national leadership to introduce those lists as soon as possible on the assumption that they would give exporters a chance to quickly negotiate deals involving approved items without a need for seeking each time individual authorization each time. In other words, it was their expectation that the Lists should bring about a much simplified procedure.[62] The lists were finally introduced in late summer of 1998.

That the List of approved for export weapons and military hardware required by law did not materialize in time is hardly surprising. Since the Russian government has been consistently trying to accommodate the needs of individual manufacturers pushed to the brink of bankruptcy by authorizing on an *ad hoc* basis the export of their top-of-the-line products, the introduction of restrictive Lists would have made the overall system more rigid to operate and less susceptible to the interests of both bureaucracy and producers. It is much easier to make individual decisions as a favor to individual manufacturers without the List rather than on top of the List.

In the meantime, there were numerous reports about defense plants exerting pressure on the government for inclusion of their products in List No. 1. The "Sukhoi" Design Bureau actively lobbied for its new reconnaissance and attack SU-32FN aircraft, yet to be fully inducted in Russia's Air Force. According to Rolan Martirosov, "Sukhoi" Chief Designer, this aircraft has a great export potential to littoral states because its mission is to track and destroy surface ships and submarines at a considerable distance from the shoreline. With one in-flight refueling its range is extended up to 4,500 miles. SU-32 FN is currently armed with the "Moskit" ("Sunburn" by NATO designation) supersonic anti-ship missile and will be able to carry the "Alfa" new generation supersonic missile.[63] Another example involves the Moskit itself. A ban on exporting air-based and sea-based Moskits was reluctantly lifted by the Russian military after numerous démarches by the administration of the Far Eastern region where they are manufactured. Professor Igor Seleznev, General Director of the Raduga Design Bureau, where Moskits were developed, claimed that not a single Western country had ever succeeded in producing a comparable weapon system. The Moskit 3M-80E modification was part of the package deal with China, which was scheduled to receive in 1998 up to 30 missiles. In addition to the Progress main assembly plant in Arsenyev (Russia's Far East), about 300 Russian subcontractors were involved in this Russian-Chinese deal.[64]

The Provision attached to Yeltsin's Decree No. 907 also covered some new ground in regulating agreements on military-technical cooperation. Such agreements can be negotiated only if authorized by the president upon recommendation from the government. They can be supplemented by separate subagreements between cooperating departments or agencies acting as counterparts, provided these subagreements are cleared by the Ministry of Defense and specifically mentioned in the text of the main agreements. The government has the power to authorize negotiations leading to interdepartmental subagreements after the Ministry of Foreign Affairs, jointly with other interested bodies of the federal executive branch, makes an appropriate submission. With international agreements in place, the government can set up bilateral and multilateral intergovernmental commissions on military-technical cooperation in order to implement their provisions.[65]

The Procedure for Granting to Russia's Organizations the Right to Trade with Other Countries in Military Products attached to Yeltsin's Decree No. 907 dated August 20, 1997, outlined major requirements for applying and receiving this trading privilege. Decisions to grant the right are made by the Coordinating Council, but must be subsequently approved by the government. The Ministry of External Economic Relations (transformed into the Ministry of Trade maintains a register of entities certified to trade in military products. They are either designers and manufacturers of these products or federal state unitary enterprises specified by Presidential Decrees. No other intermediaries are permitted. Any information-sharing, including promotion and marketing efforts, must be cleared in advanced with the Defense Ministry.[66]

This block of regulations was later expanded and specified. Each decision made by the Coordinating Council and approved by the prime minister to grant the right listed export-intended products designed or manufactured by the individual applicant and the types of work and services to be performed. For example, Government Resolution No. 1847-R, dated December 31, 1997, accorded the right "to sign contracts through the established procedure" to the Rubin Design Bureau in St. Petersburg. Such resolutions are valid for three years. It authorized the Rubin Bureau to carry out R&D, maintenance and modernization; repair and operation, training, and other types of work and services as regards Rubin-designed submarines of the three projects 877, 636, and 641. The next generation of Amur-type submarines was also included in the resolution, but the permitted scope of military-technical cooperation was limited to R&D. It must be stressed that the Amur-type submarine is primarily intended for export as Amur-1650. In terms of its stealthiness, sonar equipment, and other modern features, the boat is likely to be superior to all preceding models. It will be armed with the latest cruise missiles, torpedoes, and mines.[67] This may be another example of exporting top-of-the-line weapons without proper consideration of security implications.

Two more documents under this heading appeared in 1998. The first one was Government Resolution No. 244, dated February 21, 1998, which approved the statute of the registar for defense institutes and plants that were granted the right to participate in military-technical cooperation. The second was Yeltsin's Decree 327, dated March 30, 1998, which specified the procedure for submitting relevant applications to the Coordinating Council to get this right.[68] Efforts to prioritize this particular segment of the new model should not come as a surprise. According to former Economics Minister Yakov Urinson, who was its main architect, designers and manufacturers empowered to participate as independent entities in the area of military technical cooperation should constitute the top tier of the model, with the designated three intermediaries providing support and services at the second tier.[69] It usually worked the other way around in the framework of the previous model.

The Statute of the Coordinating Council also attached to Yeltsin's Decree No. 907, dated August 20, 1997, provided a clear definition of the future interagency process. However, the council was set up not as a decision-making agency but rather as a deliberating body that is supposed to develop a variety of proposals for the president and the government. The following ministries and services were represented in the council chaired by the prime minister: Ministry of Economics, Ministry of Foreign Affairs, Federal Security Service, Russian Space Agency, Ministry of Defense, Ministry of Finance, Ministry of Atomic Energy, Presidential administration, Ministry of Foreign Economic Relations (now Ministry of Trade), Security Council, and Foreign Intelligence Service.[70]

As the "centralized multiactor model" continued to evolve, there was no lack of criticism about its effectiveness. What most critics would like to emphasize was that the aggregate volume of weapons export dramatically dropped from over $3 billion in 1996 to barely $2 billion in 1997. Despite claims to the contrary by the arms trading elite, the value of lost contracts in the second half of 1997 and first half of 1998 was estimated by some experts at about $3 billion. After a series of hearings and in anticipation of new ones, the Duma Defense Committee drafted a resolution urging the government to rectify the situation as soon as possible. Among the reasons for low efficiency of military-technical cooperation, Duma deputies named the absence of clearly formulated and formalized goals and principles of state policy in the area of military-technical cooperation and insufficiently vigorous methods of ensuring state monopoly and control. It was implied that the federal ministries and agencies whose mandate is to promote trade and economic cooperation had failed to prioritize weapons trade. In the view of the Defense Committee, Russia's weapons trade is "sporadic, unsubstantiated, and spontaneous."[71]

The August 1998 economic and financial crisis and the subsequent change of government have had a deep impact on Russia's weapons export policies and practices. On the one hand, the ruble devaluation was expected to make Russia's products even more competitive and easier to sell. On the other, in the absence of government-sponsored credits the manufacturers had no choice but to turn to outside financial institutions for support. Latters' policy of charging unprecendentedly high annual interests ranging from 20 percent to 30 percent brought to naught not only the devaluation advantage but also radically increased the actual cost. Moreover, Russia's search for new buyers was seriously hampered by the growing perception of Russia as a country in the midst of a long-term crisis likely to default on its international debts.

In the crisis situation the weakened federal government had to face a growing trend of individual regions and producers increasingly becoming more independent players in military-technical cooperation. With the government virtually bankrupt, the regions had more incentives themselves or felt pressure from manufacturers to develop their own channels of dealing with potential and existing buyers. This would certainly boost the "multiactor" component of the currently evolving model of Russia's military-technical cooperation.

It was not surprising that the adjustment, introduced by the government to the legal basis of military-technical cooperation on December 1998, was designed to strengthen the "centralized" component. Yeltsin's Decree No. 1488, dated December 7, 1998, replaced the Coordinating Interagency Council with a new Presidential Commission of Military-Technical Cooperation chaired by Prime Minister Primakov.[72] The attached statute of the Commission defined it as a deliberating and consultative body whose mission would be to develop laws, recommendations, and other documents for the President, who thus assumed once again a position to control, and to regulate the process of military-technical cooperation. One of the two deputies of the Chairman specifically referred to in the decree was Yuri Maslukov, first Deputy Prime Minister in charge of economic matters including the military-industrial complex, who was widely known for his ardent support for Russia's defense industry and far-reaching ideas aimed at restoring its original vitality and technological process. Though there are grounds to expect continuity in finalizing the "centralized multiactor model" of Russia's military-technical cooperation, more changes in its leadership and policies are just a matter of time. It should not come as a surprise that the left-of-the-center government of prime minister Primakov will attempt to revitalize the defense industry and even more aggressively stimulate weapons export. In the latter area the government is likely to use its full weight without visibly transgressing the limits of what it perceives as Russia's international commitments.

CONCLUSION

The arms trade and military-technical cooperation mean much more for Russia than for any other major weapons supplier. Second only to oil and gas sales in terms of budget revenues, exports of military products have so far prevented the defense industry from a total collapse that would certainly destabilize the country and lead to dangerous social turmoil. Moreover, military reforms and weapons modernization programs would have been considerably hindered or delayed had not Russia succeeded in generating weapons export revenues. For strategically and economically weakened Russia, the arms trade is providing important leverage for maintaining old partnership-type relations with other countries and forging new ones. Exporting weapons and expanding military-technical cooperation enable Russia to project itself as a high-tech source globally in the absence of other economically competitive options. To some extent, weapons sales, in addition to nuclear power and space cooperation, have become yet another important trapping of Russia as a great power.

There are basically three types of military-technical cooperation currently practiced by Russia. The first type is focused on reintegrating the defense industry potential of the former Soviet republic without which Russia is unable to manufacture the bulk of its defense products. This type of military-technical cooperation is hardly a direct cash-generating activity but serves important security purposes in the CIS framework, reinforces general reintegration trends, and contributes to keeping the Russian defense industry afloat and relatively competitive. The second type involves weapons exports, licensed production, services, and training for old and new recipients, mostly in Asia, the Middle East, and South America. This type of cooperation is undoubtedly very important to Russia as a revenue source. In order to compete successfully in world markets, Russia has been increasingly offering for sale its most state-of-the-art weapon systems, sometimes ignoring possible implications for its own national security. The third emerging type is military-technical cooperation with industrialized countries. It is Russia's expectation that such cooperation might eventually generate R&D-related savings, facilitate marketing prospects, and pave the way for some other dual-use or civilian projects to follow suit. This is Russia's response to the globalization trends in defense production worldwide and reflects its willingness to acquire a niche in the evolving international division of labor.

Overall, Russia and its defense industry are becoming dangerously dependent on weapons sales. Its emphasis on weapons exports and resultant vulnerabilities are not unique compared to those of other weapons producers, but they are alarming because of Russia's still overmilitarized economy, economic stagnation, and dramatically decreased GNP. Two major recipients of Russian-manufactured arms—China and India—which account for almost three fourths of its exports, are getting powerful leverage, enabling them, if necessary, to wrestle important concessions from Russia. If Russia fails to diversify its arms trade and find new markets, this growing dependency threatens to have an impact on its foreign and security policy.

The three models of controlling weapon exports with which the Russian leadership has been experimenting since 1992 have one common denominator: how to establish a workable balance between better incentives and more breathing space for manufacturers and strict state control for the government. The current "centralized multiactor model" that started to emerge in mid-1997 is far from being perfect and requires major adjustments. As the pendulum was swinging away from the overly centralized approach of the preceding "centralized uniactor model" toward more leeway for individual producers, there reappeared a risk of the opposite extreme—increased competition for foreign sales and poor coordination among Russian arms manufacturers that were licensed to participate in military-technical cooperation (as of mid-1998 there were 16 of them). As long as Russia maintains excessive defense production capabilities and does not move aggressively toward their consolidation, getting an export contact at any cost will remain the only option for survival.

As an important profit-generating activity and policy tool, Russia's weapons export system cannot be immune to all the ups and downs of

Russia's transition period. Russian arms sales strategy and decision-making have been subject to considerable restructuring and numerous personnel changes. There have been cases of corruption, illegal transfers, and violations of legal norms. The entire system of governance in Russia is still inchoate, being a result of the yet to be completed nation-building process. Under the circumstances, the arms trading business cannot be an oasis of perfection in a sea of problem-prone policies and their implementation.

NOTES

1. Press Conference with Yevgenii Ananyev, General Director of the State Unitary Company "Rosvooruzhenie," *Interfax News Agency* (April 28, 1998).
2. Yeltsin's address before the Federal Assembly is quoted from the text published in *Rossiiskaya Gazeta* (February 25, 1994).
3. The International Institute for Strategic Studies, *The Military Balance 1997/98* (Oxford University Press, 1997), p. 265.
4. Press conference with Vice Premier and Minister of Economics Yakov Urinson, ITAR-TASS News Agency, (February 12, 1998).
5. Yuri Karnakov, "Generals Continue CIS Integration," *Russkii Telegraf* (April 3, 1998).
6. For more information, see Igor Khripunov and Mary Matthews, "Russia's Oil and Gas Interest Group and Its Foreign Policy Agenda," *Problems of Post-Communism* (May-June 1996), pp. 38–48.
7. Yuri Maslukov, "Military-Industrial Complex Needs Help," *Nezavisimaya Gazeta* (January 17, 1998).
8. Agence France-Presse, February 7, 1998.
9. Interview with Academician Evgenii Fedosov, "Self-Isolation of Russian Scientists Is More Dangerous Than Leaks of Secret Technologies," *Nedelya* (February 16–22, 1998).
10. Anatoli Popelov, "Illusion of Prosperity," *Nezavisimaya Gazeta* (June 2, 1998).
11. Aleksandr Rybas, "A Dangerous Trend," *Nezavisimoye Voennoe Obozrenie* (February 13–19, 1998).
12. Interview with First Deputy Defense Minister Nikolai Mikhailov, *Kommersant-Daily* (April 29, 1998).
13. *Krasnaya Zvezda* (November 19, 1993).
14. Aleksandr Shaburkin, "CIS Defense Programs," *Nezavisimoye Voennoye Obozrenie* (April 4, 1998); Yurii Karnakov, "Generals Continue CIS Integration," *Russkii Telegraf* (April 3, 1998).
15. Interview with General Director of Ukrspetsexport Andrei Kukin, *Nezavisimoye Voennoye Obozrenie* (April 17–23, 1998).
16. U.S. Congressional Research Service, *Conventional Arms Transfers to Developing Nations, 1989–1996* (Washington, DC, 1997).
17. *Nezavisimoye Voennoe Obozrenie* (May 8–14, 1998).
18. *Reuters*, May 13, 1998.
19. *Interfax*, May 29, 1996.
20. Vladimir Kostrov, "Duma Is Concerned About Arms Trade," *Russkii Telegraf* (May 22. 1998).
21. "Military-Technical Cooperation," ITAR-TASS Agency, April 13–19, 1998, p. 9.
22. Aleksandr Kotelkin, "Russia and the World Arms Market," *International Affairs* (Moscow), No. 4 (1996), p. 34.
23. *Defense News* (March 30–April 5, 1998) p. 16.

24. Interview with a former official of the Ministry of Defense Industries, November 15, 1997.
25. Nikolai Zlenko, "Military-Technical Cooperation Strengthens National Security," *The Military Parade* (May-June, 1998).
26. Andrey Bagrov, "Each Propeller Reeks of Scandal," *Kommersant-Daily* (July 18, 1996).
27. *Defense News* (February 5–11, 1996).
28. Interview with an engineer from the Komsomolsk-on-Amur Aircraft Manufacturing Company (KnAAPO), August 5, 1997. (There are unconfirmed reports that KnAAPO had initiated this deal with the Chinese on its own, leaving little room for Moscow to back off when the negotiations brought out a draft agreement.)
29. Pavel Felgengauer, "An Uneasy Partnership: Sino-Russian Defense Cooperation and Arms Sales," in Andrew Pierre and Dmitri Trenin, eds., *Russia in the World Arms Trade* (Carnegie Endowment for International Peace, 1997), p. 103.
30. Igor Khripunov, "Conventional Weapons Transfers: U.S.-Russian Cooperation or Rivalry," *Comparative Strategy*, vol. 14 (1995), pp. 453–466.
31. Gennadii Gornostayev, "Condition for the Survival of Russia's Defense Industry," *Nezavisimoye Voennoye Obozrenie* (May 15–21, 1998).
32. Nikolai Novichkov, "A Blow Against Enemies and Competitors," *Nezavisimoye Voennoye Obozrenie* (April 24–May 7, 1998).
33. Ilya Bulavinov, "Russia's Smart Shell Outstarted the U.S. One," *Kommersant-Daily* (July 5, 1998).
34. "Military-Technical Cooperation," ITAR-TASS Agency, April 13–19, 1998, p. 55.
35. Press Conference with Presidential Aide Yevgenii Shaposhinkov, RIA Novosti News Agency (May 17, 1998).
36. Brooks Tigner, "Bonn Freezes FLA Future," *Defense News* (May 25–31, 1998).
37. Interview with a Department of Defense official, June 9, 1997, and December 10, 1997.
38. Heinrich Vogel, "Russia Pushes into Market," *Defense News* (June 8–14, 1998).
39. For more about Russia's external legal framework for conventional weapon transfers, see Sergey Kortunov, "The Influence of External Factors on Russia's Arms Export Policy," in Ian Anthony, ed., *Russia and the Arms Trade* (Oxford University Press, 1998), pp. 93–106; Pyotr Litavrin, "Russia, the Wassenaar Arrangement, and the Creation of International Restraints on Arms Transfers," in Andrew Pierre and Dmitri Trenin, eds., *Russia in the World Arms Trade* (Carnegie Endowment for International Peace, 1997), pp. 105–114.
40. *Krasnaya Zvezda* (November 19, 1993).
41. "Guidelines for Conventional Arms Transfers Policy," White House, Washington, D.C., (February 17, 1995).
42. Nikolai Revenko, "Regulation of Conventional Weapons Exports in Russia," in Gary Bertsch and Igor Khripunov, eds., *Russia's Nonproliferation and Conventional Export Controls: 1995 Annual Report* (Athens: University of Georgia, 1996), pp. 29–37.
43. Interview with a former staffer of the Duma Defense Committee, November 14, 1997.
44. Leonid Krapivin, "Generals Fattening on Weapons Trade," *Moscow News* (March 28–April 3, 1996).
45. Aleksandr Rybas, "A Dangerous Trend," *Nezavisimoye Voennoye Obozrenie* (February 13–19, 1998).
46. Konstantin Makienko, "The Evolution of the Institutional System of Managing Russia's Military-Technical Cooperation," *The Monitor: Nonproliferation, Demilitarization, and Arms Control*, vol. 3, no. 3 (Summer 1997), p. 28.
47. Interview with Boris Kuzyk, "Arms Experts Will Save the Defense Industry," *Business in Russia* (December 1997), p. 17.

48. *Op. cit.*, p. 18.
49. Interview with Ruslan Pukhov, January 30, 1998.
50. Viktor Klenov, "Enriched Civilizations Quit the Arms Business," *Rossiiskaya Gazeta* (February 14, 1998).
51. Vladimir Vinnikov, "Switchman Kotelkin," *Zavtra* (January 27, 1998).
52. Mikhail Viesens, "The Military-Industrial Complex: Where Is a Way Out of the Crisis?" *Russkaya Mysl* (February 11, 1998).
53. Interview with a former staffer of the Duma Defense Committee, November 14, 1997.
54. "One Should Not Meddle with the President's Powers," *Rossiiskaya Gazeta* (August 12, 1997).
55. *Rossiiskaya Gazeta* (August 2, 1997).
56. *Rossiiskaya Gazeta* (January 31, 1998).
57. Igor Korotchenko, "Rosvooruzhenie Revises Its Priorities," *Nezavisimaya Gazeta* (May 13, 1998).
58. *Rossiiskaya Gazeta* (August 22, 1997).
59. Press Conference with Air Force Commander-in-Chief Colonel General Anatoly Kornukov, Interfax News Agency, June 10, 1998.
60. *Rossiiskaya Gazeta* (August 22, 1997, and August 26, 1997).
61. Yuri Golotyuk, "A Go-Ahead Has Been Given to the New Redistribution of the Weapons Export Area," *Russkii Telegraf* (May 16, 1998).
62. Aleksandr Sychev, "Russia's Defense Industry Will Survive Due to Exports," *Izvestia* (June 16, 1998).
63. "Military-Technical Cooperation," ITAR-TASS Agency, January 12–18, 1998.
64. Dmitrii Safonov, "'Moskit' Lost Its Top Secret Status," *Kommersant-Daily* (April 14, 1998); "Military-Technical Cooperation," ITAR-TASS Agency, April 13–19, 1998, p. 10 and pp. 35–37.
65. *Rossiiskaya Gazeta* (August 26, 1997).
66. *Op. cit.*
67. *Rossiiskaya Gazeta* (February 11, 1998).
68. *Rossiiskaya Gazeta* (April 8, 1998).
69. Press Conference with Vice Premier Yakov Urinson at the RF Government House, August 25, 1997, English transcript by Federal News Service.
70. *Rossiiskaya Gazeta* (August 26, 1997).
71. Vladimir Kostrov, "Rosvooruzhenie Is Set the Track of Overtaking the United States," *Russkii Telegraf* (May 22, 1998).
72. *Rossiiskaya Gazeta* (December 15, 1998).

9

EXPORT CONTROLS AND NUCLEAR SMUGGLING IN RUSSIA

Vladimir A. Orlov

The dissolution of the Soviet Union in August to December of 1991 brought about doubts regarding the ability of newly independent states' leaders effectively to control the storage, transportation, and export of fissile materials and nuclear warheads.

DISSOLUTION OF THE SOVIET UNION AND EMERGENCE OF THE THREAT OF NUCLEAR DEVIATIONS

From the international security perspective, three worst-case scenarios were distinguished. The first one is the "resurgence" scenario: "it would arise if existing nuclear weapons are inherited by a unitary actor—most likely the Russian republic—which regains strength and coherence, and becomes malign. If it becomes impossible to keep the nuclear weapons under central control, they might be divided among the republics. The second risk is the 'anarchy and civil nuclear war' scenario. A third danger might be called the 'selling out' scenario: if the control over the Soviet nuclear complex is lost, the development of a black market for nuclear technology, if not weapons, and the large-scale spread of first-hand knowledge about weapons production could result."[1]

Upon the whole, all fears proved to be overly exaggerated. The most pessimistic scenarios were avoided, though it took Ukraine three years to confirm its nonnuclear status. Furthermore, it took a majority of newly independent states much time and effort to establish their export control system for nonproliferation purposes, to say nothing about the absence of appropriate coordination on exports control issues among the CIS states, which seem to have good prospects to create what David Fisher had called "CISAtom."[2]

In that situation interim scenarios came to the fore. Fears regarding diversions of Russian-origin nuclear warheads and their smuggling to "sensitive countries" belonged to non-science-fiction scenarios. The possibility of nuclear warhead thefts from the territories of Kazakstan and Ukraine (in particular to Iran) was a more acute problem, although it was usually posed theoretically and sometimes just to deliberately aggravate the problem. According to a number of scenarios, the real problem is the appearance and further growth of smuggling CIS-origin fissile weapons-grade materials (uranium enriched to more than 80 percent and weapons-grade plutonium-239) in amounts whose total sum suffices to create a nuclear bomb by some rogue state or a terrorist group. The potential interest of a number of countries, primarily Iran and Iraq, in the Ulba Metallurgy Plant, which produces almost all containing uranium pellets for nuclear reactors, is particularly keen. For example, one expert remarked that such plants "present an interest for countries striving for nuclear weapons production . . . since, having obtained them, they would be able to skip the most power-consuming enrichment stage."[3]

As far as the Russian Federation is concerned, the approach of a majority of experts was twofold. On the one hand, it was acknowledged that Russia had inherited the Soviet export control system that was reliable even in political and economic chaos. Presidential Decree No. 388, on establishing of export control system in Russia of April 11, 1992, was considered successful, and measures of the Russian government on its implementation were characterized as "effective."[4] It was stated that no serious evidence existed of illicit export of some Russian-origin nuclear weaponry, their components, or weapons-usable materials in amounts of military significance.[5]

On the other hand, it was argued that Russia inherited about 900 facilities with fissile materials, and there are no guarantees that in a situation favorable for entrepreneurs there will be no illegal, uncontrolled exports of nuclear materials from Russia. For example, noted FSU export control expert William Potter noted: "If you are in the market for a fast-breeder reactor, enriched uranium, a little heavy water or even 'peaceful nuclear explosives,' Moscow is the place to shop."[6] The critical approach to Russia's ability to fully control its nuclear exports prevailed over an optimistic statement made by a number of Russian specialists that "the illicit export of radioactive weapons-grade materials from Russia has been absolutely ruled out."[7] Criticism was aimed mainly at Russia's "imperfect" export control laws, replete with numerous loopholes, the absence of a state system for nuclear materials protection, control, and accounting

(MPC&A), as well as poor border and customs control at many Russian frontiers and the absence of such control at the borders with CIS states.[8]

It should be pointed out that the Russian export control system was considered to be one of several "weak links," but not the weakest one, in a chain that was called upon to stop illicit export of nuclear materials. However, by most estimates, the legal mechanisms of 1991, early 1992, and 1993, including Presidential Decrees and approved export control lists, had almost eliminated the possibility of large-scale illegal nuclear export. The system of control, under which agreements were issued from Minatom and licenses from the Ministry of Foreign Economic Relations, had practically eliminated all shady companies from the "nuclear trade." At last, the requirement to name the end user legally prevented nuclear export to the countries of nuclear proliferation concern: Iraq, North Korea, and Libya.

In other words, concerning the possibility of the "illegal export of nuclear materials," one should understand that the likelihood of being detected violating Russian export control laws was minimal (for example, incorrect license registration, misleading or inaccurate applications, and so on). It was assumed that this risk was not large, or at least no higher than in the United States: ". . . but neither does America have an unblemished record in this respect."[9] Legitimate concern was aroused by absolute ignorance of export control norms by private, governmental, and quasi-governmental companies that were flourishing in Russia in 1992 and 1993, as well as by various criminal groups, and even specific individuals ready to directly smuggle weapons-grade materials. That is why top priority was given to activities and measures of the customs and law enforcement bodies (the Security Ministry and the Ministry of the Interior) rather than to the activities of the export control services in Russia (in particular, the Ministry of the Economy). At the time, this appears to have been a reasonable approach.

The first wave of international media campaigns regarding "nuclear smuggling" from Russia began in 1992. Here is a typical example: in January, 1992, an employee of Italian TV and radio was offered "5 kilos of Russian plutonium" in Switzerland.[10] Italy, Switzerland, and Austria were most often named as transition routes for Russian-origin nuclear smuggling. The deputy public prosecutor of the Italian city of Como, Romano Dolce, accused Russia of "nuclear smuggling" (including highly enriched uranium, plutonium, and the so-called "red mercury") until the fall of 1993, when he was arrested on a charge of being an accomplice to an international criminal ring involved in shady transactions with counterfeit dollars and bank certificates, as well as weapons, drugs, and even radioactive materials.[11] Russia had evidently nothing to do with that. The first wave of accusations that Russia was unable to stop nuclear smuggling subsided very quickly. Nevertheless, the situation with

MPC&A at Minatom's facilities was, at the time, completely overlooked.

One can only make a guess about objectives of the hyperactive international campaign in the press, on TV, and at scientific conferences, all accusing Russia of the inability to control its nuclear exports. According to one of the versions, the matter in point was a collision of economic interests and, in particular, the desire of some large Western uranium companies to undermine the reliability of highly enriched uranium export control in Russia in order to prevent a Russian company, *Tekhsnabexport*, from entering the international uranium market and selling its uranium at very low prices.[12] According to another version, it was an attempt to convince Russia and other New Independent States of the complete deficiency of their national systems of nuclear export control and of nuclear MPC&A, in order to penetrate into this area, which Russia considers to belong to national security.

Finally, these concerns might be genuine to a certain extent and based, if not on smuggling cases, then at least on statements made by specific Russian "entrepreneurs" from quasi-governmental companies; for example, by the Cheteck company president, Mr. Dmitriyev.[13] This concern appears to have been partly brought about by the situation where all Russian governmental institutions were going through a grave crisis and a number of Minatom structures were very near to economic collapse: salaries were not paid, and a number of key facilities had almost gone on strike.[14] The austere situation provoked employees who worked at facilities dealing with radioactive materials to steal those materials. It was not accidental that 1992 turned out to be the year when, at Minatom and Goskomoboronprom, not only did enterprises experience deficits of fissile materials and ionizing sources of radiation, but also the thefts of such materials were revealed.

The second wave of the international media campaign aimed at branding Russia as a source of "nuclear smuggling" was in the summer of 1994, when three cases of alleged nuclear smuggling were revealed in Germany.[15] The Munich case, which was the last one of note, became the climactic event for those who considered Russia to be the key source of nuclear smuggling in the world. Nevertheless, hardly two weeks had passed since the scandalous arrest, when it was said that the Russian origin of the plutonium was not proved, in the best case, or was invented by German special services, in the worst one.[16] The second wave regarding nuclear leakage gradually abated, and today, according to the Russian leadership, "serious experts of foreign special services have reported to officials that nuclear security in Russia is at an appropriate level. . . . There are no grounds to be concerned with the possibility of radioactive materials smuggling."[17]

Any efforts to exercise political pressure on Russia, especially the pressure applied in August of 1994, detracted from those who sincerely wanted Russia to have effective export controls. Discrepancies between the accusations of Russia and the facts gave grounds for Russian officials to deny fully the possibility of nuclear thefts.[18] First, Russia had to convince the world community that it is a reliable successor of the USSR in matters of physical protection, control, and accounting of fissile materials and nuclear warheads. Second, the government implemented measures aimed at thwarting criminal rings inside Russia from attempting to steal and smuggle fissile materials, since nobody ever succeeded in doing so. Third, the leadership of Russia was concerned with the two waves of international campaigns aimed at discrediting Russia's capabilities effectively to control fissile materials that are on its soil (the first wave was in 1991 and 1992, the second was in August 1994). Since there was no convincing proof that fissile materials detained in the West (Italy, Switzerland, Germany) were of Russian origin, the leadership of Russia considered that it had been done for political objectives (to discredit Russia as a reliable successor of the USSR), as well as for economic ones (to prevent Russian state companies from entering the world uranium market). President Yeltsin's former Aide on National Security, Yuri Baturin, pointed out, "In the majority of cases, detained buyers, sellers or middlemen were connected with German special services. I think that it is a special operation, and its aim is to convince the public and leaderships of a number of states that Russia is the leading source of nuclear danger and it is necessary to set up a number of international controlling bodies over its nuclear production."[19]

CLASSIFICATION OF NUCLEAR THEFTS AND COUNTERACTION MEASURES

Nevertheless, it should be admitted that pressuring Russia to give priority to problems of counteracting nuclear smuggling also had certain positive effects. It was primarily the United States and Germany who forced Russia to discuss these problems publicly at the official level, in the press, and at scientific conferences.

There are obvious signs that the Russian leadership, who did not seriously consider problems of nuclear smuggling even in 1992, has been changing its stance toward these problems since the end of 1992 and the beginning of 1993. Reports of Russian law enforcement bodies and federal special services have also contributed to such changes. The reassuring tones of the end of 1991 and the beginning of 1992 grew into warnings at the end of 1993, after the thefts of fuel rods at naval bases near Murmansk, home of the Russian Navy Northern Fleet, in July and November 1993. Reports of this kind have become regular since then. As a result, since 1993 the Russian leadership has considered counteraction of nuclear thefts and smuggling to be a key problem in respect of national security.

The leadership's stance was, to a considerable extent, formulated by Yuri Baturin in the fall of 1994:

If the whole country is in chaos, it is impossible to declare that all industries are in order. That's why I would not stake my head that we have one-hundred-percent reliable control at all nuclear materials storage facilities. The problem of nuclear materials smuggling should be separately discussed because of its potential threat to the world's peace and security. The United States and the world community give priority to prevention of this threat and decreasing the possibility of acquiring of these dangerous materials by rogue states or terrorists. So far, we have not had grounds to say that in the CIS there are organized criminals who are involved in the smuggling of weapons-grade nuclear materials. Nevertheless, there is such a threat. If no measures are taken, there may be a catastrophe.[20]

At the same time, it would be reasonable to rule out the ambiguities in terminology and find out what arouses the most concern of the Russian leadership today and what is likely to arouse this concern in the future. Is it nuclear smuggling? Or is it Russian criminal rings that seek contacts with their likes in Italy, in the Balkan Peninsula, or in the Near East, and ship large amounts of uranium enriched to 90 percent? Such smuggling is very unlikely, and here is why. Let us look into the terms. "Theft" and "smuggling" should be differentiated. By "theft" we mean an act of illegal carrying or driving away of fissile materials or nuclear warheads from the territory of a nuclear facility. "Smuggling" is the illegal export of fissile materials or nuclear warheads from the territory of the Russian Federation to the territory of any other state, including the CIS states.

Thefts of fissile materials can be grouped as follows:

1. According to the *nature of the fissile materials* involved: thefts of low-enriched uranium (LEU); thefts of highly enriched uranium (HEU) and weapons-grade plutonium; thefts of other nuclear materials; and thefts of nuclear warheads;
2. According to the *amounts* of stolen material: insignificant amounts that do not pose a serious danger to national and international security; amounts that are insufficient for the creation of a nuclear device, though presenting danger to national and international security; amounts that are sufficient for the creation of a nuclear device;
3. According to the *type of facility* where theft takes place: Minatom enterprises; defense ministry facilities; enterprises and facilities of the defense industry complex; and other facilities;
4. According to the *aim of thefts*: thefts for terrorist (group or individual) purposes; thefts for personal profit;
5. According to the *outcome*: prevented thefts (criminals are detained and the stolen material is recovered); unprevented thefts (criminals are not arrested, the stolen material is not found).

Since the dissolution of the Soviet Union in December of 1991, the total number of thefts of fissile materials in Russia varies, according to various sources, from 19 to 31 cases.[21] Approximately 95 percent of all cases are thefts of low-enriched uranium. About 60 percent of all thefts were committed at Minatom facilities (according to the data, 19 thefts had been committed at Minatom facilities before January 1, 1995).

According to Alexei Pushkarenko, a Federal Security Service high-ranking official:

> There have been thefts, but not of weapons-grade plutonium. In 1993 and 1994 the bodies of the Federal Counterintelligence Service have worked out 27 cases along these lines, and the Ministry of Internal Affairs worked cases somewhere in the order of 100. However, scandals (both at home and abroad) flare up on account of fissionable materials generally, including isotope products for medicine, construction, and so on. The Germans include even rare earth metals in the list of radioactive materials to be detained.[22]

Furthermore, according to Yevgeny Maslin, then head of Defense Ministry's 12th Directorate (nuclear weapons): "Not a single nuclear warhead has been stolen in Russia, and not a single nuclear warhead has been lost."[23]

According to official data, there were two cases of LEU thefts in 1995. No thefts of weapons-grade materials were detected.[24] At the same time, various institutions describe the situation differently. Thus the State Customs Committee, which has been supervising nuclear smuggling issues only since 1995 (before it had been domain of the Federal Frontier Service), is very skeptical about its ability to prevent nuclear thefts. A State Customs Committee high-ranking official believes that "it is easy to name heavy water just water in a license, while we have very limited capabilities to detect a lie."[25] Nevertheless, in 1995, Russian customs officials detained radioactive material that was legally exported, but its enrichment degree turned out to be higher than the one indicated in the license. The criminals have been arrested, and the case is being investigated.

There have been 12 thefts of ionizing emission sources (isotopes of cesium, iridium, and cobalt) at enterprises of the defense industry. Not a single theft was committed by terrorists. It is supposed, moreover, that all unprevented thefts were committed in order to profit by selling nuclear materials either in Russia or in ex-Soviet republics.

One cannot be sure about the ratio of prevented to unprevented thefts because there is no effective nuclear materials control and accounting system. Thus, a theft of heat-extracting assemblies in Severomorsk, Murmansk, in November 1993 could have remained undetected for another few years if there had not been obvious traces of burglary on the storage door:

> Another problem is the method of examining for the presence of, for example, the heat-extracting assemblies. That is usually restricted to examination of the integrity of the seal. What is a plastic seal? It would take me about seven minutes to take it off and affix it again. Nine

tenths of the containers with heat-extracting assemblies were last checked during loading at the plant. Approximately once in two days the person in charge of the storage checks the safety of the containers by eye: he lifts the tarpaulin to see whether there are footprints or anything is scattered around. In other words, except by accident, the theft in Murmansk might have been discovered in ten, maybe more, years.[26]

According to the official point of view, all thefts of fissile materials should be classified as prevented. As far as we know, there are a few thefts that remain undetected. All told, nineteen Russian citizens were convicted of thefts of fissile materials. Sixteen cases of such thefts have been investigated.

CAUSES OF NUCLEAR THEFTS

Specialists from the law enforcement bodies have named six causes of nuclear thefts. The first is poor physical protection: insufficient number of ditches; absence or shortage of detectors; poor lighting conditions; insufficient safeguards; and relatively unrestricted movement in and around access to the facility. The technical means of MPC&A remain at 1980 levels, when the threat of nuclear terrorism and nuclear smuggling was minimal. Current technical means of MPC&A have to be upgraded in the shortest possible time at practically all nuclear facilities. Certain drawbacks make thefts of fissile materials possible, if they are known to thieves and the theft is well planned, though it is practically impossible to steal nuclear warheads. The current system of fissile materials control and accounting does not guarantee immediate detection of a theft. The present system of customs control makes it possible to smuggle small as well as large amounts of fissile materials, especially into or through former USSR territories—primarily the Baltic and Transcaucasian states.

Second, the acute shortage of funds allotted for MPC&A specifically aimed at counteracting thefts of fissile materials remains a significant problem. Furthermore, funds allotted for departmental efforts are insufficient. U.S. aid (the Nunn-Lugar Cooperative Threat Reduction Program) sufficed to equip only a few Russian enterprises with modern instruments (for example, portal monitors). Without large-scale Western aid, Russia will not be able to improve MPC&A at Minatom and Defense Ministry facilities, except when U.S. specialists are denied access to secret facilities for security considerations. Without large-scale Western aid, it will be impossible to equip Russian Customs with necessary equipment.

Third, a problem area is the low wages of, and frequently the lack of payment to, MPC&A personnel. As Viktor Murogov, then Director of the Institute of Physics and Power Engineering and currently IAEA Deputy Head, stated:

Sergey Stepashin [then director of Federal Security Service] visited our institute, and we demonstrated our security system and nuclear material protection. He carefully studied it and then reported to the State Duma that our system is good and reliable and that nothing can be stolen from our facility. As a result, the Duma decided that we did not need further funds to enhance security since everything is so good. Following this logic, it would have been better if Stepashin had said that there was complete disorganization at the institute. Indeed, according to accepted norms, everything is "good and reliable" at our institute. However, we understand that these norms were adopted ten years ago. We know the drawbacks and know how to improve this system so that it can work at its potential. For example, we know how many more guards we need. We agree on this. They also agree. And then they add: "Give us seven billion rubles for housing and we will provide you with security protection. We have to recall guards from Kamchatka, they will retire, and you will build houses for them." And such problems we have all the time. Of course, we cannot resolve the security problem in this way.[27]

Fourth, not all facilities have special railway tracks. Public roads are sometimes used for transportation.

Fifth, there is a shortage of reliable containers. AT-400-type containers are needed. In other cases there is either no protection of containers against assaults (in and under fire) or no protection for guards.

Sixth, the lack of interagency coordination is still a problem. There is no mechanism for interagency coordination to counteract thefts and smuggling of fissile materials. The Nuclear Weapons Commission in the Prime Minister's administration does not handle such problems. The Russian Security Council interagency commissions do not coordinate such activities since they only collect and prepare general analytical data. Neither Minatom nor the Defense Ministry have an efficient model of counteracting thefts of fissile materials and warheads, although the situation in the Defense Ministry (the 12th Department) is very favorable for resolving these problems. Gosatomnadzor is partly passive and partly isolated from the interplay between the controlling departments. The Defense Ministry manages its oversight independently. The law enforcement bodies, primarily the Federal Security Service (the Directorate for Counterintelligence Support of Strategic Facilities) and the Interior Ministry (IM) (for example, operations at the Chepetsk mechanical plant), have been contributing much in this direction. Nevertheless, their activities lack coordination—exchange of fire between FSS and IM officials while a seller of LEU was being detained in Moscow in June 1995 serves as a shining example of the complete absence of interagency coordination.

TYPICAL CASES

The following cases of nuclear thefts have been confirmed and may be considered to be typical.[28]

The Smirnov Case

After graduating from the Moscow Chemistry and Technology Institute, Smirnov worked as an engineer, a junior researcher, a foreman, and a techniciane in the Eko-Luch scientific-manufacturing association (Podolsk) workshop just before he committed the crime. He had good knowledge of the technological process of radioactive raw materials processing and a great deal more. The investigation discovered that Smirnov took advantage of flaws in the accounting of raw materials and processed products, whose weight increases by 23 percent after calcification. The guards' "leniency" also played into his hands. Each time he stole 50 to 70 grams of technological surplus, accumulating more than 1.5 kilograms of uranium-235 in a few trips, which he hoped to sell at a profit. Smirnov also stole three containers for radioactive materials storage.[29]

The Yatsevich Case

Special product storeman Yatsevich, who worked in workshop No. 103 at the All-Russian Scientific Research Institute of Engineering Physics (Chelyabinsk-70), colluded with engineer Shelomentsev, who worked in the same workshop, and stole a half-finished product made from natural uranium-238 weighing 5.5 kilograms. Yatsevich also stole other valuable materials. Subsequently, investigators discovered an interesting detail: after inventory, Yatsevich had never reported a surplus or deficit of materials he was in charge of. Apart from uranium, he had stolen 151 grams of platinum, 13.5 kilograms of titanium, and 49.5 kilograms of tantalum. The explanation turned out to be very simple: the so-called routine monitoring was the main form of MPC&A, which gave Yatsevich the opportunity to steal the fissile materials.[30]

The Vasin Case

An unemployed worker, Vasin, was detained in Arzamas-16 with 5.1 kilograms of uranium-238. He was attempting to sell the uranium in Ukraine through various intermediaries, but failed. When the uranium's composition was examined, it turned out that it was of local origin, from the All-Russian Scientific Research Institute of Power Engineering Physics. Unfortunately, the investigation failed to detect who stole the nuclear material, when, and under what conditions.[31]

Further Cases

- Almost three kilos of HEU (more than 90 percent enrichment) were detained in the Czech Republic on December 14, 1994. However, the "Russian connection" has yet to be confirmed.
- In May 1993, a container full of beryllium was delivered to Vilnius from Ekaterinburg via Obninsk and Moscow. It is highly likely that

there were about 150 grams or more of uranium-235 also within the container.[32] This particular case contains more questions than answers; however, even if there were no HEU in the container, it is worrisome that beryllium, which is a dual-use material, could be illegally exported from Russia by the ton.

- Six grams of weapons-grade plutonium-239 mixed with 50 grams of metallic alloy were detained in Tengen, Germany, on May 10, 1994. The plutonium might be of Russian origin; however, a Russian connection in that case has not been established.
- A seller of LEU was arrested in Moscow June 7, 1995, while a Federal Security Service official was handing him over $600,000 for two kilograms of uranium.[33] According to some reports, however, he may have been a seller of nonradioactive materials, and there may have been a deliberate information leakage to the media in order to confuse his accomplices, who have not yet been detained. This case is still being investigated.

One of the numerous questions raised by the last case is whether a "nuclear mafia" exists. If not, should we expect one to emerge and assume the shape of the international drug mafia that spreads its tentacles all over the world, from Colombia and Mexico to Azerbaijan and Georgia? Such prospects, added to fissile materials, would be truly daunting.

Regarding nuclear smuggling, General Alexey Pushkarenko, of the Federal Security Service Office (FSB), said:

> At the talks with our German colleagues we said that the myth about the existence of a nuclear materials "black market" in Germany was created by the noise raised in the German press. The prices named in publications on another seizure of nuclear materials varied from $60,000 to $80,000 per kilo. This is what might initiate the flow of criminal nuclear materials into Germany. It appears that the Germans have created a problem for themselves. What is dangerous here is that the noise may provoke an avalanche-like supply of such materials to Germany and no special services will be able to get the situation under control.[34]

At the same time, there is no unanimous opinion about the existence or nonexistence of an organized "nuclear and missile" criminal community when it comes to specific groups and individuals with the intentions (and the possibilities) to obtain nuclear materials and even nuclear warheads for blackmail and terrorist purposes. Yevgeny Maslin, then Head of the Defense Ministry 12th Directorate (which is in charge of nuclear weapons), believes that the scenarios now being staged in Hollywood may take place in Russia in the near future:

> What is theoretically possible [at Defense nuclear facilities] and what we always should be ready for is robbery of railway cars transporting nuclear warheads. But why? For [Chechen leader] General Dudayev to be able to threaten all of us with "his own nuclear weapon?" Though it

is a very powerful weapon for blackmail, it is technically impossible to use such a warhead since the possibility of nuclear radiation is very high. Not only pro-Dudayev forces may try to obtain a nuclear warhead. I would repeat that we do not rule out such a possibility and we take it into consideration in our everyday routine, in improving the criteria for choosing and training people, and in introducing a new generation of code-blocking devices. We have to pay attention to the problems of counteracting nuclear smuggling since there were a few thefts of fissile nuclear materials at Minatom facilities and in the North Fleet. Although all checks have shown that it is impossible to make a nuclear bomb out of those materials, the thefts still took place and we have to continue. A decision was made to improve the facilities and transportation security as well as in order to increase appropriate financing. In the units under my control, thousands of well-trained personnel are on guard daily to ensure against nuclear smuggling and terrorism.[35]

Thus it can be assumed that there has been no reliable data on international, Russian, or mixed criminal rings that are professionally involved in fissile materials smuggling from Russia. No states or organizations of terrorist nature that might be potential buyers of Russian-origin fissile materials have demonstrated their interest in such materials, except for India's interest in beryllium and Iran's interest in heavy water. The lack of a large-scale demand for Russian fissile materials makes smuggling operations unprofitable and also highly risky to organized criminal rings, while the smuggling of rare and rare earth metals, as well as drugs, brings high profits and relatively low risks. Therefore, statements attesting to the existence of such a demand are, in a word, groundless. At the same time, demand for "nuclear brains" and "nuclear technologies" (know-how) will be increasing, though such "supply" is very limited and under complete and effective control.

Thus far, thefts of proliferation concern have been rare. It should be taken into consideration that the majority of data regarding such cases is classified as secret and that what appears in the press is either inauthentic or unchecked, or deliberate (which means doubtful), leakage.

THE SHORT-TERM THREATS AND PREVENTIVE MEASURES

At present we do not have a complete knowledge of the nuclear security level at Minatom and Defense Ministry Facilities. Nevertheless, it follows from a preliminary acquaintance with the situation that risks regarding the possibility of nuclear thefts in Russia will be increasing if not today, then at the end of the 1990s. According to Alexander Mytsikov, who is assistant to the General Public Prosecutor of Russia and knowledgeable about dozens of nuclear theft cases and an even bigger number of cases of violations of norms and nuclear safety and security requirements at Minatom's facilities, "the security level at some facilities has even decreased for the last years."[36]

One of the key problems in this connection is the absence of civilian independent control over military facilities where nuclear materials are concentrated. Conflicting opinions are given during discussions on this subject. On the one hand, there is the idea of single control and supervision by the Defense Ministry, in the belief that this is the only organization able, in these turbulent times, to prevent the leakage of Russian military-use nuclear materials abroad. This was President Yeltsin's viewpoint when, in July 1995, he signed an order that deprived Gosatomnadzor of control functions at defense ministry facilities.

There is another viewpoint, however. Nikolai Filonov, a former commander of a nuclear maintenance unit, says that "nuclear maintenance units are integrated not only into the Russian Defense Ministry, but into the whole society. That is why current processes cannot but affect their functioning, and it is imprudent to claim that there are no ground for concerns about the safety and reliability of nuclear weapons. Such claims can be considered as an attempt to conceal the true state of affairs."[37]

Addressing those who struggle for the limitation of Gosatomnadzor to those functions that the Nuclear Regulatory Commission (NRC) performs in the United States, he notes:

> But are situations in the United States and Russia equal? Are the U.S. officers who operate nuclear warheads unpaid for months (I do not speak about other kinds of allowances) and do they have to sell empty bottles and pick up mushrooms in the woods and hills in order to feed their wives and children? Have there been any cases in the United States when people who repair nuclear-powered vessels were driven to despair because they were unpaid for months and were sued for a threat of terrorist act? Isn't it worrisome that officers who refused to serve on board the ships (and who finally left ships) and in combatant units are sent to continue their service in a number of nuclear maintenance units of the Armed Forces? All 100 percent of the thefts of radioactive materials (even those not intended for the creation of a nuclear charge) have been committed by insiders, who directly worked with those materials. This phenomenon is well illustrated by the case where three nuclear heat-extracting assemblies were stolen in the North Fleet.[38]

Alexander Kanygin, who worked as an official in the Yaroslavl regional office of Gosatomnadzor and who has worked in Gosatomnadzor for 27 years, says that "recently there are more telephone calls from GAI (civilian traffic police) posts: 'We have stopped a suspicious military column with the "Radiation danger!" sign, but the military do not show us any documents, they refuse to say what and where they are driving allegedly because it is "top secret, examination is prohibited".'" According to Kanygin, "military units treat the storage and use of nuclear materials very poorly in comparison with facilities under Gosatomnadzor's control. The personnel is poorly trained. The impact of nuclear materials on people and environment is not analyzed. Guarding of secret facilities is unreliable."[39]

To all appearances, it is the absence of information transparency and the impossibility of carrying out elementary civilian control at the majority of dangerous nuclear facilities that hold real danger. It is very unlikely that Gosatomnadzor's control would undermine the security of the nuclear-weapons complex of Russia. But the ban on making public any information related to serious attempts at nuclear thefts from military facilities can result in a distorted idea about the situation and makes it impossible promptly to detect the weakest links through which nuclear materials can disappear from a facility or enterprise with the help of a well-organized group, including insiders of this facility or enterprise.

It is obvious that thefts can be prevented through an effective system of nuclear materials control and accounting (SNMC&A). According to Alexander Rumyantsev from the Kurchatov Institute in Moscow:

> as long as the nuclear fuel cycle exists, there will be inevitable operations loss of nuclear materials (NM) during the phases of their processing and use. Figures from a plutonium-processing reactor will always exceed figures on plutonium output from a reprocessing plant. The quantity of NM supplied by a producing plant to a nuclear power plant (NPP) will always be less than the real quantity that determines power production. It is a well-known law of mankind and of the production this mankind created, it is called the "difference in data of a sender and receiver," or just "difference in data of a seller and buyer." This law has not only been confirmed by Russian experience. Improvement of measuring methods results in a change of data on real quantities of NM. It is important to find out possible mistakes in measuring and to seek ways to minimize them, as well as to find reasonable and valid explanations for those differences [in data] that have already been discovered.[40]

The current SNMC&A does not make it possible to do this. Thus, the current system in Russia objectively contributes to the concealment of the real causes for NM "deviations" that are ascribed to legal operations and losses accruing to routine and inevitable errors inherent in the technological means designed to monitor, control, and account for nuclear materials and technologies.

There has been, nevertheless, some modest progress in the process of improvements of the SNMC&A. For example, the cooperation between the Kurchatov Institute in Moscow and Gosatomnadzor made it possible to carry out in January 1996 a physical inventory (PI), which was in fact the first one in Russia's recent history, at one of the installations at the Kurchatov Institute. Gosatomnadzor inspectors made selective measurements of nuclear materials and statistically processed the available bulk of nuclear materials that contained uranium with 96-percent enrichment. The PI was conducted in the presence of inspectors from the USNRC. The PI results confirmed statements of the Kurchatov Institute's staff and were acknowledged positive.

It is difficult, however, to overestimate the scope of the task of creating a SNMC&A of NM and radioactive substances in Russia. According to some estimates, the number of material balance arrears at Russian nuclear installations may reach 1500 to 2000. Procedures for beginning inventory (BI) and physical inventory (PI) should be worked out for each material balance area. Practically the majority of material balance areas should be equipped with devices for prompt measuring of NM and computerized SC&As. Priorities are to be established in strengthening nuclear installations with upgraded SC&A. Personnel at nuclear installations should be trained to conduct BI and PI. Sizes and contents of registration and accounting documents are to be uniformly established and standardized, thereby expediting the prompt notification of the state organs with data on available NM quantities and their locations.

A long-range objective is the creation of a center for processing SNMC&A information. The creation of a state system of nuclear materials control and accounting and a state system of radioactive substances and radioactive wastes control and accounting, as well as appointing bodies that will conduct this control and accounting, constitute a no less difficult objective. Nuclear materials are currently at the disposal of several Russian ministries and agencies, including Minatom. Whether the SNMC&A will become a nonagency state system that will receive information directly from nuclear installations, or the bureaucratic approach will win and the state system will become just a consumer of departmental SC&A, only the future will show.

THE THREAT OF NUCLEAR THEFTS AND EXPORTS CONTROL

As we have pointed out before, the problem of nuclear thefts has very little to do with the problem of export control system improvements as one facet of the overall nonproliferation effort.

First of all, though nuclear materials are stolen primarily by specific workers of nuclear facilities for profit, these workers lack the ability to sell the goods abroad. There is no evidence that organized criminal rings are interested in nuclear smuggling, although periodic assertions appear from, as a rule, German sources, that "an (international) nuclear mafia exists. It involves Germans, Bulgarians, Austrians and Russians, people from the Near and Middle East countries, (primarily) former Soviet top officials who use their old contacts for the crime."[41] Nothing has been heard of license forgery or attempts by commercial firms to export Russian-origin nuclear materials in significant quantities. There have been cases where nuclear exports were detained by customs, but they are not numerous.

Secondly, there are no buyers. Only in some cases have foreign diplomats (for example, Nam Ge Uk, an official from the North Korean embassy) "persuaded" Russian missile and nuclear scientists to work in their countries.[42] Nevertheless, nothing has been reported on attempts of representatives from "rogue states" to contact Russian workers from nuclear facilities or Russian companies. At the same time, one cannot be one-hundred-percent sure that representatives from some Near and Middle East countries have not been probing into the possibilities of strategic materials illicit export at some Russian nuclear fuel cycle facilities.

Thirdly, criminals have been gradually, but surely, shifting their interest in nuclear materials from purely commercial profit to the use of these materials for murdering rivals or for nuclear blackmail or terrorism. For example, in 1992, the Russian Ministry of Security warned the public that the threat of nuclear sabotage was not only a scenario for the Hollywood movies. Representatives of the ministry wrote in an article published in a governmental daily in 1990 to 1992: "The directors of Kursk, Smolensk, and Rostov NPPs received letters with threats to explode or to seize the plants." Then chemical weapons came on the scene. In 1995, Ivan Kivelidi, a leading Russian businessman and head of the Roundtable of Russian Business and of Rosbusinessbank, was killed in Moscow in his office. Later, Governor Dmitry Ayatskov of Saratov Oblast stated that a top secret modern chemical substance from Shikhany—a major storage facility of chemical weapons in Russia—was used by killers (most probably, a phosphororganic or amedefira-phosphoro-acidic substance). His sensational statement was not denied by the investigators, who had just concluded their investigation. Although Stanislav Nesterov, head of the local administration of Shikhany said, "This is a modern CW with a secret formula. I do not know of any confirmed cases of selling it at or near the NII Orgsintez Institute," investigation has been delayed "for reasons of national security." Furthermore, one of the Aum leaders on trial in Tokyo stated that the sect obtained sarin gas special technologies in Russia, with the direct assistance of the former Secretary of the National Security Council, Mr. Lobov. However, Russian law enforcement agents, who have carried out their own investigation, have never confirmed those statements.

"Caucasian terrorism" has become threat number one for federal authorities. Numerous e-mail requests and descriptions of explosives and CW production were registered as emanating from Chechnya addresses as well as from the Caucasian Diaspora in the Middle East. On November 21, 1995, Chechen terrorist Shamil Bassaev planted a container with radioactive cesium-137 in Izmailovo Park in Moscow. The only practical, but very efficient, purpose of putting that source of low radiation in Moscow was to threaten the Russian public, a public conversant with the Chernobyl disaster. Finally, Chechen terrorist leader Bassaev switched from radioactive threats to nuclear ones: "We have no nuclear weapons in Chechnya. But in 1993 I was offered the opportunity to buy a nuclear explosive for $1,500,000."

The Caucasus region has also produced such financially influential and politically ambitious ethnic-criminal mafias as the Ingushetian, Abkhazian, and Kurdish ones. In some of the areas, these groups can freely transfer drugs, arms, and strategic raw materials. Anyone interested in smuggling issues should pay attention to Nazran International Airport. Nazran is a small town and capital of Republic of Ingushetia, which is part of Russia but has no declared border with its neighbor Chechnya. Nazran has official duty-free status and is a center of criminal activities in the region. From Nazran International, there are regular and charter flights to Turkey, Greece, and other states of the Mediterranean and the Middle East. At the airport checkpoints, there is practically no control over transferred goods, and this has already attracted attention by criminal groups allegedly associated with the "international mafia"—in particular in reference to charter flights from Nazran to Antalya in Turkey and Nazran to Athens.

The *Komsomolets* nuclear submarine, buried after the accident of April 7, 1989, at a 1,685-meter depth in the Norwegian Sea, housing two nuclear warheads (total 6 kg Pu-239 and 116 kg enriched uranium), has also become a subject of concern. As one expert put it, "terrorists will need a few hours to take one warhead, about one day to take the second one. Unauthorized activities in this area have recently been detected."

Russian law enforcement agencies have become increasingly concerned about the intensive and developing ties between ethnic terrorist groups and organized crime in Russia, on the one hand, and the international criminal community, on the other. Currently, most of the international cooperation involving the Russian mafias is directed at financial operations, drug trafficking, and illegal conventional arms sales. As a result, the Russian criminal community has established close ties with Italian, Colombian, and Arab criminal and clandestine groups. The roots of this illegal trade connect Badakhshan in Tajikistan, Abkhazia, Chechnya, and Ingushetia with Cali, Antigua, Peshawar, Yemen, Laos, and Estonia.

As General Valynkin, head of the 12th Main Directorate (nuclear weapons) of the Russian Defense Ministry, has stated, "We cannot exclude the possibility of unauthorized access [by individual terrorists and terrorist groups] to Russian nuclear warheads in storage or in transit in the future." He believes "it could lead to a nationwide crisis and would be impossible to prevent given the instruments we [at the Defense Ministry and Russian Government] now have." Moscow Mayor Yuri Luzhkov has said that "he is concerned about possible accidents and even sabotage at the nuclear facilities in Moscow. As the former FSB Director Gen. Barsukov believed, sabotage attempts against NPPs, other nuclear facilities, and CW facilities, as well as attempts to seize WMD [currently in Russia] are quite possible."

In other words, in the mid-1990s, Russia has become one of the most vulnerable areas of the world, both subject and object of WMD threats.

Therefore, the key question in this regard is: What should be done to avoid such a catastrophe, and, consequently, what has been done already by the Russian government, what efforts have succeeded, and what efforts have failed?

According to the law on terrorism adopted by the State Duma: "Terrorism is qualified as an attempt upon the lives of political and state leaders, the use violence or the threat of violence against citizens or institutions with the aim of destroying the constitutional order, destabilizing state order, and/or threatening the overall security of the state." The law on terrorism does not include any special provisions for combating and preventing terrorism and the measures to prevent it. These situations, in part related to nuclear weapons, are regulated by the draft Law on the Creation, Functioning, Destruction and Security of Nuclear Weapons, and in particular, by Chapter 3, "The State management and regulations of activities in the area of security of nuclear weapons" (Articles 17 to 20), and Chapter 5, "Regulations of relations in cases of accidents with nuclear weapons and at the nuclear defense facilities" (Articles 24 to 26).

The Ministry of Defense has the following major concerns related to the NBC (nuclear, biological, chemical) terrorism threat: the possibility of nuclear accident by "technological terrorists"; attack by a terrorist group with the aim of seizing fissile materials of category No. 1, which may assist in the construction of nuclear device(s) by terrorists; and operations by criminals from non-Russian CIS countries who worked for the Soviet Ministry of Defense Nuclear-Technical Forces in the 1980s and know characteristics of the facilities, transportation details, and ways of accessing nuclear warheads.

As results of analysis made at the Center for Policy Studies in Russia (PIR) in 1996 and 1997 show, the most vulnerable points related to fissile materials at the Minatom and Ministry of Defense storage facilities as well as to nuclear warheads are insufficient and, in some places, nonexistent physical protection; secure transportation means; and a lack of a safeguards culture at the closed cities (nuclear facilities such Arzamas-16).

As for the physical protection at Minatom facilities, despite Russian-U.S. cooperation, 70 percent of all such installations are in use longer than their instructions demand and should be changed or upgraded, and 20 percent are in use for periods two to three times longer than their instructions demand and should be dismantled immediately. It is now impossible to maintain their capabilities. The completely outdated equipment includes communications and alarm systems at the facilities. Most of the checkpoints still have no metal and/or nuclear and/or explosive detectors. As First Deputy Minister of Minatom Lev Ryabev put it:

> PP of the majority of the facilities does not meet requirements of the regulations which have entered in force in Russia in recent years, and the PP at nuclear installations and materials is not sufficient against possible terrorist attacks. The PP at military nuclear facilities does not pre-

vent potential accidents with explosion of nuclear materials and radioactive contamination of the territories of up to 100 km from the facility.

Thousands of individuals fired from the facilities and currently unemployed still have their permission passes to enter the facility. Private companies are located in the territories of secret nuclear facilities and research institutes, and there is no real control over their activities and personnel.

Transportation has become critical problem mostly for the Ministry of Defense in the process of continuing the dismantlement of nuclear warheads. In Russia, where nuclear warheads are traditionally transported on land only, there is lack of special armored fire trucks. Most of the transport railcars are operating with expired dates. By the year 2000, the Ministry of Defense is expected to have only 362 railcars. The total number of railcars produced for 1993–97 is 38, and the total destroyed because of expired dates, 223. Railroads for NW transportation are also a problem: they were never modernized before, and in every facility there are about 10 to 12 km of such railroads.

In late 1996, social tensions increased in the Ministry of Defense facilities, and in Minatom-operated closed cities and NPPs in the summer of 1997. Results of an inspection by the Central Inspectorate concluded that state supervision over the security of nuclear weapons in one of the facilities of the 12th Main Directorate of the Defense Ministry last fall demonstrated that officers and soldiers were paid no salary for three months and received no compensation for food during eight months. The military units that worked with nuclear warheads suffered from starvation. There were even fainting fits because of starvation. Officers had no special slippers for work in the special area with nuclear warheads—it is prohibited to work there in ordinary footwear, and there were no funds for slippers, so the officers who were paid nothing were taking money from their wives' salaries to buy slippers.

In June 1997, engineers from the Smolensk NPP organized a march to the Moscow White House and demanded a salary increase, as well as funds for safety and security improvements at the plant. Their action attracted public attention, was supported by specialists from other NPPs, and met with sympathy by numerous Minatom-related research institutes.

To prevent the threat of the NBC, particularly nuclear terrorism, Russia should implement a number of both immediate and long-term measures. These include allocation of more funds for improvement of physical protection of fissile materials and warheads as well as their transportation for fiscal year 2000; the development of national data banks; the improvement of Materials, Protection, Control and Accounting (MPC&A) of fissile materials; the improvement of the safety culture in facilities and enterprises dealing with the NBC weapons, components, and technologies; the enforcement of intelligence activities against terrorist groups; the identification and limitation of sources of funds for terrorist groups when and where possible; increasing consultations and data exchange among the states of the international community; increasing interagency coordination, in particular in the area of data exchange, such as the recently founded Interagency Antiterrorism Commission; and the training of special anti-NBC-terrorism groups.

The latter represents one of the most critical aspects of preventing the threat. The structure that is responsible for anti-nuclear-terrorism activities has the name Vympel, also known as the Directorate V of the Federal Security Service (FSB). In August 1997, Vympel organized a simulation drill with the code name Atom-97. It was a training exercise designed to prevent potential terrorist attack at the Kola NPP and at the atomic icebreaker *Siberia* (both located in the Russian northwest). In its simulation of sabotage against the NPP, the "terrorists" managed to conquer it for some time, but were not able to explode it or create any significant radioactive danger. In the *Siberia* exercise, "terrorists" attacked and occupied the *Siberia* and took hostages. They were attacked from the surface by the Murmansk surface fleet, by the Vympel paratroopers by air, and from under the sea by the Vympel military scuba divers. As General Dmitry Gerasimov of the FSB concluded, "Unfortunately, the threat of nuclear sabotage in Murmansk Oblast [region] still exists."

Unfortunately, it should be admitted that fairly efficient Russian laws that aim at control over sensitive, especially nuclear, exports would prove helpless against smugglers who attempt to export nuclear materials abroad. Indeed, nuclear materials are formally exported on the basis of licenses from the Ministry of Trade with Minatom approval. Only a very limited number of enterprises, all of which are well known, have access to these licenses. It is very difficult to conjecture about motives in illicit nuclear export. "'Shady' dealers, half-criminals, and criminals can hardly count on obtaining those licenses, since the times of anarchy that ruled in the end 1991 and through the beginning 1993, when it was possible to obtain documents for export of even such a mythical product as red mercury."[43] It is even more difficult to track illicit (or, more precisely, secret) nuclear exports to, for example, the so-called "rogue countries," which can be made at the state level, bypassing Russian and international laws. Such speculations err on the side of cheap press sensationalism.

In other words, the export control regime for nonproliferation purposes that has formed in Russia practically rules out illicit nuclear export through its legislation mechanisms and practical regulation. At the same time, however, the export control system appears to have a weak link, though it is a crucial one, which is almost the only one vulnerable place in the "outer export control circle." It is customs services and the state borders.

From the standpoint of nonproliferation and the counteraction of potential nuclear smuggling, the most acute problem facing the Russian export control system is the technical equipment at the "outer control circle" of its final frontier: customs and their management of the national borders. It is evident that this is a costly matter. At the same time, flaws in customs control make it possible for nuclear materials, though in small quantities, to leak outside the Russian Federation to, for example, the New Independent States, and it will be more difficult to monitor their movements from there. Russian State Customs Committee officials confidentially admit that they cannot counteract potential theft of radioactive substances, including weapons-grade materials, primarily for technical reasons. Apart from the lack of technical equipment, customs is affected by two other factors: logistical constraints (which gives customs officers no time to check correspondence of papers—correspondence between a product mentioned in a license and a product that is in fact exported from the country) and bribe-taking. Could one guarantee that customs services will be able efficiently to prevent attempts (if there are any) to export radioactive materials abroad in the short term? This is unlikely. At the same time, it should be admitted that this is not only Russia's problem. While Germany, the United States, and a number of other states have established effective customs control over sensitive exports, a number of other states with significant inventories of NM cannot provide safeguards against illicit exports.

Thus it can be assumed that, provided safeguards in the "outer circle" cannot be much counted on, special attention should be paid to the "inner circle," in other words, to effective and full-scale physical protection, control, and accounting of nuclear materials and warheads. Here moves are necessary and possible. Since MPC&A was introduced at the Institute of Physics and Power Engineering (IPPE) Obninsk and in the Russian Scientific Center of the Kurchatov Institute, even the theoretical possibility (in case of IPPE) of smuggling has been practically ruled out.

CONCLUSION

For a long time, Russian officials have denied that there are insufficient levels of nuclear security of Minatom or Ministry of Defense-operated nuclear installations. Moreover, they insist that the "antismuggling campaign" was orchestrated by the U.S. and German intelligence services and espoused a purely economic objective by unfavorably portraying Russian nuclear exporting state companies. It was not until April 1996 that Russia, for the first time, officially recognized that the problem of nuclear smuggling—in other words, the possibility of unauthorized access to nuclear installations—was not a fiction created by Russia's purported enemies, but was a very real problem for the Russian political and military leadership.

Although it is partly correct that some elements of the two "antismuggling campaigns" in the West in 1992 and in 1994 were based on purely political objectives and not upon sound and credible evidence, it would have been absolutely wrong to declare that all the threats of nuclear leakage from Russia were artificial and unrealistic. In 1995, *Yaderny Kontrol* editors disclosed two instances of nuclear materials thefts from the North Fleet, both involving enriched uranium (one case involved uranium enriched to 36 percent). Subsequently, governmental officials acted in three different directions. First, they invested modest funds toward improving the MPC&A climate in the North Fleet. Second, they requested U.S. assistance, resulting in the creation of a fully modern MPC&A system at two storage facilities. Third, Russian officials prohibited the dissemination of all information related to cases of nuclear smuggling, explaining that it was done "in interests of national security." The official prohibition, moreover, was prompted specifically by suggestions that organized crime or ethnic terrorists would use detailed information about weak points in the MPC&A system.

Despite all efforts, cases of nuclear leakage continue. Thus, in 1996, at the Tomsk Institute of Nuclear Physics of the Tomsk Polytechnical University, Gosatomnadzor discovered the loss of one fuel assembly with uranium enriched to 90 percent. The material was never recovered. Local experts said recovering the material would be impossible, and the case was closed.

Accurate accounting at the facilities is an even more serious problem for the federal government. In 1997, in Murmansk, nine cases of incorrect data regarding quantities of fissile materials (for instance, fuel rods and spent nuclear fuel) were detected. For example, the recorded amount of fuel rods at the floating bases of Imandra and Lotta was "significantly less" than indicated in the accounting documents. In 1996, as a result of six Gosatomnadzor inspections at the *Mashinostroitelny Zavod* (Machine-Building Plant) at Elektrostal, weight checks of the nuclear materials demonstrated three cases of surplus LEU (total weight 8.4 kg) and three cases of surplus of HEU (total weight 895 g) when compared to the accounting documentation at the facility, which produces nuclear fuel rods and is now in the process of being equipped with a computerized U.S. MPC&A system.

It is clear that, for instance, 145 g of weapons-grade HEU from the Tomsk Institute could be smuggled by criminals with either commercial (which seems less probable) or terrorist purposes. At the same time, it is important to mention that even now, Russian officials mostly continue to divide the problem into two parts. According to interviews with many of officers at the Federal Security Service (FSB), Minatom, and the Ministry of Defense, on the one hand they recognize how significant a problem the threat of nuclear terrorism in Russia is—in particular, after terrorist acts committed by separatist Chechens in 1995 and 1996—and, on the other hand they do not recognize that this problem has its roots in a weakened system of accounting, control, and physical protection of both weapons-grade fissile materials and nuclear warheads. Until these problems are addressed and effectively managed, Russia will continue to pose a proliferation threat to national, regional, and international security.

NOTES

1. Matthias Dembinski, "The Threat of Nuclear Proliferation to Europe," in K. Bailey and Robert Rudney (eds.), *Proliferation and Export Controls* (London: University Press of America, 1993), p. 1.
2. "NIS and Nonproliferation," Seminar sponsored by Program for Nonproliferation Studies of the Monterey Institute of International Studies. Kyev, November 1992.
3. William Potter, "Improving Nuclear Materials Security in the Former Soviet Union," *Arms Control Today* (January-February 1993).
4. Interview with Vladimir Sementsov, head of Economy Ministry's Export Controls Office, by the author, November 1993.
5. Potter, "Improving Nuclear Materials Security in the former Soviet Union."
6. William Potter, "Russia's Nuclear Entrepreneurs," *New York Times* (November 7, 1991), p. A29.
7. Gennady Evstafiev, "Devyat voprosov o yadernom nerasprostranenii," *Yaderny Kontrol*, no. 1 (January 1995), p. 14.
8. Vladimir A. Orlov, "Mechanisms of Export Controls of Nuclear Materials in the Russian Federation and Illicit Nuclear Export," presentation at a conference in Monterey, March 1992.
9. Jan Hoekema in Bailey and Rudney, *op.cit.*, p. 83.
10. Paolo Biondani, "Uranovaya Okhota," *Literaturnaya Gazeta* (November 3, 1992), p. 15.
11. "Criminal Ring Uncovered," *Izvestiya* (October 27, 1994), p. 7.
12. Interview with Viktor Mikhailov, Minister for Atomic Energy of the Russian Federation, by the author, May 1992.
13. Vladimir Dmitryev, President, Chetek Corporation: Conference on Research of Radioactive Pollution. Ottawa, Canada, April 23–24, 1991.
14. *Ibid.*
15. *Rossiyskiye Vesti* (July 28, 1994), p. 2.
16. May 10, 1994, Tengen: one fifth ounce of plutonium, apparently a sample, seized at private home. German businessman arrested. He said he was prepared to sell larger amounts.
17. June 13, 1994, Landshut: trace amount of plutonium, apparently a sample, seized. German businesswoman, five Czech and Slovak men arrested. August 10, 1994, Munich airport: 12 ounces of plutonium seized from flight from Moscow. Two Spaniards, one Colombian arrested as alleged couriers. See also: William C. Potter, "Before the Deluge? Assessing the Threat of Nuclear Leakage from the Post-Soviet States," *Arms Control Today* (October 1995), p. 10.
18. Mark Hibbs, *Bulletin of Atomic Scientists* (November-December 1995), p. 6–7.
19. Yuri Baturin, "Vnutrennikh ugroz bezopasnosti Rossii bolshe chem vneshnikh," *Segodnya* (October 14, 1995), p. 2.
20. *Ibid.*
21. Anton Surikov, "Yaderny Chemodanchik s Troinym Dnom," *Yaderny Kontrol*, no. 8 (August 1995), p. 16; *Yaderny Kontrol*, no. 1 (January 1995), p. 2.
22. *Moskovskiye Novosti*, no. 54 (August 13–20, 1995), p. 20.

23. *Yaderny Kontrol,* no. 9 (September 1995), p. 6.
24. *Yaderny Kontrol,* no. 11 (November 1995), p. 1, 7.
25. An unofficial interview by the author.
26. *Yaderny Kontrol,* no. 2 (February 1995), p. 13.
27. *Yaderny Kontrol,* no. 8 (August 1995), p. 10–11.
28. A list of the most serious cases of nuclear proliferation and nuclear security concern can be found in the article by William Potter, "Before the Deluge," *Arms Control Today* (November 1995), p. 15. It should be noted that *Yaderny Kontrol* published a version of this article with a more detailed description of some cases: William Potter, "Otsenivaya opasnost yadernykh hischeniy iz gosudarstv byvshego Sovetskogo Soyuza," vol. 13, no. 15, p. 11–13.
29. *Yaderny Kontrol,* no. 9 (September 1995), p. 3.
30. *Kommersant-Daily* (October 28, 1994), p. 14.
31. *Moskovskiye Novosti,* no. 58 (October 30–November 6, 1994).
32. *Izvestiya* (October 9, 1993), p. 1
33. *Yaderny Kontrol,* no. 9 (September 1995), p. 3
34. *Yaderny Kontrol,* no. 5 (May 1995), p. 9.
35. *Segodnya* (May 25 1995), p. 6.
36. *Izvestiya* (August 20, 1996), p. 1
37. *Segodnya* (May 25, 1995), p. 6
38. *Ibid.*
39. *Yaderny Kontrol,* no. 5 (May 1995), p. 7.
40. *Yaderny Kontrol,* no. 15 (March 1996), p. 12.
41. *Yaderny Kontrol,* no. 16 (April 1996), p. 12.
42. *US News & World Report* (October 23, 1995).
43. Documents that prove unlimited possibilities of specific enterprises and companies to lobby governmental and even presidential decisions on exports of "red mercury" are fully given in Alexandr Gurov, *Taina krasnoi rtuti* Kommerchesky vestnik (Moscow, 1995).

10

RUSSIA AND THE MISSILE TECHNOLOGY CONTROL REGIME

Alexander Pikayev

TRADITIONAL SOVIET ATTITUDES TOWARD MISSILE PROLIFERATION

Developments before the Missile Technology Control Regime

Until the late 1980s, the Soviet Union did not follow any well-defined policy toward the proliferation of missiles and accompanying technologies. In the late 1950s, Moscow decided to provide the People's Republic of China with various missile hardware and their technologies. Reportedly, in 1956 the USSR sold to Beijing two tactical R-1 missiles and their blueprints, shorter-range R-2 missiles, and R-11FM SLBM. Besides that, Chinese students were able to smuggle blueprints of R-5 and R-12 IRBMs back to China. This transmission of hardware and technologies played an important role in developing the first Chinese DF-1 ballistic missile.[1] There was also evidence that Moscow transferred to the Chinese blueprints of the V-2 missile acquired in occupied Germany after World War II.

The Chinese syndrome, which affected the Kremlin after relations between the USSR and China drastically deteriorated in the early 1960s, forced the Soviet Union to pursue a more restrictive policy toward exporting missiles and, especially, their technologies. After the Chinese case, until the 1990s there was no evidence of missile technology sales. Until the 1970s the Soviet Union halted deliveries of missile hardware as well. However, Moscow later resumed transfers of tactical missiles to its allies and clients. It delivered conventionally armed shorter-range SS-23 ballistic missiles to

Bulgaria, Czechoslovakia, and East Germany. Besides Warsaw Pact states, obsolete tactical Scud and Frog missiles were exported to Third-World clients, particularly to Iraq, North Korea, Yemen, and Afghanistan.

To a certain extent, the relaxed Soviet policy was a reaction to the development of indigenous missile capabilities by Israel, South Korea, Pakistan, Iran, Taiwan, Brazil, Argentina, and South Africa. A need was perceived to balance the progress achieved by the countries of "capitalist orientations" by building missile capabilities in allied nations. Also, the Soviet Union might try to discourage its clients from pursuing their own missile programs, particularly through cooperation with other Third-World states, by providing them with assembled Soviet-made weaponry. If so, this tactic of providing final products without the know-how did not prevent some of the recipients from developing their indigenous missile programs based on Soviet hardware. A manifest example of such a flawed policy is represented by the Iraqi Al Hussein missile, which was developed from Scud technology after the USSR stopped their shipments to Baghdad in 1980 as a result of the Iran-Iraq War.[2] Furthermore, the 1989 Scud deliveries to Afghanistan could be partially explained by the Pakistani nuclear program, which, according to some U.S. officials, in 1986 to 1988 became capable of making its own nuclear explosive devices.[3]

The inability to control the use and reexport of military technologies, including missile hardware, by recipient countries gradually brought the Soviet authorities to an understanding of a need to establish certain policies toward their deliveries. This need was reflected by the establishment of an export control department in the powerful Gosplan economic planning ministry in the 1980s. However, those efforts were not accompanied by an actual restraint in missile exports.

U.S.-Soviet MTCR Discussions: 1987–1990

The Soviet attitude started to change after the G-7[4] decided to establish the Missile Technology Control Regime (MTCR) in April 1987. The regime was directed primarily against Scud exports—the only widely available system in the international market that was able to deliver 500 kilograms at a range of more than 300 kilometers. At the same time, the Reagan administration was mainly concerned by developments in the Third World, where a growing number of countries had gained access to missiles, and three nations—Israel, India, and South Africa—already possessed nuclear weapons technology. A solution to the Indian and, to a lesser extent, South African—and indirectly, even Israeli—case was problematic without cooperation from the Soviet Union. This dilemma forced Washington to initiate a double-track approach toward Moscow: trying to convince it to adopt a more restrictive approach in its missiles exports without involving it in the MTCR as a full-fledged member due to the Cold-War rationale.

In Moscow, the MTCR met with a controversial response as well. On the one hand, since 1987 the Soviet Union had felt quite uncomfortable after Israel developed the Jericho missile, which was capable of hitting targets in the southern and western regions of the USSR.[5] On the other hand, much more advanced nuclear and conventional capabilities against Israel, as well as other missile proliferators, provided Moscow with a reliable feeling of security. Also, there were fears that the regime was aimed against Soviet foreign policy interests and represented an additional COCOM-type tool of depriving Moscow's access to high technology.

In May 1987, the United States approached the Soviet Union with the prospect of joining the MTCR. As a result, discussions took place in London in May 1987. The Ministry of Foreign Affairs prepared an internal memo, which was quite critical of the regime. The memo referred to the fact that potentially important WMD delivery vehicles such as manned aircraft were exempted from the MTCR. It also said that since the regime did not prohibit existing contracts, it in fact endorsed continued U.S.-Israeli strategic cooperation. Thus, the regime seemed useless for dealing with the only threat that existed, at that time, to Soviet security—the Israeli Jericho program. Finally, the memo expressed fears that the regime could undermine Moscow's relations with friends in the Third World. Further criticism was concentrated on the fact that the MTCR lacked a verification and enforcement mechanism; therefore compliance with it could become a subject of considerable disagreement.

On September 27, 1988, the Soviet Union sent the U.S. a memorandum on limiting missile proliferation. In developing the U.S.-Soviet INF Treaty, concluded a year before, Moscow had proposed the establishment of a global ban on all missiles with a range of less than 5,500 kilometers. Besides that, the memorandum suggested the founding of the World Space Organization, aimed at monitoring transfers of peaceful space technology permitted by the MTCR.[6] The memorandum could be hardly evaluated as very realistic. First, a global ban on all missiles with a range of less than 5,500 kilometers would lead to dramatic reductions in the nuclear arsenals of the other nuclear powers—China, France, and the United Kingdom. Yet it was well known that their adherence to the proposal was impossible, given those countries' reluctance to agree on even modest binding restraints to their nuclear forces' modernization programs. Second, reference to the World Space Organization—the idea that the Kremlin had promoted since 1986 as a part of a campaign aimed at halting the Strategic Defense Initiative (SDI) program, which became an ideological sanctuary for the Reagan administration—could only confirm suspicions in Washington that the initiative had a purely propagandistic nature.

It seems that the implicit linkage contained in the September 1998 memorandum between the MTCR and ballistic missile defenses prevented Washington from discussing the issue with the Soviet Union for the next year and a half. Most likely, the United States did not want to raise the missile proliferation issue due to concerns that Soviet diplomats would use it for bargaining during ongoing U.S.-Soviet nuclear and space talks in Geneva.

The sides returned to discussing missile proliferation only in February 1990, when Soviet Foreign Minister, Eduard Shevardnadze, and U.S. Secretary of State, James Baker, signed a joint statement suggesting that Moscow apply a national export control regime corresponding to that of the MTCR. The document also suggested that both sides "adhere" to the MTCR's rules.[7] During a summit between Presidents George Bush and Mikhail Gorbachev in June 1990, Moscow became more cautious. In a joint statement on nonproliferation, both countries declared their support for the objectives of the MTCR and called for other nations to observe the "spirit and guidelines" of the Regime. According to the statement, the two presidents were "taking measures to restrict missile proliferation on a worldwide basis, including export controls and other internal procedures." However, contrary to the Baker-Shevardnadze statement, the word "adhere" was not mentioned.[8]

The June 1990 Joint Statement represents the first international document where Moscow agreed to observe the "spirit and guidelines" of the MTCR. However, it was not a binding obligation, nor did it contain any clearly specified commitments from the Soviet side to follow the regime's provisions. But from 1990 to 1993 the United States pretended that this vague and declaratory document was Moscow's commitment to adhere to the MTCR rules, and thus USSR/Russia's missile exports must conform to the regime.

DEBATES ON RUSSIA'S ADHERENCE TO MTCR: 1990–1995

U.S.-Russian Disagreements Surrounding the Indian Deal

Russia's adherence to the MTCR proceeded against the background of a painful dispute with the United States concerning sales of cryogenic rocket engines to India. The contract (Agreement No. 800/1–50) was formally signed on January 18, 1991, between the Soviet organization Glavkosmos (established as early as 1984 as a Directorate within the Ministry of General Machine Building) and the Indian Space Research Organization (ISRO). Glavkosmos intended to sell the KVD-1 engine, designed and manufactured by the Isayev Design Bureau (*KB Khimicheskogo mashinostroyeniya imeni Isayeva—Khimmash*). It was based on an engine developed in the 1960s for the canceled L-3M manned lunar mission.[9] Russia was to assemble and deliver two operational engine blocks and two dummy engines for testing purposes; transfer production technology and equipment to allow India to build its own engines; and supply training and consultation services. The first of the engines was to be delivered in 1994, and the second in 1995.[10] By 1996 to 1997 India was to be able to build its own engines with the production technology and training transferred under the deal.

The deal prompted an energetic diplomatic exchange even before its formal conclusion. The U.S. approached the Soviet side immediately after learning about the negotiations in December 1990. Washington claimed that the agreement covered a Category I item of the MTCR Annex, sales of which are unambiguously prohibited. Moscow responded that, although nominally covered by Category I, the sale was permissible because the technology involved had no conceivable military application. The engines used nonstorable liquid oxygen and liquid hydrogen, which had never been used as fuel for ballistic missiles because of the lengthy preparation time in transferring the missile onto alert status. They were also designed for peaceful space activity; India gave assurances that it would not use the deliveries for military purposes.

It seems, however, that Soviet diplomacy made a mistake by accepting the U.S. logic that the deliveries violated the MTCR guidelines. At that time, the USSR was not a member of the regime. Despite significant enlargement of the MTCR in 1990, when it was joined by six Western European NATO members[11] and Australia, there was no intention to invite the Soviet Union to formally join the regime. The June 1990 Joint Statement, to which the U.S. side frequently referred as containing the Soviet obligations to observe the MTCR rules, was very vague and, in fact, reflected a broad *intention* by Moscow to support missile nonproliferation. This *intention* was not formalized in any bilateral or multilateral *agreement*, similar to those later concluded between the United States, Israel, China, and Ukraine. This dilemma placed Washington in a delicate situation: it accused the Soviet Union of violating the regime, a regime in which Moscow neither participated nor was invited to join.

It is worth mentioning that the nonbinding nature of the 1990 Joint Statement was, in fact, well understood by the United States. Starting from February 1992, the Bush administration repeatedly urged Russia to adhere formally to the MTCR guidelines through bilateral arrangements similar to those that were reached between the U.S. and Israel and China in 1991 and 1992.

The Soviet side also missed another important point. The engines represented an inseparable part of the rocket stage, and thus were exempted from Category I of the MTCR Annex. This was the argument used by the United States in 1996, when Russia complained about U.S. missile deliveries to Turkey.[12]

Before the Soviet collapse in December 1991, an exchange of diplomatic papers and formal notes between Moscow and Washington was taken routinely and kept at a low profile. However, immediately after the formal disintegration of the USSR, the U.S. side evidently decided to increase the pressure. Already in January 1992, Washington had threatened sanctions if the Indian deal was not immediately abandoned. On March 6, Secretary of State Baker notified the Russian Ambassador to the U.S., Vladimir Lukin, that, unless the deal was canceled by April 3, sanctions would be introduced against Glavkosmos. Although on April 9 President Yeltsin ordered a temporary halt to the deal, on May 6, the Bush administration imposed sanctions against Glavkosmos and ISRO. Washington even refused to postpone sanctions until the question was resolved during discussions within the U.S.-Russian working group established earlier with the sole aim of resolving disagreements around the ISRO deal.

U.S. pressure was met in Moscow with great anxiety and pique, and, in fact, represented the first major dispute between Russia and the United States after the Soviet collapse. In the eyes of some Russian reformers, Washington ignored the extraordinary situation related to the dissolution of the Soviet Union, a time when the Kremlin's immediate task was to save the country from a famine. Due to the collapse of the Soviet bureaucratic institutions, a lack of law enforcement mechanisms, and the emergence of thousands of kilometers of new, transparent borders with the Newly Independent States (NIS), the Yeltsin administration was hardly able simply to suspend the deal. Furthermore, U.S. pressure put the issue at the forefront of confrontations between President Yeltsin and the Supreme Soviet. The threat of sanctions provided the opposition with attractive anti-Yeltsin arguments, which further eroded the position of Russia's first reformist government, led by Yegor Gaidar, and restricted potential Kremlin maneuvering in the domestic political field.

In 1991 the Bush administration introduced sanctions twice: first, on June 25, 1991, against Chinese and Pakistani organizations following M-11 deliveries to Islamabad; and second, on September 25, 1991, against South African and Israeli organizations. The sanctions forced both Israel and China to conclude arrangements with the United States whereby they were obliged to adhere to MTCR standards without being admitted as full members to the regime.[13] The May 1992 sanctions against Russia were clearly based on those two precedents. However, Moscow emerged as a special case: as a result of sanctions, it decided to proceed with the Indian deal and, contrary to China and Israel, refused to adhere to the MTCR guidelines on a bilateral basis.

There is only a single example of outside interference by other members of the MTCR into the U.S.-Soviet dispute. On October 1991, delegations from the United States, Canada, France, and Japan met with the Soviet delegation and expressed strong concern about the Indian deal. The démarche demonstrated support from the other regime's parties for the U.S. position—that the deal was incompatible with the Soviet willingness to abide by the MTCR standards and that it contradicted the regime's guidelines.[14] However, the absence of similar multilateral steps after the Soviet collapse shows that the other members preferred to keep their distance from the controversy.

Recognizing the shortcomings of U.S. policy toward Russia in 1991 and 1992, together with a lack of support from U.S. allies, the Clinton administration decided to change course. Soon after coming to power in early 1993, the Clinton administration began a review of the U.S.-Russian relationship toward missile nonproliferation. The modified U.S. approach included the following:

- Washington finally decided not to insist on the cancellation of the whole Indian contract; rather, it was willing to accept halting deliveries of blueprints and other "technology parts of the deal," while deliveries of hardware would be permitted to continue;
- The U.S. threatened to broaden sanctions by imposing them on other Russian enterprises involved into the deal;
- An evident linkage was established between Russia's adherence to the MTCR guidelines through bilateral arrangements, on the one hand, and U.S.-Russian space cooperation as well as opening international market for commercial launches for Russian enterprises, on the other;
- Finally, the administration accepted the idea of granting Russia full membership in the MTCR after it promised to adhere to the regime's guidelines through bilateral arrangements with the United States.

Evidently, this new balance of incentives and penalties looked much more attractive to Moscow than Washington's previously ill-coordinated and rigid policy. If implemented, the Russian space industry could expect to receive considerable income from activity in international markets and through cooperation with U.S. companies. At the same time, enterprises participating in the Indian deal would also benefit from continuation of the most profitable part of the contract. Politically, for the first time Russia was offered full membership in the elite export control regime. In broader terms, it marked progress in achieving a key priority of post-Cold-War Moscow diplomacy: gaining access to Western high technology through waiving COCOM-type restrictions on its export to Russia.

After another round of diplomatic exchanges, as well as the Kremlin's domestic political maneuvering, the dispute was finally settled. On July 16, 1993, as a result of highly complicated negotiations between delegations headed by Yuri Koptev, Director of the Russian Space Agency, and Lynn Davis, Undersecretary of State, held in Washington, D.C., both sides signed a set of several agreements, among them two bilateral memoranda of understanding concerning Russia's adherence to the MTCR guidelines and conditions of continuing the Indian contract. The latter permitted Moscow to deliver complete cryogenic rocket engines but not production technologies. In the adherence memorandum, Russia secured its cooperation with other Soviet successor states; it was also obliged to bring its national legislation into line with the MTCR by 1996, with an understanding that after that Moscow would be accepted as a full member of the regime. Simultaneously, Koptev signed a separate agreement on commercial space launch services and an understanding on a cooperative U.S.-Russian space flight program and international space station. On September 2, the memoranda were formalized by Vice President Al Gore and Russian Prime Minister Viktor Chernomyrdin.

The compromise was met with criticism in both countries. In the United States, some experts expressed concerns that Washington had retreated from its initial position that Category I transfers to a country of proliferation concern were *de facto* banned, the fear being that such an arrangement could be used as a precedent by other MTCR members. If that scenario occurred, the regime's restrictive nature would be significantly eroded. However, those fears were not realized: no MTCR member stated its desire to consider the Russian-Indian case a precedent. Second, there were extensive speculations that by November 1, 1993— the deadline for implementing the Washington arrangements— Glavkosmos would be able to deliver to India up to 60 percent of all technological data. But even if so, the July 1993 compromise deprived India of full access to Russian liquid fuel expertise, which significantly devalued the previously received blueprints.

In Russia, the anti-Yeltsin opposition described the compromise as a complete surrender. On July 21, the Supreme Soviet passed a resolution calling for future obligatory ratification of all Russia's obligations under the MTCR. But the Parliament's dissolution on October 4, 1993, removed the Washington arrangements from the forefront of national debate, and the July resolution lost its practical importance.[15]

Other U.S.-Russian Disagreements during 1993 to 1995

From September 1993 until Russia's formal adherence to the MTCR on August 8, 1995, the sides have had to solve some other relatively minor problems. Among them were:

- The sale of a precision-tracking Shipwheel radar and the provision of assistance in developing SLBM technologies to India;
- The sale of a Start launching system to South Africa;
- Sales of missile parts and the provision of expertise for Syria;
- Deliveries of missile fuel to Libya via Ukraine;
- Deliveries of fiber-optic sensors, RD-120 engines, and other missile technologies to China;
- Provision of assistance in the design and manufacturing of missile nose cones to Brazil.

Given the sensitive nature of the problems, there is a lack of reliable data on how they were resolved, or whether some of these cases really took place. Most likely, some issues such as assisting in developing Indian SLBMs, or missile technologies and expertise deliveries to Syria, were raised in the negotiations context as a last ditch effort to obtain additional details on the amended contract on cryogenic engines or to prevent increasing numbers of engines being sold to India in compensation for canceling deliveries of production technologies and expertise.[16]

In late 1993, the United States claimed the Shipwheel radar could be used during tests of Indian ballistic missiles. According to Washington, the radar is controlled by Category II of the MTCR Annex. On February 16 to 17, 1994, during the second round of consultations on implementing the September 1993 agreements, Moscow responded that the radar was not covered by the Annex because it could not provide measurements of in-flight velocity and missile position in real time.[17]

In 1994 Russia also declared the U.S. concerns regarding the above-mentioned deliveries to Syria, China, and South Africa and assistance in developing Indian SLBMs to be groundless. According to Moscow, these activities were consistent with the MTCR standards and national regulations. Russia accused Washington of attempting to gain more information about its potential exports to the Third World. Later, the U.S. side had to recognize that those cases did not represent a clear violation of the MTCR.

Russia continued using Start-1 and Start-2 launchers (based on Topol SS-25 ICBM technology) for commercial satellites. Under a contract signed in 1996, the launchers will deliver payloads from the Space Port Canada site located in Northern Manitoba until late 1998. Moscow will maintain control over the boosters.[18]

In 1994, the Grafit Research Institute was accused by U.S. officials of providing critical expertise to Brazil in the designing and manufacturing of missile nose cones. Another institute, *TsNIIMash* (Central Research Institute for Machine Building), was accused of helping Brazil to develop an advanced testing facility and assisting in guidance and control design. On May 15, 1995, sanctions were imposed on foreign entities whose names and nationalities were not published for reasons of national security. The sanctions most likely involved Russian and Brazilian enterprises. However, the Clinton administration decided not to enter into a dispute with Brazil and, given its improved stance in nuclear nonproliferation, opened the door for its full membership in the MTCR. Subsequently, in May 1995 the sanctions were waived. After both Russia and Brazil entered the regime, in October 1995 they signed a bilateral agreement on defense cooperation, which provided a legal base for future missile-related transfers.[19]

Russia formally applied for MTCR membership during the regime's plenary session in Stockholm on October 4 to 6, 1994. In the spring of 1995, the United States and France blocked Russia's formal accession to the MTCR, perhaps due to disputes surrounding the Brazilian contract. Subsequently, during the fifth session, on June 28 and 29, 1995, of the Gore-Chernomyrdin Commission, Washington announced its support for Moscow's entry. Russia was officially accepted as a full member on August 8 and attended its first plenary meeting in its new capacity in Bonn on October 10 to 12, 1995.

BUILDING MISSILE EXPORT CONTROLS IN RUSSIA

Since 1992, Russia has established a developed system of controlling exports of missile technologies according to its obligations under the MTCR. However, owing to the extraordinary economic and political situation that emerged as a result of the Soviet collapse and the unprecedented transformation toward a democratic system and market economy, Moscow faces certain problems in effective implementation of its national export control guidelines. These problems related to the following:

- The legislative base for export control has not been completed yet: the export control system relies largely on governmental regulations rather than on laws passed by the Federal Assembly, the Russian Parliament;
- Existing legislation contains some ambiguities and loopholes that complicate the implementation of adequate law enforcement measures;
- Bureaucratic instability exists at the federal level, and exporters circumvent governmental regulations;
- Ambiguities and deficiencies of the international missile control regime cause difficulties in independently monitoring possible violations and their nature.

Russia's Missile Export Control Regulations

The establishment of the national system of controlling missile exports started well before the Russian Federation joined the MTCR in August 1995. The first Soviet public legislative act on controlling missile proliferation was issued on April 5, 1991. A decree signed by President Mikhail Gorbachev established a new mechanism for controlling the export of sensitive technologies, including missile delivery systems. In particular, the decree stipulated the creation of the Department for Export Control in the then Ministry of the Economy and Forecasting in order to draft a list of missile technology. The list was drafted, but due to bureaucratic delays it did not enter into force until the Soviet Union disintegrated in December 1991.[20]

A year later, on April 11, 1992, President Boris Yeltsin signed Presidential Decree No. 388, "On Measures to Establish an Export Control System in Russia." This decree provided the initial legal basis for creating a system of nonproliferation export controls in the country. With reference to both Russian national interests and international nonproliferation obligations, the decree resolved to establish export controls for materials, equipment, and technologies that can be used in the development of, among other things, missiles and their components.

The first Russian missile export control list was approved on January 11, 1993, by Presidential Directive No. 29-rp. The list was entitled "A list of equipment, materials and technologies which are used for creating missile weapons, whose export is controlled and is a subject of licensing."[21] The Russian side claimed that the approved list was compatible with MTCR standards and guidelines, and in some cases, was even more detailed.[22] However, the United States disagreed. In the opinion of the U.S., the list's restrictions could be circumvented by exporting missile technologies labeled for "civilian use." Washington made modifying the list a necessary condition for Russia's accession to the MTCR. As a result, on April 25, 1995, prior to Moscow's incorporation to the regime, a new missile list was approved by Presidential Directive No. 193.

In 1996, Moscow decided to send a message to Washington that it had further tightened its missile export control regulations in accordance with Russia's obligations under the MTCR. On August 16, 1996, the new missile list was approved not by a Presidential Directive, but by a Presidential Decree—the highest act that, constitutionally, could be issued by an executive branch of power in the Russian Federation. According to Presidential Decree No. 1194, "On Control of Exports from the Russian Federation of Equipment, Materials, and Technology Used to Develop Missile Weapons," a new control list for exports of equipment, materials, and technologies used to produce missiles, in accordance with Russia's accession to the MTCR in 1995, was approved. The decree also instructed the Cabinet of Ministers to draw up a new statute of procedures to control the export of equipment, materials, and technologies used in the production of missiles.

Initially, the statute of procedures was established on January 27, 1993, by Government Resolution No. 70, "On Approval of the Statute Regulating Control of Exports from the Russian Federation of Equipment, Materials and Technology Employed to Develop Missile Weapons." This resolution approved the export licensing procedures for equipment, materials, and technologies used to produce missiles capable of delivering payloads of at least 500 kg to a range of at least 300 km. The resolution also defined the export licensing authority and guidelines for missile exports. Later on, modifications to the statute were approved on November 19, 1993, by Government Resolution No. 1178 and on May 24, 1995, by Government Resolution No. 521.

In order to fulfill Presidential Decree No. 1194, on September 13, 1996, Government Resolution No. 1100, On Amending the Statute Regulating Exports from the Russian Federation of Equipment, Materials, and Technology Used to Develop Missile Weapons, was adopted. This resolution approved the most recent statute regulating export of missile technologies. According to the resolution, the statute is similar to the one for other dual-use commodities and technologies. The exporter must apply for a license to the Federal Service for Currency and Export Control (VEK). The service considers the application and asks other agencies for approval (among them, the Ministry of Foreign Affairs, the Federal Security Service, and the Ministry of Defense). In cases of approval by VEK, the exporter can approach the Ministry of Industry and Trade (MPT), which is in charge of issuing formal licenses. The license is given for a single transfer only. Separate departments of the MPT are responsible for licensing exports of military and civilian missile technologies. In order to provide more effective control, recent applications must be sent only to the central offices of both VEK and MPT. (Earlier, the applications could be delivered to regional branches of those agencies.) Producers in some remote areas, such as Siberia, complain that the new system requires their representatives to travel to Moscow twice in order to receive one license. However, the number of licenses issued for missile exports is still quite limited, and the current centralization efforts do not, reportedly, affect the exporters considerably.[23]

Other regulations restrict the unauthorized reexport of dual-use commodities and technologies, including missiles. On October 11, 1993, Governmental Resolution No. 1030, On Controlling the Fulfillment of the Obligations to Guarantee the Use of Imported and Exported Dual-Use Goods and Services for Declared Purposes, was adopted. It approved the procedures for monitoring the fulfillment of obligations regarding the end use of dual-use imports and exports. The statute covered both measures to prevent the unauthorized reexport of dual-use items from Russia and measures to prevent the unauthorized reexport from a foreign country of dual-use items imported from Russia.

As a reaction to U.S. criticism on illegal deliveries of Russian missile technologies to Iraq (see below), on November 7, 1997, Government Resolution No. 1403, "On Control Over the Export to Iraq of Goods, Dual-Use Technologies, and Other Materials Subject to International Mechanisms for Permanent Oversight and Control," was adopted. It defined the rules and procedures for the export of controlled goods and technologies to Iraq in accordance with U.N. Security Council resolutions that either restrict or forbid the export of sensitive goods and technologies to Iraq. In accordance with this resolution, it is forbidden to export any items to Iraq intended for use in activities that are forbidden by the U.N. Security Council.[24]

It should be noted that one can find a significant correlation between the adoption of new missile export control regulations in Russia and the state of the U.S.-Russian relationship. The April 1991 Gorbachev decree was issued as a reaction to initial U.S. criticism toward the Glavkosmos-ISRO deal. A year later, Presidential Decree No. 388 coincided with Secretary of State Baker's ultimatum on introducing sanctions against Glavkosmos and, most likely, was aimed at softening Washington's disappointment. Presidential Directive No. 29-rp was issued only a few days after the Bush-Yeltsin summit in early January 1993.

National Missile Export Control Legislation

While the regulatory base of Russia's missile export control system has been developed, its legal component will have to be improved. The only existing federal law formalizing the role of the export control system in Russia's foreign and security policy and its foreign economic relations is the Federal Law No. 153-FZ, "On State Regulation of Foreign Trade Activity," which entered into force on October 13, 1995. This law includes three articles that are relevant to nonproliferation export controls: Article Two provides a list of the basic terms of export controls; Article Six provides for federal jurisdiction in determining policy and procedures for export control of, among other things, missile delivery systems; Article Sixteen provides basic principles for export control regulations, stating that the export control system in Russia has been instituted to protect national interests and to fulfill international obligations regarding the nonproliferation of weapons of mass destruction.

This law was adopted by the State Duma on July 7, 1995, approved by the Federation Council on July 21, 1995, and signed by President Boris Yeltsin on October 13, 1995. An earlier draft of the law, adopted by the Duma in May 1995, was vetoed by President Yeltsin because the bill required that export control lists be approved by federal law. In the final version of the law, that provision was removed.

A basic Law on Export Controls was drafted by the Federal Service for Currency and Export Controls and circulated among relevant agencies in the fall of 1997. The draft law has been sharply criticized by some government agencies, including Minatom, and analysts believe this draft will have to be drastically revised before submission to the Duma, which approved the draft in late fall 1998.[25]

On January 1, 1997, a new Russian Criminal Code entered into force, which provided a legislative basis for criminal prosecution of some missile export control violations. The code was adopted by Federal Law No. 63-FZ, Criminal Code of the Russian Federation, which was signed by the President on June 13, 1996. This law contains some provisions that address violations of missile export controls. In particular, Article 189 provides criminal penalties for the illegal export of technologies, scientific-technical information, and services that could be used to develop weapons of mass destruction and the means of their deliveries. It is punishable by up to three to seven years imprisonment. The minimum penalty is established by fines ranging between 700 and 1000 times the level of the minimum wage (as of July 1998, approximately 58,000 to 83,000 Russian roubles, or 9,300 to 13,400 U.S. dollars).

At the same time, the Criminal Code, does not, in fact, contain any clear penalties for illegal export or contraband of missile hardware, which is contained in export control lists. For instance, Article 188, introducing penalties for contraband, does not mention missiles and their components at all. The article's language permits exporters to qualify their export as contraband only if the goods remain undeclared or if they attempt to escape customs control. However, if the missile-related commodities were declared as, say, ferrous metals or scrap, it would leave few chances for initiating a criminal investigation against the exporter.[26]

In a similar way, Articles 225 and 226 provide penalties for inadequate protection, stealing, and racketeering of weapons of mass destruction, but do not include penalties for executing the same crimes against means of their deliveries. Article 234 provides penalties for illegal production, processing, purchasing, possessing, transporting, and selling of poisonous substances other than drugs, and their production and processing equipment. Those criminal activities are punishable by up to a maximum of eight years of imprisonment. Indirectly, those provisions might apply to highly toxic missile fuel and the equipment for its production and processing. But the jurisdiction of the article on illegal export of missile fuel and related equipment could be disputed on the grounds that Article 234 is part of Chapter 25, devoted exclusively to crimes against public health and morale, and thus it does not cover illegal transboundary transfers.[27]

Loopholes in the Criminal Code related to illegal missile exports could be explained by several factors. First, during the preparation of the Criminal Code, the Russian law enforcement establishment remained unaware of relatively new policy areas such as the MTCR. Second, bureaucratic instability deeply affected the efficiency of interagency coordination. Third, the Duma Committee on Security, where the Criminal Code was first considered, is traditionally controlled by the parliamentary left and nationalist majority. In 1992 and 1993, representatives of this political spectrum actively supported an anti-MTCR campaign in the Supreme Soviet. Therefore, the lack of provisions penalizing illegal missile exports could reflect the deliberate attitudes of those groups that were not identified by the Yeltsin administration as supporters of missile nonproliferation.

In order to meet criticism on the inadequacy of the Criminal Code in preventing unauthorized missile exports, on July 16, 1998, President Yeltsin formally required the government to accelerate its activity on modifying the code with the aim of enforcing its provisions against illegal missile transfers. In the requirement, the president also appealed for the rapid completion of the new export control legislation.[28] As in previous cases, the move coincided with discussions in the U.S. Congress on overruling a veto by President Clinton of a bill that imposed sanctions against Russian companies suspected of missile cooperation with Iran (see below).

POST-1995 U.S.-RUSSIAN DISPUTES ON MTCR COMPLIANCE

Since Russia was permitted to join the MTCR on August 1995, disputes between Moscow and Washington on alleged Russian missile exports to "rogue states" have continued. They covered several episodes, such as:

- Illegal deliveries of gyroscopes from dismantled SS-N-18 SLBMs to Iraq;
- Unauthorized export of Scuds to Armenia;
- Chinese attempts to buy SS-18 ICBM technology;
- Cooperation between some Russian enterprises and Iran in the missile area;
- A proposed deal on deliveries of the S-300 air defense system to Cyprus.

At the public level, the United States expressed the biggest concerns over the Iraqi and Iranian cases. The Chinese case was subject to an official US démarche; however, the episode now seems to be closed. There is no available data on whether the Scud deliveries to Armenia became the subject of U.S. official objections. The most famous source on congressional criticism did not mention the Armenian, Chinese, and Cyprus issues at all.[29]

Cyprus

According to this deal, Russia will sell to Cyprus an unspecified number of S-300 air defense interceptors—a more advanced analog of the U.S. Patriot PAC-2 interceptor. The systems were to be delivered to the recipient between August and November 1998. This issue is not considered within the MTCR framework. The S-300s cannot be qualified as "missiles," since they are exclusively designed to intercept aircraft as well as some tactical cruise and ballistic missiles. Their range is 150 kilometers—below the 300-km threshold established by the MTCR guidelines. The deal was officially approved by the Russian authorities; as a member of the MTCR, Russia is exempted from sanctions if a non-Category I missile transfer was approved according to the national procedure. Finally, U.S. cooperation with Israel on the antimissile Arrow system as well as Washington's own Patriot deliveries to South Korea established a precedent on exempting air defense interceptors with a range of less than 300 kilometers from consideration under the MTCR guidelines.

U.S. objections to the S-300 deliveries complicate the political environment for the Yeltsin administration in responding to challenges directly related to the MTCR. Since the 1991 to 1993 controversy over the ISRO-Glavkosmos deal, a widespread opinion had emerged in Russia that Washington uses international nonproliferation regimes for purely commercial reasons: as a tool of dishonest competition used against Russian companies in world markets. Although this opinion might not be well grounded in the Indian case, some other elements of U.S. policy helped that view to survive. For instance, in 1995 Washington objected to Russo-Brazilian missile cooperation at a time when it was already known that Brazil would join the MTCR within several months.

The S-300 dispute led to the further solidification of that position. The deal remains compatible with Russia's nonproliferation obligations, and this is not disputed even by the United States. Furthermore, according to views popular among the Republican majority on the Capitol Hill, antitactical missile defenses are stabilizing and purely defensive weapons—they do not kill people, just other weapons. However, the attempts of tiny Cyprus to improve its air defenses—which sounds quite logical given the occupation of 40 percent of the island's territory by much more powerful Turkey—led to a nervous reaction in the U.S. This is believed to be especially illogical because Cyprus cannot be considered as a "rogue" state: the country is a first-wave candidate for membership in the European Union. Under those circumstances, an argument gained momentum in Russia that Washington objects to the deal for purely commercial reasons: to compel Cyprus to buy the U.S.-made Patriots and to undermine Russia's high-tech exports. This further affects Moscow's responsiveness to other U.S. concerns, such as Russia's nuclear and missile cooperation with Iran.

China

In May 1996 the United States warned Russia not to sell SS-18 ICBM technology to China. The SS-18 is considered to be the most powerful Russian land-based ICBM, possessing the world's highest-capacity throw-weight and the ability to carry up to ten multiple independently targeted reentry vehicles (MIRVs). In Russia it is known under the abbreviation R-36M UTTH. The missile system must be destroyed under the U.S.-Russian START II Treaty, an arms control agreement signed in January 1993 but still awaiting ratification in the Russian Duma.

Not surprisingly, the information was met with significant concern among Russian lawmakers. By a majority of votes, the Duma requested that the Chernomyrdin government testify as to whether the deal had taken place. In its response, the government denied the deal. However, Russian officials later recognized that the Chinese really approached Moscow, and perhaps Kyev, and tested the ground as to whether they could buy some elements of SS-18 technology. Russian authorities responded negatively.[30]

Iraq

In November 1995, at the Amman airport, Jordanian authorities intercepted 115 sets of gyroscopes and accelerometers (components of guidance systems for ballistic missiles) on their way to Iraq. Their cost was estimated by UNSCOM experts at approximately $25 million. According to the U.S. and U.N. officials, the goods were clearly marked as made in Russia. A month later, on December 9, 1995, the Iraqis, in order to preempt similar UNSCOM action, removed another 30 sets of gyroscopes from the Tigris river. They were identified as gyroscopes from SS-N-18 SLBMs.[31] In Russia these are known as the R-29R missile; deployed on Project 667 BDR (Delta III) strategic nuclear submarines, it can carry up to three MIRVs. Due to aging and under the conditions of the START I Treaty, the submarines are gradually being decommissioned, and their missiles are being destroyed.[32]

Initially, Moscow was surprised by the incident and disputed the Russian origin of the equipment. Moscow started its own investigation. As a result some leakages were made, acknowledging cases of smuggling. It was found that the gyroscopes originated from the Research and Experimental Institute of Chemical Machine Building located in the city of Sergiyev Posad, 60 kilometers to the northeast of Moscow. The facility is involved in eliminating the SS-N-18s. The deal was reportedly arranged by the Arab community in Russia, and particularly, by a middleman named Weam Abu Ghabriyeh, of Lebanese or Palestinian origin. A private Russian optics company, TASM, directed by a retired general, was allegedly also involved. In order to penetrate through customs control, the equipment was declared as "electrical measurement tools." As mentioned above, this was a way to circumvent provisions of the 1997 Criminal Code. Therefore, although the prosecution has started, there are doubts that the smugglers will face any criminal penalty; due to ambiguities in the legislation, it would be impossible even to finish the prosecution formally.

According to some analysts, the investigation did not find evidence that Russian authorities were involved in the case. The Clinton administration tends to support that conclusion. However, the Russian side has yet to provide a formal report for UNSCOM.[33]

Armenia

In 1997, then Chairman of the Duma Defense Committee, General Lev Rokhlin, accused the Russian Armed Forces of selling up to 32 Scud tactical ballistic missiles to Armenia from 1994 to 1996. On July 1, 1997, then Prime Minister Viktor Chernomyrdin stated that his government had not approved the deal. Moreover, under President Yeltsin's Decree of September 9, 1993, all arms deliveries to Armenia and Azerbaijan were suspended until a peaceful solution to the conflict over Nagorno-Karabakh could be found. According to General Rokhlin, the sales were approved by then Russian Minister of Defense Pavel Grachev.[34]

Upon Rokhlin's statements, the Office of the Military Prosecutor initiated an investigation of the affair. In 1998 it was most likely shelved, partly because of the political situation. Deep and ongoing reductions of military manpower (in 1997 and 1998 the number of military personnel in all armed forces will be reduced from 1.8 to 1.2 million) naturally led to disappointment among officers. In order to avoid possible unrest, the authorities decided not to bother the military establishment by investigating some potentially scandalous criminal affairs in which top generals might be involved. Moreover, in 1998 Pavel Grachev, who still enjoyed support from airborne troops, was nominated as a presidential representative to Rosvooruzheniye, a state-owned monopoly responsible for Russia's arms sales. In July 1998 General Rokhlin, the initiator of the scandal and a key promoter of the investigation, was killed in his country house near Moscow.

The delivered Scuds cannot carry nuclear warheads. Armenia possesses no industrial capabilities permitting it to increase the range of the missiles. Given Yerevan's special relations with both Moscow and Washington, it is hard to imagine that it would take a risk by reexporting the missiles to, say, Iran or Iraq. Furthermore, as a member of the CIS, Armenia represents a special case. As the capital of one of the successor states of the Soviet Union, Yerevan has a right to claim its share of former Soviet arsenal of conventional weapons, including the Scuds. During the 1992 and 1993 talks with the United States, Moscow consistently stated that its missile cooperation with other CIS countries represented a special case and should not be a subject of MTCR restrictions. Nevertheless, although the Armenian case *per se* was not evaluated as a subject of proliferation concern in either Russia or the United States, it highlighted the clearly insufficient legal environment in Russia for preventing illegal missile exports.

It could be asserted that illegal sales of Scuds might qualify as a "criminal" activity, penalized by the Article 222 of the 1997 Criminal Code, which provides punishment for illegal sales of armaments of up to eight years of imprisonment.[35] However, since the Criminal Code does not mention missiles directly, such jurisdiction could be disputed, especially if the Scuds were delivered to Armenia without warheads. In other words, the presence of warheads defines missiles as "weapons," without the warhead a missile could be considered just a "delivery means" of the weapon.

Another serious problem is related to the inadequacy of the legal mechanisms regulating conventional arms exports originating from armed forces stockpiles and held by the military. In Moscow's bureaucratic language, such exports are defined as "international military and technical cooperation." Due to disagreements between influential lobbying groups, the Bill on International Military and Technical Cooperation, which used to regulate such activity, has been shelved in the Duma Defense Committee since 1995.

After the failed coup in Moscow in October 1993, the military reaped a great deal of political leverage and became bureaucratically strong enough to rebuff the attempts to implement civilian monitoring of their activities. From the civilian side, the regulatory mechanism was disaggregated by Presidential Decree of December 31, 1994, under which the State Committee for Military and Technical Cooperation was established. However, it was not clear as to how the responsibilities of the new agency in the missiles export control area would correlate to that of the VEK. Also, the prerogatives of the committee were contested by Grachev's Ministry of Defense.

Besides the internal directives of the Ministry of Defense, there is no regime regulating deliveries of armaments and military equipment to Russian military bases abroad and guaranteeing their transfers to local allies, unauthorized by top federal authorities in Moscow. In Armenia, Russian Armed Forces deployed two military bases; in addition, the Armenian border with Turkey and Iran is protected by the Russian Federal Border Service. Thus, in 1994 to 1996, the military could easily avoid civilian export control authorities by claiming, for example, that the missiles were being delivered to Russia's military bases in Armenia, which have extraterritorial status.

Iran

Since 1994 the United States has raised concerns over the alleged cooperation between various Russian enterprises and Iran in the missile area. However, in 1995, contrary to Russo-Brazilian cooperation, the Iranian link was not mentioned as a pretext for delaying Russia's accession to the regime. This reflects the fact that Washington did not possess real and compelling evidence of such cooperation at that time. In June 1995, during a regular meeting of the Gore-Chernomyrdin Commission, the U.S. side raised the issue of Russo-Iranian cooperation, mainly in the area of conventional arms sales. In response, Prime Minister Chernomyrdin offered not to conclude new deals on conventional arms transfers to Iran and to finish existing contracts within two years. This pledge was not formalized in any binding agreement and represented Russia's unilateral offer. Although later Washington broadly interpreted the Chernomyrdin's pledge as an obligation to halt any military cooperation with Iran, Moscow has never confirmed it and has proceeded with implementing existing contracts, including the construction of a nuclear power plant in Büshehr.

Since February 1997, media reports have appeared, frequently citing Israeli intelligence sources, alleging that Russia was delivering R-12 (SS-4) missile components to Iran. In June 1997 the Clinton administration officially confirmed that in 1996 Russia, together with China, represented the main source of deliveries of missile technologies to Iran. However, it failed to specify detailed cases of illegal missile transfers.[36] President Clinton personally raised the issue during the U.S.-Russian summit in March 1997 and at the first G-8 meeting in Denver in June. He was followed by Vice President Gore and Secretary of State Albright. In July the United States and Russia commenced formal discussions on the issue. On the U.S. side the talks were initially led by Frank Wisner, and later by Robert Gallucci, and on the Russian side, by Yuri Koptev, Director of the Russian Space

Agency. In 1997 and 1998, the consultations were held, on average, on a bimonthly basis. During these consultations the United States reportedly provided Russian authorities with a list of specific MTCR violations. In 1998 ferroalloys of Russian origin, which could be used for producing missile systems, were intercepted in Azerbaijan.

Similar to the Iraqi case, Russian authorities initially denied the allegations of illegal activity. According to statements of the Ministry of Foreign Affairs of July 9, 1997, Russia did not cooperate with Tehran in the missile area, as this violated the MTCR norms. The ministry also said that information on illegal activities by some enterprises was verified by "competent agencies," but the facts were not confirmed.[37] Subsequently, President Yeltsin, Prime Minister Chernomyrdin, and Foreign Minister Primakov repeatedly denied that Moscow had approved any missile-related exports that violated the MTCR guidelines to Iran.

At the same time, Russia reacted positively to the U.S. démarches by launching a Federal Security Service (FSB) investigation. In October 1997, an anonymous Russian official recognized for the first time that there had been episodes that could have led to illegal transactions of missile technology; however, the cases had been discovered at an early stage and all of them suspended. Particularly, the FSB intercepted an Iranian attempt to receive components for liquid-fuel missiles from the Samara-based Trud Scientific and Production Association. On November 14, 1997, an Iranian national was detained by Moscow police when he attempted to receive technological blueprints of unspecified missile components. However, according to some reports, the Iranian was deceived and provided with nonsecret documentation. Some analysts maintain that the detention was the result of a sting operation made by the Russian secret service.[38]

In the spring of 1998, both houses of the U.S. Congress overwhelmingly approved the Iran Missile Proliferation Sanctions Act, which would sanction foreign companies in cases of "credible evidence" of their missile cooperation with Iran. President Clinton vetoed the bill. Under threat of overruling the veto, Moscow reacted rapidly. In July, President Yeltsin ordered the establishment of a commission led by Yakov Urinson, Minister of Economy, with the sole aim of investigating allegations of illegal cooperation with Iran against the following nine Russian organizations:

1. *Inor* Research Center, accused earlier in selling to Iran ferroalloys necessary for missile production;
2. The Moscow-based *Polyus* Research Institute, which allegedly attempted to deliver missile guidance systems;
3. *Grafit* Research Institute;
4. *Tikhomirov* Institute;
5. *Glavkosmos*;

6. The Novosibirsk-based *Komintern* plant;
7. The Baltic State Technological University of St. Petersburg;
8. *MOSO* company; and
9. *Europalace-2000* enterprise.

President Yeltsin announced that if the investigation demonstrated that the enterprises were involved in illegal activity, their managers would be punished by administrative or even criminal measures. On its side, on July 15, 1998, the Clinton administration threatened that, pending the results of the Russian investigation, the organizations could be sanctioned by the United States as well, though American assistance to seven of the nine organizations had already been suspended.[39]

The list of organizations differs considerably from those often mentioned in the U.S. media and semiofficial reports circulated earlier in 1997 and 1998. The investigation list does not include such regularly mentioned "proliferators" such as *TsAGI*, *Trud*, or Rosvooruzheniye. This suggests that the 1997 investigation did not detect any violations in their activities. The available data permits the following conclusions to be drawn.

First, in many cases, evidence of alleged violations referred to in the preliminary negotiations between the enterprises and the Iranians was absent. All negotiations were compatible with Russian regulations which, as mentioned above, required the enterprises to apply for an export license after a contract is concluded. Governmental approval of the preliminary negotiations and the contract itself is necessary only for critical nuclear exports. In cases of missile transactions, the export control authorities cannot prevent the signing of the contract; they can, however, block implementation.[40] This explains why the 1997 FSB investigation did not bring about significant results, despite a sincere effort—as the FSB had demonstrated in an earlier incident involving an Iranian national in November 1997—to prove its efficiency.

Second, the existing cooperation took place in areas that are not regulated by the missile list. For example, the Central Aerodynamic Institute (*TsAGI*) was accused of delivering aerodynamic tubes to Iran. However, Category II of the MTCR restricts sales of such tubes with a velocity of air stream of 0.9 m or more.[41] The tubes with less velocity are not restricted by the regime; therefore, the fact of the tube deliveries *per se* does not necessarily mean that the MTCR was violated.

Third, the presence of university and research institutes in the investigation list indicated that the concerned activity included students' education and contacts between scientists. However, the human aspect of missile proliferation is not regulated by the MTCR. Authoritative U.S. sources recently confirmed that the "Russian assistance to Iran had been largely in the form of research grants and scientific partnership programs."[42]

Thus, illegal Russian cooperation with Iran had most likely a much more limited nature than was portrayed in 1997 and 1998. It seems, moreover, that the real aim of the United States and its allies was to halt an activity that did not directly violate the MTCR and was not regulated by the regime. The main concern was most likely associated not so much with a limited leakage of fragmented missile hardware and blueprints, but rather with the prospects that through scientific and university cooperation with Russia, Tehran would be able to build a community of professional missile experts, which represents the main prerequisite for obtaining indigenous missile capabilities.

This conclusion explains the controversies surrounding Washington's maneuvers around Russo-Iranian missile cooperation. The United States did not want to make public the details of suspected noncompliances, as this would raise suspicions that many of the cases could hardly be evaluated as violations of the MTCR. The wording of the congressional act established a low threshold for imposing sanctions by using the definition of "credible evidence" rather than, say, "MTCR violations." Again, this can be interpreted as a desire of U.S. lawmakers to affect an activity that might be not restricted by the regime.

LESSONS FROM THE U.S.-RUSSIAN MTCR DEBATES

Since 1991, the U.S.-Russian dialogue has contributed significantly to the building of a national missile export control regime in the Russian Federation. Significant progress has been achieved in developing missile export control lists, all of which currently meet the requirements of the MTCR guidelines. Furthermore, a normative base for regulating export control procedures has been established. However, additional improvements are needed in the following areas:

- Consolidating the legal basis for missile export controls by adopting two basic federal laws on export control and on international military and technical cooperation;
- Actions designed to prevent illegal transactions must be accompanied by modifications in the 1997 Criminal Code, which currently lacks provisions penalizing illegal missile exports;
- Stricter civilian control is required of missile transfers from military stockpiles; particularly, control should be enforced over missiles stored and deployed in military bases located outside Russia;
- Domestic discussions are needed on the desirability of upgrading missile export controls to the level of provisions established for critical nuclear exports;
- The bureaucratic export control system must be stabilized.

The U.S.-Russian dialogue facilitated Russia's accession to the MTCR and Wassenaar Agreement, thereby expediting Moscow's access to Western high technologies. Besides that, it promoted the commercialization of the Russian missile industry and helped it to gain benefits from participating in international space launches. Given the poor state of the Russian economy, the number of confirmed cases of illegal missile exports from Russian entities remains surprisingly low. The majority of alleged cases of illegal activity were shown to be in compliance MTCR guidelines.

The undeviating policy of the Bush administration on the Glavkosmos-ISRO deal, which lacked both incentives and penalties, helped to consolidate a strong anti-MTCR coalition in Russia. Further démarches from Washington, particularly on the Brazilian and Cyprus deals, as well as on the MTCR-compliant aspects of Russo-Iranian cooperation, further undermined the credibility of U.S. warnings and complicated efforts aimed at upgrading national missile export control legislation.

The MTCR does not restrict some aspects of missile-related activities, a subject of growing concern in the United States. Washington's attempts to solve the problems on a bilateral basis and through sanctioning the concerned activities, even if they are compatible with the MTCR, is gradually eroding Russian commitment to the regime. Therefore, U.S. objections against Russian international cooperation in areas that are not adequately restricted by the MTCR undermine the missile nonproliferation regime and, thus, U.S. efforts and interests in that area. It seems that a more sustainable solution could be found through consolidating the regime itself, including negotiating stricter missile export guidelines between the members.

Finally, the painful U.S.-Russian disputes on whether certain cases violate or do not violate the MTCR indicate the lack of an independent body monitoring regime compliance. In the presence of such a body, it would be much more difficult for Moscow to portray every U.S. warning as a reflection of dishonest competition and a policy of double standards.

NOTES

1. John W. Lewis and Hua Di, "China's Ballistic Missile Programs. Technologies, Strategies, Goals," *International Security*, vol. 17, no. 2 (Fall 1992).
2. Most likely, halt of the Scud deliveries to Iraq was the first example when economically profitable Soviet missile export was sacrificed for political reasons—in order not to jeopardize emerging relations with Iran after the 1979 Islamic revolution there.
3. Alexander A. Pikayev, Leonard S. Spector, Elina V. Kirichenko, and Ryan Gibson, *Russia, the US and the Missile Technology Control Regime* (London: The International Institute for Strategic Studies, 1998), *Adelphi Paper* 317, p. 86.
4. The United States, Canada, France, Italy, Japan, West Germany, and the United Kingdom.
5. See Leonard S. Spector and Jacqueline R. Smith, *Nuclear Ambitions: The Spread of Nuclear Weapons 1989–1990* (Boulder, CO: Westview Press, 1990), Chapter 3.
6. Alexander A. Pikayev, et al., *Russia, the US and the Missile Technology Control Regime*, pp. 14–15.

7. "Joint Statement Issued by Secretary of State Baker and Foreign Minister Shevardnadze, Moscow, February 10, 1990," *American Foreign Policy Current Documents, 1990* (Washington, DC: US Department of State, 1991), p. 369.

8. "Joint Statement Issued by the Governments of the Soviet Union and the United States, 4 June 1990," *ibid.*, p. 73.

9. ANSER, "Proton Launch Vehicle Analysis 1997" (Rosslyn, VA: ANSER Center for International Space Cooperation, 1997).

10. Sergei Ivanov, "Glavkosmos Head Criticizes India Rocket Deal Cancellation," *Komsomolskaya pravda* (July 31, 1993). "Cryogenic Engine for Rocket Technology Developed," *Delhi All India Radio Network* (April 27, 1993), in FBIS-NES-93-080, (April 28, 1993), p. 68. Alexander A. Pikayev, et al., *Russia, the US and the Missile Technology Control Regime*, pp. 21–22.

11. Belgium, Denmark, Luxembourg, the Netherlands, Norway, and Spain.

12. Author thanks Gennady Khromov for providing this detail.

13. Elaine Sciolino, "US Lifts Its Sanctions on China Over High Technology Transfers," *New York Times* (February 22, 1992), p. 1. David Hoffman and R. Jeffrey Smith, "President Waives Sanctions for Israel," *Washington Post* (October 27, 1991), p. A1.

14. See "US Rocket Deal," Associated Press, 8 May 1992.

15. Alexander A. Pikayev, et al., *Russia, the US and the Missile Technology Control Regime*, pp. 53–55, 57–58.

16. In order to compensate India for amending the initial contract in accordance with the July 1993 Washington arrangements, Glavkosmos agreed to increase the number of engines to be sold from the initial two to seven; two of them will be provided for free.

17. Alexander A. Pikayev, et al., *Russia, the US and the Missile Technology Control Regime*, pp. 65–66.

18. Viktor Mizin, "Russian Missile Proliferation Dilemmas: Fears and Possible Cures (A Case Study in a Non-Proliferation Model Design)," unpublished manuscript, Center for Nonproliferation Studies, Monterey Institute of International Studies, pp. 30–31.

19. Wyn Bowen, "Brazil's Accession to the MTCR," *The Nonproliferation Review*, vol. 3, no. 3 (Spring-Summer, 1996); Alexander A. Pikayev, et al., *Russia, the US and the Missile Technology Control Regime*, pp. 78–79.

20. Elina Kirichenko, "The Evolution of Export Control Systems in the Soviet Union and Russia," in Gary Bertsch, Richard Cupitt, and Stephen Elliott-Gower (eds.), *International Cooperation on Nonproliferation Export Controls: Prospects for the 1990s and Beyond* (Ann Arbor, MI: University of Michigan Press, 1994), pp. 163–179.

21. See the Russian text of the directive and the list in Aleksandr Pikayev (ed.), *Rossiya, SShA, Kitai, Ukraina i rezhim kontrolya za raketnymi tehnologiyami* [Russia, the US, China, Ukraine and the Missile Technologies Control Regime] (Committee for Critical Technologies and Non-Proliferation, 1995), pp. 32–59.

22. *Ibid.*, p. 9.

23. Author's discussion with Russian export control specialist, Moscow, July 1998.

24. For the Russian text of the resolution, see *Rossiiskaya Gazeta* (November 18, 1997), p. 4.

25. Author's discussion with a Russian official from the State Duma, July 1998. *Nuclear Successor States of the Soviet Union. Status Report on Nuclear Weapons, Nuclear Materials and Export of Sensitive Technologies*, Number 5 (Carnegie Endowment for International Peace and Monterey Institute of International Studies, March 1998), Table II-A.

26. *Ugolovny kodeks Rossiiskoi Federatsii (ofitsial'ny tekst)* [Criminal Code of the Russian Federation (official text)], (Rolf Airis Publishing House, 1996), pp. 97–98.

27. *Ibid.*, pp. 117–119, 122.

28. Prezident Rossii dal porucheniie pravitel'stvu uskorit' podgotovku i vneseniie v Gosdumu proekta federal'nogo zakona ob eksportnom kontrole [Russia's President Requested the Government to Accelerate Preparation and Submitting of the Federal Law on Export Control to the State Duma], RIA-Novosti, *Goriachaya liniya*, July 16, 1998, http:/www.ria-novosti.com/ruproducts/hotline/1998/07/16-010.htm.

29. "The Proliferation Primer," A Majority Report to the Subcommittee on International Security, Proliferation and Federal Service. Committee on Governmental Affairs. U.S. Senate (January 1998).

30. In 1996 the author prepared a draft text of the request while working as a senior staffer in the Duma Defense Committee. Author's discussion with a Russian official, Moscow, April 1997.

31. "The Proliferation Primer."

32. For more detailed data on Russian ballistic missiles, see Aleksander Pikayev, "Vypolneniye Rossiyey Dogovora SNV-1" [Russia's Compliance to the START I Treaty], Chapter 1 in *Razoruzhniye i bezopasnost. Rossiia i mezhdunarodnaia sistema kontrolia nad vooruzheniiami: razvitiie ili raspad. Yezhegodnik IMEMO 1997-98* [Disarmament and Security. Russia and International Arms Control System: Development or Disintegration. IMEMO Yearbook 1997–98] M. (Nauka, 1997), pp. 14–28.

33. "The Proliferation Primer," Viktor Mizin, "Russian Missile Proliferation Dilemmas," pp. 31–33; author's discussion with Dr. William Potter, Parnu, Estonia, February 1998; author's discussion with Russian missile expert, Moscow, January 1998.

34. *Izvestiya* (June 1, 1997); *Nezavisimaya gazeta* (May 14, 1997).

35. *Ugolovny kodeks Rossiiskoi Federatsii (ofitsial'ny tekst)* [Criminal Code of the Russian Federation (official text)] (Rolf Airis Publishing House, 1996), pp. 115–116.

36. Director of Central Intelligence, *The Acquisition of Technology Relating to Weapons of Mass Destruction and Advanced Conventional Munitions: July-September 1996.* June 1997, Washington, DC.

37. Zayavleniye MID RF, *O doklade TsRU po voprosam nerasprostraneniya OMU i noveishikh sistem obychnykh vooruzheniy* [Statement of the RF MFA On the CIA Report on Non-Proliferation of WMD and Advanced Conventional Weapons] (July 9, 1997).

38. "The Proliferation Primer"; author's discussion with a Russian missile expert, December 1997.

39. Steven Erlanger, "Russian Arms Firms Face U.S. Sanctions," *Moscow Times* (July 17, 1998); "Rossiya ne dopustit utechki voiennykh tehnologiy" [Russia Will Not Permit Leakage of Military Technologies], *Segodnya* (July 17, 1998); The Proliferation Primer, "Prezident Rossii dal porucheniie."

40. Author's discussion with a Russian export control specialist, Moscow, July 1998.

41. Aleksander Pikayev (ed.), *Rossiya, SShA, Kitai, Ukraina i rezhim kontrolya za raketnymi tehnologiyami*, p. 48.

42. Steven Erlanger, "Russian Arms Firms Face U.S. Sanctions."

11

RUSSIA AND THE WASSENAAR ARRANGEMENT: A NEW MULTILATERAL EXPORT CONTROL REGIME FOR CONVENTIONAL WEAPONS AND DUAL-USE ITEMS

Elina Kirichenko and
Dmitriy Nikonov

During the post-World-War-II years, the policies of export control over conventional weapons, military hardware, and items used for their development were evolving as elements of national security in the Cold War, both in the United States and the Soviet Union. Concerned with the possible ramifications of nuclear war, capable of destroying life on Earth, nuclear powers managed to overcome disagreements and enact the Nuclear Nonproliferation Treaty (NPT), aimed at restraining the spread of nuclear weapons and technologies and limiting the number of nuclear states. The trade of conventional weapons and sensitive dual-use technologies, however, remained hostage to, and a tool of, ideological confrontation between the two political systems. With the U.S. leadership, the Western states formed a Coordinating Committee on Export Controls (COCOM) to prevent the transfer of strategic items and technologies of possible military applicability to the Communist Bloc. For the same purpose, the Soviet Union vehemently guarded its strategic items and technologies through mechanisms of its heavily centralized planned economy and security agencies.

The end of the Cold War changed the element of strategic rivalry between the Soviet Union and the United States. In return, it created a number of New Independent States (NIS), some of which (Russia, Ukraine, and others) had the potential of producing and exporting advanced weaponry and technologies. Given the modern sophistication and destructiveness of conventional weapons, their accumulation is no less a serious threat to international security than proliferation of the weapons of mass destruction (WMD).

These conditions prompted the creation of a new multilateral export control regime, the Wassenaar Arrangement, whose task is to strengthen regional and international security by means of raising countries' awareness of transfers of weapons and dual-use technologies to other countries, particularly in situations when peace and international security are in jeopardy. In that respect, the function of Wassenaar Arrangement is to control the export of conventional weapons and dual-use goods and technologies in order to make a decisive step toward the New World Order. At the same time, there are a number of economic factors undermining the effectiveness of export control mechanisms and urging their revision from the national and international security standpoints:

- Technologies, information availability, and social needs (values) are the primary driving forces of today's world. It is important for the interests of national security not only to understand the short-term aspects of these forces, but also to envision the long-term tendencies of development and interlacing of these three forces. Fundamentally, new technologies and informational infrastructure will form new social needs, as well as thinking and reality perception by individuals, and will determine differently national competitiveness and national interests, and retailor the geopolitical space.

- Access tĭo foreign technologies and information is an essential factor in maintaining both national competitiveness and security; from a long-term standpoint, this factor will become critical.

- Scientific progress accelerates the international diffusion of advanced technologies. An increasing number of countries are becoming more technologically developed; the world market of dual-use goods and technologies continues to expand. Naturally, the availability of analogous items and technologies on the world market and multilateral coordination of national export control policies provide better grounds for their effectiveness.

- Internationalization of scientific and technical knowledge is increasing. This is facilitated by the activities of the multinational corporations: search for new external markets and expanded selection of locations for R&D and production facilities eclipse the national identification of technologies, thereby making the implementation of national export regulation more difficult.

- The civilian sector has overtaken the military in some areas of generating the latest technologies that have important military applicability, particularly in computer production. Export controls therefore concern almost all science and technology-related producers. States face the difficult dilemma of balancing facilitation and limitation of exports in the interest of international security.

MULTILATERAL CONTROLS IN RETROSPECT

Export controls occupy a special part in the politics of foreign economic regulation of any developed country. They are based on the proscrip-
tion/permit (or licensing) procedure of export of certain goods and
technologies found in special control lists. Exports are understood
expansively, including all foreign economic operations covering transfers of controlled items and technologies. Restrictions are imposed to
ensure national security and to address internal economic problems
(such as commodity shortages) or foreign policy goals (such as implementation of international economic sanctions).

The specificity of an export control system, such as the opportunity to
cut off the flow of advanced technologies and to respond quickly to adver-
sarial actions, made it an irreplaceable instrument of the West's foreign
policy during the Cold War. Even nowadays many associate the phrase
"export controls" with the discriminatory policies of COCOM. The
Coordinating Committee on exports of strategic items to the socialist
countries was the first (founded in 1949, with the headquarters in Paris)
popularly known multilateral "gentlemen's agreement" on export controls, but not the only one. In the 1970s and 1980s, a number of formal
and informal multilateral export regulation regimes appeared that made
it their goal to stop the proliferation of WMD—the Australia Group,
MTCR, the Zangger Committee, and the Nuclear Suppliers Group (NSG).

A list of armaments, nuclear equipment, and materials, and the so-
called international industrial list, which included dual-use items and technologies, were developed within COCOM. The dual-use list was replaced
in 1991 by the Core List, which included nine categories: electronics, material processing, advanced composite materials, telecommunication and
information security equipment, sensors and lasers, navigation and avionics systems, naval navigation technologies, and engines. Control over
exports of items included in the list was carried out on the basis of national legislative acts and export regulation mechanisms. Until recently, U.S.
control lists were much more extensive than international lists.

The United States has played a special part in multilateral export regulation. It was not only the initiator of COCOM, but also the driving
force of this informal organization, influencing enormously the formation of its collective policy. Since the mid-1980s, the United States, realizing that export controls can be effective only if coordinated with all
dual-use goods suppliers, set out to make the multilateral control system
more complex. COCOM remained its core; the United States, however,
had a number of bilateral agreements whereby the American partner
pledged to comply with COCOM regulations, developed national export
and import control mechanisms, instituted the issuance of import end-
user certificates, and checked whether the supplied items were used for
declared purposes.

The so-called "black lists" of companies and countries suspected of violating COCOM regulations and re-exports of dual-use items controlled by the United States became important pressure tools. The scope of multilateral controls was expanding because of the aggressive outward thrust of the U.S. export regulation legislation, which, in turn, was based on the attractiveness of the American market and technologies for partners around the globe. Japan improved its export control system after a highly publicized case of Toshiba Machine Company, which, after accusations of violating multilateral export regulations, was banned for three years from selling its products on the American market and seeking U.S. government contracts. States that created effective export control systems and consistently coordinated their actions with COCOM received a "reliable partner" status and were treated more like members of the organization.

The issue of COCOM's obsolescence and lesser effectiveness was discussed even before the collapse of the Soviet Union. As economic interdependence and internationalization deepened, rapid proliferation of advanced technologies and commodity analogs on the world market became an international reality. Not only do export self-limitations undermine the competitiveness of national exporters, they also create a barrier for domestic producers on the way to foreign technologies: "exports" are interpreted expansively, and export control systems include all forms of foreign economic relations. At the same time, the issue of nonproliferation of WMD is becoming the key element of national and global security concepts and, accordingly, of export control policies.

In the early 1990s, the question of how to use COCOM experience to strengthen international regimes of WMD nonproliferation was widely discussed. Some experts suggested reorienting COCOM's activities and fusing it with other international regimes.[1] Over the last three years of its existence, COCOM's position had undergone considerable evolution. Restrictions on 350 out of 600 items had been eliminated or downgraded. For the first time in the history of the organization, one of the controlled countries—Hungary—was lifted from control lists. Also, the export of computers and communication equipment was liberalized significantly.

The dissolution of the Warsaw Pact, disintegration of the USSR, and the appearance of Russia and other independent nations changed the geopolitical situation. The collapse of the old world order, based on the opposition of two world superpowers, occurred so swiftly that the global community failed to realize promptly the necessity of reconsidering many political and economic concepts, doctrines, and strategies, particularly export control policies, as part of global and national security. The old mentality did not allow the acknowledgement of Russia as an equal economic partner or to lift restrictions and dismantle institutions created in the years of blind confrontation.

On June 1, 1992, delegates at the meeting of COCOM states made two important decisions: first, to liberalize control over exports of telecommunications equipment; and second, to create a forum on cooperation in export controls of modern technologies with the participation of the former socialist countries, including Russia and China.

COCOM members outlined the membership and activities of the so-called New Forum; the U.S. State Department prepared a document clarifying its position on some key issues:[2]

- New Forum participants would not become COCOM members; the forum would be a supplement to COCOM;
- COCOM would not lift restrictions toward forum participants, but would stimulate "much greater access of the latter to advanced Western goods and technologies";
- The Department of State did not see a contradiction in the fact that forum participants were invited to cooperate on export controls while some restrictions toward them remained. One of the goals of the forum—to work closely on issues of export control policy—included assistance in creating appropriate reliable national systems;
- The United States did not intend to use the forum as means to limit the access of developing countries to technologies that they need for their economic development;
- The forum would supplement but not duplicate the existing non-proliferation regimes (the London Club, the Australia Group, MTCR).

As the White House officially announced, the goals of the forum reflected new strategic relationships, particularly with Russia and other republics of the former Soviet Union. These goals were: much more expanded access by the participants to advanced Western technologies; development of guarantee procedures against transfers of sensitive items for military use to uncontrolled consumers; assistance to new members in the creation of national export control systems; and further cooperation in developing common approaches toward export controls.[3]

The preservation of COCOM and export restrictions on a variety of civilian goods were taken by Russia at the time as the unwillingness of the West to allow her access to new technologies from the standpoint of commercial interest. Russia could not see how one could join the forum as an equal partner.[4] COCOM appeared increasingly obsolete.

On November 17, 1993, 17 COCOM members decided that, beginning April 1, 1994, COCOM would be replaced with the new body, with a new political direction and organizational structure. Russia was invited to participate. Despite the amusing selection of the date [April 1 is April Fools' Day—*trans.*], the event itself was historic. The West did not just plant a bomb under one of the relics of the Cold War. The new multi-lateral export control regime over sensitive dual-use technologies and weapons, which could scarcely be called COCOM's successor, was formed not on ideological orientation, but on global tasks of preventing the proliferation of WMD and strengthening international security.

In 1994 and 1995, five rounds of negotiations on the future of the new multilateral regime were conducted in Wassenaar, a suburb of The Hague. The negotiations included former COCOM members and countries that received, according to the U.S. laws, the status of "reliable partner" (Austria, Ireland, New Zealand, Finland, Switzerland, and Sweden), as well as a number of countries formerly targeted by COCOM restrictions.

Russia's acceptance into the New Forum was delayed until the second half of 1995, primarily because of the tough position of the United States, Canada, and, to some extent, the United Kingdom. These countries explained their resistance with the necessity to obtain from Russia additional concessions on her military and technical cooperation with certain countries (primarily with Iran) and to ascertain the effectiveness of the Russian export control system.[5]

Having decided to join the Wassenaar Arrangement, Russia developed a new list of certain raw materials, materials, equipment, technologies, and scientific and technical information that can be used in the development of weapons and military hardware, and adopted procedures for controlling these items. In addition, Russia introduced the mechanism of import certification. The official Russian position was that Russian export control system now met international standards.[6]

The West, however, was concerned with Russia's economic and political instability, which could undermine the effectiveness of the established export control system. The absence of appropriate control mechanisms over WMD proliferation in other NIS countries and border transparency between them and Russia were also causes for concern.[7] At the same time, some members of the New Forum were quite realistically pointing out that without including such a significant producer of arms and sensitive technologies as Russia, the new organization would be pointless; besides, that would cut off all leverage to influence Moscow's policies.

Russian-Iranian cooperation was also a major impediment to Russian involvement in the Wassenaar Arrangement. In September 1994, President Boris Yeltsin announced during his visit to New York that Russia would refrain from signing new arms deals with Iran. After another meeting of the two presidents in Moscow in May of 1995, the U.S administration stressed that old contracts that Russia continued to honor did not destabilize the region. Finally, Vice President Al Gore and Prime Minister Victor Chernomyrdin agreed on Russia's joining the Wassenaar Arrangement at their meeting in June 1995. Russia viewed becoming a full-fledged member as an indicator of the West's desire for

Russia's integration into the world community. However, the participants could not agree on the items to be included in the proscription lists. Russia believed it unfair that she should support restrictions without having participated in putting the lists together.

On December 19, 1995, representatives of 28 countries including Russia agreed to create the new multilateral export control regime, to be called the Wassenaar Arrangement, over conventional weapons and sensitive dual-use items and technologies, with the secretarial headquarters in Vienna. From January 1996, the preparatory committee began putting together control lists and developing the principles of organizational activity. On July 12, 1996, the participants of the Vienna meeting agreed on adopting the Wassenaar Arrangement; at that point 33 countries participated.

The Wassenaar Arrangement would have been created even without Russia's participation. It is, however, in the interests of both the international community and Russia herself that the latter joined and participates. Russia recognizes that it is easier to promote national interests from within the organization. Although the 1988 U.S. Law on Trade and Competitiveness has a clause urging to create among COCOM members an area "free of export licensing," this idea has never been implemented. And although it does not exist in the new Wassenaar organization either, participation in it opens up a way of legally obtaining advanced technologies.

The sphere of conventional arms export controls has until recently lacked international legal basis. The former COCOM had a Munitions List, but the restrictions were directed against the Warsaw Pact countries. The United Nations has a Conventional Weapons Register. Consultations among the five permanent Security Council members resulted in the Guidelines for Conventional Weapons Transfers, which state that the exporters pledge to avoid sales that can aggravate an armed conflict, raise tensions or introduce a destabilizing military potential into a region, violate an international embargo, support international terrorism, or be used other than for the purposes of national defense.

It was not possible, however, to agree on effective control over arms transfers in the world or on enhanced information-sharing on these transfers (such as, for example, on types and modifications) within the framework of the Conventional Weapons Register. The United States, in this respect, greatly emphasized the arms component in the formation of the new organization.

RUSSIA'S VIEWS AND THE WASSENAAR ARRANGEMENT

Joining the Wassenaar Arrangement is viewed as an agreement of a state to adhere to policies of nonproliferation of WMD and to control the exports of sensitive dual-use items and conventional weapons in accordance with adopted agreements. The Wassenaar Arrangement aspires to enhance cooperation on the prevention of acquisition of arms and dual-use items for military end-use purposes if the situation in a certain region or the policies of a certain state become an issue for concern of the international community.

For Russia, it was very important that the new regime would not replicate COCOM, created during the Cold War. Russia believed, for example, that the new regime should not rely on a defined list of proscribed countries. It became known from the press that the U.S. Undersecretary of State Lynn Davis presented a list of countries of special concern to the United States due to suspicions of their using imported equipment for military purposes; these were, first of all, Iran, Iraq, North Korea, and Libya. The United States, however, was not successful in persuading other partners to adopt this list of "rogue states."

Naturally, it was difficult to put together the control list of dual-use items. Having the goal of maintaining international security and preventing WMD proliferation in mind, no state wants to undermine the competitiveness of its exporters. The whole list is subdivided into two: dual-use items, and sensitive items and technologies; the latter has a special section of highly sensitive items.

Procedural issues separated Russia and the United States on several occasions. As some observers reported, the firmness of the Russian delegation encouraged other members to be more independent and active than they used to be within COCOM, where the United States dominated. On some issues Russia often enjoyed the support of France, Italy, Germany, and Japan.[8] Russia successfully defended the principle of preeminence of national legislation in resolving key issues. The United States suggested simple majority vote as a general principle of voting; Russia, however, insisted (again, successfully) on proclaiming consensus as the regime's voting procedure.

The largest obstacle was the mechanism of notification on transfers of listed items. The United States insisted that such information, which concerned both arms and dual-use technologies, should be shared. The Russian delegation opposed such a notification procedure, believing that the information could be used for commercial purposes by competitors. Russian military representatives were the most resolute opponents of this preliminary notification mechanism, which is not surprising since the two countries are the main competitors on the world arms markets. Russian military representatives also disputed more frequent and detailed notifications than was necessary according to the UN regulations.

After Russia withdrew her arguments with regard to the notification mechanism, participants of the July 1996 meeting adopted the so-called Initial Elements, which confirmed the establishment of the new multilateral regime. The participants agreed to meet and share information regularly, in order to seek understanding on the issues of preventing excessive stockpiling of conventional weapons and sensitive technologies in certain countries and regions that could pose a threat to peace and international security. The participants will coordinate their export control efforts based on this information.

The Initial Elements have two basic list components: dual-use items and conventional weapons. The document provides for the procedure of notification on transfers of dual-use items to nonparticipating states, and on license denials as regard the goals of the multilateral regime. For sensitive technologies, notifications are issued "on individual basis," that is, within 30 but no later than 60 days after the date of denial. These notifications, however, do not compel other members to refuse to sell similar items. Wassenaar members have not adopted a rule in effect among the members of the Nuclear Suppliers Group, which states that although the final decision on license issuance is made by an individual country based on its understanding of the problem, all members agree not to allow such exports without prior consultations with the government that had refused export of such items or technologies for certain reasons (a "no-undercut" rule). After prolonged discussions, the Wassenaar Arrangement members agreed only to inform each other on such exports within 30 to 60 days. Notification of license denials for exports of nonsensitive dual-use items will be shared in aggregated form biannually.

The regime provides for sharing the information on arms sales every six months. The data is based on the U.N. Register classification, which divides all weapons into seven categories. The exchange within the Wassenaar Arrangement provides, however, more information, such as identifying modifications and types of weapons. At the same time, participants failed to agree on whether to provide such information before the sale or transfer of the arms, on which the United States insisted.

The Wassenaar Arrangement offers a set of principles and rules for its participants. But again, the restrictions prescribed by international institutions and sanctions against violators are carried out through national mechanisms, based on national laws. As Sergei Kislyak, head of the Russian delegation and Director of the Department of Security and Disarmament of the Russian Federation (RF) Ministry of Foreign Affairs, said in his 1996 interview, radically new mechanisms of export controls in the area of arms and dual-use items have been established, which, unlike similar old mechanisms, are not directed against any particular country or group of states. The new regime provided by the Wassenaar Arrangement is designed on different principles from its COCOM predecessor, and is somewhat akin to the nuclear export control regime, which encourages states to exercise more responsibility in solving these important issues.[9]

It may well be expected that fine-tuning of the new organization will face difficulties. First, the new regime consists in fact of two different components: weapons and dual-use technologies. They concern the interests of a large number of exporters. As far as conventional weapons controls are concerned, the regime is in its embryonic stage. So far the members have merely enhanced the degree of information sharing. Besides, the Wassenaar members have effectively divided in two groups: the six large arms exporters (the United States, Russia, Germany, France, the United Kingdom, and Italy), which account for 90 percent of arms sales in the world, and the rest of the members, which view the export control problem from the standpoint of consumers rather than producers. Even the six supplier countries failed to agree on preliminary delivery notifications, and conventional weapons continue to be the most vulnerable part of the international nonproliferation regime. Its effectiveness is also questioned by the absence of China in the new regime.

RUSSIA'S EXPORT CONTROL SYSTEM

Participation in the new organization implies that a country has a system of export controls oriented toward preventing proliferation of WMD. The United States has always introduced additional unilateral restrictions; the U.S. lists are still more comprehensive than the international ones. The Soviet Union, naturally, controlled any foreign economic transfers as part of the command-administrative system, particularly weapons and items possessing military significance. In the early 1980s, the Soviet Union developed a list of strategically important items. The USSR initiated and coordinated export control policies in the Warsaw Pact countries. After declaring independence, Russia had to develop a new export control system, given the country's transition to market economy, emergence of the private sector, and the liberalization of foreign economic activity, on the one hand, and the necessity of integration into the world economy, on the other.

An amazing paradox is that after World War II the West was erecting and strengthening barriers to stop sharing technologies with the Soviet Union; now it offers Russia assistance in developing an effective export control system. Russia is one of the first NIS countries to have developed such a comprehensive export regulation system. Five control lists have been developed encompassing items and technologies that are, or can be, used for military production as well as for the production of nuclear, chemical, and biological weapons and means of their delivery. These lists are adopted by the government and approved by the president. Another adopted list of weapons and military hardware includes items subject to mandatory export licensing.

Control of Dual-Use Technologies

Russia has created an export control system over dual-use technologies that meets the requirements of multilateral WMD nonproliferation regimes, with a legal base in the form of laws, presidential decrees, and governmental decisions,[10] along with control lists, licensing procedures, and an implementation control mechanism. In order to carry out unified state policies and to coordinate and provide organizational and methodological support of export control efforts, the RF government created an Interagency Commission on Export Controls (RF *Exportkontrol*).

In 1994 the RF government adopted a control list and the Procedures for Controlling the Exports from the Russian Federation of Certain Raw Materials, Materials, Equipment, Technologies and Scientific and Technical Information that Can Be Used for Developing Arms and Military Hardware. A new list of controlled items was adopted in August 1996, which basically repeats the last COCOM list. On October 7, 1996, the government signed the new version of the Procedures on Export Controls.

Exports of dual-use goods and services are carried out only with single licenses, by authorization of the Department of Foreign Economic Activity of the Ministry of Trade and RF *Exportkontrol*. A decision of the latter provides grounds for issuing a license; it also issues a decision on the possibility of reexport. The State Customs Committee submits to the working group of RF *Exportkontrol* information on the actual export shipments of dual-use goods and services across the border. The Criminal Code has been supplemented with provisions for criminal liability for violations of export control regulations.

In order to export Russian dual-use items, the importer must provide guarantees that they will not be used, directly or indirectly, for developing weapons and military hardware, and will not be reexported or transferred to another party without the written consent of the exporter. The guarantees must be documented at the state official level.

In October 1993, Russia introduced procedures to control the adherence to guarantees to use imported and exported dual-use goods and services for declared purposes. Due order of obtaining the Russian import, delivery confirmation, and end-user certificates was also established. According to this, the Ministry of Trade is responsible for the issuance of import certificates, and the State Customs Committee is responsible for delivery confirmation certificates. The Russian exporter, in turn, must include in the signed contract a provision for the right to conduct inspections of the use of the exported items in declared purposes. Requests for such inspections are sent through the RF Ministry of Foreign Affairs.

Formation of the Russian Weapons Export Controls

Penetration into new arms markets has recently become an important strategy of Russian foreign trade. The world arms market has been sharply and unavoidably declining, which only strengthens competition for the sales of arms and military hardware. After the disintegration of the Soviet Union, foreign arms trade was in a serious crisis. Unlike the Soviet Union, Russian agreements on military and technical cooperation and arms sales are not ideologically based but are driven by commercial interest. In the mid-1990s, Russia made significant efforts to sign sales agreements with those developing nations that could pay in hard currency for their purchases. According to the U.S. Congressional Research Service, Russia's arms transfer agreements in 1996 were valued at $4.6 billion (second to the United States), and actual deliveries at $2.9 billion, tied for third with France after the U.S. and the United Kingdom.[11] None of the countries, including Russia, is going to let this area of trade slip through its fingers.

The procedures for Russia's Military and Technical Cooperation with Foreign Countries, along with the Law on Military Conversion, adopted in May 1992, established the initial normative foundation for state export and import regulation of arms, military hardware, work, and services. At that time, the Interagency Commission on Military-Technical Cooperation was making decisions in that area. The Directorate for Military-Technical Cooperation of RF Ministry of Trade issued export licenses. A special department responsible for technical assessment of export applications was created within the ministry.

According to the 1995 Procedures for Licensing Exports and Imports of Military Designated Items, Work and Services, foreign trade operations began to be carried out in accordance with the decisions of the RF government and licenses issued by the State Committee on Military and Technical Policy. Licenses issued exclusively to legal entities of the Russian Federation in due order granted the right to conduct foreign trade operations in the military and technical sectors. The same committee carried out registration of such entities. This mechanism is presently dismantled, and a department within the Ministry of Trade responsible for weapons export licensing was reestablished.

During the entire period of Russia's independence, there has been a continuing discussion on whether the state should hold the monopoly on foreign arms trade or simply regulate it by means of licensing. Various agencies fought for responsibilities within the export control system; small wonder that the licensing mechanism changed several times in the 1990s.

Naturally, the effectiveness of an export control system depends not only on its perfection, but also on a number of economic and political factors. An export control system is certainly not immune from the economic and financial hardships endured by a country.

Russia, as is the case with many other developed countries, presently faces problems of developing a strategy of export controls in the context of reconsidering its national security. How should export control effectiveness be assessed? How should contradictory tasks of promoting national goods on the world market and honoring international obligations of nonproliferation of WMD, international technological development (which implies, among other things, access to foreign technologies), and restrictions on transfers of critical technologies be balanced? Russia has a long way to go in learning to stand by her interests in multilateral regimes. And unfortunately, these problems sometimes cannot be resolved by diplomatic skill. The most vulnerable link in the chain of the Russian export control system is the weak mechanism of balancing and coordinating different interest groups. The industrial lobby in the United States has great influence over the decision-making process and the formation of policies and the export control system at different levels: during congressional hearings, licensing (participation in putting together control lists), and international negotiations (participation in delegations, preparing draft agreements). In Russia, participation by the actual producers in business circles is minimal. This is explained not only by the desire of the bureaucratic apparatus for an easy life, but also by the absence of business culture and experience among Russian businessmen. Bogged down by numerous taxes and restrictions, they often fail to understand the goals of export controls, and view control lists as just another bureaucratic obstacle. On the other hand, the state itself does not have a defined concept of national security, which makes it difficult to set certain goals during international negotiations (it is particularly unclear what should be accounted for in the formation of control lists).

RUSSIA'S FUTURE IN THE WASSENAAR ARRANGEMENT

Given the size of her defense industrial complex and her share in the world conventional arms market, Russia's active membership in the Wassenaar Arrangement will remain crucial to the regime's success. The obstacles and controversy encountered by both Western nations and Russia on the way into the Wassenaar Arrangement show that this membership is unlikely to be without controversy; the subsequent resolution of the issues, on the other hand, proves that differences are not insurmountable. Many factors are likely to affect the success of the new regime; we cannot predict what these factors will be and how their effects will manifest. We can assume, however, that the factors that are likely to affect the success of the Wassenaar Arrangement are the original motives for Russia to have sought membership and for the West to have offered it.

Since cooperation implies participation by at least two parties, we should examine the motives of both Russia and the Western partners (the United States in this case, as it was the principal opponent of several Russian proposals) that drove their actions during the formation stage of the new regime. Theories of international relations provided several explanations of actions undertaken by states on the international arena to achieve certain goals.

The *realist* school of thought argues that states act to maximize their security and interest in terms of power. Although realism is usually connected with explanations of conflict rather than cooperation, certain cases of cooperation may be argued to enhance the security of particular states, such as, for example, building alliances.[12]

The *rational-institutional* school of thought believes that states are likely to cooperate if they perceive that certain inducements may be obtained as a result of such cooperation, or economic incentives have been promised or delivered to them by their partners conditional upon their cooperation.[13]

The *domestic pressure* school of thought does not really treat states as single entities (unlike the two previous approaches), but assumes that much of what is known as foreign policy is in fact a product of domestic politics in a particular country—a result of intertwining of preelection politics, ethnic or religious division in the society, political culture, and so on.[14]

Finally, the *liberal community identity* theory suggests that states are likely to cooperate and form similar foreign policies with states that they share a common identity with,[15] or, as is the case with Russia, if they are striving to be identified as a part of a desirable community or group of states.

These theoretical approaches can be translated into four possible factors explaining Russia's involvement in the Wassenaar Arrangement: (1) realist—considerations of national security; (2) rational-institutional—expectations of economic benefit; (3) domestic pressure—effect of domestic politics; and (4) liberal community identity—search for a new identity among Western democracies. Let us consider these four.

First, although Russia proclaimed that it presently faces no major external threat,[16] it is safe to assume that her national security would be enhanced if provisions of the Wassenaar Arrangement were to be fulfilled by all members. Indeed, Russia may not be expecting to be challenged in a large-scale war by a serious adversary at this time. States, however, are usually not inclined to view with benign indulgence attempts at heavy militarization near their borders or in the areas of their national interest. And since the Wassenaar Arrangement targets precisely that kind of behavior through control of transfers of conventional weapons and dual-use items, the fact of participation in the regime can only facilitate Russia's security.[17]

In addition, with participation in the Wassenaar Arrangement, there is a possibility of sanctioned exports of weapons and technologies to certain long-term Russian weapons buyers such as China, India, countries of Latin America and Europe, and South East Asia. A new strategic plan for expanding Russian arms market for advanced weapons systems, focusing on Asia, Latin America, and the Middle East, was announced by Rosvooruzhenie, Russia's major arms trader.[18] Such exports are less likely to cause objections from the United States and the West. By becoming actively engaged in arms trade within close proximity to her borders,

Russia will be able to exercise effective and substantial control of the regional balance of power, undoubtedly in her favor.[19] Indirectly, Russia's security can also be enhanced through closer cooperation with members of the regime, which implies less likelihood of conflict.

Second, the question whether Russia expects tangible economic benefits from participation in the Wassenaar Arrangement remains an issue for debate. On the one hand, Russia can benefit in the long run, by utilizing closer relationships and increased trust among the members of the arrangement in order to obtain the latest Western technologies, investments, and contracts. Conversely, trade policies that violate provisions of the export control regime will lead to restrictions on all sales of advanced technologies to Russia, as well as severance of the existing economic assistance programs. This prospect, however remote, is bound to attract the consideration of the Russian leadership.

On the other hand, the cash-stripped Russian defense industry views conventional arms exports as the only means of staying afloat in the widespread economic crisis and lack of government contracts and subsidies.[20] In that respect, any impediment to free export of weapons will not be welcomed by either the Russian defense industrialists or the government. The issue is further aggravated by the wage nonpayment crisis in the Russian economy, in which wages to R&D and defense enterprises have lagged behind for several months.[21]

Realizing the dilemma, the attempts of the Russian government to negotiate a suitable agreement with, mostly, the United States during the initial stages of Wassenaar Arrangement are quite understandable. Russia cannot afford to be left out of the arrangement, but would like to keep as much of a free hand as possible in conducting her arms exports within the confines of the regime.

Third, admitting that Russia's actions in the international arena are that of a unitary player certainly simplifies attempts of analysis. It is very likely, however, that given the current state of controlled chaos in Russian politics, multiplicity of political forces at play, and anecdotal evidence of high-level government corruption, Russian foreign policy, especially in cooperation with the West, is a constantly changing vector-sum effort. Joining the Wassenaar Arrangement should, therefore, be approached from that perspective as well.

Several relevant key factors can be singled out from the current Russian political palette, as well as from the period of the most heated debate over the provisions of the new agreement (1994 to 1996). The government of Boris Yeltsin, who at the time was preparing for his reelection campaign, had to tread rather carefully, both to ensure Russia's participation in the Wassenaar Arrangement and not to facilitate the opposition's outrage. For reasons discussed further, the government believed it necessary to secure Russia's active role in the new regime. Such actions, however, could most certainly be viewed by the mainly conservative Duma as "betrayal" of the Russian national interests and another evidence of the "treacherous character" of the "Yeltsin regime."[22] This opposition stance is unlikely to have reflected genuine position on the issue, but rather was a part of preelection rhetoric. The government managed to placate these fears by maintaining a tough stance in negotiations with the United States on key issues of the new arrangement and by showing every evidence of being protective of Russia's national interests.

On the other hand, this tough position of the government was probably due to its own accord: since 1992 it had become clear that Russia can obtain more benefits from the West by taking a firm stance and negotiating from it to a more desirable compromise.

Another interested party, undoubtedly, was the military-industrial complex, ridden by numerous financial and economic problems. It is unlikely that defense industries would be willing to curb their potential arms exports through Russia's participation in the regime unless the government provided certain incentives in return for support, such as, for example, more liberal export licensing, possible beneficial cooperation with Western companies, or assurances that formal obligations in the arrangement are unlikely to affect export policies at all.

Fourth, although the arguments of the liberal community identity theory concern states that already share common identity and therefore foreign policy, they can also be used in the case of Russia. The question whether Russia belongs with the West or the East, or has a place in the world altogether of her own, has been a highly debated and painful one. Ever since the first attempts at Westernization by Tsar Alexei Romanov and later Peter the Great in the late 1600s and early 1700s, the ideological split between Westernizers and Slavophiles highlighted Russian political life for centuries, unencumbered even by the 70-year history of Communist rule. Manifestations of this dispute are visible even now, in the clearly traceable pro-Western moods of today's Russian liberals as opposed to radical nationalist, Communist, and right-wing centrist parties, who advocate Russia's unique and special role in world history.

Russia's euphoric statements with regard to her finally becoming a part of the community of civilized states marked the early 1990s, once the obstacle of Communism was no longer there. It soon became obvious, however, that neither was Russia yet ready (or even fit) to become fully democratic in the Western sense, nor was the West willing to abandon caution in dealings with its former adversary. Without a doubt, the West hailed the ongoing economic and political reform in the former Soviet Union but wasn't quick to move from words to deeds in altering its policies to reflect the new reality.

Disenchantment with the "romantic period" of the U.S.-Russian relationship has caused Russia to refocus her foreign policies from an approach almost exclusively geared to the West to a more balanced and pragmatic, all-encompassing approach, with special emphasis on renewed partnership with former allies in the East such as China and India.

Recognition by the West as an equal partner still remains an important factor of prestige. After the Cold War, Russia was hurt by, if not military, nevertheless, a defeat, and at the same time was in search of a new identity. Hence, Russia's insistence on becoming a *de jure* member of the G-7 group of industrialized states,[23] demands for special treatment in relationships with the expanding NATO, and constant assertions in public speeches by Russian officials of Russia's status as a great power and her industrial and military potential.[24]

Membership in international organizations, especially of such exclusive nature as the Wassenaar Arrangement, is considered by Russia as another sign of acknowledgment of her status as a powerful state, an important player in international relations. From this perspective, active participation in the Wassenaar Arrangement and the reassertion of her independent position on key issues during negotiations are perfectly comprehensible.

To sum up the argument, Russia's eagerness to participate in the Wassenaar Arrangement indicates that the benefits of such participation—cooperation with the West, possible long-term economic benefit, association with a desirable community of states, and enhanced national security—outweigh the costs, such as limitations on arms or technology transfers and loss of the badly needed immediate cash revenues. And even these costs do not constitute a great problem, since whereas the provisions of the arrangement are rather strict with regard to sensitive goods and technologies, they leave much of conventional weapons exports to the discretion of national authorities, stipulating only a lenient notification mechanism among the members.

On the part of the United States and the West, involving Russia in a conventional weapons control regime has several advantages. First, the new export control regime would have been a stillborn child without Russian participation, given her current potential as a major weapons and technologies exporter. Regardless of how much the West is displeased with the necessity to compete with Russia for arms markets, it is still easier to manage the relationship within mutually recognized boundaries of an international agreement than to have to deal with a "rogue" Russia selling weapons and technologies left and right.

Second, by increasing her involvement in a Western-oriented alliance, the West tries to ensure that its overall relationship with Russia in the future remains amiable and manageable. Failure to do so would most certainly mean further isolation and alienation of Russia and a possibility of renewed Cold-War hostility.

The Western position can thus be explained from at least some of the earlier stated theoretical perspectives. By involving Russia, the Western states (and especially the United States) enhance their security, both directly through improved relationships and indirectly by controlling transfers of weapons to the West's existing and potential adversaries.

Participation in a Western alliance also facilitates improvement in Russia's overall economic condition through transfers of Western technologies, thereby making her a more desirable and predictable market for goods and investments—a benefit of the end of the Cold War that has so far not been very effectively used.

CONCLUSION

The global experience shows that unilateral national export restrictions are ineffective. The challenge of increasing the effectiveness of nonproliferation export controls can only be addressed through improving multilateral international cooperation. By limiting supplies of sensitive technologies, export controls remain an important element of nonproliferation policies.

The success of the Wassenaar Arrangement will depend on a number of factors, some of which have been stated in this chapter. Other factors, however, cannot be predicted, but still are anticipated. As the level of technological development evens out, and more states become capable of producing sophisticated weaponry and technologies, will the current front-runners of the industrialized world have to deal with much more numerous and therefore less controllable potential proliferants? Will the large numbers of members, higher diversity of the new regime, and the lack of ideological thrust in its policies, compared, for instance, to COCOM, lead to disputes among its members and to eventual collapse? Will the rising global economic and military powers such as China challenge the goals of nonproliferation and render all efforts to control proliferation null and void? These are the issues that future researchers will have to deal with.

But to return to present-day issues, given the internationalization of scientific knowledge and the appearance of new suppliers of dual-use technologies, supply will always meet the demand. It is essential, therefore, along with improving multilateral export control regimes, to search for other accents in the international concept of nonproliferation of WMD. The governments of the member-countries will have to make great efforts to make the Wassenaar Arrangement a cornerstone of the new economic order.

NOTES

1. L. Spector and V. Foran, "Preventing Weapons Proliferation: Should the Regimes Be Combined?" *The Stanley Foundation* (October 22–24, 1992).
2. "COCOM Approves U.S. Proposals for Cooperation Council," *Export Control News* (June 30, 1992), pp. 5–6.
3. Statement by M. Tutwiler, U.S. State Department, Office of the Assistant Secretary (June 2, 1992).

4. See, e.g., Victor Presnyakov and Vyacheslav Sokolov, "Export Controls: Economic Needs v. Proliferation Concerns," *FBIS-USR-92-167* (December 31, 1992), pp. 91–93.

5. Pyotr Litavrin, "Russia and the New Forum to Replace COCOM," in Andrew L. Pierre and D. Trenin (eds.), *Russia in the World Arms Trade: Strategy, Politics, Economics* (Moscow Carnegie Center, 1996), p. 146.

6. Rustam Safaraliev, "Russian Export Control Is Taking Its Place in the Multilateral System," *The Monitor: Nonproliferation, Demilitarization and Arms Control*, vol. 1, no. 3 (Fall 1995), pp. 1–3. Mr. Safaraliev was Deputy Director of Russia's Federal Currency and Export Control Service.

7. In 1992 heads of the CIS states signed in Minsk an agreement to coordinate the issues of export control over raw materials, materials, equipment, technologies, and services that can be used in the development of WMD and missile delivery systems. Practical implementation of this agreement, however, has been difficult.

8. Elmar Guseinov, "New COCOM Is Born Amidst Moscow-Washington Debate," *Izvestia* (April 16, 1996), p. 3.

9. Info-Tass, AIST-87 (July 13, 1996).

10. In RF it consists of the 1995 "Law on State Regulation of Foreign Economic Activity," the 1992 Presidential Decree "On Measures to Create Export Control System in Russia," as well as about 60 other normative acts.

11. Richard F. Grimmett, *Conventional Arms Transfers to Developing Nations*, 1989–1996, CRS Report for Congress (August 13, 1997).

12. Hans Morgenthau, *Politics Among Nations* (New York: Alfred Knopf, 1973), pp. 4–15; Hans Morgenthau, *Dilemmas of Politics* (Chicago: The University of Chicago Press, 1958), pp. 54–55.

13. Robert O. Keohane and Joseph Nye, *Power and Interdependence* (Glenview, IL: Scott, Forseman and Co., 1989), p. 262; Robert Keohane, *International Institutions and State Power: Essays in International Relations Theory* (Boulder, CO: Westview Press, 1989).

14. See Matthew Evangelista, "Issue Area and Foreign Policy Revisited," *International Organization* (Winter 1989), vol. 43, no. 1, pp. 148–149; Michael Mastanduno, David Lake, and John Ikenberry, "Toward a Realist Theory of State Action," *International Studies Quarterly*, vol. 33, no. 4 (December 1989), pp. 463–464.

15. Michael Doyle, "Liberalism and World Politics," *American Political Science Review*, vol. 80, no. 4 (December 1986), pp. 1151–1170; Emanuel Adler and Michael N. Barnett, "Security Communities," a paper delivered at the Annual Meeting of the American Political Science Association (September 1–4, 1994).

16. "On National Security," Address of the President of the Russian Federation to the Federal Assembly, *Nezavisimaya Gazeta* (June 14, 1996).

17. The Initial Elements of the Wassenaar Arrangement target, among other "destabilizing accumulations" of conventional weapons.

18. Most recent examples of these advances include the sale of 10 Mi-17 helicopters to Colombia, S-300 air defense missile systems to Cyprus (*OMRI*, February 4, 1997), agreement with China on licensing and plant construction for SU-27 fighter aircraft, possible long-term cooperation with Greece, (Reuter's, January 4, 1997), and China's order to purchase Russian SS-N-22 advanced antiship missiles and four Sovremenny-class destroyers, *AFP*, April 15, 1998), etc.

19. For a discussion of Russia's security scenarios, see Roland Goetz, "Russian Security Options and their Price," *Aussenpolitik*, vol. 47, no. 3, pp. 254–259.

20. Boris Kuzyk, President Yeltsin's aide on military-technical cooperation with foreign countries, said that by selling arms abroad, Russian defense industry could supply up to 60 percent of its needs for maintaining research capabilities, which would bring some relief on the strained federal budget (UPI, October 6, 1996). Overall, Russia's aggregate military production in 1996 was only 12.8 percent of

the 1991 level. The average monthly wage at defense enterprises was 579,000 rubles (app. $100), compared to 965,000 rubles in the industrial sector. *Nezavisimaya Gazeta* (January 23, 1997).

21. Russia owed up to $88 billion (500 trillion rubles) in unpaid wages and pensions (UPI, February 24, 1997).

22. Quotations are attributed to frequent political rhetoric of the time. The term "regime" usually bears a negative connotation in Russian political vocabulary.

23. In the Russian media, the group was routinely called G-8, an implicit evidence of wishful thinking.

24. This was very visible in Russia's new National Security Doctrine outlined in the Presidential address (see note 16).

PART IV

CONCLUSION

12

CONCLUSION

*Gary K. Bertsch
and William C. Potter*

The contributors to this volume have detailed the magnitude and complexity of current export control problems in the former Soviet Union and have identified the initial steps taken to confront the challenge. Ironically, given the West's prompting to encourage the growth of a free enterprise system in the NIS, the movement in that direction has in some respects aggravated the export control situation. The erosion of effective state controls over the export of sensitive defense commodities and the rise of private entrepreneurs eager to exploit a chaotic and "wild East" marketplace have combined to raise the stakes and the difficulties of nonproliferation export regulations. Although the lack of connectivity to date between suppliers and would-be end users of WMD technology and components has limited the number of confirmed proliferation-significant exports of contraband, there is little reason to believe that this luck will continue indefinitely.[1]

Further compounding the export control challenge are the signs of new strains in the U.S.-Russian nonproliferation relationship. Although the United States and Russia often cooperated closely on nuclear export and nonproliferation policy during the Cold War, in its aftermath their partnership has begun to deteriorate. Symptoms of this unraveling include major disputes between Moscow and Washington over Russian nuclear and missile exports to Iran, Russia's nuclear exports to India; disagreement about the activities of the United Nations Special Commission on Iraq; lack of meaningful intelligence-sharing regarding illicit trafficking in nuclear material; and the absence of cooperation on important regional security issues in South Asia, the Middle East, and North Korea.

Especially ominous are increasing pressures in both Russia and the United States to give priority to short-term economic and political consideration rather than long-term international security nonproliferation export control objectives. This tendency is apparent in U.S. readiness to waive tough economic sanctions against Pakistan and India following their nuclear tests, to postpone ratification of the Comprehensive Test Ban Treaty, and to ignore the steps that must be taken immediately to shore-up a very fragile nuclear Non-Proliferation Treaty regime. It also is reflected in the failure on the part of both the administration and Congress to recognize the direct relationship between the growing Russian economic crisis and the potential for catastrophic WMD proliferation and terrorist use.

The tendency to emphasize economic and political considerations over nonproliferation objectives is equally, if not more, pronounced in Russia. Among recent examples are Russian nuclear trade with India and the failure to prosecute the exporters of missile components and technology to Iraq.

The Indian case involves Russia's reaffirmation in May 1998 that it planned to continue its nuclear power cooperation with New Delhi by subsidizing the sale of two nuclear power reactors despite India's nuclear weapons tests. This decision, which followed Russia's amendment of a domestic export control regulation that precluded nuclear exports to states lacking "full scope" or comprehensive IAEA safeguards, sent precisely the wrong signal to the international community regarding the benefits of NPT membership and nuclear weapons abstinence.

The Iraqi case involves the Russian government's reluctance to prosecute those involved in missile transactions with Iraq after the Gulf War, and may represent the litmus test of the seriousness with which the Kremlin today takes its nonproliferation obligations.[2] Although not all of the details of this case have been revealed, the following facts are known.

On November 10, 1995, the Jordanian government intercepted a shipment of 240 Russian missile-guidance gyroscopes and accelerometers bound for Iraq. The next month, between December 16 and 30, a team of Iraqi scuba divers was directed by UNSCOM to dredge the Tigris River near Baghdad. They pulled out more than 200 additional missile instruments and components, many bearing clearly identifiable serial numbers in Cyrillic script. These items, like those recovered earlier in Jordan, had come from dismantled Russian submarine-launched ballistic missiles (SS-N-18s) designed to deliver nuclear warheads to targets more than 4,000 miles away.

The Russian government initially denied that the gyroscopes were Russian, notwithstanding their serial numbers. Moscow also encouraged a rumor that the instruments had been stolen from a Ukrainian manufacturer. Following UNSCOM Chairman Rolf Ekeus's visit to Moscow in early February 1996, however, Russian authorities grudgingly acknowledged that the equipment might be of Russian origin. Although they denied that the Russian government was involved, they agreed to initiate a criminal investigation, which began on April 9, 1996.

Two years later the case was abandoned. Russia's main internal security agency, the Federal Security Service (FSB) closed their case in October 1997, and in February 1998 the government investigation was formally concluded. No prosecutions were recommended. The prosecutor's office said it could not establish that a felony had been committed since the gyroscopes were "scrap metal" once they were removed from decommissioned missiles. Exporting scrap metal, even to an embargoed country, was not worthy of further prosecutorial effort. Besides, the FSB argued, technically there was no criminal provision under which the case could be prosecuted.

One possible explanation for the government's decision to drop the case was a desire to conceal the true extent of the Moscow-Baghdad missile relationship. This relationship continued from 1993 through at least mid-1995, involved repeated meetings between Iraqi representatives and senior officials from such well-known Russian military industrial enterprises as Energomash, Mars Rotor, Almaz, and Graphit, and resulted in negotiations over millions of dollars of draft contracts for missile technology transfers, including missile engines, missile design, and manufacturing capabilities that could have supported a complete intermediate-range missile development program—from training to production to assembly.

Fortunately, most of these draft contracts or protocols do not appear to have been implemented thanks to the defection in August 1995 of Saddam Hussein's son-in-law, Hussein Kamel, and UNSCOM's discovery of a portion of Iraq's missile procurement network. The ability of Iraq to negotiate the contracts in the first place, however, reveals the vulnerability of the Russian military establishment to any foreign buyer with a good line of credit. The deepening economic crisis in Russia can only exacerbate these vulnerabilities and increase the likelihood of nuclear material, missile, and chemical weapons leakage and braindrain. The tremendous economic pressures to obtain hard currency at any price also will make it very difficult for the Russian government to close the growing discrepancy between its declared nonproliferation policy and its practices and will impede closer cooperation with the United States in combating a variety of proliferation challenges.

The strains in the U.S.-Russian relationship are increasing at a time when the global nonproliferation regime is under siege. Unless there is renewed and heightened cooperation for nonproliferation on the part of the world's two leading military powers, the battle against the spread of dangerous weapons could well be lost. Among the steps that should be taken to renew U.S.-Russian cooperation for nonproliferation are revival of biannual nonproliferation bilaterals and the investment of more U.S. resources in export control assistance.

During the mid-1970s the United States and the Soviet Union initiated a series of consultations on nuclear nonproliferation matters and often worked closely together in international forums to tighten export restraints and to gain greater adherence to the NPT. In the Reagan and Bush administrations these consultations also included regular bilateral meetings held approximately every six months involving the U.S. Ambassador for Nonproliferation, other senior U.S. nonproliferation specialists, and their Soviet counterparts. Unfortunately these regular, narrowly focused bilaterals have been replaced in recent years by the much more diffuse Gore-Chernomyrdin/Primakov Commission. One low cost but important step in reviving U.S.-Russian nonproliferation cooperation is to resurrect the biannual nonproliferation bilaterals. It also would be desirable to revive the post of U.S. Ambassador for Nonproliferation and to have the occupant of that post coordinate U.S. nonproliferation policy. These measures, by themselves, would not mend the unraveling of U.S.-Russian cooperation for nonproliferation, but may be necessary conditions for concentrating bureaucratic attention on the problems and providing a dedicated forum for addressing the difficulties.

Increased U.S. government support to the NIS in the export control sector also is very important. The vast majority of the NIS are experiencing acute economic and political crises and frequently lack the requisite funds and expertise to develop and enhance their export control systems. As such, resources should be available to the key U.S. agencies—the Departments of Commerce, Defense, Energy, and State, and the U.S. Customs Service—to fund high-impact programs. Furthermore, U.S. efforts—governmental and nongovernmental—to train a new generation of nonproliferation experts are particularly important. Export control specialists also are particularly important if the progress made to date in the export control sector is to be sustained.

"Dangerous weapons and desperate states" is a global problem and, therefore, a global responsibility. Far more international attention and multilateral action are necessary. Yet, the most important things that can be done are national and local. Russia, Ukraine, and other NIS have a responsibility to do more themselves. They must continue their work to complete the legal and organizational bases of export controls. They must strive to find the resources to train the personnel and staff the weapons control structures upon which nonproliferation efforts are based, and they must make a greater effort to ensure that adequate resources are available to their export controllers. They also must demonstrate a greater political will—at the highest levels—to enforce those export control regulations already on the books.

The 1997 National Research Council study on the proliferation challenge posed by the NIS called attention to the considerable gap between NIS plans for effective export controls and their implementation.[3] Not surprisingly, it has been much easier to declare the existence of an effective weapons control program than to implement one. The Moscow-Baghdad missile relationship is only a recent illustration of how much room remains for improvement.

As the contributors in this volume point out, government and business officials in the NIS need to strike a better balance between trade and security. On the part of the governments of the NIS this means elevating the place that nonproliferation occupies in the hierarchy of national policy objectives. For the United States and other Western nations, greater sensitivity is needed about the legitimate export demands of the NIS. Too often Western lectures about the need for the NIS to undertake more stringent nonproliferation export controls are undermined by the erection of artificially high barriers to NIS exports of nonsensitive commodities. To be sure, achieving the right balance between trade and security is no easy task. Given the weapons of mass destruction arsenal of the NIS, however, the consequences of failure could be catastrophic.

NOTES

1. On this issue, see Emily Ewell, "NIS Nuclear Smuggling since 1995: A Lull in Significant Cases?" *The Nonproliferation Review* (Spring-Summer 1998), pp. 119–125.
2. See Vladimir Orlov and William C. Potter, "The Mystery of the Sunken Gyros," *The Bulletin of the Atomic Scientists* (November–December 1998), pp. 34–39.
3. *Proliferation Concerns: Assessing U.S. Efforts to Help Contain Nuclear and Other Dangerous Materials and Technologies in the Former Soviet Union* (Washington, DC: National Academy Press, 1997), pp. 17–18.

PART V

APPENDICES

APPENDIX 1

PROLIFERATION CONCERNS

*Assessing U.S. Efforts to Help Contain Nuclear and
Other Dangerous Materials and Technologies
in the Former Soviet Union*

OFFICE OF INTERNATIONAL AFFAIRS
NATIONAL RESEARCH COUNCIL

EXECUTIVE SUMMARY

The successor states of the former Soviet Union (FSU), particularly Russia, have enormous stocks of weapons—usable nuclear material and other militarily significant commodities and technologies. Preventing the flow of such items to countries of proliferation concern and to terrorist groups is a major objective of U.S. national security policy.

Russian officials have acknowledged two dozen incidents of thefts and attempted thefts of nuclear-related items in Russian facilities, including several cases involving small quantities of fissile material. Such incidents support U.S. government assessments that, as a result of the dissolution of the Soviet Union, nuclear weapons technologies are now more accessible to nations and subnational groups seeking to acquire such weaponry than at any other time in history.

Missile components traceable to the FSU have been intercepted in Jordan en route to Iraq. Also, the Aum Shinrikyo cult, which released sarin gas in the Tokyo subway in 1995, obtained a helicopter and other support equipment from Russia, presumably for use in related activities.

Other than such anecdotal evidence, reliable information is not available about the quantities and types of sensitive commodities leaving the FSU—as items of trade or as contraband. But the stakes are so great that it is only prudent to assume that significant transfers of sensitive items are a serious possibility.

This study reviews the effectiveness of U.S. bilateral programs initiated in the early 1990s to support the efforts of Russia, Ukraine,

243

Kazakstan, and Belarus in strengthening two important mechanisms for controlling the diffusion of militarily sensitive items, namely:

- Systems for materials protection, control, and accountability (MPC&A) of highly enriched uranium and plutonium, with program efforts to date having emphasized improved safeguards approaches at the facility level; and
- Export control systems covering many types of sensitive items, including dual-use items, with the programs having given primary attention to regulatory and enforcement capabilities at the national level.

Russia, Ukraine, Belarus, and Kazakstan are the focus of this effort because almost all of the fissile material of concern and the bulk of other militarily sensitive items arising from the days of the Soviet Union are found in these countries. Also, these countries were singled out for a range of U.S. cooperative security efforts in the FSU in view of the past deployment of nuclear weapons on their territories.

CHALLENGES IN CONTROLLING MILITARILY SENSITIVE ITEMS

Containment of "Direct-Use" Material

This study addresses efforts to upgrade the security of stocks of unirradiated uranium enriched to a level of 20 percent or greater (referred to herein as highly enriched uranium or HEU) and of separated plutonium of weapons grade or reactor grade (referred to herein as plutonium). HEU and plutonium are suitable for use in constructing a nuclear weapon without further enrichment or chemical reprocessing; they are thus called direct-use material. Such material is located in hundreds of buildings at widely dispersed sites; most are in Russia, but a few are in Ukraine, Belarus, and Kazakstan.

The study considered various bilateral programs involving U.S. specialists directed to the protection of HEU and plutonium, particularly those managed on the U.S. side by the Department of Energy (DOE). It did not address programs of the U.S. Department of Defense (DOD) concerning direct-use material in weapons or in other forms under the control of the Russian Ministry of Defense. The study did examine DOE efforts to address the security of nuclear fuel of the Russian Navy and civilian icebreaker fleet.

The difficulty in obtaining direct-use material is a principal technical barrier preventing countries of proliferation concern, as well as subnational groups, from acquiring a nuclear weapons capability. Many other components are required to construct a nuclear weapon, but most probably can be more readily obtained than direct-use material. Efforts to prevent wide diffusion of all critical items needed for nuclear weapons have of course been pursued by the United States.

Several kilograms of plutonium or several times that amount of HEU are required to construct a nuclear weapon, with the quantity depending on the composition of the material, type of weapon, and sophistication of the design. Details aside, the necessary amounts are very small compared to the many hundreds of tons of direct-use material present in the FSU, with much of it stored under uncertain and, in some cases, inadequate security arrangements. Most of the material is HEU, which is of particular concern. HEU can be used in weapons of primitive design and is more readily concealed during transport than plutonium since its radiation signature is easier to shield.

Given the small quantities of direct-use material required for nuclear weapons, the first challenge is to ensure that *all* such material is brought under effective MPC&A systems. Then the systems must have the integrity to ensure that materials are used only in an authorized manner.

Controlling Exports of Sensitive Items

Effective regulatory systems for controlling exports of many types of sensitive commodities and technologies from the Soviet successor states to questionable destinations also are of critical importance. The second focal point of this study is therefore the set of bilateral programs directed to improving systems for controlling exports of such items from Russia, Ukraine, Belarus, and Kazakstan.

Hundreds of enterprises and institutes developed and produced sensitive commodities in the four countries. A large number of these facilities, as well as dozens of warehouse and trading organizations, have old and new inventories of sensitive materials and equipment and also possess technical design information. The economic pressures to sell these items are intense.

National systems should effectively control exports of sensitive commodities and technical data, in accordance with international norms that recognize the importance of both nonproliferation goals and legitimate trade. Of special concern are international transfers of controlled items to inappropriate end users by (a) smugglers and (b) enterprises or trading organizations that violate national export control requirements.

While providing important guidance for regulating exports of many items, the existing international agreements on export control call for prohibitions or restrictions on transfers of only the most critical items. These agreements emphasize the need for transparency of international transfers rather than limitations on exports of most weapons-related items and dual-use commodities; for these items, each government, though required to establish an export licensing system, retains the prerogative to decide when an export is appropriate. Thus, if diffusion of sensitive items to countries of proliferation concern and terrorist groups is to be contained on a broad basis, the governments of Russia and the other successor states must be committed not only to establishing internationally acceptable export control machinery, but also to achieving nonproliferation goals in their national decisions on specific exports of militarily significant items.

Of special note, Russia inherited a large storehouse of facilities, equipment, and technology related to biological and chemical warfare, and many of these items should be carefully controlled. While the U.S. Government has undertaken limited efforts to help contain such items, a review of such activities was beyond the scope of this study.

U.S. RESPONSE FOR SECURING SENSITIVE ITEMS IN RUSSIA, UKRAINE, BELARUS, AND KAZAKSTAN

The U.S. Policy Context

THE INTERNATIONAL EXPORT CONTROL REGIMES

For a number of years the United States in concert with its traditional allies, has taken a variety of steps to reduce the likelihood that militarily sensitive items would move freely in international commerce. Central to this effort has been strong support for the establishment and operation of international control regimes covering exports of selected commodities and related technical information in the following areas: nuclear, chemical, biological, and advanced conventional weapons systems; missile systems; and other strategic items with both military and civilian applications. The regimes also cover the technologies needed to design or manufacture commodities in the foregoing categories.

These regimes provide a very important framework for the establishment of national export control systems. They require licensing of all items that have been identified as being of concern to the international community. Therefore, they greatly complicate the efforts of states of proliferation concern or terrorist groups in obtaining access to sensitive materials, equipment, or technical data. Table 1.1 identifies the international control regimes.

These regimes have established approaches for addressing export controls that have become the norms in the free market economies. Thus, even though the four countries are not members of some of the regimes, they appreciate the need to adopt similar practices if they are to be recognized as responsible trading partners.

BILATERAL ACTIVITIES

The United States has established bilateral programs with each of the four successor states to help prevent the diffusion of sensitive material and equipment, particularly direct-use nuclear material. Through such programs, the U.S. government has encouraged the key industrial countries of the region to conform as soon as possible to the requirements of the international regimes. Also, the United States has mounted diplo-

TABLE 1.1   Participation in International Control Regimes

REGIME[a]	RUSSIA	UKRAINE	BELARUS	KAZAKSTAN
Nuclear				
Non-Proliferation Treaty (NPT)	Ratified in 1970 (NWS)[b]	Ratified in 1994 (NNWS)[c]	Ratified in 1993 (NNWS)[b]	Ratified in 1994 (NNWS)[b]
NPT Exporters Committee (Zangger Committee)	Member since 1971			
Nuclear Suppliers Group (NSG)	Member since 1974	Member since 1996		
Biological				
Biological Weapons Convention Australia Group (Biological and Chemical)	Ratified in 1975 Has stated that its controls are consistent with requirements	Ratified in 1975[d] Has stated that its controls are consistent with requirements	Ratified in 1975[d]	
Chemical				
Chemical Weapons Convention	Signed in 1993	Signed in 1993	Ratified in 1996	Signed in 1993
Missile				
Missile Technology Control Regime (MTCR)	Member since 1995	Adherent since 1994		
Dual-Use Technologies				
Wassenaar Arrangement	Member since 1996	Member since 1996		
Conventional Weapons				

[a] Nuclear Weapons State (NWS) Party: Under the NPT, states that detonated a nuclear explosion prior to January 2, 1967, are classified as nuclear weapons states. They are permitted to retain nuclear weapons and are not required to accept comprehensive International Atomic Energy Agency (IAEA) inspections of their nuclear activities.
[b] Non-Nuclear Weapons States (NNWS) Party: These states are prohibited by the NPT from manufacturing or possessing nuclear weapons and are required to accept IAEA inspections of all nuclear activities.
[c] The Ukranian and Belorusian Soviet Socialist Republics each ratified the convention.

Source: U.S. Department of State.

matic efforts to discourage proposed sales of certain sensitive items, even though such sales are not prohibited by the regimes (e.g., the Russian sale of nuclear reactor components to Iran).

The MPC&A programs that are the focal points of this study are carried out in the broader context of a large number of programs supported by the U.S. government. Related efforts include programs directed at reducing nuclear material stockpiles through American purchases of stocks of HEU from Kazakstan and Russia, assessing the feasibility of terminating production of plutonium in nuclear reactors in Tomsk-7 and Krasnoyarsk-26, supporting cooperative projects that encourage civilian production activities at weapons-oriented enterprises, and providing economic incentives for FSU weapons scientists and engineers to redirect their efforts to peaceful pursuits rather than be tempted to look abroad for customers for their weapons know-how.

Bilateral Cooperation in Containment of Direct-Use Material and Export Control

While some of the foregoing activities moved forward on a cooperative basis in the period from 1992 to 1994, the U.S. government had considerable difficulty establishing significant cooperative programs in MPC&A and export control, despite the availability of a mandate and funding from the U.S. Congress. Nonetheless, during this period, American experts from both the public and the private sectors took advantage of limited opportunities to acquaint officials of the region with Western approaches in both fields.

In time, administrative and political problems in the FSU and in Washington diminished. Since the beginning of 1995 a number of U.S. government agencies have undertaken sizable bilateral programs directed at MPC&A and export control. Tables 1.2 and 1.3 summarize the activities under U.S. government programs to date.

The characteristics of the two programs are very different. MPC&A systems concentrate on a single item—direct-use nuclear material. They limit access to areas where material is located and provide for strict control and accountability of the material. The types and locations of the facilities of interest are generally well known. The systems are designed to prevent theft or diversion of direct-use material at the facility level and in transit between facilities and, when such prevention fails, the prompt detection of missing material. Table 1.4 presents the key elements of an MPC&A system.

Export control activities, by contrast, embrace many different types of materials, equipment, and technical data. They include establishment of a legal framework, a licensing procedure, enforcement mechanisms with programs for detecting and prosecuting violators of export control laws and regulations, and programs to inform exporters of their obligations. The numbers of interested government agencies and affected facilities

TABLE 1.2   MPC&A Program Activities in the FSU Supported by DOE (as of July 1996)

Russia	*Government-to-Government:*
	Activities at eleven Minatom sites (two fuel fabrication plants, one breeder reactor, three reactor technology institutes, five research institutes); support for Obninsk Training Center
	Agreement with GAN:
	Regulatory document development; MPC&A information system; MPC&A equipment; activities at six non-Minatom sites.
	Laboratory-to-Laboratory:
	Activities at eight Minatom sites (three plutonium sites, three uranium enrichment sites, two nuclear weapons labs, one research and development institute); activities at Kurchatov; activities at two naval fuel storage facilities (Northern and Pacific fleets) and the icebreaker fleet; transportation security
Belarus	Activities at one site (research institute)
Kazakstan	Activities at four sites (one low-enriched uranium fuel fabrication plant, one power-breeder reactor, two research institutes)
Ukraine	Activities at four sites (one power reactor complex, three research institutes)
Uzbekistan	Activities at one site (research institute)
Latvia	Activities at one site (research institute)
Lithuania	Activities at one site (power reactor complex)
Georgia	Activities at one site (research institute)

Source: U.S. Department of State.

TABLE 1.3   U.S. Export Control Program Activities Involving Russia, Ukraine, Belarus, and Kazakstan Supported by the U.S. Departments of State, Commerce, Energy, and Defense, and the U.S. Customs Service

Policy-level exchanges to emphasize the importance of enactment and enforcement of export control legislation

Training on the essential elements of comprehensive export control laws and enforcement regulations (except Russia)

Computer automation of export control licensing procedures and provision of enforcement equipment (except Russia)

Workshops on international nonproliferation export control regimes and associated control lists

Seminars on government outreach to nongovernmental entities and manufacturing organizations on export control and nonproliferation

Training and equipment for supporting enforcement activities

Lab-to-lab programs, including technical exchanges, directed to nuclear-related exports

Source: U.S. Departments of State, Commerce, and Energy.

TABLE 1.4   Components of an MPC&A System

	PHYSICAL PROTECTION	CONTROL	ACCOUNTING
Detection and assessment (sensors, alarms, and assessment systems such as video)	X	X	
Delay (barriers, locks, traps, booths, active measures)	X		
Response (communications, interruptions, neutralization)	X	X	
Response team	X		
Entry-and-exit control (badges, biometrics, nuclear material detectors, metal detectors, explosive detectors)	X	X	
Communications and display	X		
Measurements and measurement control (weight volume, chemical analysis, isotopic analysis, neutron, gamma, calorimetry)		X	X
Item control (barcodes, seals, material surveillance)		X	
Records and reports			X
Inventory		X	X
Integrated planning, implementation, and effectiveness evaluation	X	X	X
Supporting functions (personnel, procedures, training, organization, administration)	X	X	X

Sources: NRC committee and publications of the U.S. Department of Energy.

are very large. Table 1.5 presents the elements of an export control system as set forth in the Common Standard developed by the former Consultative Group and Coordinating Committee for Multilateral Export Controls (COCOM). This standard has been widely accepted by Western governments.

Within these two programs the U.S. agencies measure progress toward the goal of nonproliferation by (a) the amount of direct-use material contained in secure MPC&A systems and (b) the extent to which functioning export control regulatory systems, including enforcement mechanisms, have been established. The agencies are well aware that such measures do not indicate the seriousness of the remaining vulnerabilities in the systems, nor do they reflect the more limited progress that would be achieved without U.S. involvement. Still, the agencies recognize their usefulness as indicators of the scope of the programs and of program accomplishments.

TABLE 1.5   Common Standard for Export Control (The Common Standard Level of Effective Protection, Developed by COCOM)

Prelicensing Requirements

Adequate manpower and equipment available to the licensing authorities
Lists of controlled products published nationally
Legal and regulatory bases for controls with sanctions for violations
Awareness by industry of the objective of controls
Specification of information required on license applications
System of import and delivery verification certificates and end-use statements
Capability to review license requests and to evaluate parties to transactions, specifications of products to be exported, and any inherent risks

Postlicensing Requirements

Legislation should include provisions enabling national authorities to:

- deter, prevent, and punish illegal exporters;
- carry out checks after licenses are issued; and
- monitor licensed exports (inspect goods, seize suspect shipments, apply sanctions).

At the enforcement level, national authorities should provide:

- necessary financial and other resources;
- adequate training of personnel; and
- support for development of a capability to compile, assess, and distribute relevant information and to take into account all available sources of information.

Source: U.S. Departments of State, Commerce, and Energy.

FINDINGS AND RECOMMENDATIONS TO THE U.S. GOVERNMENT CONCERNING COOPERATION IN MPC&A

The committee considered but did not use structured criteria for evaluating the effectiveness of the cooperative programs. Both the joint efforts and the related activities of the governments and at the facilities are evolving rapidly. Thus, progress attributable to cooperation is not quantifiable. Also, the optimum upgrade programs against which to judge the impacts of U.S. efforts cannot be easily framed, given the political and economic uncertainties in the four successor countries and our incomplete knowledge of the status of Russian facilities. Therefore, the committee's judgments are largely qualitative in nature and are intended to provide an overall sense of the impact of cooperation.

General Findings

After initial delays of more than two years, due primarily to a lack of interest in Moscow in cooperative arrangements that the United States considered equitable and essential, progress attributable to the joint efforts of U.S. and Russian specialists in MPC&A greatly accelerated in 1995 and 1996. DOE estimates that U.S. specialists have gained access to some of the many buildings at approximately 90 percent of the sites where direct-use material is known to be located outside the Russian Ministry of Defense complex and have initiated cooperative interactions to address many of the most pressing MPC&A issues at these sites.

This is a significant political and organizational achievement, considering (a) the complexity of the tasks in transforming the Soviet approach to MPC&A, which had relied primarily on controlling people, to an approach that increasingly relies on technical measures and (b) the history of secrecy throughout the Soviet nuclear complex. But while improvements have been made at selected facilities, the task has not been completed at any Russian facility and serious efforts are only beginning at most facilities. DOE estimates that *tons* of direct-use material are contained in internationally acceptable MPC&A systems and that *tens of tons* are in partially acceptable systems, but adequate MPC&A systems for *hundreds of tons* must still be installed. Thus, the challenge now is to extend the organizational and political achievements to significant technical improvements, a process that is only beginning.

In Ukraine, Belarus, and Kazakstan, cooperative efforts have already achieved easily discernible technical improvements. Of special interest, DOE announced in 1996 that it had completed MPC&A upgrades at the Institute of Nuclear Power Engineering in Belarus, the only known facility in Belarus with direct-use material.

Several other accomplishments for which the United States can take considerable credit illustrate the importance of the program to date. Building 116 at the Kurchatov Institute of Atomic Energy in Moscow and a building at Arzamas-16 have become MPC&A models, attracting the attention of hundreds of Russian officials and specialists responsible for MPC&A programs. The Russian Ministry of Atomic Energy is using the MPC&A training center at Obninsk as the focal point for upgrading the skills of specialists from throughout the country. American specialists have successfully taken the first steps in initiating cooperative programs with Russian specialists from naval reactor fuel storage facilities and from highly sensitive nuclear weapons assembly and dismantlement facilities. In Kazakstan, the government has committed to installing complete MPC&A systems at its nuclear facilities as quickly as possible. In Ukraine, American specialists have been given access to a previously closed facility at the Sevastopol naval base, while upgrade activities proceed at the two other principal nuclear facilities.

Nevertheless, the size of the Soviet nuclear complex was enormous, and much remains to be done. The need for American specialists to continue to support upgrading of MPC&A systems until such time as the institutions in all four successor countries are willing and able to continue on their own is very clear. Even in Belarus, where all upgrades are in place, visits by American specialists are important to ensure that they are maintained as designed.

Having overcome significant political, cultural, and organizational hurdles, and in the absence of dramatic political change, the cooperative program should be in position to make significant progress over the next several years. As the program moves into the next stage of rapid implementation, certain overarching principles should guide cooperative efforts:

- For the near term it is essential that the United States *sustain* its involvement until counterpart institutions are in a position to assume the full burden of upgrading and maintaining MPC&A programs over the long term.
- Emphasis should be on upgrading the skills of specialists in the four countries, relying on local expertise and whenever possible local equipment, and establishing viable long-term funding sources—in short, actions to *indigenize* the implementation activities.
- Drawing on cooperative efforts to date, the governments and institutions in the FSU should *simplify* the problem by reducing the direct-use material of concern and consolidating the remaining material at fewer sites and fewer locations within sites.
- The cooperative programs should include more concerted efforts to *minimize the possible routes to bypass* the MPC&A systems.
- The participating specialists should *enhance the program* in several areas to increase the effectiveness of their joint efforts.

I. Sustain the U.S. Commitment to the Program

Finding: The continued flow of U.S. funds in the near term is essential because of the limited ability of the four governments to finance MPC&A upgrades. The next few years will be a critical period for upgrading systems to an acceptable level, and U.S. specialists are in a unique position to help ensure that such upgrades are given high priority and installed in a prompt and effective manner. The current level of U.S. funding of MPC&A programs is about $100 million annually.

Recommendation: *Continue to fund MPC&A efforts in the FSU at least at the level of fiscal year 1996 for several more years and be prepared to increase funding should particularly important high-impact opportunities arise.*

II. Indigenize MPC&A Capabilities

Finding: Once the U.S. program ends, the cooperating governments must be committed and able to assume full responsibility for funding and maintaining upgraded MPC&A systems. The challenge is great, as economic shortfalls even for basic program support limit the domestic funds available for MPC&A. Nevertheless, ministries, institutes, and individuals must be prepared to implement adequate MPC&A programs and have access to income streams that will permit them to continue their efforts in the long term.

Recommendation: Continue to emphasize the importance of MPC&A as a nonproliferation imperative at the highest political levels in the FSU.

Recommendation: Prior to initiating MPC&A projects at specific facilities, obtain assurances at both the ministry and the institute levels that the upgrade programs will be sustained after improvements have been made. Financial incentives, such as support for related research activities, should be considered as a means to stimulate long-term commitments.

Recommendation: Involve institute personnel to the fullest extent possible in determining how to use available funds for upgrades.

Recommendation: Give greater emphasis to near-term training of local specialists.

Recommendation: Reward those institutes that are making good progress in upgrading MPC&A systems by giving them preference for participation in other U.S.-financed cooperative programs.

Recommendation: Encourage the establishment of new income streams that can provide adequate financial support for MPC&A programs in the long term, such as earmarking for MPC&A programs a portion of the revenues from Russian sales of HEU.

Recommendation: Rely increasingly on domestically produced and locally available equipment for physical protection, detection, analysis, and related MPC&A tasks.

III. Simplify the Problem

Finding: The challenge of controlling small amounts of direct-use material located in hundreds of buildings, including many in a poor state of repair, seems overwhelming. If the amount of material and the number of storage areas could be substantially reduced, the time and costs involved in installing MPC&A systems also could be significantly reduced.

As for Russia, the previously noted U.S. programs concerning purchase of HEU and alternative energy sources for the plutonium production reactors at Krasnoyarsk-26 and Tomsk-7 are directed to reducing the amount of direct-use material in the country. Very limited discussions have addressed the other large source of plutonium production—the nuclear fuel rod reprocessing plant at the Mayak complex. The Russian government has shown no interest in terminating this activity. A remaining challenge is consolidation of material.

Outside Russia, the future use of the small remaining stocks of direct-use material is uncertain at best. Retaining these stocks requires significant MPC&A expenditures and continued vigilance over the possibility of theft.

Recommendation: In Russia, encourage consolidation of direct-use material in fewer buildings, at fewer facilities, and at fewer sites.

Recommendation: Take steps to encourage the removal of all HEU at research facilities outside Russia, including the purchase of HEU when appropriate.

Recommendation: For research reactors outside Russia where important and adequately financed research programs are planned in the foreseeable future, support conversion of the reactors so that they can use low-enriched uranium instead of HEU.

IV. Minimize the Possibilities to Bypass MPC&A Systems

Specific Finding: If an MPC&A program is to be effective, all relevant organizations and all sources of direct-use material must be addressed. Of special concern, large stocks of direct-use material are located at some Russian facilities that have not yet become active participants in the bilateral program.

However, as facilities become involved in the program, there is uncertainty among both Russian and American specialists as to the precise amounts of direct-use material present. For example, at some facilities there was a practice of maintaining stocks of material "off the books," and at these and other facilities the inventory records may be unreliable. Previous control systems may not have given sufficient attention to scrap and off-specification material. Also, during a period of political and economic turmoil and expanded criminal activities, the possibility of efforts by irresponsible persons to remove material from the MPC&A systems while the systems are being evaluated for upgrades or even after such systems are in place cannot be ignored.

An important oversight agency in Russia, the State Nuclear Regulatory Committee, Gosatomnadzor (GAN), suffers from a shortage of well-trained inspectors, qualified staff, and necessary analytical and related equipment, as well as uncertain administrative responsibility with regard to military-related activities.

Recommendation: Ensure that all stocks of direct-use material are encompassed in the program, including icebreaker nuclear fuel, supplies at naval facilities, and off-specification and scrap material.

Recommendation: Encourage rapid development of a comprehensive national material control and accounting system in Russia and the prompt incorporation of all existing direct-use material into that system.

Recommendation: In Russia, increase support of GAN as an important independent agency by assisting it in developing MPC&A methodologies, training inspectors, obtaining staff support from research institutions, and procuring necessary equipment for MPC&A inspections.

Recommendation: Encourage a system of incentives, possibly including monetary rewards, that will stimulate participants in MPC&A programs to report promptly to central authorities any irregularities in the implementation of MPC&A systems.

Recommendation: Emphasize the importance of developing a culture among MPC&A specialists that does not tolerate shortcuts or exceptions in implementing MPC&A systems.

V. Enhance the Program

Finding: A number of initiatives will enhance the effectiveness of U.S. efforts.

The threats of theft and diversion in the FSU differ significantly from those in the United States. The general economic and crime situation in the FSU raises the prospect of different threat scenarios than in the United States. Moreover, there are differences in the facilities that affect susceptibility to the loss of material. In the FSU, many buildings where direct-use material is stored are in poor repair, long perimeters with inadequate protection characterize some sites where material is located, and old accounting systems of dubious reliability are used at some facilities. Some local specialists are not prepared to absorb sophisticated technologies. Modest immediate enhancements at a large number of facilities may be more important than major investments at a limited number of storage locations.

Another area of concern is the vulnerability of direct-use material during transport—a topic that has not been a priority in past cooperative efforts. Trucks and other vehicles that are not suitable for transporting direct-use material are in use, and the rigor of the accounting systems for tracking the movement of material is of concern.

Also, the continued isolation of some facilities where MPC&A upgrades are needed limits the opportunities for specialists at one facility to learn from the experiences of their colleagues at other facilities.

Finally, several agencies are usually involved in providing security for direct-use material, including responding to incidents and alarms. In Russia, the Ministry of Interior and the Federal Intelligence Service do not appear to be adequately involved in designing MPC&A upgrades, a task left largely to specialists of the Ministry for Atomic Energy or of the other concerned research organizations.

Recommendation: Emphasize MPC&A approaches that respond to threat scenarios that are appropriate for the FSU, recognizing that they may differ from the threat scenarios used in the United States.

Recommendation: Recognize that in the near term it may be necessary to install systems that fall short of internationally accepted standards in anticipation of subsequent refinements. In this regard, use appropriate MPC&A measures, whether they involve high-tech or low-tech approaches.

Recommendation: In Russia, give greater attention to MPC&A of direct-use material during transport within and between facilities.

Recommendation: Promote greater communication and cooperation among ministries and facilities involved in MPC&A in each of the countries where bilateral programs are being implemented.

Recommendation: In Russia, encourage more active involvement of the Ministry of Interior in the planning, testing, and implementation of physical security systems.

FINDINGS AND RECOMMENDATIONS TO THE U.S.GOVERNMENT CONCERNING COOPERATION IN EXPORT CONTROL

General Findings

After initial delays of more than two years owing to interagency uncertainties and procurement problems in Washington and to a lack of readiness in the FSU to initiate serious collaboration, U.S. efforts have stimulated interest and action at the policy and technical levels to strengthen export control systems in Russia and to establish new systems in Ukraine, Kazakstan, and Belarus. American specialists and their counterparts have developed a high degree of mutual confidence that their joint efforts are producing important results in critical areas, and enthusiasm of government officials of the four cooperating countries is high for the joint programs. The joint efforts, undertaken at relatively low cost, have been particularly important in developing the legal bases for export control, training cadres of specialists in a variety of relevant fields, and installing systems for more efficient processing and validation of license requests. Despite these early accomplishments, much remains to be done in the development of comprehensive and effective export control systems in the four countries.

Several specific examples illustrate how American involvement has triggered new activities. In Russia, a number of enterprise managers are applying American experience in establishing new internal mechanisms to ensure compliance with regulations. U.S. support has been very important in facilitating the membership and participation of Ukraine in the Nuclear Suppliers Group and the Wassenaar Arrangement. Belarus regulatory authorities and the customs service have used American computer hardware and software in establishing information systems that have greatly enhanced their capabilities to process and track export control cases. In Kazakstan, the insistence of American specialists that presidential decrees and regulations be codified into law has provided the country with a stable legal base for export control that should withstand political shocks.

But American specialists can continue to play an important role—in many cases a pivotal role—in establishing systems that in time should conform to the requirements of the international control regimes. For example, interagency regulatory mechanisms are in place in each of the four countries, but additional experience is needed to ensure the effective integration of all international control lists into the review processes. Although the customs services have greatly expanded their manpower, training of new personnel remains a priority. A few areas deserve special emphasis during the next several years:

- Cooperative efforts should reflect the need for the four successor countries to *complete the legal, organizational, and manpower infrastructure* for regulating exports of critical items.

- The importance of the governments' continuing to *strengthen implementation and enforcement capabilities* is very clear.
- Since not all aspects of export control can receive immediate attention, priorities should *focus additional efforts on urgent problems*, including (a) the need to control the most sensitive items first; (b) the opportunities for promoting stewardship and internal compliance at the enterprise level; and (c) the importance of participation by adjacent states of the FSU in regional approaches to combat smuggling and unsanctioned transshipments of sensitive items.
- Preventing the diffusion of certain types of technical data can sometimes be more important than containing sensitive commodities, and higher priority should be given to efforts to *control sensitive technical information.*
- An important need is the evolution of a cadre of export control officials who *give adequate weight to proliferation concerns* in their decision-making. Governments must not only have regulatory systems that operate in conformity with the procedural requirements of the international regimes but must also reflect a commitment to nonproliferation goals in their export decisions.

I. Support Completion of the Legal, Organizational, and Manpower Infrastructure for Effective Export Control

Specific Finding: A starting point for controlling exports of sensitive items is a legal and organizational structure that provides the capability for policy and regulatory development, licensing activities, and enforcement. Each of the four successor countries is in the process of broadening and codifying the legal basis for its programs and of providing an operational system that is staffed with well-trained specialists. This long-term effort requires continued attention over a number of years. The United States has the most fully developed export control infrastructure in the world and is in a strong position to contribute in many ways. Over the long term, however, the four countries must assume responsibility for ensuring that improvements are sustained.

Budgetary support in the United States for bilateral export control programs is in constant jeopardy because funding is provided through the relatively small budget of the Department of State. The fiscal year (FY) 1996 budget level of $10 million for export control cooperation worldwide, together with other funds already in the pipeline from previous appropriations to DOD, has sustained an adequate level of activity in the FSU, but the reduction of funding to less than $5 million for FY 1997 jeopardizes future progress.

Further confusing the budget situation, the U.S. Customs Service and DOE recently received special appropriations to cover some of their activities in cooperative programs, while the Department of Commerce, which has much to contribute, has no access to special funds.

Recommendation: Continue to fund export control efforts in the FSU at least at the level of FY 1996 for several more years and be prepared to increase funding should particularly important high-impact opportunities arise.

Recommendation: Ensure that adequate resources are available to the Department of Commerce, as well as to the Departments of State, Defense, and Energy and the U.S. Customs Service, so that specialists with unique expertise can continue to participate in the programs.

Recommendation: Emphasize in bilateral discussions at all levels the importance of developing capabilities to meet international requirements for export control and to ensure adherence to all relevant aspects of the international control regimes.

Recommendation: Negotiate an intergovernmental agreement with Russia to help ensure the long-term stability of bilateral cooperation in the field of export control.

Recommendation: Support the strengthening of institutions in the FSU that provide training and advisory services for government agencies and enterprises involved in export control.

Recommendation: Involve interested American universities and non-governmental organizations, when appropriate, in promoting training and research related to export control that involves specialists from the FSU.

II. Strengthen Implementation and Enforcement Capabilities

Specific Finding: In each of the four successor countries there is a considerable gap between the requirements and plans for export control activities and the implementation of effective programs for fulfilling those requirements, particularly in the area of enforcement. Joint programs have imparted momentum in the overall efforts of the four countries, but there are still many weaknesses. Also, it appears that there have been very few successful prosecutions of violators of export control regulations. U.S. experience has shown that highly visible prosecutions can capture the attention of many exporters.

Recommendation: Continue to cooperate with counterpart agencies that have received computers and related equipment to ensure that automated licensing and customs tracking systems are installed and used as planned.

Recommendation: Expand bilateral cooperation among customs officials, emphasizing training and demonstration programs that can have multiplier effects in view of the vast responsibilities of the customs services.

Recommendation: Share with enforcement counterparts information on procedures used in the United States to collect evidence and prosecute parties found to be violating export control laws.

Recommendation: Encourage high-visibility prosecutions of export control violators in the four countries so that local exporters become aware of the consequences of violations of export control laws and regulations.

III. Focus on Critical Commodities, Stewardship and Compliance at the Enterprise Level, and Regional Approaches

Specific Finding: In addition to providing the basis for comprehensive approaches to export control, strategies should focus on immediate solutions to reducing the likelihood of diffusion of sensitive items. In this regard, an emphasis on layers of protection for the most sensitive items could help reduce the most serious concerns. In addition to national review procedures and checks at customs control points, control of items at the enterprises and institutes and improved capabilities for intercepting items en route to their final destinations, including during transit through neighboring countries, could both deter and complicate the efforts of parties intent on theft or diversion of controlled items.

Recommendation: Emphasize control of the most sensitive items by targeting educational and enforcement efforts on the organizations most likely to handle such items.

Recommendation: Encourage the strengthening of surveillance at the enterprise level through enhanced capabilities of on-site customs officials.

Recommendation: Expand interactions between officials of American companies and foreign enterprises responsible for internal export compliance programs and for industrial security and demonstrate to foreign counterparts how the U.S. private sector participates in the development of new export control regulations.

Recommendation: Encourage local officials involved in the Customs Union in the FSU to strengthen approaches for monitoring transshipments of controlled items.

Recommendation: Participate in cooperative programs with countries of Central Asia that emphasize the importance of countering smuggling and inappropriate transshipments of sensitive items.

IV. Increase Attention to Control of Technical Data

Specific Finding: Some nations and subnational groups of proliferation concern could benefit significantly from access to technical data about the design, manufacture, and/or integration of weapons system components. Yet this threat is receiving relatively little attention in the FSU. While Russia, in particular, still protects documents classified for military reasons, there is less attention to restrictions on unclassified technical data that should be controlled pursuant to international agreements concerning exports of sensitive items. Some sensitive information is considered to be intellectual property and subject to limited distribution in the absence of patent or copyright protection, but controls on such information are uncertain at best. At the same time, data controls should not unnecessarily inhibit the exchange of information that is not explicitly subject to controls and that is central to the viability of international scientific endeavors.

Recommendation: Encourage counterparts in the four countries to strengthen national regulatory and organizational frameworks for regulating flows of technical data subject to export controls.

Recommendation: Develop and disseminate "model" technical data provisions that could be used by institutions in the FSU in contracts with domestic or foreign organizations involving controlled items.

V. Encourage Full Consideration of Proliferation Issues in Export Control Decisions

Specific Finding: While bilateral activities have concentrated on establishing the machinery for export control activities, they have devoted little effort to the policy considerations that should underpin decisions, other than consistency with the limited requirements of the international regimes. Such discussions are the subject of separate diplomatic discussions when specific issues arise. Given economic realities, the governments of the successor states inevitably give less weight than would the United States to restricting trade with nations that pose proliferation risks. The involvement of strong nonproliferation advocates in the FSU in interagency deliberations can help ensure that appropriate attention is given to international security concerns in export control decisions.

Recommendation: Ensure that continuing consultations on the importance of export control activities in meeting nonproliferation objectives become an integral component of U.S. bilateral relations with the successor states in both the short and the long terms, as has been the case with relations between the United States and its traditional allies.

Recommendation: Promote bilateral discussions of the relationships between exports of sensitive items and proliferation concerns in many forums, at the governmental and nongovernmental levels.

Recommendation: Support the development of cadres of nonproliferation specialists in the FSU who have strong linkages with both policy officials in their countries and colleagues abroad.

The returns during 1995 and 1996 on U.S. investments in bilateral programs in MPC&A and export control were significant. U.S. agencies now have in place an extensive web of international arrangements involving very supportive foreign counterparts. The base of international experience can facilitate future program efforts that contribute directly to nonproliferation objectives.

Cutting across all program elements is the need for the United States to emphasize *cooperative* rather than *assistance* programs. This approach will help ensure that the countries will be ready to assume full responsibility for upgrading and maintaining systems that are internationally acceptable.

Despite the progress through bilateral efforts, the size of the tasks in each of the countries remains great. Reducing to an acceptable level the risk of unsanctioned transfers of weapons-related items from the FSU to states of concern or to terrorists will require many years of effort at the international, national, and facility levels by governments and specialists throughout the region. Continued participation by American specialists in the activities of these countries can accelerate the process while also providing the United States with valuable linkages to important organizations and institutions. American national security interest will be well served by a continuation of these two relatively inexpensive programs.

APPENDIX 2

EXPORT CONTROL
DEVELOPMENTS IN RUSSIA,
UKRAINE, BELARUS,
AND KAZAKSTAN

This appendix is derived from *Arms on the Market: Reducing the Risk of Proliferation in the Former Soviet Union,* Gary K. Bertsch and Suzette R. Grillot, eds. (New York: Routledge, 1998). It represents a summary of the export control developments in the former Soviet Union—with particular attention to Russia, Ukraine, Belarus, and Kazakstan—and the means by which such developments are measured and assessed. This work results from a long-term evaluation project at the Center for International Trade and Security at the University of Georgia.

INTRODUCTION

Since the demise of the Soviet Union and subsequent end of the Cold War, government and scholarly communities have paid increasing attention to the potential proliferation threat emanating from the former Soviet region.[1] Almost overnight, the massive military-industrial assets of the Soviet Union came under the jurisdiction of 15 fledgling states instead of one established government. The question of who would inherit, safeguard, and control the stockpile of weapons of mass destruction (WMD) and the associated materials, equipment, technology, and expertise posed problems for the security relations of both the New Independent States (NIS) and the international community. Of special concern was *how* the 15 successor states—especially Russia, Ukraine, Belarus, and Kazakstan—would control exports of military and dual-use items (goods, services, and technologies with both military and commercial applications), given both economic and political instability.

263

All the states of the former Soviet Union possess at least some elements of a national export control system. Furthermore, developing effective export control systems (regulations, processes, and practices governing the transfer of military or military-enabling dual-use items, technologies, or information) for all the NIS has become an important objective in the effort to reduce the risk of proliferation of weapons of mass destruction.[2] These systems differ, however, in the degree to which they have developed all elements of an export control system, which include licensing procedures, control lists, international regime participation, catch-all provisions, training mechanisms, bureaucratic processes, customs authority, verification procedures, penalties for export control violators, and information-gathering and -sharing methods. They also differ in the extent to which they have moved beyond mere policies for each of these elements toward actual implementation.

EXPORT CONTROL DEVELOPMENT EVALUATION: METHODOLOGY

The University of Georgia project analyzed and evaluated NIS export control measures using a general quantitative tool that we created based on Western, nonproliferation export control "common standards."[3] Because individual states develop and implement national systems of export control, it is possible that states may inconsistently create and apply export control measures. Such inconsistencies or gaps in export control systems decrease the effectiveness of export control as an international nonproliferation tool.

For export controls to be a useful tool for preventing proliferation, states must interpret and implement controls with some degree of uniformity.[4] Accordingly, "common standards" for export control development and implementation, which emerged throughout the Cold War era, serve as a basis for state export control systems. In particular, the earliest export control regime, the Coordinating Committee for Multilateral Export Controls (COCOM), began to establish in 1949 the rules, norms, and procedures that permit member states to manage their economic competition while focusing on the security threats posed by common enemies.[5] Through their participation in COCOM, states were encouraged to develop common lists of controlled commodities, as well as other national procedures that evolved into the "common standards" for national systems of export control. The standards provided COCOM members a guide for the creation of comprehensive and consistent national export control practices and allowed for the evaluation of national export control systems.[6] These "common standards," therefore, serve as a point of departure for our measurement of export control development.[7]

Drawing on various documents that Western government officials have in the past used to describe levels of national export control devel-

TABLE 2.1   Elements of an Export Control System

Licensing System	Control Lists
Regime Adherence	Catch-All Clause
Training	Bureaucratic Process
Customs Authority	Import/Export Verification
Penalties	Information-Gathering and -Sharing

opment, particularly a COCOM questionnaire used to evaluate member and cooperating states, the University of Georgia research team elicited ten elements of an export control system. The ten elements are distinct from one another, but mutually reinforce and represent key components of an effective export control system (see Table 2.1).

Each element is comprised of three subparts: (1) policy and/or legal foundation; (2) institutions and procedures; and (3) behavior (implementation). The first subpart concerns the existence of nonproliferation export control laws and decrees that provide a legal basis for the country's control of sensitive exports. The second subpart rests on the notion that policies may be effective only if institutions and procedures exist for implementing them. Do officials and/or bureaucracies, for example, exist that are responsible for export control development and implementation? The third subpart reflects the necessity for actual export control behavior. Are export control policies and procedures, in other words, actually in use?

With the ten elements of an export control system in mind, the University of Georgia research team devised a questionnaire for the measurement of export control development in a given country. The 72-item questionnaire allowed us to calculate levels of export control development with the use of a rating scheme that ranges from no development (0) to some development (.5) to compliance with Western standards (1). Because some export control elements may be more significant in the effective operation of an export control system, we developed relative weightings that indicate the importance of certain elements. We created the weightings based on surveys of governmental officials, nongovernmental experts, and industry representatives. We asked the respondents to list the ten elements according to their importance using a scale from 1 (most important) to 10 (least important).[8]

To calculate the weights we averaged the rank scores for each element and subtracted that number from 10. The Licensing System element, for example, received the highest score (2.53), and the Catch-All Clause element received the lowest average score (8.8). The relative weights, therefore, calculated to be 7.47 and 1.2, respectively. To arrive at a total weighted score that represents a country's level of export control development based on common standards, we averaged the tallies for each

TABLE 2.2 Development of NIS Nonproliferation Export Controls (Percentage Compliance)

COUNTRY	EXPORT CONTROL SYSTEM STATUS IN 1997
Russia	84%
Ukraine	78%
Belarus	74%
Latvia	74%
Estonia	70%
Lithuania	65%
Kazakstan	64%
Armenia	50%
Kyrgyzstan	36%
Georgia	30%
Azerbaijan	29%
Uzbekistan	17%
Turkmenistan	10%
Tajikistan	10%

element, multiplied the averages by the weights, then added the weighted scores for a total measurement that may then be compared to the "ideal" or "perfect" score,[9] as well as to the scores of other states.[10] Using our method for measuring export control development, we were then able to determine the level at which states comply with Western, common standards in export control. For a summary of the University of Georgia's evaluations of the new independent states (NIS), see Table 2.2.

TRENDS OF EXPORT CONTROL DEVELOPMENT IN RUSSIA, UKRAINE, BELARUS, AND KAZAKSTAN

Based on the empirical evidence resulting from the University of Georgia research, it is apparent that some elements of an export control system are consistently more developed. A clear example of this can be seen in the Licensing and Control Lists elements, which tend to be the most developed. This is not especially revealing given that an export control system lacks a foundation without a licensing system for sensitive exports and some type of control list that specifies the items requiring an export license.

Enforcement mechanisms also represent a critical component of any export control system. We find that the export control systems in Russia, Ukraine, Belarus, and Kazakstan have relatively underdeveloped enforcement structures—which include Customs Authority, Verification, Penalties, and Catch-All—in comparison to other aspects of their systems.

Domestic agencies also play a central role in determining the level of export control development. Concerning the closely related elements of Bureaucratic Authority and Information-Gathering and -Sharing, we find that they are strongly correlated with overall levels of export control development. For example, in Ukraine and Russia, which have rather high levels of overall development, bureaucratic processes are relatively elaborate and decision-making is often interagency in nature.

In the area of information-gathering and -sharing, most of the states score comparatively low, which reflects the legacy of Soviet secrecy. Many of the FSU states are hesitant to share information with other states about the number of licenses issued and denied and prosecutions of export control violations. This may stem from fear that such information could reflect poorly on their export control systems if, for example, there have been no prosecutions and few license denials. Even in Russia, information on export licenses of strategic technology is regarded as "sensitive." Russia has yet to report any denials of export control violations to the NSG and it lobbied against important information-sharing provisions that were to have been introduced into the Wassenaar Arrangement. However, some states, such as Russia and Ukraine, have undertaken educational efforts designed to inform exporters of strategic technology about national export control laws and regulations.

Until exporters in the FSU come to understand export control procedures, there remains the very real threat that they will unknowingly provide technology, equipment, and other items to proliferants. Throughout the FSU, the majority of enterprises exporting strategic technology remain to varying degrees under state control, which should make efforts to regulate exports more manageable. The challenge, however, comes in the legal structure of the FSU that gives these enterprises greater freedom to pursue international contracts and to market their wares abroad. Moreover, many enterprises who struggle in efforts to find foreign buyers employ the services of middlemen and export consultants who are adept at eluding regulations of all kinds, including export controls.

Although the information-sharing element remains underdeveloped throughout the FSU, an even more pressing task is training export control personnel. Only Russia, which inherited a small Soviet export control cadre, had a personnel base upon which to build. Other states have been faced with learning the many facets of export control from scratch. The United States and other Western countries have provided training (through seminars, conferences, on-site training, the provision of equipment, and so on) for many agencies and officials in the FSU. The existence of most training efforts in the FSU can be largely attributed to these assistance efforts.

Russia

Russia has developed a relatively sophisticated export control system in comparison to the other states of the former Soviet Union. Although Russia did inherit much of the Soviet export control bureaucracy, the Soviet experience was not capable of coping with Russia's privatizing economy, which provided exporters with increased autonomy, including the opportunity to negotiate and sign contracts with foreign companies. In 1992, Russia's export control system was only 40 percent compatible with the ideal type outlined in our methodology section. However, since 1992, Russia has made significant strides toward enhancing its system to meet the challenges of a market economy and increased international high-technology trade. By 1997, the Russian system was 83 percent compatible with the ideal export control system.

Russia's lists of controlled technologies and weaponry correspond to those advocated by the multilateral export control arrangements, which include the Nuclear Suppliers Group (NSG), the Missile Technology Control Regime (MTCR), the Wassenaar Arrangement, and the Australia Group. Russia inherited the Soviet Union's status as a member of the NSG, and its representatives have been active within the arrangement since Russia's independence. In 1993, following the settlement of a conflict with the U.S. over a contract to transfer missile technology to India, Russia signed a Memorandum of Understanding that stated its intention to comply with MTCR guidelines. In 1995, Russia was accepted as a member of the MTCR. Russia's pledge to curtail arms transfers to Iran also paved the way for Russia's admission into the Wassenaar Arrangement. Prior to this, Russia participated in the COCOM Cooperation Forum, a multilateral arrangement that was established to aid the states of the former Soviet Union in formulating export control policies in the wake of the Cold War. Although Russia is not a member of the Australia Group, it is an adherent to the guidelines of the arrangement following the issuance of decrees in 1992 regulating exports that can be used for developing chemical and biological weapons.

In the 1990s, Russia has also undertaken numerous other steps to implement a system of nonproliferation controls. Customs and licensing officials received training by the United States and other Western governments. Customs laboratories were opened in locations around Russia for analyzing seized materials. Equipment was installed at various customs posts for detecting illicit transfers of radioactive materials. An amendment was added to Russia's Criminal Code that renders export of materials or equipment that can be used to make weapons of mass destruction punishable by three to twelve years' imprisonment. In 1994, the government established procedures for issuing import certificates and conducting end-user checks, both of which are elements of an effective nonproliferation verification system. Finally, conferences have been organized to inform industrialists about export control procedures and violations.

Despite Russia's progress, there are several challenges that must be addressed in order for Russia further to enhance its export control system. First, government agencies tasked to control strategic exports are both underfinanced and understaffed. For example, the Federal Service for Currency and Export Control has only a small cadre of about 25 employees to review licenses and has difficulty retaining them because of low salaries that cannot compete with jobs in the private sector. The Ministry of Foreign Affairs often finds it difficult to send the desired representation to international conferences because of budget limitations. Furthermore, the Russian Federal Border Service was allotted less than half of what it requested for 1996 and remains ill-equipped to thwart smuggling operations. Overall, Russia's agencies involved in export control have only a small fraction of the staff that their Western counterparts possess.

Organized crime and government corruption render attempts to control sensitive exports from Russia especially difficult. Agencies charged with enforcing controls—the Interior Ministry and the State Customs Committee—are reported to be among the most corrupt.[11] The Russian General Prosecutor's Office recorded over 1,700 violations by customs officials in 1994 which led to 138 criminal cases brought against officers charged with accepting bribes and misuse of their office. Officials charged with licensing exports and personnel responsible for guarding borders face the temptation of lucrative bribes offered by exporters and importers wanting to circumvent the system and avoid duties. According to estimates by Russia's Customs Committee, about 30 percent of all exports bypass customs.[12] As state enterprises of the military-industrial complex privatize or form side ventures to promote export, the risk of such activity increases. Russia has not effectively coped with such illegal activity either. There is no evidence that violators of export control have been identified and punished. Russia also lacks trained personnel within its embassies to carry out inspections to ensure that technologies originating in Russia are being used for declared civilian purposes. The enforcement of export control regulations in Russia will likely suffer until the general political and economic environment stabilizes.

Ukraine

The system of nonproliferation export controls in Ukraine has undergone major changes since its inception in 1992. Given the deleterious political and economic environment, export control developments have been remarkably steadfast. Despite inheriting WMD materials and technologies, Ukraine did not fall heir to, as did the Russian Federation, a system of export controls. Consequently, relative to Western export control systems, moderate and confined development is to be expected, in spite and because of Western assistance. The evolution of the system, nevertheless, continues to be part and parcel of the overall state-building process.

Overall, lacking an institutional history upon which to draw reference, Ukraine encountered and continues to face many challenges to its export control system development effort. Nevertheless, substantial progress has been made. Based on a quantitative analysis of export control development in 1998, Ukraine ranked a score of 35.41 out of an ideal 41.82, or an 83 percent compliance rate with Western export control standards. Furthermore, when examining overall development over time, a longitudinal study also suggests a progressive pattern. In other words, since 1992, Ukraine has evinced a steady evolutionary path in the development of its export control system. However, the individual elements of the system, examined individually, reveal an inconsistent rate of development.

Despite Ukraine's progress, logistical problems and proliferation risks remain to be overcome. Several reports have chronicled illicit transfers of sensitive goods and technologies to such destinations as China, Iraq, Libya, and Syria. The export control agencies are understaffed, under-equipped, and undertrained. Furthermore, owing to parliamentary wrangling over the 1997 budget, funds were not disbursed until July, thereby impeding export control activities. Organized crime and government corruption remain formidable obstacles to export control development. For example, in late 1996, top officials in the Ministry of Foreign Economic Relations were arrested for bribe taking and for issuing licenses to export "strategic raw materials." The exporting community is not well versed in its export control obligations. Internal compliance mechanisms, for instance, are not a common feature at Ukrainian enterprises. Additionally, porous, understaffed borders add to the dilemma. Lax enforcement and limited overseas representation further diminish export control effectiveness.

Belarus

Since its independence in 1991, Belarus has made a fairly consistent effort to control its inventories of dangerous weaponry and sensitive materials, equipment, and technologies—despite not having inherited the means by which to do so. Belarus, in fact, was among the first of the former Soviet states to develop a national system of export control. After signing CTR agreements with the United States, Belarus has taken numerous steps to prevent the unlicensed proliferation of its nuclear and other materials—including its adoption of an export control law in January 1998. Although domestic political struggles and economic crises have often overshadowed the importance of export control in Belarus, the country has made significant progress in developing an export control system that is 73 percent compatible with Western standards.

Belarus has come a long way in its campaign to develop a national system of export control. With nothing to build upon (no policies, procedures, institutions, or personnel), Belarus developed from scratch an export control system that is nearly compatible with Western common standards. Despite many deficiencies and shortcomings, such as the lack of resources, adequate training, reasonable and enforceable penalties, and export control personnel without divergent interests and priorities, Belarusian officials seemingly remain (at least in the short term)committed to the continued development, implementation, and enforcement of nonproliferation export control policies practices and procedures.

Despite Belarus's export control accomplishments, many challenges lie before Belarusian leaders, and before Western nations that are particularly concerned about preventing the spread of dangerous weapons and weapons-related items. In general, domestic political unrest and economic crises in Belarus may continue to derail its export control efforts due to an increased emphasis on export promotion and a decreased commitment in human and material resources to export control. Unfortunately, unfavorable domestic developments in Belarus may further relegate export control activities to an even lower priority position, creating the possibility that such activities may become lost and irretrievable. Moreover, the nonproliferation export control culture that has slowly developed in Belarus may wane if export control policies are left unimplemented and institutions are left understaffed and underfunded. Given these realities, the West can ill afford to isolate Belarus and, in the process, turn a blind eye to an export control system that is not fully developed. Because international nonproliferation efforts depend on the consistent and comparable implementation of national export controls, Belarus cannot be ignored.

Kazakstan

Constructing a system to control the export of sensitive technologies and materials is a natural part of constructing a self-sustaining government, and much progress has been made in Kazakstan toward the goal of building a viable, solid system of export control. Considering the handicaps present in Kazakstan, its system of export control has developed quite well over the past six years. Kazakstan is still in the middle of a long process of building a functional export control system consistent with Western standards.

When breaking down the Kazakstani system of export control element by element, as the University of Georgia study does, differentiations can begin to be drawn. By August 1998, Kazakstan had a system that is 59 percent complimentary with Western standards of export control development. While this is far from what would be considered a system without faults, for a country that began from scratch some six years before, it has made tremendous strides. In 1992, for example, Kazakstani controls were at a level only 28 percent consistent with Western standards. Thus, in a six-year period, Kazakstan more than doubled its level of development. When considering that in 1994, Kazakstan's level of export control development was only 34 percent compatible, one sees that most of this development has taken place in the last four years, which is very encouraging.

Kazakstan has done a commendable job in developing a fairly well-functioning export control system in just a short period of time. For a country in 1992 that had a basically nonexistent system, Kazakstan has come a long way toward developing something close to Western standards in export control development. Furthermore, even without many necessities present in the West, such as adequate financing, quality personnel with expertise in this area, and lack of technology to enforce export control provisions appropriately, Kazakstan appears to remain committed to further developing its export control policies, bureaucracies, and procedures.

That being said, there are many challenges that lie ahead of the further development of export controls in Kazakstan. Issues such as the lack of regulatory legal bases for export control, the lack of attention given to international supplier regimes, and the strong possibilities that exist for corruption within the system are just some of the problems that Kazakstan must deal with if it is to significantly improve its export control system in the near future. It does appear as if one of the important contributing factors to the development we have seen thus far in Kazakstan is the attention paid to the issue of nonproliferation and export control by the West. It is safe to say that as long as the West continues to push and support Kazakstan in its efforts to develop a solid system of export control, Kazakstan will continue down the path of further development and safer licensing and enforcement procedures.

NOTES

1. See, for example Graham Allison et al., *Avoiding Nuclear Anarchy: Containing the Threat of Loose Russian Nuclear Weapons and Fissile Material* (Cambridge: The MIT Press, 1996); Gary K. Bertsch, ed., *Restraining the Spread of the Soviet Arsenal: NIS Nonproliferation Export Controls 1996 Status Report* (Athens: University of Georgia, 1997); William Potter, "Before the Deluge: Assessing the Threat of Nuclear Leakage from the Post-Soviet States," *Arms Control Today* 25, 8 (October 1996), pp. 9–16; Zachary Davis and Jason Ellis, "Nuclear Proliferation: Problems in the States of the Former Soviet Union," *CRS Report for Congress* IB91129 (June 28, 1995); United States General Accounting Office, "Weapons of Mass Destruction: Reducing the Threat from the Former Soviet Union: An Update," GAO/NSIAD-95-65 (June 1995); United States General Accounting Office, "Nuclear Nonproliferation: U.S. Assistance to Improve Nuclear Material Controls in the Former Soviet Union," GAO/NSIAD/RCED-96-89 (March 1996); and U.S. Congress, Office of Technology Assessment, *Proliferation and the Former Soviet Union*, OTA-ISS-605 (Washington, D.C.: U.S. Government Printing Office, September 1994).

2. On the importance of export control as a long-term challenge requiring continuous development and modification to address the changing domestic and international environment, see Gary Bertsch and Igor Kbripunov, *Restraining the Spread of the Soviet Arsenal: Export Controls as a Long-Term Nonproliferation Tool*, Center for International Trade and Security, University of Georgia, March 1996; and the Statement of Gary Bertsch before the Permanent Subcommittee on Investigations, Committee on Government Affairs, United States Senate, March 13, 1996.

3. For a complete and detailed description of this measurement tool for export control development, see Cassady Craft and Suzette Grillot with Liam Anderson, Michael Beck, Chris Behan, Scott Jones, and Keith Wolfe, "Tools and Methods for Measuring and Comparing Nonproliferation Export Control Development," Occasional Paper of the Center for International Trade and Security (Athens: The University of Georgia, 1996); and Grillot and Craft, "How and Why We Evaluate Systems of Export Control," *The Monitor: Nonproliferation, Demilitarization and Arms Control* 2, 4 (Fall 1996).

4. On the importance of transparent compliance among regime members, see Oran Young, *International Cooperation: Building Regimes for Natural Resources and the Environment* (Ithaca: Cornell University Press, 1989); Karl Deutsch, "Power and Communication in International Society," in Anthony de Reuck and Julie Knight, eds., *Conflict in Society* (Boston: Little, Brown, 1966); and Arthur Stein, "Governments, Economic Interdependence, and International Cooperation," in Philip E. Tetlock et al., eds., *Behavior, Society, and International Conflict* (New York: Oxford University Press, 1993).

5. COCOM was created in 1949 to control the transfer of military-related materials, equipment, technology, and know-how to the Soviet Union, its allies, and (later) China. Original COCOM members included Belgium, Canada, Denmark, France, Italy, Luxembourg, the Netherlands, Norway, the United Kingdom, the United States, and West Germany. Portugal joined in 1951, Japan in 1952, Greece and Turkey in 1953, Spain in 1985, and Australia in 1989. In 1995, COCOM members disbanded the informal organization and replaced it with the Wassenaar Arrangement on Export Controls for Conventional Arms and Dual-Use Goods and Technologies, which continues to control sensitive, militarily relevant exports to questionable end-users. "Common standards" for export control practices were also enhanced by the Nuclear Nonproliferation Treaty (NPT) in 1968, the Nuclear Suppliers' Group (NSG) in 1976, the Biological and Toxin Weapons Convention (BWC) in 1972, the Australia Group (AG) in 1985, the Missile Technology Control Regime (MTCR) in 1987, and the Chemical Weapons Convention (CWC) in 1993. Each of these treaties and arrangements contributes to the overall nonproliferation regime, which seeks to prevent the spread of nuclear, chemical, and biological weapons, technologies, material, and equipment, as well as their means for delivery. For a discussion of each of these arrangements, see Leonard S. Spector and Virginia Foran, "Preventing Weapons Proliferation: Should the Regimes be Combined?" A Report of the Thirty-Third Strategy for Peace, U.S. Foreign Policy Conference, October 22–24, 1992.

6. The "common standards" approach was also employed to assess and evaluate "third countries" who were seeking to cooperate with COCOM controls. On COCOM's "third country initiative" program, see Panel on the Future and Design and Implementation of U.S. National Security Export Controls, Committee on Sciences, Engineering and Public Policy, *Finding Common Ground: U.S. Export Controls in a Changed Global Environment* (Washington, D.C.: National

Academy Press, 1991), p. 123; and Gary Bertsch, Richard Cupitt, and Steven Elliott-Gower, eds., *International Cooperation on Nonproliferation Export Controls* (Ann Arbor: University of Michigan Press, 1994) pp. 34–39; 50.

7. The nonproliferation regime's common standards serve as a reasonable model of internationally accepted export control practices, policies, and procedures. We do not suggest, however, that such a model is a perfect example of export control practices, nor that it is without flaws. Nonetheless, the multilaterally accepted export control procedures that COCOM and the other regimes established have been and continue to be well accepted and can, therefore, serve as a basis for evaluation and comparison.

8. For a different weighting method that focuses on control list items, see "Some Details on the Proposed Method for List Construction and Review," Appendix J of *Finding Common Ground.*

9. The "perfect" weighted score of 41.82 represents 100% compliance with Western common standards. This score does not suggest, however, that the system itself is "perfect" or that such a system would allow zero proliferation. A perfect score simply suggests that a country's export control system is comprised of Western-style export control policies, institutions, and procedures that are in place and in practice. The score does not reflect, in other words, an individual level of export control *effectiveness*—only an individual level of development.

10. For details concerning the various avenues of comparison, see Craft et al., "Tools and Methods"; and Grillot and Craft, "How and Why We Evaluate Systems of Export Control."

11. Testimony of Gary Bertsch, Director of the Center for International Trade and Security at the University of Georgia, before the Permanent Subcommittee on Investigations Committee on Government Affairs, 13 March 1996.

12. *Ibid.*

CONTRIBUTORS

Derek Averre is Research Fellow at the Center for Russian and East European Studies, University of Birmingham, United Kingdom. He is currently working on a government-funded project on post-Soviet industry and science and disarmament issues.

Gary K. Bertsch is the University Professor of Political Science and Director of the Center for International Trade and Security. He has served as a Fulbright Professor in England, as an IREX (International Research and Exchanges Board) Professor in Yugoslavia, and as Chairman of the Education Committee of the American Association for the Advancement of Slavic Studies. Professor Bertsch directs the Center's multiyear project on "Export Controls in the 1990s." From 1995 to 1997 he served on the National Research Council's Committee focusing on Dual-Use Technologies, Export Controls, Materials Protection, Control and Accountability in the former Soviet Union. He has published 15 books, including *International Cooperation on Nonproliferation Export Controls* (University of Michigan Press, 1994), coeditor and contributor; *Export Controls in Transition* (Duke University Press, 1992), coeditor; and *Reform and Revolution in Communist Systems* (Macmillan, 1991), author.

Dastan Eleukenov is an advisor to the Kazakstani Ministry of Foreign Affairs and to the Center for Nonproliferation Studies at the Monterey Institute of International Studies. He was formerly Chief of the Department of International Security and Arms Control in the Ministry of Foreign Affairs of the Republic of Kazakstan. He also served as Deputy Director of the Kazakstan Institute for Strategic Studies and was a visiting fellow at the Monterey Institute of International Studies and Stanford University.

Maria Katsva is a researcher at the Center for International Trade and Security at the University of Georgia. She was former Associate Editor of the Russian language monthly *Nuclear Control* and editor of the Russian language quarterly *Problems of CW Destruction in Russia.*

Igor Khripunov is Associate Director of the Center for International Trade and Security at the University of Georgia in Athens. His previous professional career was with Russia's Foreign Ministry and United Nations Secretariat in New York.

Elina Kirichenko is Head of the North American Department at the Institute of World Economy and International Relations, Russian Academy of Sciences, Moscow. She is an expert in foreign trade policies, multilateral nonproliferation regimes, and Russian export controls. She provides consulting services to the Russian government and Russian and foreign businesses.

Ural Latypov is Deputy Prime Minister of Belarus, and was formerly a Vice President of the Development and Security Research Institute of Belarus. He received his doctoral degree in law from the Institute of State and Law of the

Academy of Sciences of the former Soviet Union. He is an expert on antiterrorist and law enforcement issues.

Dmitriy Nikonov is a Russian Ph.D. student in Political Science at the University of Georgia and a Research Assistant at the Center for International Trade and Security. He specializes in international relations, Russian politics, export controls, and conventional arms trade issues.

Vladimir A. Orlov is a Russian journalist and political scientist. He is Director of the Center for Policy Studies in Russia, a Moscow-based private research and publishing institution. He is also an editor of *Yaderny Kontrol* (Nuclear Control) monthly journal.

Vyachaslau Paznyak is Director of the International Institute for Foreign Policy in Minsk, Belarus. His area of research is weapons nonproliferation and international security. He has been a visiting scholar at a number of U.S. universities and nongovernmental institutions.

Alexander Pikayev is Director, Section on Arms Control and Non-Proliferation, IMEMO, and Director, Program for WMD Control and Non-Proliferation, Carnegie Moscow Center. From 1994 to 1997 he was a senior professional staff member in the Russian Duma Defense Committee. He is a coauthor of *Russia, the U.S. and the Missile Technology Control Regime* (London: The International Institute for Strategic Studies, 1998), *Adelphi Paper* 317.

William C. Potter is a Professor and Director of the Center for Nonproliferation Studies at the Monterey Institute of International Studies. He also directs the MIIS Center for Russian and Eurasian Studies. He is the author and editor of numerous books, including *Nuclear Profiles of the Soviet Successor States* (1993), *International Nuclear Trade and Nonproliferation* (1990), *International Missile Bazaar: The New Suppliers' Network* (1994), and *Dismantling the Cold War: U.S. and NIS Perspectives on the Nunn-Lugar Cooperative Threat Reduction Program* (1997). His present research focuses on nuclear exports, nuclear safety, and nonproliferation problems involving the post-Soviet states. He is a member of the Council on Foreign Relations and the International Institute for Strategic Studies, and served (1995–1997) on the National Research Council's Committee on Dual-Use Technologies, Export Controls, Material Protection, Control and Accountability.

Anatoli Rozanov is Professor of International Relations at Belarusian State University, Minsk. His areas of research include Belarusian security policy, new European security structures, and strategic studies. He has been a visiting fellow at a number of U.S. institutions.

Keith D. Wolfe is a Ph.D. student in Political Science at the University of Georgia and a Research Assistant at the Center for International Trade and Security. He specializes in NIS security and political affairs and in Kazakstan's nonproliferation export control system.

Victor Zaborksy is a Senior Research Associate at the Center for International Trade and Security at the University of Georgia in Athens. He is former Assistant Professor at the Institute of International Relations, Kyev University (Ukraine). His area of research is nonproliferation export control regimes.

INDEX